JANUARY 2008 THROUGH DECEMBER 2008

352

Financial Decisions for Retirement

Insurance Achievement Study Notes

At press time, this edition contains the most complete and accurate information currently available. Owing to the nature of advanced designation examinations, however, information may have been added recently to the actual test that does not appear in this edition. Please contact the publisher to verify that you have the most current edition.

This publication is designed to provide accurate and authoritative information in regard to the subject matter covered. It is sold with the understanding that the publisher is not engaged in rendering legal, accounting, or other professional services. If legal advice or other expert assistance is required, the services of a competent professional should be sought.

If you find imperfections or incorrect information in this product, please visit *www.schweser.com* and submit an errata report.

352: FINANCIAL DECISIONS FOR RETIREMENT, JANUARY 2008 THROUGH DECEMBER 2008
© 2008 DF Institute, Inc., d/b/a Kaplan Schweser. All rights reserved.

Published by DF Institute, Inc., d/b/a Kaplan Schweser

Printed in the United States of America.

ISBN: 1-60373-217-9 / 978-1-60373-217-8

PPN: 4535-8IA8

08	09	10	9	8	7	6	5	4	3	2	1
J	F	M	A	M	J	J	A	S	O	N	D

Definitions of the Terms to Know are adapted from Littell, David A., and Kenn Beam Tacchino, *Financial Decisions for Retirement*, Second Edition. Bryn Mawr: The American College Press, 2007.

Contents

Introduction

" *Only the curious will learn and only the resolute overcome the obstacles to learning.* "

—Eugene S. Wilson

A HELICOPTER VIEW

Welcome

Course Components

Test Tips

Study Tips

WELCOME

Welcome to Kaplan Schweser's Insurance Achievement Study Notes for *352: Financial Decisions for Retirement*. We congratulate you in your quest to enhance your industry knowledge and broaden the scope of your career with an advanced designation.

Your goal in this course is to master the required reading and understand the material so you are able to apply the concepts and theories you've learned. The study package you have purchased has been carefully crafted to get you through even the most challenging concepts. All of our materials implement Kaplan Schweser's proven method of LEARN · PRACTICE · RETAIN™ to ensure that you LEARN the curriculum, PRACTICE new skills, and RETAIN key concepts. By following this approach, you will be fully prepared for success.

The Study Notes, such as this guide, provide clear, concise presentations of the most current and essential exam content. Supplemental to the Study Notes are online tools including SchweserPro™ QBank and InstructorLink™—convenient, simple-to-use programs that will greatly enhance your studies. You will find more information about the online tools and what they entail in the following pages.

Best wishes in your educational efforts. Rest assured that you have selected the industry leader as your partner in self-study. As you will experience, Kaplan Schweser has much to offer:

Extensive knowledge. Kaplan Schweser's high-quality materials are considered the gold standard and are used by dozens of top universities.

Expert instructors. Kaplan Schweser's educators have more than 400 combined years of financial planning training and consulting experience.

Flexibility. Our self-study and instructional methods are customizable to fit your particular learning style and schedule.

Structure. Kaplan Schweser's products are designed to provide a logical and well-planned approach to the study process.

Advanced technology. Our innovative technology provides convenient access to live instruction, efficient online study tools, and the opportunity to interact with other students.

To learn more about Kaplan Schweser study solutions, please visit our Website, *www.schweser.com*.

COURSE COMPONENTS

This course contains two essential components: the Insurance Achievement Study Notes you are holding in your hands plus a variety of online tools that will make your studies as efficient and effective as possible.

How the Study Notes are Organized

Insurance Achievement Study Notes are the main study tool you will use to supplement the required texts for your designation program. Diligent study of this material is critical to passing your designation exam on the first try.

The Study Notes are organized into specific assignments that reflect the main topics of your designation exam. These assignments contain core content on basic principles you will find on the exam. Each assignment begins with a Helicopter View that provides an overview of the topics covered in the assignment and a listing of the Terms to Know for the assignment. Be sure to focus on learning these terms as you go through the assignment.

Each assignment includes a detailed outline of the topics covered in the required reading. Leading off each section of this assignment are key points designed to keep you focused on the important points in the outline. At the end of each assignment, Highlights reinforce important principles. Also included at the end of each assignment are the definitions of the Terms to Know covered in the assignment and review questions that will help you begin to think of the material in terms of the exam you will take at the end of your studies. In addition, each assignment includes a Zoom In that specifically focuses on one key principle covered in the assignment. Make sure you understand the concept covered in the Zoom In before you move on to the next assignment.

Exams and Online Tools

Once you have read the material in the Study Notes, build on that knowledge using Kaplan Schweser online solutions.

SchweserPro™ QBank: Our drill and practice bank has more than 500 online questions to help you prepare for the exam, plus the ability to personalize the experience further with study notes and custom exams. It's the perfect study tool for at home, in the office, or even on a laptop during your commute or travel.

InstructorLink™: Use the Schweser Library of on-demand streaming video to reinforce your readings, then return for a weekly blog from content experts, searchable FAQs, online office hours, and study calendars.

You will find these tools and more at *www.schweser.com*.

352: Financial Decisions for Retirement

352: Financial Decisions for Retirement is a practical, grassroots course that covers important areas in today's growing financial planning marketplace. Some critical areas you must master for this designation exam are annuities, pension distributions, retirement investing, Social Security, and some key aspects of insurance, particularly Medicare. 352 is an important course for adding value to your client base. Understand the big picture as well as the fine points for your two-hour, 100 multiple-choice question designation exam.

The key assignments for this course are:

- Assignment 2: Social Security

- Assignment 3: Tax-Advantaged Retirement Plans

- Assignment 4: Nonqualified Plans and IRAs

- Assignment 6: Investing Before Retirement

- Assignment 9: Annuities and Retirement

- Assignment 11: Planning Issues in Pension Distributions

- Assignment 13: Insurance Issues for Seniors

TEST TIPS

Passing your designation exam depends not only on how well you learn the subject matter but also on how well you take exams. You can develop your test-taking skills—and improve your score—by learning a few test-taking techniques.

- Read the full question.

- Read all answers carefully and avoid jumping to conclusions.

- Interpret the unfamiliar question.

- Identify the intent of the question.

- Memorize key information.

- Understand the material.

- Beware of changing answers.

- Pace yourself.

Read the Full Question

Careless reading during your study and on your exam can be a significant obstacle to passing the exam. You cannot expect to answer a question correctly if you do not know what it is asking. If you see a question that seems familiar or easy, you might anticipate an answer, mark it, and move on before you finish reading it. This is a serious mistake. Be sure to read the full question before answering it—questions are often phrased to trap test takers who assume too much without reading the full question. You should understand the question and why it is being asked.

Read All Answers Carefully and Avoid Jumping to Conclusions

To avoid being misled by seemingly obvious answers, make it a practice to read each question carefully and each answer choice twice before marking your answer.

Look for qualifiers or clue words embedded in the question that provide a hint as to how to answer each question. Examples of qualifiers include the words *if, not, all, always, never, none,* and *except.* These questions can be answered correctly only by taking into account the qualifier. If you ignore the qualifier, you will probably not answer the question correctly.

Qualifiers are often combined in a question. Some that you will frequently see together are *all* with *except* and *none* with *except*. In general, when a question starts with *all* or *none* and ends with *except*, you are looking for an answer that is opposite to what the question appears to be asking. In other words, the question may provide three statements that are true and one that is false. To get this type of question correct, you mark the false choice as the correct answer. The key, as with all questions, is to read the full question to make sure you understand what is being asked (in this case, whether you are being asked to mark the sole true choice or the sole false choice).

Interpret the Unfamiliar Question

Do not be surprised if at first some questions on the exam seem unfamiliar. If you have studied the material in this program, you will have enough information to answer all the exam questions correctly. An obstacle may be understanding what the question is asking.

Very often, questions present information indirectly. You may have to interpret the meaning of certain elements before you can answer the question. Also, be aware that the exam will test you on the same concept in different ways. A question may ask you to identify a concept, or it may ask you to apply it to a sample fact situation.

Identify the Intent of the Question

Many questions on the exam supply so much information that you lose track of what is being asked. This is often the case in story problems. Learn to separate the story from the question.

Spend the time to identify what the question is asking. Of course, your ability to do so assumes you have studied sufficiently. There is no method to correctly answer questions if you have not studied the material and don't thoroughly understand the topic covered in the question.

Memorize Key Information

Reasoning and logic will help you answer many questions, but you will have to memorize a good deal of information. The Highlights at the end of each assignment and the Terms to Know listed at the beginning indicate some of the most important principles for memorization.

Understand the Material

Memorization is important, but it is even more important to understand how concepts are applied. A designation exam tests your ability to apply concepts, and questions are designed for that purpose. Moreover, concept questions are easier to answer if you know the theory. Memorization is the beginning, not the end, of your study.

Beware of Changing Answers

If you are unsure of an answer, your first hunch is likely to be correct. Do not change answers on the exam without good reason. In general, change an answer only if you:

- discover that you did not read the question correctly; or

- find new or additional helpful information in another question.

Pace Yourself

Some students will finish the exam early, and some will not have time to answer all the questions. It is to your advantage to answer all 100 questions. Watch the time carefully (your time remaining will be displayed on your computer screen) and pace yourself throughout the exam.

Do not waste time by dwelling on a question if you simply do not know the answer. Make the best guess you can and mark the question for review. Return to the question if you have time after answering the questions you do know. Make sure that you have time to read all the questions to ensure that you can answer the questions you know.

Test-Taking Strategy

Apply a three-step game plan. You should attack your designation exam with a three-step plan. Go through your 100-question multiple-choice designation exam three times. Answer those questions that you know the first time you go through the exam. Do not guess and do not work on any math problems. On the second time through, answer questions you skipped if you can. Save the impossible questions for your third time through. The third time through the exam is your last time. If you can't answer a question, this is the time to guess. Make sure you've answered all the questions before you are done.

Take one minute to answer each question. Because you must answer 100 questions in a two-hour time frame, you could have 72 seconds for each question if you were going through your exam only once. However, because you need to go through your exam three times, take one minute to read and answer each question the first time you go through your exam. If you spend only one minute on each question, you will have 20 minutes to review your exam and work on the questions you skipped.

Remember: Ability is what you're capable of doing. Motivation determines what you do. Attitude determines how well you do it.

A Closer Look at the Designation Exam

The computer-administered designation exam will have 100 multiple-choice questions with four responses (A, B, C, and D). There is only one correct answer to each question. One or two wrong answers may be close to correct, and one or two wrong answers will be clearly incorrect (which you will quickly spot). You are to select the one response that is most correct. You will have two hours to complete your 100-question designation exam. Do not rush through the exam. Use every minute. Read carefully.

There are three types of questions on your exam: straight-answer questions, multiple-option questions, and all-except questions. There are typically 33 straight-answer questions on your exam, 34 multiple-option questions, and 33 all-except questions. Occasionally you will find more straight-answer questions and fewer multiple-option or all-except questions. Do not worry about the types of questions being asked. Rather, focus on the question at hand and apply your test tip strategies to answer the question correctly. Here are samples of each type of question, with a little strategy associated with each.

Straight-answer questions. Here is an example of a straight-answer question:

A life insurance contract is a(n)
A.   aleatory contract
B.   unilateral contract
C.   contract of adhesion
D.   bilateral contract

A straight-answer question has one answer that correctly states a key point from your studies. Three of the choices are false. The false choices are called distractors because they distract you and impede you in your quest for the right answer.

These are the hardest question types, and they come at the beginning of the test, so don't get discouraged. These are difficult because they are the hardest to write for the question writer. It's tough to come up with three totally bogus choices that don't seem bogus.

So make sure you read all four choices. If you recognize one as clearly correct and three as clearly incorrect, great news. Often, it will be less clear. Make sure you eliminate the clearly wrong choices. That will increase your odds tremendously.

Multiple-option questions. Here is an example of a multiple-option question:

A life insurance contract is which of the following type of contract?
I.   Aleatory contract
II.   Unilateral contract

A.   I only
B.   II only
C.   Both I and II
D.   Neither I nor II

Multiple-option questions are hard because of the multiple-option structure. Don't be confused by it. This type of question is really two true-false questions rolled into one, and it pays to break the question into two pieces. You should know if I and II are true or false before you even look at the A, B, C, and D choices.

All-except questions. Here is an example of an all-except question:

All of the following are characteristics of a life insurance contract EXCEPT
A.   an aleatory contract
B.   a unilateral contract
C.   a contract of adhesion
D.   a bilateral contract

Except questions tend to be the easiest of the three question types, but you may not realize that fact because they occur at the end of the exam when you are tired. Don't spend so much time on the first two sections that you don't have time for these questions. Here's where you will get a lot of points.

The only tricky part about except questions is that, in a sense, you are looking for the single *wrong* answer among three correct answers. This can confuse you, so take your time. Read the full question. Find the three correct statements and the one incorrect statement. Mark the incorrect statement as the right answer. It sounds a little backwards, but once you understand the pattern, these are easier than the rest.

STUDY TIPS

You may be an old hand and a quick study, or it may have been years since you've prepared for an exam. Here are a few tips we recommend to make your study most effective.

Read the Entire Assignment

It is important you read the complete text of each assignment so you can understand the fundamentals of each principle covered in the assignment. Terms to Know and Key Points at the beginning of each assignment, and the Highlights at the end of each assignment direct you to the sections in the assignment that cover the most important principles. Understanding the basics of these principles will better prepare you to take the exam.

Terms to Know are repeated at the end of each assignment along with definitions. It is important that you know the terminology in this course.

Look for Question Areas as You Read Each Assignment

You can prepare for the actual exams even before you take any practice exams by identifying question areas as you read each assignment. It will be obvious to you what principles and terms will be covered on the designation exam when you review each assignment. Key question areas will most likely be those topics covered in the Key Points, Examples, Highlights, Terms to Know, Zoom Ins, and sample exam questions included in each assignment. Write down these question areas on a separate sheet of paper as you read each assignment so you can create your own set of Terms to Know for the exam.

Take the Practice Exams

Memorizing the key information and Terms to Know in each assignment is important. However, you must also learn how to apply these principles by taking practice exams. Answering practice exam questions under testing conditions comparable to what you will experience on the designation exam will better prepare you to sit for the actual exam. Take as many exams as possible, and allow yourself only two hours to complete each exam. The more exams you take under simulated conditions, the more likely you are to pass the actual designation exam.

Review Practice Exam Questions that You Answered Incorrectly

When you finish taking a practice exam, review the questions you answered incorrectly. Review the exam answers and rationales as well as the sections of your Insurance Achievement Study Notes referenced in the explanations. It is important that you study all areas in an assignment. However, as you get closer to the actual exam date, you should narrow your study to your areas of weakness rather than reviewing all the material again.

Repetition Is Key

You may notice that each of the concepts in this course is repeated many times in different ways. A concept may appear in the outline, Key Points, Zoom Ins, Highlights, Terms to Know, and the online study tools. This repetition serves two purposes. First, it helps you learn. Second, if you don't understand the concept in one context, you might understand it in another.

Overview of Retirement Planning

" When I was a boy of 14, my father was so ignorant I could hardly stand to have the old man around. But when I got to be 21, I was astonished at how much the old man had learned in 7 years."

—Mark Twain

A HELICOPTER VIEW OF ASSIGNMENT 1

TERMS TO KNOW

Active life expectancy	Eldercare locator	Life span
Activities of daily living (ADLs)	Elderly dependency ratio	Older Americans Act (OAA)
Age Discrimination and Employment Act (ADEA)	Financial gerontology	Phased retirement
Baby boomers	Fiscal welfare	Respite care
Continuity theory	Geriatric care manager	Rollover
Crisis theory	Graying of America	Social assistance
Downsize	Instrumental activities of daily living (IADLs)	Supplemental Security Income (SSI)
Echo boomers	Lentigo	

1.1 OVERVIEW OF AGING IN AMERICA

Key point   Today's seniors live longer than seniors in the past. Their lives are more active, but health is a major issue for most seniors.

Key point   Successful retirement planners realize that retirement raises other important issues besides money: financial matters should not be isolated from the personal and emotional issues that also arise prior to and during retirement.

1.11   Increasing numbers:

  a.   The **graying of America** (the concept of population aging) is indicated by the fact that 35 million people are at least age 65 (13% of the population).

  b.   By the year 2030, the number of individuals age 65 and over will double.

  c.   By the year 2040, 20% of all Americans will be age 65 or over.

  d.   Most individuals 65 years of age or older are women (i.e., 58%) and women account for 70% of individuals who are 85 years of age or older.

1.12   Changing population characteristics:

  a.   Seniors today have different characteristics than seniors of the 1950s.

     (1)   Higher levels of education.

     (2)   Longer life expectancy: one out of every nine **baby boomers** (individuals born between 1946 and 1964) is anticipated to live until at least age 90.

        (a)   The current life expectancy is 76 years, up from 49 years in 1900.

        (b)   Scientists estimate that the human **life span** (longest possible life expectancy) is at least 120 years.

        (c)   **Active life expectancy** is longer: 80% of individuals over age 65 can perform the standard activities of daily living without help from others—almost 9% more than in 1982.

  b.   The number of people who are 100 years of age or older will reach 1.1 billion by 2050; only 66,000 individuals in the US are currently over age 100.

     (1)   The quality of life at age 100 is expected to be relatively healthy.

1.13   Aging and caregiving.

  a.   Five general characteristics of caregivers in the United States:

     (1)   72% of caregivers are women.

     (2) $2 billion is spent annually to care for aging relatives.

     (3)   Nine out of ten baby boomers consider caring for an aging parent a top life priority.

     (4)   Caregivers are not always healthy and young (e.g., a 75-year-old child may have to care for a 95-year-old parent).

1.14   Other changes affecting retirement:

  a.   Sweeping changes are expected to occur in patterns of consumption of services and products, wealth transfer, travel and leisure, and health management.

    b. Retirees' responsibilities for caregiving—for their parents, children, and grandchildren—is another changing area of retirement.

1.15 **Financial gerontology** (the study of the dynamics of relationships between economic forces and gerontological trends) focuses on these areas:

    a. Biology of aging, health, and wellness.

        (1) For planning purposes, a key factor is **active life expectancy** (measure of number of years a person can expect to live without a disability).

    b. **Elderly dependency ratio** (number of persons age 65 and older per 100 persons of working age), which will increase from 20 per 100 in 1990 to 30 per 100 in 2030. The number of **echo boomers** (those born between 1977 and 1994) is increasing as well, and now is estimated to be 72 million.

    c. Economic status: impressive gains in wealth are distributed unevenly.

    d. Retirement age and timing; living arrangements.

    e. Transition from work to retirement; two theories:

        (1) **Crisis theory:** views loss of work as negative experience that deprives clients of meaningful status in society because occupational role is major source of personal validation.

        (2) **Continuity theory** (more prevalent): sees retirement as a positive experience because it stresses that personal identity persists as it expands into other roles.

    f. Employment prospects and age discrimination.

        (1) **Age Discrimination and Employment Act (ADEA):** federal law enacted in 1967 prohibiting discrimination against employees over 40 years old; law theoretically prohibits firing, demoting, or reducing salaries of older employees without good cause.

    g. Other areas of concern: family, social, and government support; geographical migration; responsibilities for raising grandchildren; understanding differences between male and female clients.

1.2 OVERCOMING CHALLENGES TO RETIREMENT SECURITY

Key point Four major challenges to retirement security include biological changes, lack of investment and financial knowledge, retirement system shortcomings, and unique risks for women.

Key point Retirement planning will become an increasingly important area of business for financial planners.

1.21 Biology of aging:

    a. Biological changes range from mundane, such as **lentigo** (spots and discoloration appearing on the face, hands, and arms of persons over age 50) to chronic (physical limitations, frailty, and increased likelihood of dependence and disease).

        (1) Serious changes include arthritis, dementia, hearing impairments, heart disease, loss of muscle mass, and vision problems.

(2) Genetic, behavioral, and social factors influence how people react to changes in their bodies.

b. Seniors often need long-term care to assist with **activities of daily living (ADLs)**, such as bathing, dressing, mobility, and self-feeding.

(1) Some older individuals may also need help with **instrumental activities of daily living (IADLs)**: doing housework, grocery shopping, managing finances and medications, preparing meals, and using transportation.

c. Findings from a longitudinal study of aging disprove many misconceptions.

(1) Many diseases and losses of function previously thought to be age-related can be slowed or stopped by lifestyle changes.

(2) Only 10% of people over age 65 develop dementia.

(3) More elderly people than young people exercise regularly.

(4) There is no single pattern of aging; it varies widely among individuals.

1.22 Lack of investment and financial knowledge.

a. Most people lack investment knowledge or do not know how much to save for retirement.

(1) 71% of workers say they do not know as much about investing as they would like.

(2) Many retirement plan participants barely keep up with inflation because they invest too conservatively.

b. Workers are uninformed about many other key retirement planning issues:

(1) Long-term care insurance.

(2) Annuitization.

(3) Retirement tax rules.

c. According to the Employee Benefits Research Institute (EBRI), aggregate retiree income shortfall could be over $500 billion in the decade following 2020; people today have to finance retirements that will last an average of 15 to 20 years.

1.23 Retirement system shortcomings.

a. Shift from defined-benefit plans (e.g., a life annuity beginning at a specified normal retirement age) to defined-contribution models (e.g., 401(k) plans) means more risk for employees/retirees.

(1) Defined-benefit plans dropped from 175,000 in 1975 to 36,000 in 2001; bottom line: decline in wealth needed for retirement.

b. Preponderance of money invested in employer stock means lack of diversification and overexposure in company stock by a significant group.

(1) Employee's risk is doubled because investment risk and job security are centered on one company (consider Enron).

c. Employers are increasing premiums and cutting back on retiree medical coverage.

d. Private pensions are generally more available to employees of medium- and large-sized companies than to those who work for small businesses.

e. Social Security is becoming vulnerable as ratio of workers to retirees diminishes.

f. Pension Benefit Guaranty Corporation (PBGC) also has potential liabilities.

1.24 Unique risks and tendencies for women.

    a. Women face some unique problems that affect the ability to finance retirement.

        (1) For every 100 women over age 85, there are only 39 men.

        (2) Women make up 58% of individuals over 65 and 70% of individuals 85 or older.

        (3) Women of all ages are more likely to be poor than men.

        (4) Women are less likely to have pensions from work; if they do have pensions, they are more likely to invest assets too conservatively.

        (5) Women have lower earnings overall, hindering retirement savings.

        (6) Women live longer and are more likely to be single or widowed (widowed men are seven times more likely to remarry than women).

        (7) Women have more caretaking responsibilities and are more likely at all stages of life to forgo income opportunities to care for loved ones.

    b. Risks are lessened by the fact that women are more likely than men to ask others for help and to receive social support.

1.3 CLIENT'S PERSPECTIVES ON THE RETIREMENT PLANNING PROCESS

> **Key point** Five overlapping stages in retirement planning from the client's perspective are saving, visualizing and identifying needs, making decisions, adapting to retirement lifestyle, and coping with dependency and frailty.

1.31 Saving:

    a. Ideally, begins soon after client begins work career.

    b. Motivation often comes from planner, whose role is to encourage saving and to make sure retirement savings are not used for other purposes.

    c. Key planning service: encourage client to use **rollovers** (tax-free transfers from one tax-qualified vehicle, such as an employer plan, to another, such as an IRA) when changing jobs.

1.32 Preparing and visualizing needs:

    a. Starts at any age, but the earlier the better.

    b. Savings motivation comes mostly from client in this phase (e.g., increased 401(k) contributions or paying off mortgage before retirement).

    c. Planner's role is to alert clients to future needs.

1.33 Decision making:

    a. Age sometimes, but not always, drives decision of when to retire.

    b. Planners should educate clients that money and health are more accurate drivers of retirement timing.

    c. Other areas planners should educate clients about:

        (1) When to start Social Security.

        (2) How to allocate pension distributions.

        (3) How to convert assets into retirement income; in particular, should clients **downsize** (sell their home to free up assets for retirement use while they move to more senior-friendly housing)?

1.34 Adapting to retirement and making transition to new lifestyle:

    a. Often accompanied by increased spending, travel, new pursuits.

    b. Caregiving responsibilities often become a new "career."

    c. Client's financial situation becomes more income poor and asset rich.

    d. Planners should notice client's emotional needs during transition and advise on how to adjust spending plans and whether to move near family or to a continuing care retirement community.

1.35 Coping with dependency and frailty:

    a. Dependency and frailty can occur at any age; involve health issues, caregiving for spouse, and loss of mobility (either physical or having to forfeit driver's license).

    b. Clients tend to become lonelier and more emotionally dependent in this phase; close access to community and medical services becomes more important.

    c. Planner's role:

        (1) Counsel clients so they can have resources for financial independence.

        (2) Direct clients to other organizations for non-financial needs.

1.4 PLANNER'S PERSPECTIVES ON THE RETIREMENT PLANNING PROCESS

Key point Six steps a planner must consider in retirement planning are to: establish a good working relationship, help the client determine goals, evaluate financial status, develop and present the plan, assist in implementation, and monitor the plan periodically.

Key point Successful retirement planners realize that they must often educate clients about alternative strategies for achieving their goals.

1.41 Establish good working relationship with client:

    a. Understand aging process and nonfinancial issues related to senior living.

    b. Supply clear descriptions of services, planning process, and necessary documents.

1.42 Determine goals and expectations:

    a. Listening is important.

    b. Educate clients and help them become more specific about options.

1.43   Evaluate and analyze client's financial status:

    a. Make inventory of client's current situation and stated goals.

    b. Determine assets, liabilities, securities holdings, and annual income.

    c. Use other client documents as fact-finding tools, such as wills and trusts, Social Security statements, employer benefit statements, employer summary plan descriptions, and long-term care policies.

    d. Assess client's risk tolerance and exposures.

    e. Analyze client's needs and determine whether client has:

        (1) Adequate disability insurance and long-term care insurance.

        (2) Investment allocations aligned with goals.

        (3) Sufficient savings.

        (4) Sensible tax planning strategies.

1.44   Develop and present the retirement plan:

    a. Include health care and housing.

    b. Compare and contrast various alternatives.

    c. List priorities.

    d. Assess tax strategies and distribution options.

1.45   Implement retirement plan:

    a. Assist client in implementing recommendations.

    b. Help client coordinate with other professionals, such as **geriatric care managers** (social service professionals with expertise in developing and coordinating care plans for elderly persons), accountants, attorneys, and real estate agents.

1.46   Monitor retirement plan periodically:

    a. Assess changes in client's personal circumstances, such as births, deaths, divorce, illness, or job changes.

    b. Inform client of relevant changes in tax laws and benefit and pension options.

1.5 FOUNDATIONS OF RETIREMENT SECURITY

Key point Retirement income is most secure when it comes from several sources. Three basic sources, often thought of as the legs of a three-legged stool, are Social Security, employer-sponsored retirement plans, and personal savings.

1.51   Additional factors that help retirees climb the ladder to retirement security are:

    a. Proper planning.

    b. Insurance solutions.

    c. Social assistance and fiscal welfare.

    d. Part-time wages.

    e. Inheritances.

f. Other forms of support, such as home equity, rental property, family business assets, life insurance proceeds from a deceased spouse, or cashing out a whole life policy.

1.52 Social Security.

   a. Covers 90% of Americans age 65 and older.

   b. Social Security alone won't provide enough income for higher-income employees, because Social Security replaces a smaller percentage of their salary.

   c. Social Security provides an average income replacement ratio of only 43%, so it should not be relied on exclusively even for lower-income retirees.

   d. Social Security should be supplemented by other income sources.

1.53 Employer-sponsored retirement plans.

   a. Three types: defined-benefit plans, defined-contribution plans, and private pension plans.

   b. Almost 95 million Americans are covered by two types of company-sponsored retirement arrangements: defined-benefit plans or defined-contribution plans.

   c. Number of Americans covered by defined-benefit plan type is dropping.

   d. Defined-benefit plans offer more advantages to employees:

   (1) Place more risk on employers, who can withstand market cycles better.

   (2) Based on worker's final average salary, and so usually account for pre-retirement inflation.

   (3) Often provide a significant replacement ratio (percentage of final salary) for a long-term employee in form of an annuity.

   (4) Can be based on employee's service before plan was established.

   e. Defined-contribution plans, such as 401(k)s, place more risks on employees but are becoming more common. Some characteristics:

   (1) Money allocated to individual accounts for each worker; employer contributes either a fixed or discretionary amount.

   (2) Based on career average salaries and thus do not fully account for pre-retirement inflation.

   (3) Many defined-contribution plans offer investment alternatives, but workers are often not well informed about choices.

   (4) They are more transportable than defined-benefit plans, and there are no penalties when moving fully vested benefits from one employer to another.

   (5) Lump-sum distributions are common but often are not used wisely.

   (6) No penalties when moving fully vested benefits between employers.

   f. Private pensions are third type of company-sponsored retirement plan.

   (1) About 30% of retirees have pension income.

1.54 Personal savings.

   a. Once accumulation goal is set, three things affect saver's ability to reach it:

   (1) Length of accumulation period (consider the effects of compounding).

(2) Rate of return (obviously, more is better).

(3) Amount invested (an investment of $0 returns $0).

b. Savings rate in United States decreased from 7.4% in the 1960s to less than 5% in the most recent 10-year period, well below many other developed countries.

c. Over 50% of people who have reached age 65 have interest income.

d. About 25% of people who have reached age 65 have dividend income.

1.55 Proper planning is essential because most workers have inadequate financial and investing knowledge.

a. Plan sponsors often hesitate to provide advice because of fiduciary liability concerns.

b. Financial services professionals have major opportunity to meet retirement planning needs and expand their client base; Internet will supplement but not replace direct advice.

1.56 Insurance solutions: seniors often lack key protection.

a. Clients with long-term care insurance, Medigap coverage, and adequate property protection will be more secure.

b. A recent estimate says that an average 65-year-old couple retiring today will need $190,000 to cover medical expenses over the next 20 years, not including long-term care, dental care, or over-the-counter medications.

1.57 Social assistance and fiscal welfare.

a. Planners need to help clients understand fiscal and social benefit programs:

(1) **Fiscal welfare**: an indirect payment to individuals through the tax system, such as the retirement savings contribution credit.

(2) **Social assistance**: a type of social benefit administered by the Social Security Administration (SSA) with eligibility criteria designed partly to encourage able-bodied poor persons to work by providing minimal benefits, such as supplemental security income.

(3) **The Older Americans Act (OAA):** a law that created programs to help seniors live independently; administered by the federal Administration on Aging (AoA) and by State Units on Aging (SUA).

b. Retirement savings contribution credit is a tax credit of up to $1,000 ($2,000 if married filing jointly); see IRS form 8880.

(1) Serves as savings incentive for lower-income clients, who must be at least age 18 and not full-time students or dependents on another person's tax return.

(2) Available if client makes an eligible contribution to any of the following:

(a) Traditional or Roth IRA.

(b) 401(k), 403(b), or 457 plan.

(c) A SIMPLE or a salary reduction SEP (SARSEP).

(3) Credit is a percentage of qualifying contribution amount; highest rate is for taxpayers with least income (see Figure 1-1).

(4) To compute retirement savings credit, subtract amount of distributions clients received from retirement plans from contributions they have made.

ZOOM IN   **Defined-Benefit vs. Defined-Contribution Retirement Plans**

Defined-Benefit Plans	Defined-Contribution Plans
Characteristic: Provides a specified benefit, usually a life annuity beginning at a specified retirement age	Characteristic: 401(k) plan is common model; employer contributes either fixed or discretionary amount
Advantages to employees: 1. Employers bear more risk. 2. Usually cover preretirement inflation because are based on worker's final average salary. 3. Can be based on employee's service before plan starts.	Disadvantages to employees: 1. Employees bear risk of poor investment choices. 2. Do not fully account for inflation because are based on career average salaries. 3. Many workers are ill-informed about investment choices. 4. Lump-sum distributions are fairly common (especially with job changes) and often are not used wisely.

FIGURE 1-1

Retirement Savings Contributions Credit

Credit Rate	Income for Married Filing Jointly	Income for Head of Household	Income for Others
50%	Up to $30,000	Up to $22,500	Up to $15,000
20%	$30,001–$32,500	$22,501–$24,375	$15,001–$16,250
10%	$32,501–$50,000	$24,376–$37,500	$16,251–$25,000

   c. **Supplemental Security Income (SSI)** pays monthly income to clients who are 65 or older, blind, or disabled.

      (1) Maximum federal amounts: close to $600 for individuals, $900 for couples. There may be additional state benefits.

      (2) Recent statistic: Almost 4% of population age 65 and older receives an average of $4,200 in SSI benefits.

      (3) Benefits are needs based; planners must conduct client financial inventory and then work with SSA to determine eligibility. Rules are complex but generally include the following qualifying criteria:

         (a) Client must have limited resources and income.

         (b) Assets limited to $2,000 for individuals, $3,000 per couple, but do not include home, care, household goods, and other items.

         (c) Benefit amount partly depends on place of residence.

   d. OAA helps lower-income clients with several programs:

      (1) **Eldercare locator**: provides referrals for clients, caregivers, and planners on a variety of senior living needs: 1-800-677-1116 or **www.eldercare.gov**.

      (2) Family Caregiver Support Group helps primary caregivers with referrals to five basic services including **respite care** (temporary relief from caregiving responsibilities to enable caregivers to pursue personal needs or interests).

         (a) Caregiver support is available at **www.aoa.gov**.

      (3) State Area Agencies on Aging (AAAs) help with:

         (a) Locating services that affect finances (such as Medigap counseling).

      (b) Funding transportation for doctor visits; contracting with providers for meal delivery and in-home support services; helping children find care for parents who do not live nearby.

      (c) Medicaid qualification assessments.

    (4) Nursing home ombudsman program.

1.58 Part-time wages: seniors continue to work for financial, social, and other reasons..

    a. 23% of people age 65 to 69 remain employed; 16% of people age 65 and older have earned income, with a median income of $15,000.

    b. For clients who started retirement planning late, planners can help them consider a strategy of **phased retirement**: a reduction in hours and commitments rather than an abrupt, complete removal from the workforce, or a second, part-time career.

1.59 Inheritances.

    a. Only 15% of baby boomers expect to receive an inheritance.

    b. Given the population's increasing longevity, planners should counsel clients not to count on inheritances as a financial planning tool.

HIGHLIGHTS

Highlight 1: Overview of Aging in America

- Three general characteristics of seniors today that affect retirement planning:
  (1) Higher levels of education than in previous years.
  (2) Life expectancy is longer: one out of every nine baby boomers is expected to live until at least age 90.
  (3) Active life expectancy is longer: 80% of individuals over age 65 can perform standard activities of daily living without help—9% more than in 1982. (1.12)

- Four general characteristics of caregivers in the US:
  (1) 72% of caregivers in the US are women.
  (2) $2 billion is spent annually to care for aging relatives.
  (3) Nine out of ten baby boomers consider caring for an aging parent a top life priority.
  (4) Caregivers are not always healthy and young. (1.13)

Highlight 2: Four Challenges and Threats to Retirement Security

- Biological changes:
  (1) Range from mundane to chronic (arthritis, vision problems), with need for long-term care to assist with activities of daily living being common.
  (2) Many diseases and losses of function that previously were considered age-related can be slowed or stopped by lifestyle changes. (1.22)

- Lack of investment and financial knowledge:
  (1) Many people are unaware of how much they need to save to finance a retirement that will last 15 to 20 years.
  (2) Workers are often uninformed about key retirement planning issues such as taxes, long-term care insurance, and annuities. (1.23)

- Shortcomings in the retirement system itself:
  (1) Shift away from defined-benefit plans that favor employees to defined-contribution models such as 401(k) plans.
  (2) Employers cutting back on retiree medical coverage.
  (3) Social Security system becoming more vulnerable. (1.24)

- Unique risks for women:
  (1) Women of all ages more likely to be poor than men.
  (2) Women live longer, are more often widowed, and have more caretaking responsibilities. (1.25)

Highlight 3: Five Client Perspectives on the Retirement Planning Process

- Saving: Planner's role is to encourage it and make sure retirement savings are not used up.

- Preparing and visualizing: Planner's role is to identify future needs for clients.

- Decision making: Planner should educate clients about when to start Social Security, how to convert assets into income, and how to allocate distributions.

- Adapting to retirement and making transition to new lifestyle.

- Coping with dependency and frailty. (1.3)

Highlight 4: Six Planner Perspectives on the Retirement Planning Process

- Establish good working relationship.

- Help client determine goals and manage expectations.

- Evaluate client's financial status.

- Develop and present the retirement plan, comparing various alternatives.

- Assist in implementing plans and coordinating with other professionals.

- Monitor retirement plan periodically. (1.4)

Highlight 5: Foundations of Retirement Security

- Retirement income is most secure when it is based on several sources, including Social Security, personal savings, and company-sponsored plans. (1.51–1.54)

- Additional factors that help retirees climb the ladder to retirement security:
  (1) Informed planning.
  (2) Insurance.
  (3) Fiscal welfare and social assistance, including tax credits, Supplemental Security Income, and federal and state assistance programs.
  (4) Part-time wages.
  (5) Inheritances and other forms of support. (1.55–1.59)

Active life expectancy Age at which individuals can perform the standard activities of daily living without help from others. (1.12a)

Activities of daily living (ADLs) Bathing, dressing, eating, transferring from bed to chair, maintaining continence, and using the toilet. (1.22b)

Age Discrimination and Employment Act (ADEA) Federal law enacted in 1967 prohibiting discrimination against employees over 40 years old; law theoretically prohibits firing, demoting, or reducing salaries of older employees without good cause. (1.15f(1))

Baby boomers Individuals born between 1946 and 1964. (1.12a)

Continuity theory View that sees retirement as a positive experience because it stresses that personal identity persists as it expands into other roles besides work. (1.15e(2))

Crisis theory View that sees loss of work as a negative experience that deprives clients of meaningful status in society because occupational role is a major source of personal validation. (1.15e(1))

Downsize Sell a home to free up assets for retirement use while moving to more senior-friendly housing. (1.34c)

Echo boomers Persons born between 1977 and 1994. (1.15b)

Eldercare locator Provides referrals for clients, caregivers, and planners on a variety of senior living needs. (1.57(d))

Elderly dependency ratio Number of persons 65 and older per 100 persons of working age. (1.15b)

Financial gerontology The study of the dynamics of relationships between economic forces and gerontological trends. (1.15)

Fiscal welfare An indirect payment to individuals through the tax system, such as the retirement savings contribution credit. (1.57a(1))

Geriatric care manager Social service professional with expertise in developing and coordinating care plans for elderly persons. (1.46)

Graying of America The concept of population aging. (1.11a)

Instrumental activities of daily living (IADLs) Doing housework, grocery shopping, managing finances and medications, preparing meals, and using transportation. (1.22b(1))

Lentigo Spots and discoloration appearing on the face, hands, and arms of persons over age 50. (1.21a)

Life span Longest possible life expectancy. (1.12a)

Older Americans Act (OAA) A law that created programs to assist seniors to live independently; administered by the federal Administration on Aging (AoA) and by State Units on Aging (SUA). (1.57a(3))

Phased retirement A reduction in hours and commitments rather than an abrupt, complete removal from the workforce; or a second, part-time career. (1.58c)

Respite care Temporary relief from caregiving responsibilities to relieve the caregiver who provides home care. (1.57d)

Rollover A distribution from a tax-qualified retirement plan that a participant personally receives and deposits into another plan without tax consequences (also known as an indirect rollover or regular rollover). (1.32c)

Social assistance A type of social benefit administered by the Social Security Administration (SSA) with eligibility criteria designed partly to encourage able-bodied poor persons to work by providing minimal benefits, such as supplemental security income. (1.57a(2))

Supplemental Security Income (SSI) Benefit administered by the Social Security Administration (SSA) that pays monthly income to clients who are 65 or older, blind, or disabled. (1.57c)

QUESTIONS

1. All of the following are steps in the retirement planning process from a planner's perspective EXCEPT
   A. determining goals
   B. coping with dependency
   C. analyzing information
   D. developing a plan

2. Which of the following is a disadvantage of defined-contribution plans?
   A. No penalty when moving vested funds from employer to employer
   B. Risk is shifted from employer to employee
   C. Employer may make matching contributions
   D. Participant retiring prior to full retirement age is eligible for entire account balance

3. Which of the following concerning financial gerontology is(are) CORRECT?
   A. Understanding the differences between male and female clients is not a factor in retirement planning.
   B. Active life expectancy is a key factor in retirement planning.
   C. Both A and B.
   D. Neither A nor B.

4. Which of the following is(are) a risk(s) pertinent to women regarding retirement?
   A. Women are less likely to be single, and thus are able to share retirement responsibilities.
   B. Women historically work in industries that ignore pensions.
   C. Both A and B.
   D. Neither A nor B.

5. All of the following are examples of social assistance or fiscal welfare benefits EXCEPT
   A. retirement savings contribution tax credit
   B. Supplemental Security Income
   C. part-time wages
   D. Administration on Aging caregiver support

ANSWERS

1. **B.** Coping with dependency is part of the process from the client's perspective, not the planner's, although planners should be alert to their clients' needs in this area. (1.35)

2. **B.** Another disadvantage of a defined-contribution plan is no preretirement inflation protection. (1.53)

3. **B.** Financial gerontology is concerned with a wide variety of relationships between economic forces and gerontological trends. (1.15)

4. **B.** Some of the unique risks women face in retirement are: (1) conservative approach to investments hinders savings; (2) historically work in industries that ignore pensions; (3) experience higher job turnover than men; (4) wages earned are generally lower than men's; (5) more likely to serve in caregiver roles; (6) outlive men, creating a need to save more; and (7) more likely to be single or widowed, thus unable to share retirement responsibilities. (1.24)

5. **C.** Part-time wages can be part of a phased retirement or second career but are not part of fiscal welfare or social assistance programs. (1.57)

2

Social Security

"*Knowing is not enough; we must apply. Willing is not enough; we must do.*"

—Goethe

A HELICOPTER VIEW OF ASSIGNMENT 2

TERMS TO KNOW

Average indexed monthly earnings (AIME)

Breakeven life expectancy

Currently insured status

Delayed retirement

Disability insured status

Early retirement reductions

Earnings and benefit estimate statement

Earnings test

Family maximum

Full retirement age (FRA)

Fully insured status

OASDI

Primary insurance amount (PIA)

Provisional income

Taxable wage base

2.1 THREE TYPES OF OLD-AGE, SURVIVORS, AND DISABILITY INSURANCE (OASDI) BENEFITS

> **Key point** The three main types of Social Security benefits are old age (retirement), survivors (for children and surviving spouse), and disability insurance (preretirement disability). Remember these initials: OASDI.

2.11 **Old-Age, Survivors, and Disability Insurance (OASDI)** is part of the Social Security program.

    a. OASDI: Old-Age, Survivors, and Disability Insurance; refers to parts of Social Security other than Medicare (i.e., hospital).

    b. OASDI provides three types of benefits: retirement, survivors', and disability benefits.

        (1) Retirement (old-age) benefits.

            (a) For a fully insured worker:

                ■ Full (i.e., normal) retirement age: age at which benefits may be taken without incurring benefit reductions; in 2007, the **full retirement age (FRA)** is 65 years, 10 months.

                ■ Benefits are available as early as age 62, but are permanently reduced.

                ■ The retirement age for nonreduced benefits is increasing gradually until retirement age reaches 67 in 2027.

            (b) Spouse age 62 or older:

                ■ Benefits are permanently reduced if taken before spouse reaches FRA.

                ■ Benefits are available to an unmarried divorced spouse if the marriage lasted at least 10 years and no remarriage, unless the new spouse receives Social Security benefits as a widow, widower, parent, or disabled child.

FIGURE 2-1

Full (or Normal) Retirement Age for Social Security	
Year of Birth	**Full Retirement Age**
Before 1938	**65**
1938	65 and 2 months
1939	65 and 4 months
1940	65 and 6 months
1941	65 and 8 months
1942	65 and 10 months
1943–1954	**66**
1955	66 and 2 months
1956	66 and 4 months
1957	66 and 6 months
1958	66 and 8 months
1959	66 and 10 months
1960 and Later	67

(c) Spouse of any age if he cares for at least one child of the retired worker and the child is either under age 16 or disabled and entitled to a child's benefit. (This benefit is called the mother's or father's benefit.)

(d) Dependent, unmarried children under age 18.

- Continues until 19 years of age if the child is a full-time student in elementary or secondary school.

- Disabled children of any age are eligible for benefits if the children were disabled before becoming 22 years of age.

(2) Survivors benefits (paid to survivors of a covered worker): if deceased worker was fully insured at time of death, all categories are payable.

(a) Three types of survivors benefits are available to currently insured workers as well as fully insured workers:

- $255 lump-sum death benefit: available to surviving spouse living with deceased worker at time of death; if no such spouse, $255 is payable to children eligible for monthly benefits; if no such survivors, the benefit is not paid.

- Spouse or divorced spouse caring for a child/children as in 2.11b(1)(c).

- Dependent, unmarried children as described in 2.11b(1)(d).

(b) Benefits are available to the following categories only if the deceased worker was fully insured:

- Widow or widower 60 years of age: benefits reduced if taken before FRA; available to divorced spouse if marriage lasted 10 years or longer; available to disabled spouse at age 50 if the disability began not more than seven years after worker's death or the end of the year in which entitlement to a parent's benefit ended.

- Parent 62 years of age or older who, at the time of the worker's death, was a dependent of the deceased worker.

(3) Disability benefits.

(a) Disability definition is very rigid:

- A mental or physical impairment that prevents any substantial gainful employment and the impairment has lasted or is expected to last for at least 12 months or is expected to result in death.

- Blind workers 55 years of age or older are defined as disabled if unable to perform work that requires skills or abilities comparable to those required by the work regularly performed before 55 years of age or becoming blind, if later.

(b) Waiting period: benefits begin with sixth full calendar month of disability.

(c) Definition of *disabled* is the same for disabled children of workers as for workers.

(d) Widows or widowers are defined as disabled if such persons are unable to hold any gainful employment, not just "substantial" gainful employment.

2.12 Eligibility for dual benefits.

a. A person may be eligible for more than one benefit (e.g., own retirement benefit as well as the spouse's benefit) but can only receive the higher benefit of the two.

2.13 Termination of benefits.

a. At death of worker:

(1) A recipient's benefits end at death.

(2) Family members' benefits end at death of the retired or disabled worker but family members then become eligible for survivors' benefits.

(3) Benefits of surviving spouse end upon remarriage unless the remarriage occurs when the spouse is age 60 or older.

b. Disability benefits:

(1) End at FRA; disability benefits are then replaced by retirement benefits.

(2) End if the disability ends but continue during a readjustment period consisting of the month of recovery and two additional months.

(3) For children of a disabled worker, benefits end at age 18 but can continue to age 19 if child is a full-time elementary or secondary school student.

2.14 Average indexed monthly earnings (AIME).

a. OASDI benefits (excluding $255 death benefit) are based on the worker's primary insurance amount (PIA). PIA is determined by the worker's **average indexed monthly earnings (AIME)** on which the worker paid Social Security tax.

b. Steps in calculating AIME:

(1) List the earnings on which Social Security taxes were paid for each year beginning with 1951 (or the year in which the worker turned 22, if later) and include the year of death or the year preceding disability or retirement.

(a) Use the taxable wage base if actual earnings exceed this base (see Section 2.32).

(2) Index the earnings by multiplying the earnings by the SSA indexing factor to reflect changing wage levels:

(a) The indexing year is defined according to the type of benefits: (1) for retirement purposes, the indexing year is the year a worker reaches 60 years of age; (2) for survivor or disability benefits, the indexing year is two years preceding the year of death or disability.

(b) For the years preceding the indexing year, the indexing factor is equal to the average annual covered wages for the indexing year divided by the average annual covered wages for the year to be indexed.

(c) For the indexing year and the years following, the covered earnings figure is multiplied by 1.

(3) Determine the number of years to be included in the calculation.

(a) For retirement and survivors' benefits, this number is the minimum number of quarters necessary to be fully insured minus five (usually 35).

(b) For disability benefits, this number is the minimum number of quarters necessary to be fully insured minus a specified number based on age (five quarters for workers age 47 or over; four quarters for workers age 42 – 46).

ZOOM IN	**Five Steps to Calculate Average Indexed Monthly Earnings (AIME)**

1. List the client's earnings for each year after 1950, up to the maximum taxable amount. Assume future earnings to be the same as 2007, so that the benefit will be more closely related to the value of today's dollar.

2. Multiply the earnings for each year by the Index Factor (see www.ssa.gov) to reflect changing wage levels.

3. Use the 35 best years of earnings (after indexing) to figure AIME. If the client has fewer than 35 years of earnings, use zero for each of the remaining years.

4. Add up all the indexed earnings for the years to be included.

5. Divide the total earnings by 420 (35 years × 12 months) to get the Average Indexed Monthly Earnings (AIME).

    (c) For disability and survivors benefits, up to three additional years can be excluded from calculation if the worker had no income during the year and had a child under age three in the household during the entire year; a minimum of two years must be used.

    (4) Exclude the years with the lowest indexed earnings, leaving the number of years required in the step above.

    (5) Add the indexed earnings for the years to be included in the calculation and divide by the number of months in these years (the number of years multiplied by 12).

2.15 Determination of **primary insurance amount (PIA)** and monthly benefits:

    a. After calculating a worker's AIME, PIA is the amount a worker will receive per month at normal retirement age or upon becoming disabled and the amount on which family members' benefits are based.

    b. 2007 formula for PIA: 90% for the first $680 of AIME + 32% of AIME over $680 and under $4,100 + 15% of AIME over $4,100 (annual adjustments).

        (1) Formula to determine a worker's retirement benefit is the formula for the year in which the worker reached 62 years of age.

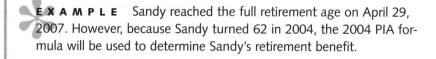

> **EXAMPLE**   Sandy reached the full retirement age on April 29, 2007. However, because Sandy turned 62 in 2004, the 2004 PIA formula will be used to determine Sandy's retirement benefit.

        (2) Formula to determine survivors and disability benefits is the formula for the year death or disability occurred, not the year benefits are applied for.

    c. In 2007, a worker with average earnings would have a PIA of $1,044 ($12,528 per year).

        (1) A person earning maximum income subject to Social Security taxes can receive about $2,116/month ($25,392/year) for retirement purposes (smaller disability and survivors benefits).

2.16   Benefits to family members as a percentage of a worker's PIA:

    a.   If the worker is retired or disabled:

        (1)   Child under 18 years of age or disabled: 50% each.

        (2)   Spouse caring for disabled child or child under 16 years of age: 50%.

        (3)   Spouse at full retirement age: 50%.

    b.   Survivors benefits if worker dies:

        (1)   Spouse caring for disabled child or child under 16 years of age: 75%.

        (2)   Dependent parent: 82.5% for 1; 75% each for 2.

        (3)   Child under 18 years of age or disabled: 75% each.

        (4)   Spouse at full retirement age: 100%.

    c.   Family maximum for retirement and survivors benefits for 2007:

        (1)   Formula: 150% of first $869 of PIA + 272% of PIA over $869 through $1,255 + 134% of PIA over $1,255 through $1,636 + 175% of PIA over $1,636.

        (2)   Family maximum is usually reached when three or more family members (including a retired or disabled worker) are eligible for benefits.

        (3)   **Family maximum** for disability benefits is lesser of 85% of worker's AIME or 150% of worker's PIA (but is never reduced below PIA).

        (4)   If the total benefits to the family exceed the family maximum, then the worker's benefit, in the case of retirement or disability, is not changed but the benefits of the other recipients are each reduced by the same percentage so that benefits are limited to the family maximum; as the number of eligible family members changes, each recipient's benefit also changes, so that the total family income is at the maximum for that family.

2.17   Five factors affecting benefits:

    a.   Benefits taken early.

        (1)   For the worker, benefits are permanently reduced by $\frac{5}{9}$ of 1% for each of the first 36 months that early retirement precedes the full retirement age, plus $\frac{5}{12}$ of 1% each month for up to 24 months thereafter.

> **EXAMPLE**   Jude was born in 1945 with an FRA of 66. If he retires in 2007 when he is age 62 (48 months before FRA), Jude's monthly benefit will be calculated as follows: 36 months × $\frac{5}{9}$ of 1% (a 20% reduction) and 12 months × $\frac{5}{12}$ of 1% (a 5% reduction). Therefore, Jude would receive a 25% reduction from his full retirement benefit by taking early retirement.

        (2)   For the worker's spouse, benefits are permanently reduced by $\frac{25}{36}$ of 1% for each month that benefits precede the full retirement age.

        (3)   For the worker's widow or widower, benefits are permanently reduced by $\frac{19}{40}$ of 1% for each month that benefits precede the full retirement age.

        (4)   If a widow or widower elects benefits at an earlier age due to disability, the benefit percentage is not reduced further.

        (5)   For the worker with a normal retirement age past FRA, benefits are permanently reduced by $\frac{5}{12}$ of 1% per month if the worker retires 3 years before normal retirement age.

b. **Delayed retirement**: A client who is eligible for benefits can choose to suspend receiving them, thus earning delayed retirement credits (DRCs) for any month from full retirement age up to age 70; the purpose is to encourage delayed retirement.

   (1) The additional benefit was 5% for persons born in 1932 and gradually increased to 8% for persons born in or after 1943.

   (2) DRCs increase the benefit for the retired worker but not for the spouse. However, DRCs earned by the worker do increase the benefit payable to the widow(er).

c. **Earnings test:** reduction tied to wages.

   (1) Benefits are reduced for beneficiaries under FRA with wages above a specified level. Reason: Social Security benefits are intended to replace lost wages but not other income.

   (2) In 2007, the limit is $12,960 in annual wages ($1,080/month) for beneficiaries under FRA (adjusted annually); reduction is $1 for every $2 in excess earnings.

   (3) If a person reaches the FRA in 2007, the limit for 2007 is $34,440 in annual wages ($2,870/month); reduction is $1 for every $3 in excess earnings.

   (4) Beneficiaries at FRA can earn an unlimited amount and not have benefits reduced.

   (5) The reduction in a retired worker's benefits applies to all benefits paid to family members (may eliminate all benefits to the worker and family members).

   (6) Reduction in benefits to family members other than the worker does not apply to earnings of other family members (e.g., a widowed mother who is employed may lose mother's benefits, but benefits received by children are not affected).

d. Cost-of-living adjustments (COLAs): 3.3% in 2007; annual increase.

e. Offsets exist for other benefits (e.g., disabled workers who also receive workers' compensation or disability benefits from other government programs; monthly benefit of a spouse or surviving spouse is reduced by two-thirds of any government pension based on earnings not covered under OASDI).

2.2 SOCIAL SECURITY ELIGIBILITY

Key point   There are three types of insured status: (1) fully insured (for retirement): 40 quarters; (2) currently insured (for survivors): 6 out of last 13 quarters; and (3) disability insured: fully insured plus minimum work requirement.

2.21 Minimum work requirements based on quarters of coverage:

a. 2007: a worker receives credit for one quarter for each $1,000 in earnings on which Social Security taxes are paid, up to a limit of four quarters per calendar year.

b. Credit for four quarters is given for as little as $4,000 ($1,000 × 4) in earnings during the year.

2.22   Three types of insured status:

   a. **Fully insured status**: when a person has 40 quarters of coverage (exceptions for workers born before 1930).

   (1) Once achieving 40 quarters, the person is fully insured for life even if covered employment under Social Security ends.

   b. **Currently insured status**: certain survivor benefits are available if a worker is currently insured even if the individual is not fully insured.

   c. **Disability insured status**: worker must be fully insured and meet minimum work requirements within a recent time period; defined as:

   (1) A worker under age 24 must have credit for six out of the last 12 quarters.

   (2) A worker between ages 24 and 30 must have credit for at least half the quarters of coverage from the time he turned 21 and the quarter disability begins.

   (3) A worker age 31 or older must have credit for at least 20 of the last 40 quarters.

   (4) Blind persons are exempt from the recent-work rules if they are fully insured.

2.3 BENEFIT FUNDING

Key point Social Security benefits are funded by the following taxes (2007 rates): (1) self-employed (SECA taxes): 15.3% on first $97,500 of income, 2.9% above $97,500; and (2) employees (FICA taxes): employer and employee split the payments on the above amounts; each pays 7.65% on first $97,500, 1.45% above $97,500.

2.31   Benefits of OASDI are financed by:

   a. Payroll and self-employment taxes on covered persons.

   b. Taxes on employers of covered persons.

2.32   Taxes (as of 2007):

   a. Employees who are on company payrolls pay FICA (Federal Insurance Contributions Act) tax.

   (1) Employee and employer each pay 7.65% of first $97,500 of employee's wages.

   (a) 6.2% is for OASDI.

   (b) 1.45% is for Medicare.

   (c) Wages above $97,500 are also taxed at 1.45% for Medicare.

   (2) The $97,500 figure is called the **taxable wage base** and is adjusted annually.

   b. Self-employed: pay SECA (Self-Employment Contributions Act) tax; 15.3% on first $97,500 of income and 2.9% on remainder (equals combined employee/employer rates).

   c. Even if Social Security benefits have begun, individuals must continue paying these taxes as long as employment continues.

   d. Social Security is funded on a pay-as-you-go basis with limited trust funds.

(1)   The tax rate and wage base have both increased significantly over time as benefit levels have increased and new benefits have been offered.

2.33   Funds are deposited into four trust funds:

a.   Old-age and survivors fund; this fund is growing but is projected to be adequate only until 2041 because of the retirement of baby boomers; for every dollar paid into Social Security, $.69 goes to this fund.

b.   Disability fund; for every dollar paid into Social Security, $.12 goes to this fund.

c.   Two Medicare funds: Part A and Part B; for every dollar paid into Social Security, $.19 goes to these two funds.

d.   These four funds receive contributions and some interest income.

e.   OASDI's expected inability to pay promised benefits in the future was partially resolved by 1983 amendments to the Social Security Act, which limited future increases in some benefits and increased payroll taxes.

2.4 WHO IS COVERED UNDER SOCIAL SECURITY?

Key point   Ninety percent of Americans are covered by Social Security; middle- and lower-income persons rely on Social Security for half or more of their income.

Key point   Persons not covered by Social Security include ministers, US citizens working abroad, railroad workers, civilian employees of the federal government who started before 1984, some state and local government employees, and others.

2.41   Nearly 90% of US workers are covered, including both employees and the self-employed.

a.   Social Security benefits replace about 40% of the average wage earner's income.

(1)   Percentage is lower for more prosperous clients; lower-paid workers are favored over higher-paid workers because of benefit structures.

b.   Middle-income and lower-income Americans rely heavily on Social Security.

(1)   Without Social Security, the percentage of American senior citizens living in poverty would increase from 10% to nearly 50%.

(2)   Social Security is more than 50% of income for two-thirds of the elderly.

(3)   Social Security is the only source of income for one-third of the elderly.

2.42   Nine categories of workers who are not covered under the Social Security program:

a.   Ministers who choose not to be covered for reasons of religion or conscience.

b.   Certain American citizens working abroad for foreign affiliates of US companies; however, US citizens working abroad directly for US employers are covered.

c.   Railroad workers covered under the Railroad Retirement Act; these workers are covered for Medicare purposes and certain other benefits.

d.   Certain civilian employees of the federal government hired before 1984.

e.   Certain state and local government employees.

f.   Workers in certain jobs (e.g., student nurses, newspaper carriers under 18 years of age, or students working at a college or university).

g. Individuals who do not meet minimum earnings requirements (e.g., self-employed persons must earn at least $400 per year).

h. Family employees, including children under 18 employed by a parent; this exclusion does not apply to employees of a corporation owned by a family member.

i. Employees having fewer than 40 quarters of coverage.

2.5 SOCIAL SECURITY BENEFIT TAXATION

Key point Provisional income (PI)—the portion of Social Security benefit subject to tax—equals adjusted gross income (AGI) plus tax-exempt interest plus one-half the Social Security benefit.

Key point There is no tax if PI is under $25,000 for a single person or under $32,000 for a joint return.

Key point If PI is under $34,000 for single person or $44,000 for a joint return, up to 50% of Social Security benefits are taxed; if PI is over $34,000 for a single person or $44,000 for a joint return, up to 85% of Social Security benefits are taxed.

2.51 History of benefits taxation: no federal income taxes on any Social Security benefits until 1984; beginning in 1994, 85% of benefits are taxed for some people.

2.52 **Provisional income:** the part of OASDI benefit subject to tax.

a. Equals the sum of the individual's tax-exempt interest for the year, adjusted gross income, and one-half of the Social Security benefits for the year.

b. No tax if provisional income is less than the base amount ($25,000 for a single taxpayer and $32,000 for a married taxpayer filing jointly).

c. Up to 50% taxed if provisional income is between the base amount and $34,000 (single) or $44,000 (married filing jointly).

d. Up to 85% taxed if the provisional income exceeds $34,000 (single) or $44,000 (married filing jointly).

2.53 Three steps to calculating the portion of benefits that is taxable:

a. Calculate provisional income.

b. Determine thresholds, based on the individual's tax filing status.

c. The amount of Social Security benefits that is taxable income is the smallest of:

(1) 50% of any provisional income that exceeds the base threshold, plus 35% of any amount in excess of the second threshold.

(2) 85% of the benefits.

(3) 50% of the benefits, plus 85% of any amount in excess of the second threshold.

> **EXAMPLE**   Jill and Jim Kingston are married and file jointly. They have $44,000 AGI (not including Social Security) plus $5,500 of tax-free bond interest and are entitled to a $16,500 Social Security benefit.
>
> To determine Jill and Jim's taxable Social Security benefits:
>
> Step 1: Provisional income equals:
>
> | | |
> |---|---:|
> | Preliminary adjusted gross income | $44,000 |
> | Tax-free bond interest | 5,500 |
> | 50% of Social Security benefits | + 8,250 |
> | Provisional income | $57,750 |
>
> Step 2: Determine income in excess of the applicable thresholds:
>
> | | |
> |---|---:|
> | Excess over base threshold ($57,750 − $32,000) | $25,750 |
> | Excess over second threshold ($57,750 − $44,000) | $13,750 |
>
> Step 3: Amount includable in taxable income is the lowest of the following three amounts:
>
> a. 50% of excess over base threshold plus 35% of excess over second threshold ([.5 × $25,750] + [.35 × $13,750]) = $17,687
>
> b. 85% of Social Security benefits ($16,500) = $14,025
>
> c. 50% of total Social Security benefits ($16,500) plus 85% of excess over second threshold ($13,750) = $19,937
>
> In this example, the second amount—$14,025 (85% of the Social Security benefits)—is the smallest and is therefore the amount that is includable as adjusted gross income.

2.6 REQUESTING BENEFIT INFORMATION AND FILING FOR BENEFITS

Key point The Social Security Administration gives workers an annual earnings and benefit statement.

Key point Social Security benefits don't begin automatically; a person must apply for them.

2.61 Annual earnings and benefit estimates.

  a. Earnings and benefit estimate statement: contains earnings and benefits data prepared by the SSA for each worker over 25 who is not receiving benefits.

  (1) Mailed to workers annually, with more detail available on the Social Security Website.

  b. Planners should instruct clients to make certain their earnings history is correct; W-2 forms for client's affected years help rectify mistakes.

  c. Additional information provided by statements:

  (1) Estimated retirement benefit the client can expect (statement will be adjusted for cost-of-living increases).

      (2) Estimated disability and survivors' benefits the client will receive.

      (3) Client's full retirement age.

2.62 Applying for Social Security benefits:

    a. Benefits are not automatic; worker must apply.

    b. Benefits should be applied for three months in advance; however, benefits can be paid retroactively for up to six months or longer for a disability.

    c. Three advantages of filing an application if worker may be eligible for benefits:

      (1) Benefit applications receive more attention than requests for information.

      (2) If benefits are denied in error, the benefits will be paid retroactively to the application date when the problem is corrected.

      (3) If a person is eligible for a different, larger benefit (e.g., as a spouse), an application must be filed to receive the larger benefit.

2.7 THE DILEMMA OF POSTRETIREMENT EMPLOYMENT

Key point Employment during early retirement can reduce Social Security benefits; income from employment can shift Social Security benefits into a higher tax category.

2.71 Returning to work after retirement may subject the worker to significant tax penalties and reduction of retirement benefits.

    a. Application of earnings test to working Social Security beneficiaries under the full retirement age will result in reduction of benefits.

2.72 Four guidelines for retirees planning to return to work:

    a. Keep income below earnings test limit so Social Security benefits are not reduced (e.g., use deferred compensation until earnings test no longer applies).

    b. Retired worker returning to work after the full retirement age is not subject to reduction in benefits, regardless of amount earned.

    c. Minimize portion of Social Security benefits subject to taxation by lowering non-employment income.

    d. If wages will exceed earnings test amount, notify the Social Security Administration in advance so benefits can be reduced in the current year; this reduction effectively lowers taxes for the current year.

2.8 WHEN SHOULD CLIENTS TAKE EARLY SOCIAL SECURITY RETIREMENT BENEFITS?

Key point Benefits are reduced if they begin before FRA.

Key point Questions to consider before deciding whether a client should take early retirement: (1) Does the client have resources to live for a longer retirement period? (2) Will the client have to return to work? (3) Is the client being forced to retire by losing a job close to normal retirement age?

2.81   Retiring workers who are fully insured: benefits are based on PIA.

  a. The retirement benefit is reduced by $\frac{5}{9}$ of 1% of the PIA for the first 36 months that benefits are received before the full retirement age and $\frac{5}{12}$ of 1% for any months beyond the first 36.

  b. **Early retirement reductions**: reduction of benefits if they begin before the full retirement age; based on specified factors; reduction is permanent unless the worker returns to work and earns more than the earnings base.

  c. The minimum age for early retirement is 62 years.

2.82   Spouse: at normal retirement age, entitled to 50% of the surviving retired spouse's PIA.

  a. The spousal benefit is reduced by $\frac{25}{36}$ of 1% of the PIA for each of the first 36 months that benefits are received before the full retirement age and $\frac{5}{12}$ of 1% after the 36 months.

  b. This percentage is applied to the 50% of the worker's PIA for which the spouse would be eligible at normal retirement age.

> ✾ **E X A M P L E**   For a spouse retiring at 62 years of age, the benefit is reduced by 25%, or $\frac{25}{36} \times .01 \times 36$ months.

  c. Spouse should calculate whether benefit is larger based on spouse's own work record: only the larger of the sums (not the total of the two) can be received.

  d. The minimum age for early retirement is 62 years.

2.83   Spousal benefits of deceased workers.

  a. Benefits are based on the greater of the spouse's PIA or the deceased worker's PIA at time of worker's death.

  b. At FRA, the spouse is entitled to 100% of the deceased worker's PIA.

  c. If the deceased spouse retired early and received a reduced benefit before the full retirement age, the surviving spouse cannot receive more than the greater of the reduced deceased spouse's benefit or 82.9% of the PIA.

  d. Benefits can begin at age 60 if spouse is not disabled; benefit is reduced by $\frac{19}{40}$ of 1% (i.e., .475%) of PIA for each month that benefits are received before FRA.

2.84   Disabled spousal benefits of deceased workers.

  a. The benefit is 71.5% of the PIA between ages 50 and 60 (no benefits available until age 50), after which the benefit equals the amount for a regular surviving spouse.

  b. At FRA, the spouse is entitled to 100% of the worker's PIA (same as for a non-disabled spouse).

2.85   Four threshold issues in determining at what age to retire:

  a. Key issue: likelihood of individual returning to work before FRA.

(1) If a person returns to work before FRA, benefits will be recalculated and a reduction will be applied.

b. Financial impact of a longer retirement period and impact on pension and Social Security benefits.

(1) Social Security benefits will be decreased by early retirement reduction factor.

(2) Level of benefits will be affected if the individual has a short working history or a significant recent increase in wages.

(3) A person should make two separate information requests from SSA: (1) early retirement, and (2) benefits beginning at FRA.

c. Economic need for early retirement by the involuntarily unemployed.

d. Noneconomic issues: lifestyle preferences.

2.86 Economic issues in electing early benefits:

a. Receiving early retirement benefits is desirable if the present value of the additional benefits received before normal retirement age exceeds the present value of the higher benefits that are forgone after normal retirement age.

b. Three factors used in computing present values:

(1) The assumed real (inflation-adjusted) discount (interest) rate, which depends on the assumed nominal discount rate and the assumed growth or inflation rate for Social Security benefits.

(a) Electing to receive reduced early Social Security retirement benefits is recommended for retiring workers if the assumed real discount rate is above 7%, for spouses if the rate is above 10%, and for surviving spouses if the rate is above 6%.

(b) Discount rate is the amount of benefits a person must receive today to prefer to postpone benefits; rate is affected by seven conditions:

- Current market rate of interest; must be determined on basis of likely investments (typically 3 to 4%).

- Individual's opportunities to use the benefits today as compared to projected uses for the benefits in the future.

- Person's health and expected quality of life.

- Person's personal life expectancy projections.

- Willingness to take risks.

- Inflation; because Social Security benefits are indexed for inflation, the discount factor must be adjusted for inflation to determine the real discount rate.

- Real discount rate $= \dfrac{\text{nominal discount rate} - \text{inflation rate}}{\text{inflation rate} + 1}$

(2) Number of months before FRA when early benefit payments will begin.

(3) The assumed life expectancy of the recipient and sometimes of the recipient's spouse.

(a) Formula for determining **breakeven life expectancy** equates present value of the reduced early retirement benefits with present value of the difference between the reduced benefits and the full benefits that would otherwise be paid after FRA and factoring in the number of years after the normal retirement age.

(b) Breakeven life expectancy rises as assumed real discount rate increases.

c. Eight planning guidelines:

(1) Disabled surviving spouse should choose reduced early benefits.

(2) Decision for a healthy surviving spouse depends on expected longevity, the assumed real discount rate, family history, and gender.

(3) If the IRS mortality factors are used, surviving spouses in normal health will usually be in a breakeven position if the surviving spouses' assumed real discount rate is between 2.5 and 3.5%.

(4) For married persons, a key concern is the joint and last survivor's life expectancy, since the spouse will continue to receive a reduced benefit if the worker chooses reduced early benefits and then dies.

(5) Decision for single retiring workers is based on person's life expectancy alone; if in normal health, worker should generally postpone retirement benefits to the FRA if assumed real discount rate is less than 4.5%.

(6) Deferring retirement benefits for nonworking spouse to FRA is usually more beneficial for spouses of surviving workers than for surviving spouses; deferring benefits until FRA is recommended for the healthy spouse of a surviving worker if the assumed real discount rate is less than 8% at age 62 or 6% at age 64.

(7) The life expectancy of the retired worker's spouse must also be considered; spousal benefits should be deferred until FRA only if neither worker nor spouse is likely to die before nonworking spouse reaches the breakeven life expectancy.

(a) Reason: the spouse of a retired worker receives a 50% benefit, but benefit increases to 100% of the worker's benefit when the retired worker dies, even if the spouse received early benefits while the retired worker was alive; this is especially relevant when the spouse is much younger or has a much longer life expectancy than the retired worker.

(8) Mortality assumptions (see IRS mortality tables):

(a) 50% chance that a person will die before reaching the life expectancy for that age and a 50% chance of surviving past that age.

(b) 25% chance that any two people will survive beyond their life expectancies.

2.9 FUTURE OF SOCIAL SECURITY BENEFITS

Key point Even if no changes are made in the system, Social Security will still be able to pay 73% of benefits in 2041.

Key point Some of the proposals to reform the Social Security system include means testing, changes to the retirement age and benefit amounts, changes to the system investment strategy, and permitting individual account plans.

2.91   Historical perspective:

   a.   The pay-as-you-go system (current workers pay for current benefits) worked in the 1940s, when worker: retiree ratio was 15:1, until the 1960s, when the ratio was 5:1.

   b.   Ratio today is 3:1; should fall to 2:1 by 2030.

   c.   In 1983, the Social Security law was changed to accumulate a surplus.

   d.   Excess earnings are invested in Treasury securities, with a 4% return rate.

   e.   The old-age trust fund needs revision but is not in a crisis.

   (1)   When baby boomers start to retire, Social Security will begin to use the surplus trust fund.

   (2)   The trust fund is expected to be exhausted by 2041.

2.92   Myth: few young people today believe there will be Social Security benefits available for retirement; truth even with no changes in current system, Social Security will still be able to pay 73% of benefits in 2041.

   a.   A nominal payroll tax increase would solve most Social Security system problems.

2.93   Social Security Advisory Council made three recommendations in the 1990s.

   a.   Maintenance-of-benefit plan:

   (1)   Beginning in 2000, invest $25 billion per year in the stock market instead of Treasury bonds.

   (2)   By 2015, invest 40% of the old-age trust fund in the stock market, mostly in corporate bonds and equity index funds.

   (3)   Change the current tax rate of 6.2% for employer and employee in 2045; divide an additional 1.6% between employer and employees.

   b.   Individual Accounts plan:

   (1)   Use an additional 1.6% from employees' pay to fund mandatory IRAs; after-tax contributions to be tax free at distribution.

   (2)   Give employees the choice of investing in stock or bond index funds.

   (3)   Moderately cut guaranteed benefits for middle-income and higher-income employees.

   (4)   Raise the age for full benefits to 67 years of age by 2011; index the age limit for changes in life expectancy.

   (5)   Invest $20 to $25 billion in the stock market annually.

   c.   Personal Security Account (PSA) plan:

   (1)   Create individual accounts to replace part of Social Security.

   (2)   Use the other 7.4% of the Social Security tax to fund a modified Social Security retirement program.

   (3)   Starting in 2000, accelerate the age for full benefits.

   (4)   Increase the age to receive early retirement benefits from 62 to 65 years.

   (5)   Incur additional federal debt to finance the transition to the new system.

   (6)   Invest $75 billion annually in the stock market.

2.94   Boskin Commission: top economists appointed by the Senate.

   a.   Claimed the consumer price index (CPI) overstates inflation by 1.1% per year.

   b.   CPI was changed in 1998 to account for half of the Commission's recommendations.

2.95   Commission to Save Social Security: 2001 report focused on privatizing the Social Security system; report offered three models, all of which proposed that privatized funds be invested in mutual funds.

2.96   Other recommended changes:

   a.   Means testing (affluence or income testing) to phase out benefits for individuals with higher income and assets.

   b.   Raise the full retirement age more quickly.

   c.   Temporarily freeze cost-of-living adjustments; known as frozen COLAs.

   d.   Change the formula for determining the PIA.

   e.   Price indexing; calculating first-year retiree benefits using inflation rates instead of the increase in wages and a worker's lifetime.

Highlight 1: Three Types of Old-Age, Survivors, and Disability Insurance (OASDI) Benefits; Social Security Eligibility

- OASDI provides three types of benefits:
  (1) Retirement (old-age) benefits.
  (2) Survivors benefits.
  (3) Disability benefits. (2.11b)

- Three types of insured status:
  (1) Fully insured status: when a person has 40 quarters of coverage.
  (2) Currently insured status: worker must have credit for at least six quarters of coverage out of the 13-quarter period ending with the quarter in which death occurs.
  (3) Disability insured status: worker must be fully insured and meet requirement of a minimum amount of work under Social Security within a recent time period. (2.22)

Highlight 2: Benefit Funding and Who Is Covered Under Social Security

Funds are deposited into four trust funds: one old-age and survivors fund, one disability fund, and two Medicare funds (Part A and Part B). (2.33)

- OASDI's expected inability to pay promised benefits in the future was at least partially solved by the 1983 amendments to the Social Security Act, which:
  (1) Limited future increases in some benefits.
  (2) Increased payroll taxes.
  (3) Eliminated some benefits. (2.33e)

- Nine categories of workers who are not covered under Social Security:
  (1) Certain ministers.
  (2) American citizens working abroad for foreign affiliates of US companies.
  (3) Railroad workers: covered under the Railroad Retirement Act.
  (4) Civilian employees of the federal government if the employees were employed by the government before 1984 and are covered by the Civil Service Retirement System.
  (5) Certain state and local government employees.
  (6) Workers in certain jobs (e.g., nursing students).
  (7) Individuals who do not meet minimum earnings requirements.
  (8) Family employees, including children under 18 employed by a parent; this exclusion does not apply to employees of a corporation owned by a family member.
  (9) Employees having fewer than 40 quarters of coverage. (2.42)

Highlight 3: Social Security Benefit Taxation

- The amount of Social Security benefits that is taxable income is the smallest of the following three amounts:
  (1) 50% of any provisional income that exceeds the base threshold, plus 35% of any amount in excess of the second threshold.
  (2) 85% of the benefits.
  (3) 50% of the benefits, plus 85% of any amount in excess of the second threshold. (2.53c)

Highlight 4: Requesting Benefit Information and Filing for Benefits

■ Three advantages of filing an application if a person may be eligible for benefits:
   (1) Benefit applications are processed more quickly than information requests.
   (2) If benefits are denied in error, the benefits will be paid retroactively.
   (3) If a person is eligible for a different, larger benefit, an application must be filed to receive the larger benefit. (2.62c)

Highlight 5: The Dilemma of Postretirement Employment

■ Four guidelines for retirees planning to return to work:
   (1) Keep income below earnings test limit so that Social Security benefits are not reduced.
   (2) Retired worker returning to work after FRA is not subject to reduction in benefits, regardless of amount earned.
   (3) Minimize portion of Social Security benefits subject to taxation by lowering nonemployment income.
   (4) If wages will exceed earnings test amount, notify SSA in advance so benefits can be reduced in the current year (lowers taxes for the current year). (2.72)

Highlight 6: When To Take Early Social Security Retirement Benefits?

■ Four threshold issues in determining at what age to retire:
   (1) Key issue: likelihood of individual returning to work before the full retirement age.
   (2) The financial impact of a longer period of retirement and the impact on pension and Social Security benefits.
   (3) Economic need for early retirement by the involuntarily unemployed.
   (4) Noneconomic issues: lifestyle preferences. (2.85)

Average indexed monthly earnings (AIME) Wages on which the worker paid Social Security tax and the basis for PIA; based on lifetime earning history. (2.14a)

Breakeven life expectancy A formula that equates the present value of the reduced early retirement benefits with the present value of the difference between the reduced benefits and the full benefits that would otherwise be paid after the full retirement age and allowing for the number of years after the normal retirement age. (2.86b(3))

Currently insured status Refers to point at which survivor benefits are available even if the individual is not fully insured; worker must have credit for at least six quarters of coverage out of the 13-quarter period ending with the quarter in which death occurs. (2.22b)

Delayed retirement When a client who is otherwise eligible for benefits chooses to suspend receiving them, thus earning delayed retirement credits (DRCs) for any month from full retirement age up to age 70. (2.17b)

Disability insured status Worker who is fully insured and meets requirement of a minimum amount of work under Social Security within a recent time period as specified by Social Security rules. (2.22c)

Early retirement reductions Reduction of benefits if they begin before the full retirement age; based on specified factors. (2.8)

Earnings and benefit estimate statement (also called Social Security statement) Contains earnings and benefits data prepared by the Social Security Administration for each worker not currently receiving benefits who is over 25 years of age. (2.62a)

Earnings test Reduction of benefits for persons under full retirement age if their work wages exceed a specified level. (2.17c)

Family maximum Usually reached when three or more family members (including a retired or disabled worker) are eligible for benefits; maximum level for disability benefits is the lesser of 85% of worker's AIME or 150% of the worker's PIA; however, the maximum is never reduced below the PIA. (2.16c)

Full retirement age (FRA) Age at which benefits may be taken without incurring benefit reductions. (2.11b)

Fully insured status When a person has 40 quarters of coverage, the person is fully insured; once achieving 40 quarters, the person is fully insured for life even if covered employment under Social Security ends. (2.22a)

OASDI Old Age, Survivors, and Disability Insurance (part of the Social Security program). (2.11)

Primary insurance amount (PIA) The amount a worker will receive per month at normal retirement age or upon becoming disabled and the amount on which family members' benefits are based. (2.15a)

Provisional income The portion of the OASDI benefit that is subject to taxation; equals the sum of the individual's tax-exempt interest for the year, adjusted gross income, and one-half of the Social Security benefits for the year. (2.52)

Taxable wage base The amount of an employee's wages that is taxed to finance OASDI and Medicare benefits; adjusted annually ($97,500 for 2007). (2.32)

QUESTIONS

1. Which of the following statements concerning Social Security is CORRECT?
   A. About 50% of the average wage earner's income is replaced by Social Security benefits.
   B. Without Social Security, the percentage of American senior citizens living in poverty would increase from 10% to nearly 25%.
   C. Social Security is more than 50% of retirement income for ⅔ of the elderly.
   D. Social Security is the only source of income for ½ of the elderly.

2. Social Security is funded on which of the following bases?
   A. Government annuity policies
   B. Fully funded retirement plans
   C. Advance funded private retirement plans
   D. Pay-as-you-go basis with limited trust funds

3. OASDI provides 3 types of benefits, including all of the following EXCEPT
   A. retirement benefits
   B. survivors' benefits
   C. disability benefits
   D. health insurance benefits

4. What is the chance that both members of a couple will survive beyond their life expectancies?
   A. 15%
   B. 25%
   C. 50%
   D. 75%

5. All of the following are types of insured status EXCEPT
   A. partially insured
   B. fully insured
   C. currently insured
   D. disability insured

ANSWERS

1. **C.** About 40% of the average wage earner's income is replaced by Social Security. Without Social Security, senior citizens living in poverty would increase to nearly 50%. Social Security is the only source of income for ⅓ of the elderly. (2.41b)

2. **D.** Social Security is funded on a pay-as-you-go basis with limited trust funds; as funds are received, the funds pay the benefits of current recipients. (2.32d)

3. **D.** The three types of benefits provided by OASDI are retirement, survivors, and disability benefits. (2.11)

4. **B.** There is a 25% chance that a couple will survive beyond their life expectancies. There is a 50% chance that an individual will survive beyond life expectancy. (2.86c)

5. **A.** The three types of insured status are fully, currently, and disability insured. (2.22)

3

Tax-Advantaged Retirement Plans

"Yesterday is a canceled check; tomorrow is a promissory note; today is the only cash you have—so spend it wisely."

—Kay Lyons

A HELICOPTER VIEW OF ASSIGNMENT 3

TERMS TO KNOW

401(k) plan

403(b) plan

Allocation formula

Annual benefit statement

Cash balance pension plan

Cash or deferred arrangements (CODAs)

Defined benefit plan

Defined contribution plan

Employee stock ownership plans (ESOPs)

Highly compensated employee

IRC Sec. 401(a)(4)

IRS Form 1099R

Money-purchase pension plan

Pension plan category

Profit-sharing category

Profit-sharing plan

Put Option

Qualified plan

Ratio test

SEP

SIMPLE

Stock bonus plans

Summary plan description

Top-heavy plans

Vesting schedule

3.1 QUALIFIED RETIREMENT PLANS

Key point   The six major plan types are defined benefit pension plans, money-purchase pension plans, 401(k) plans, cash balance pension plans, stock bonus plans and ESOPs, and profit-sharing plans.

Key point   The four major qualification requirements are vesting, nondiscrimination, funding, and plan and communication.

3.11   **Qualified plan**: plan meeting Internal Revenue Service (IRS) specifications (IRC Section 401(a)); all are pre-funded (i.e., employer sets aside money in an irrevocable trust fund that is later used to provide benefits to employees).

   a. Six types of qualified plans:

     (1) Defined benefit pension plans.

     (2) Money-purchase pension plans.

     (3) 401(k) plans.

     (4) Cash balance pension plans.

     (5) Stock bonus plans and employee stock ownership plans (ESOPs).

     (6) Profit-sharing plans.

   b. Qualified plans are eligible for special tax treatment; four benefits:

     (1) Trust is tax exempt (earnings are not taxed until distributed to participants).

     (2) Employer contributions are tax deductible to the employer.

     (3) Employee pays taxes when benefits are received.

     (4) Funds may be rolled to other tax-favored plans at end of employment.

   c. Thirteen requirements for plans to be qualified:

     (1) Plan must be written.

     (2) Apply top-heavy rules when over 60% of contributions benefit key employees.

     (3) No disproportionate benefits to highly compensated employees.

     (4) Specified funding requirements must be met.

     (5) Incidental death benefits only: if life insurance is purchased within the plan, death proceeds cannot be greater than certain limits.

     (6) Appropriate communication: plan must be communicated according to statutory guidelines to participants (includes providing a summary plan description).

     (7) Must meet limitations imposed on amount of contributions and benefits.

     (8) Enough nonhighly compensated individuals must be covered.

     (9) Spouses have rights based on qualified joint and survivor annuity requirements.

     (10) Employer may not recapture funds unless the plan is terminated and all liabilities of the plan are satisfied.

     (11) Plan is required to be permanent; however, may still be terminated or amended.

     (12) Operated solely for the benefit of employees and the beneficiaries of employees.

     (13) Participants must be vested within a particular time frame.

   d. Determination letter: may be requested from the IRS by a plan sponsor; specifies that the plan document complies with applicable laws.

(1) Plan must continue to operate within the rules to maintain qualified status once the determination letter has been received.

(2) Plan sponsor must file a Form 5500 annually with the Department of Labor (DOL) and the IRS; demonstrates compliance with rules.

Note: Both the DOL and the IRS may audit plans to ensure regulatory compliance.

e. If a plan is not compliant with the law, the IRS can disqualify the plan.

  (1) Results in severe consequences including reducing tax deductions to the employer and shifting deductions to different years.

   (a) Worst case scenario: participant is taxed on all benefits at once.

f. Six rules with the greatest influence on plan design:

  (1) Eligibility and coverage.

   (a) Minimum coverage requirements: plan must benefit a specific percentage of nonhighly compensated employees to be qualified; two types of **highly compensated employees:**

   - Five percent owner in previous or current year.

   - Employees earning over $100,000 (2007) in the previous year.

   (b) **Ratio test**: test ensuring that a plan benefits a percentage of nonhighly compensated employees equal to 70% of the percentage of highly compensated employees who benefit from the plan; four types of employees excludable from the ratio test:

   - Workers under the age of 21.

   - Employees who worked less than one year.

   - Employees who are collectively bargained.

   - Part-time employees (i.e., work under 1,000 hours per year).

> **EXAMPLE** In 2007, Moon's Marshmallow Company employs 150 individuals. Fifty employees have not yet met minimum service and age requirements; therefore, the ratio test applies to 100 employees. Thirty of the 100 employees to which the ratio test applies are highly compensated; however, only 15 of the 30 participate in the plan. Of the remaining 70 nonhighly compensated employees covered by the plan, 40 employees participate. Because one-half of the highly compensated employees participate in the plan (15 of 30), 35% (70% × 50%), or 25 (35% of 70 = 24.5), of the nonhighly compensated employees must also participate to meet the ratio test requirements. Because 40 of Moon's nonhighly compensated employees participate in the plan, the plan passes the ratio test.

   (c) Plans are not required to exclude employees; however, most plans do exclude employees not meeting minimum age and service requirements to reduce administrative costs.

  (2) Nondiscriminatory benefits.

(a) **Internal Revenue Code (IRC) Sec. 401(a)(4)**: states that benefits cannot be discriminatory in favor of highly compensated employees.

(b) Regulation permits plans to select a safe harbor design formula or test the discrimination formula for the plan annually.

- Safe harbor design: permits two types of formulas to be used.

  — Formula resulting in a benefit accrual structured as a level percentage of pay.

  — Formula integrated with Social Security: allows employers to provide marginally larger benefits to employees earning more than the Social Security taxable wage base.

(c) General nondiscrimination test: annual mathematical test; allows any type of benefit structure that meets the test.

(3) **Vesting schedule**: schedule dictating when employees have a nonforfeitable right to accrued benefits (i.e., vested) from a qualified plan.

(a) Vesting rules differ for defined benefit and defined contribution plans.

(b) Defined benefit plan vesting schedule: must be at least as favorable to employees as one of two statutory schedules:

- Five-year cliff vesting schedule: employee is 0% vested until completing five years of service, then the employee becomes 100% vested.

- Three- through seven-year graded vesting schedule: employee is 20% vested after three years of service and then receives an extra 20% vesting for each service year thereafter; 100% vested after seven years.

(c) Defined contribution plan vesting schedule: more accelerated schedule, must be as favorable as one of two statutory schedules:

- Three-year cliff vesting schedule: employee is 0% vested until completing three years of service, then the employee is 100% vested.

- Two- through six-year graded vesting schedule: employee is 20% vested after two years of service and then receives an extra 20% vesting for each service year thereafter; 100% vested after six years.

(d) Rules described in (b) and (c) above apply to employment that ends voluntarily or involuntarily; employee must be 100% vested at normal retirement age (as set by the plan) regardless of years worked.

- Plans may choose to fully vest participants upon disability, death, or an early retirement age; unlike vesting participants at retirement age, these vesting decisions are voluntary.

(e) All employee after-tax plan contributions (or pretax contributions with 401(k) plans); must be 100% vested immediately; also applies to earnings on these contributions.

- Employers must maintain separate accounts for employee and employer contributions due to this rule.

(4)   Top-heavy plans.

   (a)   Top-heavy plan: more than 60% of plan benefits are attributed to certain key employees; four special rules apply:

   ■   Top-heavy defined benefit plans must use the same vesting schedules required for defined contribution plans. (See 3.11f(3)(c))

   ■   Minimum benefits must be provided to non-key employees.

   ■   Defined contribution plans: minimum employer contribution cannot be less than 3% of the compensation of each non-key employee (if the key employee also receives at least 3%).

   ■   Defined benefit plans: minimum benefit for non-key employees must be 2% or more of compensation multiplied by the employee's years of service in which the plan was top heavy, up to 10 years.

(5)   Participant loans: all qualified plans may offer loan programs for participants.

   (a)   If a plan chooses to offer a loan program, five requirements must be met:

   ■   Compliant with specific plan loan provisions.

   ■   Highly compensated employees may not have access to loans in greater amounts than nonhighly compensated employees.

   ■   Interest rate must be reasonable.

   ■   Loans must be secured adequately: nearly all plan loans use the participant's accrued benefit for security.

   ■   Participants must have reasonably equal access to loans.

   (b)   Loans are nontaxable to the participant if three criteria are met:

   ■   Cannot be greater than the lesser of 50% of the vested account balance or $50,000.

   ■   Must be repaid within five years unless loan was taken for the purpose of purchasing a primary residence.

   ■   Level amortization schedule must be used and payments must be made at least four times per year.

(6)   Plan funding.

   (a)   Periodic contributions must be paid to the plan's funding instruments.

   (b)   Contributions made to the plan are not accessible to creditors.

   (c)   Contributions are trust property (vs. property of the corporation); must be used to pay benefits unless invested poorly or stolen.

   (d)   Amount of contributions varies by plan.

   (e)   Trustee: used if funding instrument is a trust; four duties:

   ■   Pays out benefits.

   ■   Investment of employer contributions: trustee must diversify investments to reduce risk of substantial losses.

   ■   Provides the sponsor with plan accounting.

   ■   Executes the plan according to plan documents and instruments governing the plan.

(f)   Usually subject to the Employee Retirement Income Security Act (ERISA): trustees must act solely in the best interest of the participants and beneficiaries of the plan.

■   Trustees must exercise prudence (i.e., act with skill, care, discernment, and diligence under prevailing circumstances and act as a prudent person in similar circumstances would act).

(g)   Trustee may direct the investment allocation of employee contributions or allow the employee to direct the allocation.

■   SIMPLEs, SEPs, and 403(b) plans generally allow employee-directed investment of employee contributions.

■   If the plan allows an employee to make investment decisions, the fiduciary will not be liable for the employee's decisions as long as the plan satisfies ERISA Sec. 404(c) and DOL rules.

3.12   Defined benefit vs. defined contribution plans: defined benefit plans (and recent cash balance arrangements) specify benefits that an employee will receive at retirement; defined contribution plans specify the amount of funds that will be placed by an employer in a participant's account (e.g., 10% of salary) which then determines the retirement benefit.

a.   Plan limits:

(1)   Defined benefit plan: maximum annual benefit is $180,000 (as indexed for 2007) or 100% of average earnings of employee payable at age 62, whichever is less.

(a)   When calculating the average earnings of an employee, $225,000 (as indexed for 2007) is the maximum annual amount that can be considered.

(b)   Maximum deductible contribution is based on a calculation by the plan's actuary (i.e., not based on a fixed percentage).

(2)   Defined contribution plan: maximum annual contribution per employee is $45,000 (as indexed for 2007) or 100% of employee's salary, whichever is less.

(a)   Maximum deductible contribution is one-fourth (25%) of the total compensation of all covered participants.

(b)   Employer contributions are allocated for each plan participant; these account balances grow with each contribution made by the employer and will grow (or shrink) based on investment experience of the trust fund.

b.   Differences between defined benefit and defined contribution plans:

(1)   Defined benefit plans base benefits on final average compensation, which is higher at the end of a career; defined contribution plans are considered more portable (i.e., change in employers does not change the final benefit).

> **EXAMPLE** Roger works at a company with a defined benefit plan. Roger will receive 1.5% of his final average compensation multiplied by his years of service at age 65. In 2007 at age 50, Roger has worked for 15 years and has a final monthly salary of $3,300. If Roger stops working now, he will receive $742 per month at age 65. If Roger continues to work until age 65, his final salary will be $6,000 per month (i.e., compensation is increased by 4% annually) and his benefit will be $2,700 per month. If Roger retires at age 50, he will receive less than half of the amount he would receive by retiring at age 65. If Roger changes jobs at age 50 and his new employer has an identical defined benefit plan, his monthly benefit from the second company will be $1,350 ($6,000 × .015 × 15). Roger's combined monthly benefit at retirement would be only $2,092 ($1,350 + $742) vs. the $2,700 he would have received had he stayed with the original company.

   (2) Three steps to help a client understand a defined benefit plan:

      (a) Understand the client: know the client's projected retirement age and discuss expected employment changes.

      (b) Understand the plan: know the plan's benefit formula.

      (c) Explain alternatives: show effect of alternative plans.

3.13 Defined benefit pension plans are characterized by the specific benefit formula used.

   a. Unit-benefit formula: length of service and amount of salary are counted when determining the employee's pension benefit; most frequently used, providing the highest benefits to employees who:

      (1) Work or are likely to work for the same employer for many years.

      (2) Are highly paid employees or owner-employees.

> **EXAMPLE** XYZ Corporation's unit-benefit formula states that each plan participant is to receive a monthly pension beginning at normal retirement age, paid in a life annuity of 1.5% of the final average monthly salary times the years of employment. In 2007, Nick retires after 25 years. Nick's final average monthly salary is $5,000, so his benefit is 1.5% × $5,000 × 25 years = $1,875.

3.14 **Cash balance pension plans.**

   a. Introduced in 1984; increasing trend in large corporations to change defined benefit plans to cash balance pension plans for cost savings.

   b. Benefit is defined as a single sum account balance that grows with contributions and investment experience (similar to defined contribution plans).

   c. Contributions are a bookkeeping credit only; no contributions or investment credits are actually placed in participants' accounts.

> ✱ **EXAMPLE** Gold Nugget, Inc. has a cash balance pension plan. Each participant is entitled to a single-sum benefit that is calculated as a credit of 5% of compensation annually. The credit amounts accumulate along with interest, which is credited annually based on the 30-year Treasury rate on the date the interest is calculated. Actual investment experience will not impact the benefit's value.

  d. Sponsor designs contribution formula; two characteristics:

    (1) Usually based on salary and/or years of service.

    (2) Experience credits can be on a fixed rate, floating rate, or combination.

  e. Because older employees would lose benefits if a plan were converted from a defined benefit plan to a cash balance plan, grandfather provisions are often incorporated to ensure no loss of benefits.

    (1) Employer must disclose this plan change's effect on benefits.

  f. Similar to defined contribution plans in that benefits are more portable.

    (1) However, return is always positive because return is based on a conservative rate of return rather than actual investment experience, which may be negative.

  g. Similar to defined contribution plans in that benefits are more portable.

  h. Vesting: employees must be 100% vested if employed for three or more years.

3.15 Four types of defined contribution plans:

  a. **Money-purchase pension plan:** mandatory annual employer contributions are based on a percentage of participant's compensation.

    (1) Benefits are provided by contributions plus investment earnings and funds forfeited by employees who ended employment prior to being fully vested.

    (2) Three planning considerations with money-purchase pension plans:

      (a) Because contributions are not solely based on the level of compensation at retirement, a sharp inflationary increase at the time of retirement could cause the income to be inadequate.

      (b) Unable to provide a satisfactory retirement program for participants entering at an older age; less time to accrue sufficient assets.

      (c) Sponsor is permitted to amend the plan.

  b. Stock plans: **stock bonus plans** and **employee stock ownership plans (ESOPs)** are similar to profit-sharing plans, except funds are used to purchase employer stock rather than other diversified investments.

    (1) Disastrous for the participant if the employer's stock drops in value; however, the law protects ESOP participants as well as other defined contribution plan participants.

      (a) ESOPs: once the participant is age 55 and attains 10 years of participation, he may elect (between ages 55 and 60) to diversify by moving up to 50% of the account balance into other investments.

      (b) Defined contribution plans (except ESOPs) that invest in publicly traded employer securities: participants must be given the choice to diversify investments; depends on whether the contribution is from the employee or the employer.

- Employee contributions: employee always has the right to direct his contributions to investments other than employer securities.

- Employer contributions: only employee with three years of service has the right to direct his employer's contributions to investments other than employer securities.

(2) Stock bonus plans and ESOPs distribute employer stock at retirement.

    (a) If stock is distributed as part of a lump-sum distribution, participants are taxed only on the value of the stock when placed in the plan (i.e., cost basis); increase in stock value is not taxed until stock is sold.

> **EXAMPLE** Emily has 20,000 shares of her company's stock, each share having a $20 basis. In 2007 when Emily retires, the stock is worth $25 per share. Emily chooses to receive the ESOP distribution in stock. The amount of tax that Emily owes is based on the plan's cost of $400,000 (20,000 shares × $20 per share), not the actual value, which is $500,000. Emily sells the stock in 2008 for $25 per share and will pay taxes only on the $100,000 appreciation. Emily acquired a valuable tax-timing strategy by choosing to take the distribution in the form of stock.

(3) Disadvantage of stock plans: lack of liquidity in closely held businesses.

    (a) To solve this problem, employer must offer a **put option**: an offer to repurchase the stock for at least 60 days after the distribution.

    (b) If the repurchase is not exercised, the option must be offered for an additional 60-day period the next year.

c. **401(k) plans**: a type of profit-sharing plan that allows participants to defer taxes on up to $15,500 (2007) by electing to contribute part of participant's compensation to the plan.

    (1) Also known as a **cash or deferred arrangement (CODA)**: employee delays paying tax on part of salary by placing it in a plan and not getting it in cash.

    (2) Tax on interest on contributions is deferred until retirement.

    (3) The Economic Growth and Tax Relief Reconciliation Act (EGTRRA) of 2001 increases the limit on the maximum deferral amount; after 2006, the amount will increase by $500 per year to account for inflation.

        (a) Participants over 50 years old may make special catch-up contributions.

        (b) Key point: the maximum deferral is based on the individual; one individual cannot exceed the maximum deferral amount regardless of the number of plans in which the individual participates.

Maximum Salary Deferral Amounts for 2006–2007			
Year	Maximum Deferral	Catch-up Contributions for Participants 50 Years Old and Older	Total for Participants 50 Years Old and Older
2006	$15,000	$5,000	$20,000
2007	$15,500	$5,000	$20,500

(4) Three special rules for the 401(k) salary deferral portion of a profit-sharing plan:

    (a) An additional nondiscrimination test, the actual deferral percentage (ADP) test applies to salary deferrals.

       ■ ADP test: compares deferral percentages of nonhighly compensated employees with percentages of highly compensated employees; if the test is failed, a portion of the highly compensated employee contributions may be reduced or returned.

    (b) 401(k) salary reductions can't be forfeited; 100% vested at once.

    (c) In-service withdrawals can only be made in two cases: individual has a financial hardship or has attained age 59½.

(5) Four types of contributions in 401(k) plans:

    (a) Salary deferrals.

    (b) Employer matching contributions.

    (c) Employer profit-sharing contributions.

    (d) Pre- and post-tax contributions by employees are permitted; rarely used.

(6) 401(k) plans usually provide for loans, restricted to the lesser of $50,000 or 50% of the vested account balance.

(7) Participants usually have control over investments in a 401(k) plan.

(8) Seven planning considerations when working with 401(k) plans:

    (a) Older workers can increase savings by taking advantage of the new catch-up rules and increased deferral limits.

    (b) Understand the employer match.

    (c) Roll funds to another plan when changing employment.

    (d) Borrowing should only be permitted with hardship withdrawals.

    (e) Ensure appropriate asset allocation for clients.

    (f) Exercise caution when investing in employer securities.

    (g) Pre-tax savings should be encouraged.

d. **Profit-sharing plans:** primary goal is to provide a sharing of the profits rather than to provide retirement income; six advantages to employers:

(1) Employer does not have to make contributions annually; contributions must be considered "substantial and recurring" according to the IRS.

(2) Plan can be structured so that, in years during which a certain amount of profit is not realized, no contributions are necessary.

(3) Employees (including owner-employees) may make in-service withdrawals as early as two years after funds are initially contributed by the employer.

(4) More productive employees by tying contributions to profits.

(5) **Allocation formula:** must be predetermined and definite; traditionally allocates a set percentage of compensation (e.g., 4%) to each participant.

    (a) Plan may allocate a higher level of contributions to key employees if nondiscrimination requirements are met; one effective method:

       ■ Social Security integration: plan may contribute a maximum 5.7% of compensation greater than the taxable wage base plus the amount contributed based on a percentage of total compensation; $225,000 cap (2007) reduces the effectiveness of integration.

Note: Cross testing allows an employer to test when an allocation formula is nondiscriminatory.

> **(6)**   Profit-sharing plans may be used like pension plans; employer may guarantee a contribution whether or not the company earns a profit.

3.16   Pension plans vs. profit-sharing plans: pension plan must provide retirement benefits so the employer must contribute to the retirement plan; profit-sharing plan doesn't guarantee employer payments because contributions are based on earnings.

a.   Pension plan category: three traits of plans included in this category are annual funding, limit on investments to 10% of employer stock, and no distributions during employment until age 62; includes three plans:

(1)   Cash balance pension plan.

(2)   Defined benefit pension plan.

(3)   Money-purchase pension plan.

b.   Profit-sharing category: three traits of plans included in this category are no annual funding requirements, no limit on investment of plan assets in employer stock, and in-service withdrawals (i.e., before retirement); includes four plans:

(1)   ESOP.

(2)   Profit-sharing plan.

(3)   401(k) plan.

(4)   Stock bonus plan.

c.   Two instances when funds may be withdrawn from profit-sharing plans:

(1)   Entire account balance is available once five years of service is completed.

(2)   Distributions can be made for funds that were contributed to the plan at least two years prior to the distribution.

3.2   CONSIDERATIONS WHEN PLANNING FOR RETIREMENT

Key point   The six considerations when planning for retirement are: vesting, PBGC guarantee of benefits if a defined benefit plan, early retirement, delayed retirement, portability of benefits if employment ends, and investments if a defined contribution plan.

3.21   Plan termination after retirement won't affect the employee.

a.   Three effects of plans terminated before employee's retirement:

(1)   Employee immediately becomes 100% vested in the plan.

(2)   Participant is entitled to the accrued benefit in a defined benefit plan or the account balance in a defined contribution plan.

(3)   A defined contribution plan will always have enough assets to pay the account balance (unless a trustee has absconded with the plan assets).

(a)   Participants may choose a lump-sum distribution or a deferred annuity; most choose the lump sum and roll the funds into an IRA.

■   When choosing the lump-sum option, the participant has the choice to make a direct transfer of funds (to another qualified plan or IRA) and can continue to defer taxation.

ZOOM IN   Retirement Plans Up Close

Type of Plan	Who Contributes to the Plan?	Contribution Limits	Filing Requirements	Participant Loans	In-Service Withdrawals
401(k) Plan	Employer contributions and/or employee salary deferrals. Employers are always 100% vested in their salary deferrals. Employer contributions may be vested on a graduated vesting schedule.	*Employee:* $15,500 in 2007. If employee is age 50 or over, an additional catch-up contribution of $5,000 in 2007 is allowed. *Employer/Employee:* Lesser of 25% of compensation or $45,000 in 2007.	Annual filing of Form 5500 is required.	Allowed.	Permitted, but subject to possible 10% penalty tax if under age 59½.
Profit-Sharing Plan	Employer contributions only.	Lesser of 25% of compensation or $45,000 in 2007 (and subject to cost-of-living adjustments for later years).	Annual filing of Form 5500 is required.	Allowed.	Allowed, but subject to possible 10% penalty if under age 59½.
SEP	Employer contributions only.	Lesser of 25% of compensation or $45,000 in 2007 (and subject to cost-of-living adjustments for later years).	An employer generally has no filing requirements. Annual reporting required for qualified plans is normally not required for SEPs.	Not allowed.	Allowed, but includable in income and subject to the 10% penalty tax if under age 59½.
SIMPLE IRA Plan	Employer must contribute and employee may contribute.	*Employee:* $10,500 in 2007. If the employee is age 50 or over, a catch-up contribution of $2,500 (2007) is also allowed. *Employer:* generally, dollar-for-dollar match up to 3% of pay or 2% of nonelective contribution for each employee.	Employer generally has no filing requirements. Annual reporting required for qualified plans (Form 5500 series) is not required.	Not allowed.	Allowed, but withdrawals are included in income and are subject to a 10% additional tax if the participant is under age 59½. If withdrawals are made within the first two years of participation, the 10% additional tax is increased to 25%.
Money Purchase Plan	Employer and/or employee contributions.	Lesser of 25% of compensation or $45,000 in 2007 (and subject to cost-of-living adjustments for later years).	Annual filing of Form 5500 is required.	Allowed.	Not allowed.
Defined Benefit Plan	Employer contributions generally. Sometimes, employee contributions are either mandatory or voluntary.	Deduction limit is any amount up to the plan's unfunded current liability	Annual filing of Form 5500 is required. An enrolled actuary, not an enrolled agent, must sign Schedule B of Form 5500.	Allowed.	Not allowed.

b. Participants may use funds for current needs; results in income taxation and a 10% early withdrawal excise tax if under 59½ years of age.

c. For defined benefit plans, employer may purchase annuity certificates from an insurer, who then assumes the employer's liability (up to point of termination) and guarantees payments of the vested benefit under an annuity certificate; certificate contains three items:

   (1) Starting date of annuity.

   (2) Amount of annuity.

   (3) Options available regarding the annuity.

d. For participants in a terminating defined benefit plan covered by the Pension Benefit Guaranty Corporation (PBGC), the PBGC guarantees payment of basic benefits, not to exceed the lesser of:

   (1) About $4,200 per month (for 2007).

   (2) 100% of average monthly wages during participant's five highest-paid consecutive years.

3.22 Plan provisions relating to early retirement:

a. Both age and service requirements may have to be met before a participant may take early retirement (e.g., age 55 with at least 10 years of service).

b. Although early retirement benefits are paid out over a longer period, four disadvantages must be considered:

   (1) In defined benefit plans, retirement benefits are actuarially reduced to reflect the longer payout period.

   (2) In defined contribution plans, participant taking early retirement loses several years of contributions at a higher salary.

   (3) In defined benefit plans, the number of years of service and compensation used for determining the benefit formula are lower, causing a lower benefit.

   (4) Increasing salaries offer protection against inflation that continues into retirement; early retirement stops the client's salary sooner.

c. Nine questions to address with a client considering early retirement:

   (1) What is the earliest retirement age under the plan?

   (2) What is the actuarial reduction for early retirement benefits?

   (3) What effect will lost earnings due to early retirement have on the client?

   (4) What is the minimum service requirement (if any) for early retirement?

   (5) Does an actuarial reduction reflect a true reduction for the time value of money or is early retirement partially subsidized by the employer?

   (6) How will lost buying power affect a client during early retirement?

   (7) Are there any early retirement incentives (e.g., golden handshake)?

   (8) Has the lost income from a reduction in final average salary been considered?

   (9) Is there a cap on years of service in the benefit formula?

3.23 Plan provisions relating to delayed retirement; four issues to consider:

    a. Participants working past normal retirement age will face fewer post-retirement inflation problems due to shorter post-retirement period.

    b. In defined benefit plans, an employee could receive actuarially increased benefits because of a shorter payout period.

    c. Participants of a defined benefit plan may or may not continue to accrue benefits until actual retirement (e.g., 30 years of service may be the maximum amount of service in which benefits may be accrued).

    d. Participants of a defined contribution plan will continue to receive contributions until actual retirement.

3.24 Changing employment: the best approach is to elect a direct rollover into a company-sponsored plan or IRA (permits taxes to remain deferred).

3.25 Investment of plan assets: a critical factor in determining total benefits.

    a. Defined contribution plans, 401(k) plans, 403(b) plans and SIMPLEs may permit employees (vs. a trustee) to make investment decisions, five considerations:

        (1) Make asset allocation decisions while considering the whole portfolio.

        (2) Taxation.

        (3) Identify retirement goals (e.g., amount needed for retirement, risk toleration).

        (4) Must have a complete understanding of each investment offered.

        (5) Expenses associated with investment changes and frequency of allowable changes.

3.3 SOURCE OF INFORMATION REGARDING QUALIFIED PLANS

> **Key point** The three sources of information regarding qualified plans are: summary plan descriptions (SPDs), annual benefit statements, and IRS Form 1099R.

3.31 **Summary plan description (SPD):** booklet explaining the participant's benefits.

    a. SPDs that are more a promotional tool than an explanation are illegal.

    b. Limitations, exceptions, reductions, plan restrictions, and other negative consequences must be listed.

    c. Conflict between plan and SPD: although a SPD may have disclaimers, the trend in court rulings is to bind descriptions listed in the SPD.

3.32 **Annual benefit statement:** if an employer does not automatically provide the statement, participants may submit a written request; statement shows the accrued benefit/account balance of the plan participant.

    a. Must be furnished at least once per year when requested by participant and at a participant's termination.

3.33 **IRS Form 1099R:** a form filed with the IRS when a participant or participant's beneficiary receives a lump-sum distribution.

3.34 Plan document: must be provided to participants upon request; administrator may charge for copying.

3.4 OTHER TAX-ADVANTAGED RETIREMENT PLANS

> **Key point** Three other tax-advantaged retirement plans are the 403(b) plan, the simplified employee pension plan (SEP), and the savings incentive match plan for employees (SIMPLE).
>
> **Key point** A 403(b) plan allows only tax-exempt and public school employers to participate and shares key similarities and differences with the 401(k) plan.
>
> **Key point** A SEP is funded by IRAs but allows full defined contribution limits.
>
> **Key point** A SIMPLE is funded by IRAs and has lower limits, but is easy to administer.

3.41 **403(b) plan** (also referred to as tax-sheltered annuity [TSA] or tax-deferred annuity [TDA]): similar to 401(k) plans.

  a. Three similarities with 401(k) plans:

  (1) Salary reduction is used for employee deferrals.

  (2) Allows pre-tax contributions (up to the $15,500 limit in 2007).

  (3) Plan is used in lieu of, or in conjunction with, other retirement plans.

  b. Three differences from 401(k) plans:

  (1) Testing difference: not subject to nondiscrimination testing; highly compensated employees can defer the maximum amount regardless of contributions by nonhighly compensated employees.

  (2) Only qualified tax-exempt organizations (i.e., 501(c)(3) organizations) and public schools may participate.

  (3) Plan can be funded by either mutual funds or annuity contracts only.

  c. 403(b) plans can include only salary deferral contributions or may include employer contributions as well; three differences in plan operation when omitting employer contributions:

  (1) Participant's main relationship is with the service provider vs. the plan sponsor.

  (2) Annual reporting by sponsor is not required.

  (3) Not subject to the fiduciary rules of ERISA.

3.42 Simplified employee pension plans (SEPs).

  a. **SEP**: a retirement plan that uses an IRA as the vehicle for receiving contributions; a SEP is not a pension plan, despite the name, but takes the form of a profit-sharing or 401(k) plan.

  b. Four advantages over qualified plans:

  (1) Benefit is the IRA balance; contributions are nonforfeitable.

  (2) Adopted with a simple IRS form.

  (3) Less cumbersome requirements for documentation, reporting, and disclosure.

  (4) Trust accounting ends because each participant has his own IRA.

  c. Five characteristics similar to IRAs:

  (1) Cannot invest in collectibles or life insurance.

    (2) Loans are prohibited.

    (3) IRA treatment concerning distributions is the same as other IRAs.

    (4) Participants are immediately vested and have access to benefits at any time; subject to taxation and 10% early distribution tax.

    (5) Same contribution limits as profit-sharing plans.

        (a) Maximum contribution: lesser of $45,000 (2007) or 100% of pay and no more than 25% of total compensation.

d. SEPs must cover all types of employees who meet three requirements:

    (1) Minimum of $500 (indexed for 2007) in compensation for the year.

    (2) At least 21 years of age.

    (3) Worked for employer at least three of the preceding five years.

3.43 **Savings incentive match plan for employees (SIMPLE):** alternative to 401(k) plan; easy to administer and subject to strict design restrictions.

    a. SIMPLEs are funded with IRAs; therefore, three plan requirements apply:

        (1) Participants must be 100% vested at all times in all benefits.

        (2) Assets cannot be invested in collectibles or life insurance.

        (3) Loans by participants are not permitted.

    b. Eligible employers: any type of business with 100 employees or fewer who annually earn $5,000 or more in compensation; no other qualified plan, 403(b) plan, or SEP can be maintained.

    c. Contributions:

        (1) Eligible employees can make pretax contributions up to $10,500 (2007).

            (a) Catch-up election for participants age 50 and over (2007): $2,500.

        (2) Nondiscrimination testing is not required.

        (3) Employer contribution requirement: works in one of two ways:

            (a) Dollar-for-dollar matching contribution on the first 3% of compensation deferred by the employee; employer can make a lower match for up to two years in any five-year period, if two conditions are met:

              ■ Matching contribution is not less than 1% of compensation.

              ■ Participants are notified of the lower contribution in advance of the 60-day election period prior to the beginning of the year.

            (b) A 2% nonelective contribution for all eligible employees.

    d. Three eligibility requirements:

        (1) Must cover any employee earning $5,000 in any two previous years who is expected to earn $5,000 in the current year.

        (2) Employees subject to collective bargaining may be excluded.

        (3) Participants have access to funds at all times: 25% penalty on withdrawals within first two years of plan.

3.5 SELECTING A PLAN FOR THE SMALL BUSINESS OWNER

> **Key point** A SEP is a good starting point for retirement plans for small businesses because setup and administration of the plan are easy and the contribution limit is high; however, a SEP can be costly.
>
> **Key point** A profit-sharing plan is a viable alternative to a SEP; however, a profit-sharing plan has reporting requirements and more costly administration.
>
> **Key point** Although a SIMPLE is less costly and less complicated than a 401(k) plan, it is inflexible and the contribution limit is lower.

3.51 Planning for an unincorporated business is typically the same as planning for a corporation with one exception:

    a. Maximum deductible contribution is based on net earnings vs. salary for the self-employed individual.

3.52 SEPs: an excellent starting point for retirement plans for small businesses with few employees or one employee (the owner).

    a. Six advantages to the small business in starting with a SEP:

        (1) Discretionary contributions.

        (2) Maximum deductible contribution rose to 25% of compensation.

        (3) Documentation is simple to maintain.

        (4) Terminating the plan is simple.

        (5) Easy setup and administration.

        (6) No annual reports to be filed.

    b. Three limitations to the small business in starting a SEP:

        (1) Maximum contribution: lesser of $45,000 (2007) or 100% of compensation.

        (2) If unincorporated, maximum deduction can be no more than 20% of net earnings after accounting for the Social Security deduction vs. 25% of compensation for corporations.

        (3) Total compensation considered can't exceed $225,000 cap (2007).

    c. SEPs can be costly for three reasons (not recommended for larger companies):

        (1) Contributions are always fully vested.

        (2) Allocation formula: must be a formula integrated with Social Security or a level percentage of compensation.

        (3) Part-time employees meeting requirements must be included in the plan; short-term employees can be eliminated (i.e., less than three months of work).

3.53 Choosing the profit-sharing plan: similar to a SEP yet with reporting requirements and more costly administration.

    a. Although SEPs are primarily recommended for small business owners, profit-sharing plans may be a viable alternative for four reasons:

        (1) Deferred vesting schedule may be used.

        (2) Opportunity to use a cross-tested basis to allocate contributions (i.e., business owner can receive a larger contribution than other employees).

    (3) Withdrawals may be limited.

    (4) Number of covered employees can be limited more than in SEPs.

3.54 Choosing the 401(k) plan: employers with profit-sharing plans can add a 401(k) feature to provide participants with the opportunity for greater retirement savings.

  a. Employees have the ability to make salary deferrals up to $15,500 (2007).

  b. Employers must often offer a matching contribution (e.g., employer match, profit-sharing contribution) to satisfy ADP testing requirements.

    (1) Alternatively, the employer can make a safe-harbor contribution.

3.55 Choosing the SIMPLE: less costly and complicated than the 401(k) option for the employer; six considerations:

  a. Inflexible: less flexible than the 401(k) plan.

  b. Modest employer contribution by law; however, law changes have designated increases in minimum contributions to be effective over the next several years.

  c. Participants have immediate access to retirement funds.

  d. Alternative for employers expecting to fail the ADP test.

  e. Less versatile (can't direct larger contributions to the business owner).

  f. Easier to set up a SIMPLE and easier to administer than a 401(k) plan.

3.56 Choosing the defined benefit plan: not a good choice for small businesses due to complexity and cost with one exception:

  a. Defined benefit plan is the only option in which the business owner can contribute more than the $45,000 (indexed for 2007) limit.

    (1) Maximum contribution is based on the benefit formula, participant's age, and actuarial assumptions.

Highlight 1: Qualified Retirement Plans

- Six types of qualified plans:
  (1) Defined benefit pension plans.
  (2) Money-purchase pension plans.
  (3) 401(k) plans.
  (4) Cash balance pension plans.
  (5) Stock bonus plans and employee stock ownership plans (ESOPs).
  (6) Profit-sharing plans. (3.11a)

- Vesting schedules: schedule dictating when employees have a nonforfeitable right to accrued benefits (i.e., vested) from a qualified plan; vesting rules for defined benefit plans slightly differ from those for defined contribution plans:
  (1) Defined benefit plan vesting schedule: must be at least as favorable to employees as one of two statutory schedules:
      (a) Five-year cliff vesting schedule: 100% vested at five years; 0% vested before that.
      (b) Three- through seven-year graded vesting schedule: 100% vested at seven years; 20% vested at three years and an extra 20% vested each year thereafter.
  (2) Defined contribution plan vesting schedule: more accelerated schedule; must be at least as favorable to employees as one of two statutory schedules:
      (a) Three-year cliff vesting schedule: 100% vested at three years; 0% vested before that.
      (b) Two- through six-year graded vesting schedule: 100% vested at six years; 20% vested at two years and an extra 20% vested each year thereafter. (3.11f(3))

- Pension Plans and Profit-Sharing Plans

Three types of pension plans:	Four types of profit-sharing plans:
1. Cash balance pension plan.	1. ESOP.
2. Defined benefit pension plan.	2. Profit-sharing plan.
3. Money-purchase pension plan.	3. 401(k) plan.
	4. Stock bonus plan.
(3.16a)	(3.16b)

Highlight 2: Considerations When Planning for Retirement

- Three effects of plans terminated before employee's retirement:
  (1) Employee immediately becomes 100% vested in the plan.
  (2) Participant is entitled to the accrued benefit in a defined benefit plan or the account balance in a defined contribution plan.
  (3) A defined contribution plan will always have enough assets to pay the account balance (unless a trustee has absconded with the plan assets). (3.21a)

- Defined contribution plans, 401(k) plans, 403(b) plans, and SIMPLEs may permit employees (vs. a trustee) to direct investment allocation; five considerations:
  (1) Asset allocation decisions should be made while considering the portfolio as a whole.
  (2) Taxation.
  (3) Identify retirement goals.
  (4) Must have a complete understanding of each investment offered.
  (5) Expenses associated with investment changes and frequency of allowable changes. (3.25a)

Highlight 3: Source of Information Regarding Qualified Plans

■ Annual benefit statement: if an employer does not automatically provide the statement, participants may submit a written request; statement shows the accrued benefit/account balance of the plan participant.

(1) Must be furnished at least once per year when requested by participant and at a participant's termination. (3.32)

Highlight 4: Other Tax-Advantaged Retirement Plans

■ 403(b) Plans

Three similarities with 401(k) plans:	Three differences from 401(k) plans:
1. Salary reduction is used for employee deferrals.	1. Testing difference: not subject to nondiscrimination testing; highly compensated employees can defer the maximum amount regardless of contributions by nonhighly compensated employees.
2. Allows pretax contributions (up to the $15,500 limit in 2007).	2. Only qualified tax-exempt organizations and public schools may participate.
3. Plan is used in lieu of, or in conjunction with, other retirement plans.	3. Plan can be funded by either mutual funds or annuity contracts only.
(3.41a)	(3.41b)

■ Savings incentive match plan for employees (SIMPLE): alternative to 401(k) plan; easy to administer and subject to strict design restrictions. SIMPLEs are funded with IRAs; therefore, three plan requirements apply:

(1) Participants must be 100% vested at all times in all benefits.

(2) Assets cannot be invested in collectibles or life insurance.

(3) Loans by participants are not permitted. (3.43a)

Highlight 5: Selecting a Plan for the Small Business Owner

■ Planning for an unincorporated business is typically the same as planning for a corporation with one exception: maximum deductible contribution is based on net earnings versus salary for the self-employed individual. (3.51)

■ Small Businesses Starting with a SEP

Six advantages:	Three limitations:
1. Discretionary contributions.	1. Maximum contribution is the lesser of $45,000 (indexed for 2007) or 100% of compensation per employee.
2. In 2002, the maximum deductible contribution increased from 15 to 25% of compensation.	
3. Documentation is simple to maintain.	2. If unincorporated, maximum deduction can be no more than 20% of net earnings after accounting for the Social Security deduction vs. 25% of compensation for corporations.
4. Terminating the plan is simple.	
5. Easy set-up and administration.	3. Total compensation considered cannot be greater than the $225,000 (indexed for 2007) compensation cap.
6. No annual reports to be filed.	
(3.52a)	(3.52b)

TERMS TO KNOW DEFINITIONS

401(k) plan A type of profit-sharing plan that allows participants to defer taxes on up to $15,500 (2007) by electing to contribute part of participant's compensation to the plan. (3.15c)

403(b) plan Also referred to as tax-sheltered annuity (TSA) or tax-deferred annuity (TDA); similar to 401(k) plan. (3.41)

Allocation formula A profit-sharing plan formula that must be predetermined and definite; traditionally allocates a set percentage of compensation to each participant; plan may allocate a higher level of contributions to key employees if nondiscrimination requirements are met. (3.15d(5))

Annual benefit statement A statement that shows the accrued benefit/account balance of a plan participant. (3.32)

Cash-balance pension plan Benefit is defined as a single sum account balance that grows with contributions and investment experience; contributions are a bookkeeping credit only. (3.14)

Cash or deferred arrangements (CODAs) Employee delays paying tax on part of salary by placing it in a plan and not getting it in cash. (3.15c(1))

Defined benefit plan A retirement plan specifying the benefits that an employee will receive. (3.12)

Defined contribution plan A retirement plan specifying the amount of funds that will be placed in a participant's account. (3.12)

Employee stock ownership plans (ESOPs) Similar to profit-sharing plans, except most funds are usually used to purchase employer stock rather than other diversified investments. (3.15b)

Highly compensated employee Include two kinds of employees: (1) five percent owner in previous or current year or (2) employees earning over $100,000 (2007) in the previous year. (3.11f(1)(a))

IRC Sec. 401(a)(4) Provision in the Internal Revenue Code stating that benefits cannot be discriminatory in favor of highly compensated employees. (3.11f(3)(a))

IRS Form 1099R A form filed with the IRS when a participant or participant's beneficiary receives a lump-sum distribution. (3.33)

Money-purchase pension plan A type of defined contribution plan; mandatory annual employer contributions are based on a percentage of participant's compensation. (3.15a)

Pension plan category Three traits of plans included in this category are annual funding, limit on investments to 10% of employer stock, and no distributions during employment until age 62; includes three plans: cash balance pension plans, defined benefit pension plans, and money-purchase pension plan. (3.16a)

Profit-sharing category Three traits of plans included in this category are no annual funding requirements, no limit on investment of plan assets in employer stock, and in-service withdrawals (i.e., before retirement); includes four plans: ESOPs, profit-sharing plans, 401(k) plans, and stock bonus plans. (3.16b)

Profit-sharing plan Primary goal is to provide a share of the profits rather than to provide retirement income; employer does not have to make contributions annually; contributions must be considered substantial and recurring, according to the IRS; plan can be structured so that, in years during which a certain amount of profit is not realized, no contributions are necessary. (3.15d)

Put option In a stock bonus plan, an offer to repurchase the stock for a minimum of 60 days following the distribution. (3.15b(3)(a))

Qualified plan A plan meeting Internal Revenue Service (IRS) specifications (IRC Section 401(a)); all are prefunded. (3.11)

Ratio test Test ensuring that a plan benefits a percentage of nonhighly compensated employees equal to 70% of the percentage of highly compensated employees who benefit from the plan. (3.11f(1)(b))

SEP A retirement plan that uses an IRA as the vehicle for receiving contributions; a SEP is not a pension plan, despite the name, but takes the form of a profit-sharing or 401(k) plan. (3.42a)

SIMPLE Alternative to 401(k) plan; easy to administer and subject to strict design restrictions; funded with IRAs. (3.43)

Stock bonus plans Stock bonus plans and employee stock ownership plans (ESOPs) are similar to profit-sharing plans, except most funds are usually used to purchase employer stock rather than other diversified investments. (3.15b)

Summary plan description Booklet explaining the participant's benefits in an easy-to-read format. (3.31)

Top-heavy plans More than 60% of plan benefits are attributed to certain key employees. (3.11f(4)(a))

Vesting schedule Schedule dictating when employees have a nonforfeitable right to accrued benefits (i.e., vested) from a qualified plan; vesting rules for defined benefit plans slightly differ from those for defined contribution plans. (3.11f(3))

QUESTIONS

1. All of the following are advantages to a small business in starting with a SEP EXCEPT
   A. contributions are always fully vested
   B. documentation is simple to maintain
   C. there are no annual reports to be filed
   D. plan termination is simple

2. Which of the following statements regarding SIMPLEs is CORRECT?
   A. By law, employers can only make modest contributions.
   B. Participants do not have immediate access to retirement funds.
   C. They are more versatile than a 401(k) plan.
   D. They are more costly than a 401(k) plan.

3. All of the following belong to the 6 rules with the greatest influence on plan design EXCEPT
   A. eligibility and coverage
   B. vesting
   C. participant loans
   D. federal court rulings

4. Which of the following statements concerning profit-sharing plans is CORRECT?
   A. Employees may not make withdrawals before retirement.
   B. Profit-sharing plans guarantee employer payments.
   C. Plans must provide the same level of contribution to all employees.
   D. The allocation formula must be redetermined and definite.

5. Which of the following statements concerning summary plan descriptions is(are) CORRECT?
   A. The trend in court rulings is to disallow descriptions in the SPD and uphold disclaimers in the SPD.
   B. SPDs that are more of a promotional tool than an explanation are permissible.
   C. Both A and B.
   D. Neither A nor B.

ANSWERS

1. **A.** The fact that SEP contributions are always fully vested is not an advantage for the small business owner starting with a SEP, but rather one of the reasons using a SEP can be costly. (3.52)

2. **A.** With SIMPLEs, participants have immediate access to retirement funds. SIMPLEs are less versatile and less costly than 401(k) plans. (3.55)

3. **D.** The 6 rules with the greatest influence on plan design are (1) eligibility and coverage, (2) nondiscriminatory benefits, (3) vesting, (4) top-heavy plans, (5) participant loans, and (6) plan funding. (3.11f)

4. **D.** Employees (including owner-employees) may make in-service withdrawals as early as 2 years after funds are initially contributed by an employer. The plan can be structured so that, in years during which a certain amount of profit is not realized, no contributions are necessary. The plan may allocate a higher level of contributions to key employees if nondiscrimination requirements are met. (3.15d)

5. **D.** Even though SPDs may have disclaimers, the trend in court rulings has been to bind descriptions in the SPD. SPDs that are more a promotional tool than an explanation are prohibited by law. (3.31)

4

Nonqualified Plans and IRAs

"Most of us are just about as happy as we make up our minds to be."

—Abraham Lincoln

A HELICOPTER VIEW OF ASSIGNMENT 4

TERMS TO KNOW

Active participant

Incentive stock option (ISO)

Individual retirement account (IRA)

Nonqualified stock options (NQSOs)

Phantom stock

Restricted stock

Roth IRA

Roth IRA conversion

Salary reduction plan

Section 162 plan

Spousal IRA

Supplemental executive retirement plans (SERPs)

4.1 BASICS OF TRADITIONAL IRAs AND ROTH IRAs

Key point Both traditional and Roth IRAs, which are based on compensation and may rely on a spouse's compensation, have a contribution limit of $4,000 for 2007 and $5,000 for 2008.

4.11 Two types of **individual retirement accounts (IRAs)**:

    a. Traditional IRAs have four similarities with employer-sponsored tax-sheltered retirement plans:

        (1) Permit earnings to be tax deferred until retirement.

        (2) Encourage accumulation of savings for retirement.

        (3) Allow contributions to be made with pretax dollars.

        (4) Tax-favored savings plans.

    b. Roth IRA:

        (1) Contributions are made on an after-tax basis.

        (2) Earnings are not taxed.

        (3) Qualifying distributions are tax free.

4.12 Contribution limits for both IRA and Roth IRA:

    a. Annual contribution limit (2007) is the lesser of $4,000 or 100% of compensation; limit is scheduled to increase to $5,000 (2008).

    b. Contributions do not have to be made.

    c. $4,000 limit includes annual contributions to traditional and Roth IRAs.

    d. Compensation: includes wages, fees, salaries, bonuses, and alimony; money derived from investments or retirement income is not eligible.

    e. Catch-up election: individuals at least 50 years of age are permitted to contribute an extra $1,000 per year (2007).

4.13 **Spousal IRA**: IRA contributed to by a working married person for a spouse with little or no compensation; $4,000 (2007) annual contribution limit.

    a. Three conditions:

        (1) Taxpayer must be married at the end of the year and file a joint tax return.

        (2) Spouse must earn less than the taxpayer.

        (3) The couple must have compensation that equals or exceeds contributions to the IRAs of both persons.

4.14 Timing of contributions:

    a. Allowed any time during the tax year or up to April 15 of the next year.

    b. Can be made all at once for the year or over time.

4.15 Excess contributions: any contribution to a traditional IRA or Roth IRA that exceeds the maximum contribution limit.

a. Results in an excise tax of 6% of the excess.

    (1) If excess amount plus interest is withdrawn by tax deadline, penalty can be avoided but excess amount must be included in gross income for the year.

        (a) 10% premature distribution penalty may apply to interest from excess.

4.2 TRADITIONAL IRAs

Key point Contributions to a traditional IRA are deductible unless there is an active participant in an employer plan and the income is over the threshold amount.

Key point Withdrawals from traditional IRAs are generally taxable and there is no tax on earnings while in the traditional IRA.

4.21 **Active participant**: one who participates in an employer-maintained plan.

    a. Nine types of employer-maintained plans for purposes of defining active participants:

        (1) 403(b) tax-sheltered annuity plans.

        (2) Defined benefit pension plans.

        (3) Federal, state, or local government plans.

        (4) Money-purchase plans.

        (5) Profit-sharing plans.

        (6) Stock plans.

        (7) SEPs.

        (8) SIMPLEs.

        (9) Target benefit plans.

> **EXAMPLE** Sandra's only form of retirement arrangement is a supplemental executive retirement plan (SERP), which is a nonqualified retirement arrangement. Because the SERP is nonqualified, Sandra will not be considered an active participant, even though she does participate in an employer-maintained plan.

    b. Defined benefit plans: person is active participant even if he chooses not to contribute to plan.

        (1) Two situations where the individual is not considered an active participant:

            (a) No benefits are currently accruing for any plan participant.

            (b) Individual is not eligible for the plan for the entire year.

    c. Defined contribution plans: if the plan specifies that employer contributions must be designated to the individual's account, then person is an active participant.

        (1) If profit-sharing or stock plan allows employer contributions to be discretionary, person is an active participant if a contribution is received.

(2) Includes SEPs, SIMPLEs, and 403(b) plans.

(3) Mandatory or voluntary contributions and contributions made pursuant to a salary reduction SEP, SIMPLE, 403(b) plan, or 401(k) will also trigger active participant status.

d. Entirely discretionary contributions made after the end of a year apply to the next year.

> **EXAMPLE** Brian becomes eligible for his employer's profit-sharing plan on December 31, 2007. Brian's employer makes a contribution for the 2007 plan year on May 15, 2008. Brian is not considered an active participant for the 2007 plan year; however, because the employer contributed in 2008, Brian will be an active participant for the 2008 plan year.

e. For plan years which do not coincide with calendar years: active participant status is determined by whether the individual was an active participant for the plan year ending within the calendar year.

> **EXAMPLE** Alley Gator, Inc. has a money-purchase pension plan with a plan year from July 1 to June 30. Andy becomes an active participant in the July 1, 2007 to June 30, 2008 plan year. Andy is an active participant in 2008 because the plan year ended within 2008. Andy would not be considered an active participant for 2007.

f. Participation for any part of the year renders the individual an active participant for the entire year.

4.22 Traditional IRA eligibility:

a. Persons under age 70½ who receive compensation can make an IRA contribution.

b. If neither the taxpayer nor the taxpayer's spouse is an active participant in an employer-maintained retirement plan, contributions are deductible.

(1) Even if the contribution is not deductible, interest will be tax deferred.

c. If the taxpayer is an active participant, then the contributions are deductible only if the taxpayer's adjusted gross income (AGI) falls below a certain limit.

d. If an individual is not an active participant but the individual's spouse is an active participant, then the nonactive participant's contribution is deductible if the couple's income falls below a particular limit.

4.23 Traditional IRA income level:

a. Nonactive participants can deduct IRA contributions regardless of income.

b. Deductible contributions for active participants:

(1) Married couple filing a joint return (2007):

(a) Full deduction with an adjusted gross income (AGI) of $83,000 or less.

(b) Partial deduction with AGI between $83,000 and $103,000.

(c) No deduction with AGI of $103,000 or more.

(2) Individual (2007):

   (a) Full deduction with AGI of $52,000 or less.

   (b) Partial deduction with AGI between $52,000 and $62,000.

   (c) No deduction with AGI of $62,000 or more.

c. AGI for these purposes includes Social Security benefits included in gross income and gains/losses on passive investments; does not include foreign earned income.

d. Partial deduction formula:

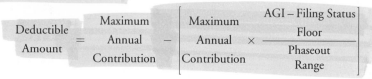

$$\text{Deductible Amount} = \text{Maximum Annual Contribution} - \left[\text{Maximum Annual Contribution} \times \frac{\text{AGI} - \text{Filing Status Floor}}{\text{Phaseout Range}}\right]$$

> **EXAMPLE** Morris is a single taxpayer with an AGI of $55,000 in 2007. He is an active participant but also makes contributions to an IRA. The maximum deductible contribution Morris can make to his IRA is $2,000.

$$\$4,000 - \left[\$4,000 \times \frac{\$55,000 - \$50,000}{\$10,000}\right] = \$2,000$$

e. For married taxpayers filing jointly, where only one spouse is an active participant (2007):

   (1) $4,000 deductible IRA contribution is allowed for the nonactive participant if the couple's AGI is $156,000 or less.

   (2) Partial deduction for participants with AGI between $156,000 and $166,000.

f. Two rules regarding taxpayers who qualify for a reduced IRA:

   (1) $200 floor: if a taxpayer is qualified to make a deductible contribution, the deductible amount is not reduced below $200.

   (2) Deductible contribution may be rounded up to the next $10 increase.

4.3 ROTH IRAs

> **Key point** A single taxpayer can contribute to a Roth IRA if his modified AGI is less than $114,000; a married couple filing jointly can contribute to a Roth IRA if their modified AGI is less than $166,000.
>
> **Key point** Contributions to a Roth IRA are not deductible.
>
> **Key point** Qualified withdrawals from a Roth IRA after five years are not taxable, and there is no tax on earnings while in the Roth IRA.

4.31 Eligibility: if eligibility requirements are met, distributions (payouts) are tax free (contributions are not deductible).

a. Maximum contribution is phased out for married joint filers with AGI between $156,000 and $166,000 ($10,000 spread is reduced on a pro rata basis).

b. Maximum contribution is phased out for single taxpayers with AGI between $99,000 and $114,000 ($15,000 spread is reduced on a pro rata basis).

Traditional IRAs vs. Roth IRAs: Questions Answered

In Publication 590, the IRS describes the key differences between traditional IRAs and Roth IRAs. The table is reproduced below. For further explanation of differences between IRAs and Roth IRAs, please refer to the chapters mentioned in the table, which can be found in Publication 590 on the IRS Website.

Question	Answer	
	Traditional IRA?	**Roth IRA?**
Is there an age limit on when I can set up and contribute to a...	Yes. You must not have reached age 70½ by the end of the year. See *Who Can Set Up a Traditional IRA?* in chapter 1.	No. You can be any age. See *Can You Contribute to a Roth IRA?* in chapter 2.
If I earned more than $4,000 in 2006 ($5,000 if I was 50 or older by the end of 2006), is there a limit on how much I can contribute to a...	Yes. For 2006, you can contribute to a traditional IRA up to: ■ $4,000, or ■ $5,000 if you were 50 or older by the end of 2006. There is no upper limit on how much you can earn and still contribute. See *How Much Can Be Contributed?* in chapter 1.	Yes. For 2006, you may be able to contribute to a Roth IRA up to: ■ $4,000, or ■ $5,000 if you were 50 or older by the end of 2006, but the amount you can contribute may be less than that depending on your income, filing status, and if you contribute to another IRA. See *How Much Can Be Contributed?* and Table 2-1 in chapter 2.
Can I deduct contributions to a...	Yes. You may be able to deduct your contributions to a traditional IRA depending on your income, filing status, whether you are covered by a retirement plan at work, and whether you receive Social Security benefits. See *How Much Can You Deduct?* in chapter 1.	No. You can never deduct contributions to a Roth IRA. See *What is a Roth IRA?* in chapter 2.
Do I have to file a form just because I contribute to a...	Not unless you make nondeductible contributions to your traditional IRA. In that case, you must file Form 8606. See *Nondeductible Contributions* in chapter 1.	No. You do not have to file a form if you contribute to a Roth IRA. See *Introduction* in chapter 2.
Do I have to start taking distributions when I reach a certain age from a...	Yes. You must begin receiving required minimum distributions by April 1 of the year following the year you reach age 70½. See *When Must You Withdraw Assets? (Required Minimum Distributions)* in chapter 1.	No. If you are the owner of a Roth IRA, you do not have to take distributions regardless of your age. See *Are Distributions Taxable?* in chapter 2.
How are distributions taxed from a...	Distributions from a traditional IRA are taxed as ordinary income, but if you made nondeductible contributions, not all of the distribution is taxable. See *Are Distributions Taxable?* in chapter 1.	Distributions from a Roth IRA are not taxed as long as you meet certain criteria. See *Are Distributions Taxable?* in chapter 2.
Do I have to file a form just because I receive distributions from a...	Not unless you have ever made a nondeductible contribution to a traditional IRA. If you have, file Form 8606.	Yes. File form 8606 if you received distributions from a Roth IRA (other than a rollover, recharacterization, certain qualified distributions, or a return of certain contributions).

4.32 After age 70½:

   a. Contributions can still be made.

   b. Minimum distribution rules requiring distribution after age 70½ do not apply.

   (1) After death, distribution rules still apply.

4.33 Two requirements for distributions from Roth IRAs to be tax free:

   a. Distribution must be made after the five-tax-year period beginning with the first tax year a contribution was made.

   b. Distributions must be made under one of four conditions:

   (1) Participant is at least 59½ years of age.

   (2) Participant has become disabled.

   (3) Distribution paid to a beneficiary because of the participant's death.

   (4) Withdrawal is used for qualified first-time homebuyer expenses:

   (a) Qualified expenses include acquisition costs of a first home for the participant, spouse, any child, any grandchild, or any ancestor of the participant or spouse.

   (b) $10,000 lifetime limit per participant.

4.34 Nonqualifying distributions are subject to income tax and a 10% penalty tax.

4.35 **Roth IRA conversions.**

   a. Four kinds of Roth IRA conversions (i.e., creation of a Roth IRA through conversion).

   (1) Distribution from traditional IRA is rolled over to a Roth IRA within 60 days.

   (2) Assets are directly transferred to a Roth IRA.

   (3) Conversion of SEP IRA or SIMPLE IRA to Roth IRA (exception: SIMPLE IRA may not be converted to Roth IRA in the first two years).

   (4) Qualified plans, 403(b) plans, and 457 plans can be directly converted to Roth IRAs starting in 2008.

   b. Who is eligible for a Roth IRA conversion?

   (1) Married persons filing separately: not entitled to a Roth IRA conversion.

   (2) Married persons filing jointly and single persons: entitled to a Roth IRA conversion from a traditional IRA if the person's AGI is not greater than $100,000 for the year (rule applies to years before 2010).

   c. Roth IRA conversion changes starting in 2010; two changes:

   (1) Income limit is eliminated; as a result, persons with a high income will be able to convert their traditional IRA into a Roth IRA.

   (2) Recognition of taxable income from conversion occurring in 2010: taxpayer can recognize all of this income in 2010 or spread the income over 2011 and 2012.

4.4 IRA PLANNING

> **Key point** The four factors to consider in choosing between Roth and traditional IRAs are eligibility requirements, deductibility of contributions, difficulty in comparing tax and investment consequences, and distribution requirements.

4.41 Eight considerations for IRA planning:

    a. Deciding between a Roth IRA or a pretax savings vehicle can be difficult.

    b. Roth IRA tax benefits are available to taxpayers who are not eligible to make a deductible IRA contribution.

    c. Special spousal rule: a married couple filing jointly with adjusted gross income (AGI) of less than $156,000 (2007) and with only one spouse covered by an employer-sponsored retirement plan can contribute the maximum amount to a traditional IRA for the other spouse.

    d. IRA-to-Roth IRA conversions create current tax liability.

    e. Maximum contribution to all traditional IRAs or Roth IRAs on an individual's behalf is $4,000 in 2007 ($5,000 in 2008).

        (1) Catch-up provision: allows taxpayers age 50 and older to contribute an extra $1,000 per year (2007).

    f. Present IRA rules are not that beneficial for high-income taxpayers but older, financially able people can influence children and grandchildren to benefit from IRA opportunities.

    g. Lower-income taxpayers do not benefit from the new IRA rules.

    h. Expenses for family education and first home buying can be made from IRAs without penalty.

4.42 Choosing a Roth IRA over a nondeductible IRA:

    a. Individuals who are only able to contribute to nondeductible IRAs have two choices: nondeductible traditional IRAs and Roth IRAs.

    b. People with a choice between nondeductible IRA contributions and Roth IRA contributions should usually choose the Roth IRA.

        (1) Tax-free distributions are clearly better than tax deferral.

    c. Two phaseout limits for Roth IRAs (2007):

        (1) Phaseout for single taxpayers: AGI between $99,000 and $114,000.

        (2) Phaseout for married couples filing jointly: AGI between $156,000 and $166,000.

    d. Taxpayers not eligible for deductible IRA contributions with a maximized 401(k) plan can use Roth IRAs to build further retirement savings.

4.43 Choosing a Roth IRA over a deductible IRA:

    a. Determining which option is best is difficult due to unknown rates of return, tax rates, and timing of withdrawals in the future.

    b. Roth IRA is best when individual will be in a higher tax bracket in retirement than at the time of contribution.

c. Distributions are not required during the participant's lifetime; if the beneficiary is a spouse, then distributions can be delayed to the death of the spouse and paid out over the expected lifetime of the spouse's beneficiaries, making the Roth IRA a powerful tool for passing income to the next generation.

d. Tax-free source of income allows participants greater flexibility in liquidating taxable assets during retirement.

e. Four individuals who should consider the Roth IRA over the deductible IRA:

   (1) Individuals concerned more with estate planning than retirement planning.

   (2) Individuals in the 28% tax bracket who will be in higher tax bracket at retirement.

   (3) Individuals in the 15% tax bracket.

   (4) Individuals who have a significant amount of tax-deferred retirement assets and wish to create a more balanced portfolio.

4.44 Four considerations in an IRA-to-Roth IRA conversion:

a. Conversions work for young people due to long accumulation period over which Roth IRA grows tax free.

b. A portion of retirement savings should be converted to Roth IRAs because non-taxable source of income in retirement can be used for retirement or estate planning purposes.

c. Another source of money (other than funds from the traditional IRA) should be used to pay conversion taxes to avoid a possible 10% premature excise tax.

d. Older persons should not disregard Roth IRA conversion since no withdrawals are required during the lifetime of the participant or the participant's spouse (if beneficiary).

4.45 Using traditional IRAs:

a. The younger a client starts investing with an IRA, the more effect those investment dollars will have at retirement.

> **EXAMPLE** Thomas contributed $3,000 per year to his IRA from the time he was age 18 until he was age 26 and then made no more contributions. Christopher, who is the same age as Thomas, contributed $3,000 per year to his IRA from the time he was 27 years of age until he was 65 years of age. Assuming a constant interest rate of 9%, if Thomas and Christopher each retire at age 65, Thomas will have more funds in his IRA than Christopher. Thomas will have $1,125,639, while Christopher will only have $927,199.

4.5 IRA INVESTMENTS AND FUNDING VEHICLES

Key point The two funding vehicles for individual retirement plans are IRA accounts (trust or custodial accounts) and IRA annuities usually issued by insurance companies.

Key point Investing IRA funds in life insurance and collectibles is not allowed; borrowing money from an IRA is also not allowed.

4.51 Three investment restrictions:

a. Investment in life insurance: not allowed.

b. Investment in collectibles: amount invested in collectibles is considered a distribution in the year invested; tax advantage is lost.

    (1) If the investment is made before age 59½, a 10% excise tax may apply.

    (2) Six examples of prohibited collectibles: antiques, rare coins, rare wines, oriental rugs, works of art, and stamps.

    (3) Two exceptions to the prohibition (i.e., are allowed):

        (a) Specified gold, silver, and platinum coins issued by the United States and coins issued under state law.

        (b) Investments in gold, silver, platinum, and palladium bullion of a quality eligible for regulated futures contract; IRA trustee must have physical possession of the bullion.

c. Three prohibited transactions:

    (1) Borrowing money from the account or annuity.

    (2) Using the account or annuity as security for a loan.

    (3) Selling property to the account.

4.52 Two funding vehicles for individual retirement plans:

a. IRA account: most popular type of individual retirement arrangement.

    (1) A written trust or custodial account whose trustee or custodian must be a bank, a federally insured credit union, a savings and loan association, or a person or organization with IRS permission to act as trustee or custodian.

    (2) IRA funds cannot be commingled with other assets.

b. IRA annuity: annuity contract usually issued by insurance companies.

    (1) Similar to IRAs, with two special rules:

        (a) Nontransferable: must be received by either taxpayer or beneficiary.

        (b) May not have fixed annual premiums, although annual fees and level annual premiums for supplementary benefits are allowed.

    (2) IRA annuities are different from IRAs in two ways:

        (a) Waiver-of-premium in the event of disability.

        (b) Life annuity payment option.

4.6 EXECUTIVE INCENTIVE OR BONUS PLANS

> **Key point**   The four types of reward plans for executives are phantom stock, incentive stock options (ISOs), nonqualified stock options (NQSOs), and restricted stock.
>
> **Key point**   Phantom stock is a bookkeeping entry that is taxed as ordinary income to the employee and deductible to the employer on the valuation date.
>
> **Key point**   An incentive stock option (ISO) is an option to purchase company stock that receives more favorable tax treatment than a nonqualified stock option (NQSO) but is not as flexible.

4.61   Executive incentive or bonus plans are offered as a reward based on the performance of company stock or specific financial objectives; not taxed to employee until benefits are received.

4.62   Four types of executive incentive or bonus plans:

a.   **Phantom stock**: a bookkeeping entry assigning units to employees just as if employees had purchased company stock; the value of the units equals the appreciation and market value of the company stock.

   (1)   The units are valued on a particular date (e.g., 15 years after the issuance of the phantom stock); on this date (i.e., valuation date), the company pays the executive in cash, stock, or a combination of cash and stock.

   (2)   Insider-trading treatment similar to stock options if the employee has control of the payment's timing.

   (3)   On the valuation date, phantom stock is taxed as ordinary income to the employee and is subject to withholding; company takes a tax deduction.

   (4)   Two disadvantages of phantom stock:

      (a)   May have a company-imposed maximum payment.

      (b)   Employee usually cannot choose when to receive payment (i.e., payment is generally at retirement).

> **EXAMPLE** In 2007, Worldview grants Sammy, the Chief Financial Officer, 250 shares of phantom stock valued at $35 per share at the time the shares are granted (i.e., $8,750). When the shares are granted, no income tax consequences occur for Worldview or Sammy since phantom stock is simply a form of deferred compensation (i.e., the phantom stock is similar to a bonus that will be received by Sammy at some future point set by Worldview). Under Worldview's phantom stock plan, the shares will be valued at the fair market value upon Sammy's retirement although some plans may specify that only the appreciation in the fair market value between the date the phantom shares were granted and the valuation date will be paid (so Sammy is getting a good deal).
>
> At Sammy's retirement, the fair market value of Worldview's stock is $50 per share. Sammy will receive $12,500 on his retirement date (i.e., the valuation date). At that time, the entire amount is taxed as ordinary income to Sammy and Worldview may take an income tax deduction for the amount for that year. If the plan specified that Sammy would receive appreciation only, Sammy would receive $3,750 ([$50 − $35] × 250 shares). Sammy would only be taxed on the $3,750 (as ordinary income) since the original bookkeeping entry involved no exchange of equity or cash (i.e., value). The only value Sammy would actually receive is $3,750 in deferred compensation, similar to a $3,750 bonus. Sammy never had access to the portion of the shares representing the original value prior to appreciation (and therefore is not taxed on that portion).

b. Incentive stock option (ISO): an option to buy company stock at a price equal to or above the fair market value (FMV) on the date the option is granted for up to 10 years.

(1) Receives more favorable tax treatment than NQSOs but is not as flexible.

(2) Three restrictions of ISOs:

  (a) Holding period requirements before sale.

  (b) Any option granted to a shareholder owning 10% or more of a company's voting stock must be priced at least 110% over the stock's FMV; in addition, the option must be exercised within five years.

  (c) Limit on value of options that can be exercised annually.

(3) May be exercised by paying cash or by tendering previously owned stock.

(4) No tax is due when the option is exercised.

  (a) The value of the stock over the option exercise price (i.e., the spread) is a tax preference item that may affect employee's obligation to pay the alternative minimum tax.

(5) Holding period requirements: if stock is held for at least two years from date option was granted and at least one year from option exercise date, the stock's increase in value is taxed at the long-term capital gains rate; otherwise, the gain realized from the date the option was granted to the option exercise date is taxed as ordinary income, with the remainder taxed as capital gain.

(6) Options granted before December 31, 1986 must be exercised in the order granted.

(7) Seven factors to consider when choosing to exercise nonqualified stock options and ISOs:

(a) Action plan must be developed.

(b) Liquidation considerations.

(c) Long-term plan must be developed.

(d) Set goals.

(e) Know the program by clarifying both the value of the options involved and choices available to the participant.

(f) Know implications of taxes, including the alternative minimum tax.

(g) Strategies for liquidation.

c. **Nonqualified stock options (NQSOs):** employee has an option to purchase shares of company stock at a given price over a given time period (e.g., 10 years).

(1) Purchase price may be at or below the stock's FMV as of the option grant date.

(2) SEC insider trading restriction: employees having access to information not available to the public and who have exercised the option to purchase stock are limited to a six-month period during which employee may sell the stock.

(a) Six months begin when option is issued and ends when stock is sold.

(3) Taxation: excess of FMV value over option price is taxed as ordinary income at the time of exercise.

(a) The corporation deducts the amount of the executive's income from the option's exercise in the year that the executive is taxed on that income.

EXAMPLE In 2003, Matt, an employee, was granted the right to purchase 800 shares of common stock at the time the stock option is used (value is $32 per share). In 2007, the market price of the stock has risen to $45 per share. If Matt exercises the option, Matt will have $10,400 of taxable ordinary income. Matt's employer will receive a tax deduction of $10,400 in 2007.

$800 \times \$45 = \$36,000$ current market value
$800 \times \$32 = \$25,600$ purchase price
Taxable ordinary income $= \$10,400$

---

(4) Vesting feature where options are not exercisable for a period of time after the options are granted; four types:

(a) Early exercise: vesting approach offered in some pre-IPO (prior to the initial public offering) firms.

(b) Cliff-vesting: options granted at a set time become vested at once.

(c) Graded vesting: a portion of the options vest each year.

(d) Vesting may be subject to the company's satisfying performance goals.

d. Restricted stock: stock given to an employee at little or no cost that is nontransferable and on which dividends are paid as long as the employee keeps the stock.

(1) Employer "stamps" restricted stock with two common restrictions:

(a) Noncompete clause: the employee must forfeit stocks if the employee quits and goes to work for a competitor.

(b) Clause stating that shares are forfeited if employee stops working prior to a specified date.

(2) Two advantages of restricted stock for the employer:

(a) Ties employee to the company through the vesting provision.

(b) Ties the benefit to the performance of company stock.

(3) Two advantages of restricted stock for the employee:

(a) Stock is secure from creditors if the company performs poorly, since stock is in the employee's name.

(b) Employee pays little or nothing for the stock: even if the stock remains level or declines, the employee gains.

(4) Taxation: employee is taxed after limitations end.

(a) Value of stock is treated as ordinary income to the employee; when the employee is taxed, the employer will receive a tax deduction.

(b) Dividends paid are treated as compensation; ordinary income to employee; deductible to the employer.

(c) Within 30 days of the grant date, employee may elect to be taxed at the time of the grant.

- Disadvantage: an employee who is taxed at the time of award and who then forfeits the stock cannot recover taxes paid.

- Advantage: an employee who pays taxes upon receipt of the stock has a better chance for long-term capital gains treatment because the one-year holding period for long-term capital gains treatment begins when the taxes are paid.

4.7 EXECUTIVE BONUS LIFE INSURANCE PLANS

Key point   An executive bonus life insurance plan, also known as a Section 162 plan, provides a bonus to an executive to use to buy cash-value life insurance.

4.71 Executive bonus life insurance plan (also known as a **Section 162 plan**): corporation pays a bonus to the executive for the executive to purchase cash-value life insurance; executive is the policy owner, the insured and the beneficiary designator.

a. Two ways a company pays out the bonus:

(1) Corporation pays premiums directly to the insurer.

(2) Bonus is paid to employee, who pays the insurer.

b. Bonus amount is deductible to company and taxable to the employee.

c. Can discriminate in favor of certain employees.

    d. Additional bonus: company may give employee a second bonus to help cover the additional tax burden imposed by a bonus plan.

4.8 NONQUALIFIED PLANS

> **Key point** The two types of nonqualified plans are supplemental executive retirement plans (SERPs) for highly compensated employees (to comply with top-hat requirements) and salary reduction plans.
>
> **Key point** Both types of nonqualified plans are taxed under constructive receipt or economic benefit doctrines.

4.81 Nonqualified deferred compensation plans: plans that enable employers to disregard IRS qualification requirements (more flexible) but deny the employer an immediate deduction for deferred compensation (no tax advantages).

    a. Employer is entitled to a tax deduction only when the employee is taxed on the benefit at time of employee's retirement.

4.82 Five uses of nonqualified plans:

    a. Shift income to future years.

    b. Provide highly compensated employees with a stand-alone benefit allowing the postponement of current income to supplement retirement income.

    c. Add an extra level of benefits to a qualified plan for executives.

    d. Disregard a qualified plan's nondiscrimination requirements.

    e. Encourage employee loyalty.

4.83 Two types of nonqualified plans:

    a. **Supplemental executive retirement plan (SERP):** complements an existing qualified plan that is not at the maximum limits.

        (1) Most popular type of nonqualified plan.

        (2) SERP must be maintained only for a particular group of highly compensated employees or management to satisfy the top-hat plan exception to ERISA.

            (a) Top-hat plan: salary reduction plan or SERP exempt from ERISA requirements; plan must be limited to top management to be exempt.

        (3) May be defined contribution or defined benefit.

    b. **Salary reduction plan:** compensation for select employees or highly compensated employees is deferred for retirement purposes.

        (1) Employee may elect to defer commissions, bonuses, or salary.

        (2) Best for employees who are currently taxed at the highest marginal rates and expect to be in a lower bracket upon retirement.

        (3) Employer must limit participation to a select group of highly compensated employees or management to be exempt from ERISA requirements.

4.84 Advantages and disadvantages of nonqualified salary deferral plan (employee, such as company executive, elects to defer compensation).

   a. Benefits of participating in a nonqualified salary deferral plan:

      (1) Greater accumulation with deferral than post-tax savings.

      (2) Investment choices in plan or promised return rate in plan.

      (3) Employer may match contributions (similar to 401(k) plan).

      (4) Withdrawal restrictions; more funds remain at retirement.

      (5) Most plan provisions are negotiated between employer and employee.

   b. Disadvantages of participating in a nonqualified salary deferral plan:

      (1) Employee must know how and when the distributions will be made when the election is made—when employee is unable to determine needs as retiree. (Section 409A rule)

      (2) Compensation arrangement may be subject to scrutiny if company hires new management.

      (3) Risk factor: benefits under the plan may not be completely paid off when the company files for bankruptcy; creditors can attach to plan funds.

      (4) Increased tax rate when employee decides to withdraw from the plan.

4.85 Taxation deferred on nonqualified plan benefits

   a. Employer gets a deduction only when an employee receives benefits.

   b. Employee may defer taxes on deferred compensation in a nonqualified plan that is subject to a significant risk of forfeiture.

      (1) Substantial risk of forfeiture: executive must satisfy a certain requirement and the circumstance that may cause the forfeiture must be likely to occur.

      (2) Examples of substantial risk of forfeiture: traditional vesting provision and requirement of executive to consult after retirement.

   c. Economic benefit and constructive receipt doctrines.

      (1) Economic benefit doctrine

         (a) Employee must report the value of any benefit in a nonqualified plan that has an identifiable FMV even if the employee does not have a present right to receive the benefit.

         (b) Employee may defer income tax on such benefits if they are payable from assets that:

            ■ Can be attached by the employer's general creditors (commonly named a rabbi trust); or

            ■ Remain the employer's property.

      (2) Constructive receipt doctrine: codified in Code Section 409A.

         (a) An employee is taxed on income he receives constructively when all of the following occurs:

            ■ Income is set aside for the employee.

            ■ Income is credited to an account established for the employee or otherwise made available.

- No substantial limits on employee's control over the income.

(b) Nonqualified plan distributions: tax may be deferred even if there is no substantial risk of forfeiture if they meet the following requirements:

- Employee deferral election rules.

- Certain distribution rules.

- Distribution acceleration requirements.

(c) Employee's election to defer compensation:

- Employee electing to defer for a year must make the election before the end of the preceding taxable year.

- Employee receiving compensation solely based on performance of services during at least a 12-month period must elect to defer no later than six months before the end of that period.

- Eligible employee may, in his first year of eligibility, elect to defer compensation for services to be performed during that year beginning within 30 days after he became eligible.

- When and how the distributions will be made must be determined when the employee's compensation is first deferred.

- An employee may elect to further defer payment of a benefit only if the deferral is made at least 12 months before the benefit becomes effective (only under limited circumstances).

(d) Distribution rules: employee may defer income tax on distributions from a nonqualified plan only if the distributions are not made before any one of the following circumstances:

- Designated time stated in the plan.

- Employee's death.

- Unpredictable crisis occurs.

- Disability.

- Ownership change.

- Key employee separated from work may not receive a distribution until six months after the separation from a public company.

(e) Distribution acceleration requirements: employee may not receive payments from the plan on an accelerated basis, except in the following circumstances:

- FICA payments.

- Payments required by conflict of interest divestiture rules.

- Payments required by a domestic relations order.

- De minimis cashout rule: interest amounts of $10,000 and under may be cashed out of the plan before 2½ months after the end of employment or December 31 of the year in which the termination occurred, whichever is later.

Highlight 1: Basics of Traditional IRAs and Roth IRAs

■ Two types of individual retirement accounts (IRAs):
   (1) Traditional IRAs.
   (2) Roth IRA: contributions are made on an after-tax basis, earnings are not taxed and qualifying distributions are tax free. (4.11)

■ Traditional IRAs have four similarities with employer-sponsored tax-sheltered retirement plans:
   (1) Permit earnings to be tax deferred until retirement.
   (2) Encourage accumulation of savings for retirement.
   (3) Allow contributions to be made with pretax dollars.
   (4) Tax-favored savings plans. (4.11a)

Highlight 2: Traditional IRAs and Roth IRAs

■ Nine types of plans that are employer-maintained plans for purposes of defining active participant:)
   (1) 403(b) tax-sheltered annuity plans.
   (2) Defined benefit pension plans.
   (3) Federal, state, or local government plans.
   (4) Money-purchase plans.
   (5) Profit-sharing plans.
   (6) Stock plans.
   (7) SEPs.
   (8) SIMPLEs.
   (9) Target benefit plans. (4.21a)

■ Two requirements for distributions from Roth IRAs to be tax free:
   (1) Distribution must be made after five-tax-year period beginning with first tax year a contribution was made.
   (2) Distributions must be made under one of four conditions:
      (a) Participant is at least 59½ years of age.
      (b) Participant has become disabled.
      (c) Distribution paid to a beneficiary because of the participant's death.
      (d) Withdrawal is used for qualified first-time homebuyer expenses. (4.33)

Highlight 3: IRA Planning

■ Four individuals who should consider the Roth IRA over the deductible IRA:
   (1) Individuals concerned more with estate planning than retirement planning.
   (2) Individuals in the 28% tax bracket who will be in higher tax bracket at retirement.
   (3) Individuals in the 15% tax bracket.
   (4) Individuals who have a significant amount of tax-deferred retirement assets and wish to create a more balanced portfolio. (4.43e)

Highlight 4: IRA Investments and Funding Vehicles

- Three investment restrictions:
  (1) Investment in life insurance.
  (2) Investment in collectibles.
  (3) Prohibited transactions, such as borrowing money from the account or annuity, using the account or annuity as security for a loan, and selling property to the account. (4.51)

Highlight 5: Executive Incentive or Bonus Plans and Executive Bonus Life Insurance Plans

- Four types of executive incentive or bonus plans:
  (1) Phantom stock.
  (2) Incentive stock option (ISO).
  (3) Nonqualified stock options (NQSOs).
  (4) Restricted stock. (4.62)

Highlight 6: Nonqualified Plans

- Five uses of nonqualified plans:
  (1) Shift income to future years.
  (2) Provide highly compensated employees with a stand-alone benefit allowing the postponement of current income to supplement retirement income.
  (3) Add an extra level of benefits to a qualified plan for executives.
  (4) Disregard a qualified plan's nondiscrimination requirements.
  (5) Encourage employee loyalty. (4.82)

- Two types of nonqualified plans:
  (1) Supplemental executive retirement plan (SERP): complements an existing qualified plan that is not at the maximum limits.
  (2) Salary reduction plan: compensation for select employees or highly compensated employees is deferred for retirement purposes. (4.83)

- Taxation of nonqualified plan benefits and economic benefit doctrine:
  (1) Employee may defer income tax on any benefit that has been handled or arranged in such a way that a cash-equivalent benefit has been provided to the employee even if the employee does not have a present right to receive the benefit if the benefit is payable from assets that:
  (a) Can be attached by the employer's general creditors (commonly named a rabbi trust); or
  (b) Remain the employer's property. (4.85)

- Taxation of nonqualified plan benefits and constructive receipt doctrine:
  (1) Employee may defer tax on any distributions from a nonqualified plan even if they are not subject to a substantial risk of forfeiture if they meet the following requirements, which must be included in the plan document governing the plan:
  (a) Employee deferral election rules.
  (b) Certain distribution rules.
  (c) Distribution acceleration requirements. (4.85)

Active participant A person who participates in an employer-maintained plan (other than a nonqualified plan) and therefore is not allowed to make deductible contributions to an IRA unless adjusted gross income falls below a certain limit. (4.21)

Incentive stock option (ISO) Option to buy company stock at a price equal to or above the stock's fair market value on the date the option is granted for a period of up to 10 years. (4.62b))

Individual retirement account (IRA) Tax-favored savings plan that encourages accumulation of savings for retirement; annual contribution limit is the lesser of $4,000 (2007) or 100% of compensation. (4.11a, 4.12)

Nonqualified stock options (NQSOs) Employee has an option to purchase shares of company stock at a given price over a given time period. (4.62c)

Phantom stock A bookkeeping entry assigning units to employees as if employees had purchased company stock. The value of the units equals the appreciation and market value of the company stock. (4.62a)

Restricted stock Stock given to an employee at little or no cost that is nontransferable and on which dividends are paid as long as the employee keeps the stock. (4.62d)

Roth IRA Individual retirement account in which contributions are made on an after-tax basis; earnings are not taxed and qualifying distributions are tax free; annual contribution limit is the lesser of $4,000 (2007) or 100% of compensation. (4.11b)

Roth IRA conversion A taxpayer can roll over money from a traditional IRA to a Roth IRA if the taxpayer's adjusted gross income is no more than $100,000. (4.35)

Salary reduction plan A type of nonqualified plan in which compensation for select employees or highly compensated employees is deferred for retirement purposes. (4.83b)

Section 162 plan Corporation pays a bonus to the executive for the executive to purchase cash-value life insurance; executive is the policyowner, the insured, and the beneficiary designator. (4.71)

Spousal IRA IRA contributed to by a working married person for a spouse with little or no compensation; annual contribution limit is $4,000 (2007). (4.13)

Supplemental executive retirement plans (SERPs) Plans that complement an existing qualified plan that is not at the maximum limits; must be maintained only for a particular group of highly compensated employees or management to satisfy the top-hat plan exception to ERISA. (4.83a)

QUESTIONS

1. Which of the following describes the use of non-qualified plans?
    A. Shifts income to later years
    B. Adds an extra level of benefits to a qualified plan for nonhighly compensated employees
    C. Tightens the nondiscrimination requirements of a qualified plan
    D. Discourages long service

2. Which of the following describes incentive stock options?
    A. Receive less favorable tax treatment than NQSOs but are more flexible
    B. The value of options that can be exercised annually is limited
    C. Must be exercised by paying cash
    D. Tax is due when option is exercised

3. All of the following are examples of prohibited collectibles for IRA investment EXCEPT
    A. works of art
    B. antiques
    C. gold coin issued by US government
    D. stamps

4. All of the following are characteristics of a Roth IRA EXCEPT
    A. maximum contribution is phased out for single taxpayers with AGI between $90,000 and $105,000
    B. contributions can still be made after age 70½
    C. maximum contribution is phased out for married joint filers with AGI between $156,000 and $166,000
    D. minimum distribution rules requiring distribution after age 70½ do not apply

5. All of the following are correct concerning contribution limits for IRAs and Roth IRAs EXCEPT
    A. contributions cannot exceed the lesser of $4,000 per year or 100% of compensation
    B. money derived from investments is not eligible
    C. $4,000 limit includes sum of annual contributions to IRA and Roth IRA
    D. money derived from retirement income is eligible

ANSWERS

1. **A.** The five uses of nonqualified plans are: (1) shift income to later years, (2) provide a standalone benefit that lets highly compensated employees defer current income to supplement retirement income, (3) add an extra level of benefits to a qualified plan for executives, (4) disregard the nondiscrimination requirements of a qualified plan, and (5) encourage long service. (4.82)

2. **B.** Incentive stock options receive more favorable tax treatment than NQSOs but are not as flexible, may be exercised by paying cash or by tendering previously owned stock, and have no tax due when exercised. (4.62b)

3. **C.** Specified gold, silver, and platinum coins issued by the United States and coins issued under state law are not prohibited. (4.51b(3))

4. **A.** Maximum contribution is phased out for single taxpayers with AGI between $99,000 and $114,000 (2007). (4.31b)

5. **D.** Contributions do not have to be made; any income earned in a given year can be contributed. However, money derived from investments or retirement income is not eligible. (4.12b, d)

5

Computing Retirement Needs

> *"Let me tell you the secret that has led me to my goal: my strength lies solely in my tenacity."*
>
> —Louis Pasteur

TERMS TO KNOW

Expense method

Golden handshake

Income requirement assumption

Replacement ratio approach

Retirement income needs

Savings step-up rate

5.1 DETERMINING NEEDS AT RETIREMENT

Key point The retirement income need is an amount needed at retirement to provide the desired standard of living.

Key point The savings rate needed is the amount that must be saved to provide for the retirement income need.

5.11 **Retirement income needs**: the amount needed during retirement to enable a client to maintain the standard of living enjoyed immediately before retirement.

   a. *Savings rate needed*: percentage of compensation that an individual must save during working years to reach the targeted retirement income.

   b. Targeted retirement income that is determined from a worksheet or computer model is not an absolute (it is an approximation).

5.2 WORKSHEET AND COMPUTER MODEL ASSUMPTIONS

Key point The seven assumptions required in most worksheets and computer models are step-up rate for savings, tax rate, age of client at death, retirement age, replacement ratio, yield expected on investmests, and inflation rate. (Memory Aid: STARRY I).

5.21 Seven assumptions required in most worksheets and computer models; the best models offer the most flexibility by allowing the financial planner to choose.

5.22 Inflation assumption.

   a. Inflation decreases the purchasing power of the client.

   b. Forecasting inflation: difficult to do accurately because other factors have a role; eight other factors that play a role in the inflation assumption:

   (1) Actual inflation rate is affected by personal buying habits.

   (2) More services than goods are purchased by retirees and services usually have higher inflation rates than goods.

   (3) Regional rates may vary from the national rate.

   (4) Long-term rates are best, but available statistical data looks at annual rates rather than long-term rates.

   (5) The medical inflation rate is double the average inflation rate: some retirees will have considerable medical expenses.

   (6) Inflation is substantial for housing costs; however, many retirees have limited housing costs (e.g., homes are owned outright).

   (7) Planning for younger clients is problematic since inflation must be considered over a long period of time (e.g., 50 years).

   (8) Which is the better proxy for clients, the CPI (consumer price index) or PPI (producer price index).

   c. Three factors to consider when setting an inflation rate:

   (1) Most planners focus on a long-term rate.

    (2) Client's risk tolerance.

    (3) The assumed rate can be changed over time based on changes in actual experience.

d. The best rate: most planners use an assumed inflation of 3 to 4%.

5.23 Retirement age assumption: the average retirement age in the United States is 62, yet most planners automatically use 65 as the retirement starting date.

a. Nine reasons for early retirement:

    (1) Financial independence: salary required to be saved to retire early.

    (2) Health: retire early while healthy or due to person's or spouse's poor health.

    (3) Downsizing of corporations.

        (a) **Golden handshake**: an employer's offer of a retirement package to an employee or group of employees to foster retirement before age 65. Incentives to encourage early retirement include the following:

            ■ Financial inducements.

            ■ Lump-sum payments based on years of employment.

            ■ Retiree health insurance payments.

    (4) Workplace conflict: some persons may retire early due to conflicts at work.

    (5) Compromise on desired standard of living: an individual wishes to stop working although the individual has not achieved desired financial status.

    (6) Death of spouse: widows retire early due to death benefits and inheritances.

    (7) Laborers and manual workers retire early due to physical demands.

    (8) Employer's retiree health care package: employees may retire early due to the employer's health care and pension package for retirees.

    (9) Two wage earners in the family: early retirement of one spouse may prompt the other spouse to retire early.

b. Seven reasons against early retirement:

    (1) The normal retirement age for Social Security purposes is increasing from 65 to 67 or from 65 to above age 65 but under age 67, depending on the person's birth date; a person affected by this change will receive lower Social Security benefits if retiring early.

    (2) Adjustment of the pension downward to offset the longer payout period that results from early retirement.

    (3) Fixed long-term liabilities (e.g., mortgage, education expenses for children) may prevent worker from retiring early.

    (4) Effect on pension benefits: if a final-average-salary formula is used, the pension is lowered because the pension would have been based on higher earnings if the worker had stayed on the job.

    (5) Loss of health insurance.

    (6) Increased exposure to inflation.

    (7) Decrease in Social Security benefits.

5.24 Longevity assumption.

a. The ideal: living on interest without ever having to liquidate the principal.

b. When estimating the length of retirement, mistakes can cause an overstatement or understatement of the amount of savings needed.

> **EXAMPLE** If a client retires at age 65 and dies at age 67, a modest amount is needed. If any evidence of the client's possible longevity had been offered to the planner, the client could have avoided an excessive savings effort. On the other hand, a client who can be expected to live to 98 or 100 will need more savings because of the length of the client's life and because of an increased exposure to inflation.

c. Seven factors in determining client's life expectancy:

(1) Socioeconomic group: higher socioeconomic status means living longer.

(2) Physical condition.

(3) Life expectancies: highest point ever in US history.

(4) Family history (e.g., longevity of parents and grandparents).

(5) Life expectancy tables.

(a) Annuity tables often overstate life expectancy but insurance tables often understate life expectancy.

(b) One-half of people outlive the projections found in tables.

(6) Internet calculators available to determine life expectancy.

(7) Probability of living from age 65 to a certain age.

d. Some planners add a "fudge factor" to the life expectancy estimate.

(1) If a client lives longer than expected without the fudge factor, no problem exists because the fudge factor makes up for the extra years.

(2) If the client does not live as long, some assets will remain for heirs.

(3) One approach to the fudge factor is to put assets into different classes.

5.25 **Income requirement assumption**: represents the planner's estimate of the level of income needed to sustain the standard of living that was enjoyed just before retirement; measured as a percentage of final salary.

a. **Replacement ratio approach**: some planners consider 70 to 80% of a person's final salary sufficient to enable the person to maintain the accustomed standard of living throughout retired life; inflation is factored in separately.

b. Two factors that influence a replacement ratio that is less than 100%:

(1) Reduced taxes: retirees often have a lower percentage of income going to pay taxes for five reasons:

(a) Social Security taxes: distributions from pensions, IRAs, retirement annuities, and similar sources are not subject to Social Security taxes.

(b) Standard deduction is increased by an extra $1,000 (in 2006) for each married taxpayer 65 years or older ($1,250 in 2006 for unmarried taxpayers older than age 65 and not filing as a surviving spouse).

> **(c)** Social Security benefits exclusion: a married taxpayer can exclude all Social Security benefits from income if the taxpayer's modified gross income plus 50% of the Social Security benefits is not greater than the base amount of $32,000 ($25,000 for single taxpayers).
>
> **(d)** State income taxation does not apply to Social Security benefits in some states.
>
> > ■ Some states provide tax relief for the elderly in the form of increased personal exemptions, credits, tax rebates, and deferrals.
>
> **(e)** Deductible medical expenses: reduced retirement income level and possible increased medical expenses enable retired taxpayers to exceed the 7.5% threshold for deductibility more easily.
>
> **(2)** Five reduced living expenses: work-related expenses, home ownership costs, no dependent children, discounts for senior citizens, and no longer saving for retirement.

c. Four living expenses that increase:

    (1) Dependents: some retirees still have dependents to support.

    (2) Expenses for medical care: increase over time for nearly all clients.

    (3) Need for services that the client could previously perform (physical work, dependent care, and unique transportation due to physical limits).

    (4) Travel, vacation, and similar changes in lifestyle.

d. The replacement ratio is preferred for younger clients because younger clients generally know the standard of living they would like to enjoy after retirement.

e. Using the replacement ratio method involves three considerations:

    (1) Apply a growth factor to the client's current salary and use a future value formula to estimate future salary.

    (2) Compare salaries of workers nearing retirement who hold jobs that the client feels he will hold in future years.

    (3) Examine current salary scales if available.

5.26 **Expense method**: estimating retirement needs by focusing on projected expenses that the retiree will have in the first year of retirement.

✱ **E X A M P L E** Upon retirement, Parker expects to have $3,000 in monthly bills, which is $36,000 annually. The retirement income he will have to maintain, then, is $36,000 worth of purchasing power in today's dollars.

---

a. General and client-specific expenses must be considered:

    (1) Five expenses that tend to increase for retirees:

        (a) House repairs, upkeep, maintenance, and property insurance.

        (b) Utilities and telephone.

        (c) Gifts and contributions.

        (d) Entertainment, travel, recreation, and dining.

        (e) Medical, dental, prescriptions, and health insurance.

(2) Nine expenses that tend to decrease for the retiree: debt repayment, alimony and child support, mortgage payments, property taxes, transportation costs, furnishings, income taxes, food, and clothing costs.

b. The expense method is preferred for clients close to retirement because clients nearing retirement can more accurately estimate post-retirement expenses.

5.27 Refining expense and replacement assumptions:

a. To account for spending patterns in old age, the replacement ratio or expense method needs to be adjusted for a downward trend in expenditures.

(1) Six expenses usually decrease even more in later retirement than in early retirement and account for an almost 20% decline in spending: insurance and pensions, food, entertainment, transportation, clothing, and housing.

(2) Five generalizations on later retirement overlooked by current models:

(a) Cost of living: some retirees move where the cost of living is lower; therefore, less money is spent for the same goods and services.

(b) Older individuals tend to lead a more sedentary lifestyle.

(c) Retirees often receive care-giving and financial help from varied sources.

(d) Nursing home costs are often covered by long-term care insurance.

(e) Replacement ratio has a greater impact when life expectancy is longer.

b. Comparing alternative models:

(1) The downward adjustment in spending by age 75 is approximately 20% of the initial level of spending during retirement at age 65.

(a) If the replacement ratio for age 65 is 80% of preretirement earnings, the age 75 ratio should be 64%.

(2) Two possible methods of correcting accumulation models:

(a) Use a weighted average to show a lower overall replacement ratio; the average will depend on the client's life expectancy.

(b) Show a reduction in annual income for consumption at age 75; the accumulation model should use separate replacement ratios for different time periods (e.g., age 65 to 74 and age 75 and older).

5.28 Financial planners must make predictions on tax rates and investment returns.

a. Ten factors that help in making predictions:

(1) Client's comfort with a certain retirement portfolio.

(2) Potential future income expected by the retiree.

(3) Ability of client to use tax-sheltered qualified plans and IRAs.

(4) Federal tax law changes that are likely to occur.

(5) Inclination to invest too conservatively in qualified plan at work.

(6) Taking the planner's investment recommendations into consideration.

(7) State income taxes that may apply to a relocated client.

(8) Possibility of inheritance.

(9) More conservative investment near and after retirement.

(10) Possibility of a lump-sum payment for retirement purposes.

     b. Many approaches consider savings as a percentage of income.

        (1) As salary increases, the annual amount saved increases.

        (2) **Savings step-up rate**: rate by which an individual can increase savings each year.

5.3 USING COMPUTER MODELS AND WORKSHEETS

> **Key point** The five steps to calculate retirement fund needs are: project retirement income from existing assets, compare with client's needs, provide inflation protection, compute sum needed at retirement, and compute amount needed to save.

5.31 Five steps in calculating retirement fund needs with typical computer software:

     a. Use existing records to project retirement income.

        (1) The planner may use a fact finder to collect the information.

     b. Compare what a client has to the client's future needs.

        (1) Retirement income status (RIS): computer model takes annual income needed at retirement minus annual income projected from existing resources.

> **EXAMPLE** Eugenia, age 60, has a salary of $100,000 in 2007. Using the replacement-ratio approach, Eugenia considers $80,000 (80%) an appropriate target. Eugenia and her planner determine that her Social Security, pension, and current savings will provide $60,000 a year. That leaves a shortfall of $20,000 annually. Computer software calculates the amount necessary at retirement to produce this stream of income over Eugenia's expected lifetime.

     c. Ensure inflation protection for income derived from existing sources.

        (1) Most sources of income will be subject to a decline in purchasing power (DIPP).

            (a) The computer model determines an additional amount needed to be saved to offset increasing needs during retirement.

     d. Compute the sum needed at retirement.

        (1) RIS calculation: most programs compute a single sum necessary to provide the RIS stream of income over the life expectancy of the retiree.

            (a) The number calculated is the present value (at retirement) of the inflation-protected RIS stream of income over the life expectancy.

        (2) DIPP calculation:

            (a) Another calculation must be used to provide an inflation-protected supplement for other sources of income that are subject to DIPP.

               ■ The number calculated is the sum of the present values of all the inflation adjustments needed for all existing-resource income that will not adjust automatically for inflation.

> **E X A M P L E** To protect against a 4% inflation rate, a first-year retirement income of $50,000 from existing non-inflation-adjusting sources must grow to $52,000 in the second year, $54,080 the third year, and $56,243 the fourth year, and continue to grow at 4% per year. The inflation adjustment for the second year, then, is $2,000, $4,080 for the third year, $6,243 for the fourth year, and so on. These inflation adjustments are discounted back to the retirement year and added together to calculate the existing-resource DIPP fund.

(3) Add the RIS and DIPP numbers: the retirement target amount represents the additional amount that the individual needs to save by retirement age to meet financial objectives.

e. Determine the amount that must be saved annually to meet the targeted amount.

5.32 Determining retirement needs using a shorthand formula:

a. The goal of the shorthand formula: to calculate the capital needed at retirement that will support a person at a constant standard of living until death.

b. Formula for capital needed (in current dollars):

$$C_r = E_r \left[\frac{1 - a^n}{1 - a} \right]$$

Where C_r = capital needed at retirement in then-current dollars

E_r = income needed in the first year of retirement in then-current dollars

r = after-tax rate of return

i = inflation rate

a = $(1 + i) / (1 + r)$

n = length of retirement

(1) E_r and C_r are in then-current dollars; to calculate E_r, specify the retirement income needed in today's dollars and adjust for the inflation anticipated between today and the year of retirement; formula: $E_r = E_t (1 + i)^b$

Where b = number of years until retirement

E_t = target retirement income in today's dollars

EXAMPLE Henry and Libby need $54,000 in their first year of retirement to maintain their standard of living. As their financial planner, you have determined to use a 4.5% inflation assumption and an 8% rate of return assumption. Retirement is expected to last 25 years. First solve for a:

$$a = \frac{1+.045}{1+.08} = .9676$$

Next use the capital needed formula:

$$\$54,000 \left[\frac{1-.9676^{25}}{1-.9676} \right]$$

$$\$54,000 \left[\frac{1-.4389}{.0324} \right]$$

$$\$54,000 \times 17.318 = \$935,172$$

Henry and Libby need $935,172 for retirement.

5.33 Assessing retirement needs through use of a consumer worksheet.

EXAMPLE Ronald and Rebecca are 15 years from retirement. Their current salary is $120,000. They also have the following resources: a defined-benefit plan of $2,000 per month, combined Social Security benefits estimated at $20,000, and $140,000 in IRAs, 401(k) plans, and mutual funds. The Zoom In includes an example of a worksheet using the case of Ronald and Rebecca.

5.34 Determining retirement needs using a planner's worksheet.

a. Three steps in using the planner's worksheet:

(1) List assumptions.

(2) List factors generated from time-value-of-money tables.

(3) Calculate the amount the client needs to save in the initial year.

EXAMPLE Ralph (age 46) and Alice (age 44) are married and have two children. Ralph and Alice both plan to retire in 19 years. Ralph will be 65; Alice will be 63. The following financial data are collected from Ralph and Alice:

(1) Ralph earns $154,000.
(2) Alice earns $38,500.
(3) Ralph's 401(k) plan contains $132,000.
(4) Ralph has no defined-benefit plan.
(5) Alice has a 403(b) plan containing $70,400.
(6) Alice will receive a pension of $1,540 per month at age 63.
(7) Ralph's Social Security retirement benefit will be $1,210 per month when he retires at age 65.
(8) Alice's Social Security retirement benefit will be $880 per month when she retires at age 63.
(9) Social Security amounts are in today's dollars.
(10) Joint savings contains $55,000 earmarked for retirement.
(11) They have sufficient savings to meet other long-term financial goals (e.g., sending children to college).

E X A M P L E (continued)

Consultation with the planner results in the following assumptions:
(1) Inflation rate: 4%.
(2) Expected duration of retirement: 25 years.
(3) After-tax rate of return before retirement: 8%.
(4) After-tax rate of return after retirement: 7%.
(5) Replacement ratio: 80%.
(6) Savings step-up rate: 6%.

Step 1 is listing assumptions on a planner's worksheet as A1 to A7:
(1) Inflation rate before retirement.
(2) Inflation rate after retirement.
(3) Number of years until retirement.
(4) Expected duration of retirement.
(5) Rate of return before retirement.
(6) Rate of return after retirement.
(7) Savings step-up rate.

Step 2 is calculating five factors based on time-value-of-money tables:

(1)	Preretirement inflation factor	2.11
(2)	Retirement needs present value factor	17.936
(3)	Current assets future value factor	4.32
(4)	Defined-benefit income present value factor	12.469
(5)	Savings rate factor	.01435

Step 3 is determining the amount clients must save in the first year:

COMPUTATIONS

(A)		Projected annual retirement budget (80% of $192,500)		$154,000.00
(B)	−	Social Security benefit (Alice and Ralph annual total)		25,080.00
(C)	=	Net annual need in current dollars		128,920.00
(D)	+	Preretirement inflation factor		2.11
(E)	=	Inflation-adjusted annual retirement need		272,021.00
(F)	+	Retirement needs present value factor		17.936
(G)	=	Total resources needed for retirement		4,878,972.00
(H)		Total in defined-contribution plans		202,400.00
(I)	+	Total private savings earmarked for retirement		55,000.00
(J)	=	Current assets available for retirement		257,400.00
(K)	×	Current assets future value factor		4.32
(L)	=	Future value of current assets		1,111,968.00
(M)		Annual income from defined-benefit plan (Alice's annual pension)		18,480.00
(N)	×	Preretirement inflation factor		2.11
(O)	=	Inflation-adjusted annual income from defined-benefit plan		38,993.00
(P)	×	Defined-benefit income present value factor		12.469
(Q)	=	Lump-sum value of defined-benefit plan		486,201.00
(R)		Total resources available for retirement (L + Q)		1,598,169.00
(S)		Additional amount needed to accumulate by retirement (G − R)		3,280,803.00
(T)	×	Savings rate factor		.01435
(U)	=	Amount needed to save—first year (24% of salary)		$47,080.00

Note: Savings in each subsequent year must increase by the savings step-up rate, 6%.

ZOOM IN

Calculation of Retirement Expenses Worksheet

1. Annual gross salary	$120,000
2. Retirement-income target (multiply line 1 by 80% target)	96,000
3. Estimated annual pension plan benefit, excluding profit-sharing plans, 403(b)s, 401(k)s, or IRAs	24,000
4. Estimated annual Social Security benefits[1]	20,000
5. Total benefits at retirement (line 3 plus line 4)	44,000
6. Income gap (line 2 minus line 5)[2]	52,000
7. Adjust gap to consider inflation (line 6 times Factor A, below)	93,600
8. Capital needed to generate extra income and eliminate gap (line 7 times 16.3)[3]	1,525,680
9. Extra capital needed to offset inflation's impact on pension (line 3 times factor B, below)	204,000
10. Total amount of capital needed (line 8 plus line 9)	1,729,680
11. Total current retirement savings (including balances in 401(k) plans, IRAs, profit-sharing plans, mutual funds, CDs)	140,000
12. Value of retirement savings (line 11 times factor C, below)	448,000
13. Net capital gap (line 10 minus line 12)	1,281,680
14. Amount needed in today's dollars on an annual basis to start saving now to cover the gap (line 13 divided by factor D, below)	36,308
15. Percentage of salary to be saved each year (line 14 divided by line 1)[4]	30.3%

Accounting for inflation, savings, and capital:

Years to Retirement	Factor A	Factor B	Factor C	Factor D
25	2.7	12.6	6.9	107.0
20	2.2	10.3	4.7	63.3
15	1.8	8.5	3.2	35.3
10	1.5	7.0	2.2	17.5

[1]Lines 3 and 4: employers can provide estimates of projected annual retirement pay; the Social Security Administration can provide estimates of Social Security benefits. Both amounts will be provided in current dollars.

[2]Line 6: if a substantial pension avoids an income gap, proceed to line 9 to compute the assets needed to account for the impact of inflation.

[3]Line 8: this computation assumes that the capital will be depleted throughout a period of 25 years.

[4]Line 15: assuming earnings increase annually (with inflation), saving a set percentage each year means that the actual amount put away will increase annually.

Note: Inflation is assumed to average 4% per year; the annual return on investments and savings is assumed to be 8%.

5.4 WEB CALCULATORS AND PROPRIETARY SOFTWARE

Key point Web calculators and proprietary software are helpful tools when assessing retirement needs and checking the accuracy of needs assessments.

5.41 Proprietary software.

    a. Planners often use software to calculate savings goals for retirement needs.

5.42 Second opinion via Internet.

    a. Log on at **www.ASEC.org** (click on savings tool).

        (1) Provides a check for accuracy.

        (2) Convincing to skeptical clients.

5.5 AN IMPORTANT RETIREMENT STUDY

Key point The Retiree Income Replacement (RETIRE) Project gives results for four groups of retirees: 65-year-old with 62-year-old spouse; 65-year-old single; 65-year-old earning 60% and 62-year-old spouse earning 40%; and 65-year-old with 65-year-old spouse.

Key point The RETIRE Project determines three types of ratios for each of the four groups of retirees: Social Security replacement ratio, gross income replacement ratio, and net income replacement ratio.

5.51 The RETIRE Project (Retiree Income Replacement Project) is a study conducted every few years to analyze retirement saving trends in the United States.

    a. The study determines current income replacement ratios based on five items: state, local, and federal income taxes; Social Security benefits, Social Security taxes, spending habits of retirees, and savings habits of retirees.

    b. The income replacement is calculated based on the preretirement standard of living, not on the amount needed to meet basic needs.

    c. Project uses two formulas to calculate the income replacement needed:

        (1) Formula A: the tax and savings model:

$$\text{Replacement ratio} = \frac{\text{PrRGP} - \text{PrRT} - \text{PrRS} + \text{PoRT}}{\text{PrRGP}}$$

           Where:

PrRT	=	Preretirement taxes paid
PrRGP	=	Preretirement gross pay
PoRT	=	Postretirement taxes paid
PrRS	=	Preretirement savings

        (2) Formula B: the tax, savings, and expenditures model:

$$\text{Replacement ratio} = \frac{\text{PrRGP} - \text{PrRT} - \text{PrRS} - \text{WRE} [+ \text{ or } -] \text{NCASE} + \text{PoRT}}{\text{PrRGP}}$$

           Where:

NCASE	=	Net change in expenditures that are age sensitive
WRE	=	Work-related expenditures

    d. The study produces results for four baseline (typical) retirees:

        (1) 65-year-old wage earner with a 62-year-old spouse.

        (2) 65-year-old single individual.

        (3) One 65-year-old spouse earning wages of 60% of total income and 40% of total income earned by the other spouse at age 62.

        (4) 65-year-old wage earner with a 65-year-old spouse.

    e. Three types of ratios are determined for each of the four types of retirees:

        (1) Social Security replacement ratio: percentage of the final salary that Social Security benefits will replace.

        (2) Gross income replacement ratio: total percentage of the final year's salary (during preretirement) necessary to meet the current standard of living during retirement.

        (3) Net income replacement ratio: the gross income replacement ratio minus the Social Security replacement ratio.

5.52 The most recent RETIRE Project (2001) findings:

    a. 65-year-old wage earner with a 62-year-old spouse:

        (1) Under Formula A: the gross income replacement ratio ranges from 76 to 85% and the net income replacement ratio ranges from 24 to 51%.

        (2) Under Formula B: the gross income replacement ratio ranges from 74 to 83% and the net income replacement ratio ranges from 23 to 48%.

        (3) The Social Security replacement ratio is the same whether computing the gross income replacement ratio or the net income replacement ratio.

    b. 65-year-old single individual:

        (1) Under Formula B, the gross income replacement ratio ranges from 74 to 82% and the net income replacement ratio ranges from 34 to 61%.

    c. One 65-year-old spouse earning wages of 60% of total income and 40% of total income earned by the other spouse at age 62:

        (1) FICA taxes are greatest; cause a lower postretirement standard of living.

        (2) Gross income replacement ratio is nearly identical for all levels of salary; however, the net income replacement ratio varies since the Social Security benefit amount is different at the various salary levels.

    d. 65-year-old wage earner with a 65-year-old spouse:

        (1) Under Formula B: the gross income replacement ratio ranges from 73 to 83% and the net income replacement ratio ranges from 17 to 44%.

        (2) Social Security benefits first paid to individuals at age 65 are 33% greater than the benefit amount paid to individuals at age 62 for early retirement.

5.53 Circulatory of the savings variable: the relationship between the gross income replacement ratio and the preretirement rate of savings.

    a. A decrease in savings during preretirement is related to an increase in consumption during preretirement and a greater gross income replacement ratio.

Highlight 1: Determining Needs at Retirement

■ Retirement income needs consist of the amount needed throughout retirement to enable a client to maintain the standard of living enjoyed immediately before retirement. Targeted retirement income that is determined from a worksheet or computer model is not an absolute. (5.11)

Highlight 2: Assumptions Required in Worksheets and Computer Models

■ Seven Assumptions Required in Most Worksheets and Computer Models (Memory Aid: **STARRYI**)

1. Step-up rate used to increase annual savings.	5. Replacement ratio.
2. Tax rate, both current and future.	6. Yield expected on investments.
3. Age of client at death.	7. Inflation rate. (5.21)
4. Retirement age.	

■ Retirement Age Assumption: Reasons For and Against Early Retirement

Nine Reasons for Early Retirement:	**Seven Reasons Against Early Retirement:**
1. Financial independence goals.	1. Normal retirement age is between ages 65 and 67.
2. Health plays a role in the retirement decision.	2. Adjustment of the pension downward to off-set the longer payout period that results from early retirement.
3. Downsizing of corporations.	
4. Two wage earners in the family.	
5. Death of spouse.	3. Fixed long-term liabilities of worker.
6. Laborers and manual workers.	4. Effect on pension benefits.
7. Workplace conflict.	5. Loss of health insurance.
8. Compromise on desired standard of living.	6. Increased exposure to inflation.
9. Employer's retiree health care package. (5.23a)	7. Decrease in Social Security benefits. (5.23b)

Highlight 3: Using Computer Models and Worksheets

■ Five steps in calculating retirement fund needs with computer software:
(1) Project retirement income from existing records.
(2) Compare what a client has to what a client will need.
(3) Provide inflation protection for income provided from existing sources.
(4) Compute the sum needed at retirement.
(5) Determine an annual savings amount to achieve the targeted amount. (5.31)

■ Know the three steps in using the planner's worksheet:
(1) List assumptions.
(2) List factors generated from time-value-of-money tables.
(3) Calculate the amount the client needs to save in the initial year. (5.34a)

Highlight 4: Web Calculators and Proprietary Software

■ Web calculators and proprietary software are helpful tools when assessing retirement needs and checking the accuracy of needs assessments. (5.41)

Highlight 5: An Important Retirement Study

■ The Retiree Income Replacement (RETIRE) Project is a study conducted every few years to analyze retirement saving trends in the United States. (5.51)

■ The study produces results for four baseline retirees:
(1) 65-year-old wage earner with a 62-year-old spouse.
(2) 65-year-old single individual.
(3) One 65-year-old spouse earning wages of 60% of total income and 40% of total income earned by the other spouse at age 62.
(4) 65-year-old wage earner with a 65-year-old spouse. (5.51d)

■ Three types of ratios are determined for each of the four retirees:
(1) Social Security replacement ratio.
(2) Gross income replacement ratio.
(3) Net income replacement ratio. (5.51e)

TERMS TO KNOW DEFINITIONS

Expense method Estimating a retiree's retirement needs by focusing on projected expenses that the retiree will have in the first year of retirement. (5.26)

Golden handshake An employer's offer of a retirement package to an employee or group of employees to foster retirement before age 65. Incentives to encourage early retirement include financial inducements, lump-sum payments based on years of employment, and retiree health insurance payments. (5.23a(3))

Income requirement assumption Represents the planner's estimate of the level of income needed to sustain the standard of living that was enjoyed just before retirement; measured as a percentage of final salary. (5.25)

Replacement ratio approach A method of estimating level of income needed to sustain the standard of living that was enjoyed just before retirement; measured as a percentage of final salary. Some planners consider 70% to 80% of the client's final salary sufficient to meet the client's needs during retirement. (5.25a)

Retirement income needs The amount needed during retirement to enable a client to maintain the standard of living enjoyed immediately before retirement. (5.11)

Savings step-up rate Rate by which a person can increase savings each year. (5.28b(2))

QUESTIONS

1. Which of the following is a reason for early retirement?
   A. Financial dependence
   B. Corporate growth
   C. Death of spouse
   D. Mental demands of the job

2. Which term applies to the additional amount needed to be saved to offset increasing needs during retirement?
   A. RIS
   B. DIPP
   C. Fudge factor
   D. Target factor

3. Some expenses tend to increase for retirees and others usually decrease more in later retirement than in early retirement. Which of the following tend(s) to decrease in later retirement?
   I. Insurance and pensions
   II. Food
   A. I only
   B. II only
   C. Both I and II
   D. Neither I nor II

4. Which of the following is(are) a goal(s) of the shorthand formula of determining retirement need?
   I. To calculate the capital needed at retirement that will support a person at a constant standard of living until death
   II. To determine the postretirement tax rate
   A. I only
   B. II only
   C. Both I and II
   D. Neither I nor II

5. Of all of the methods of calculating financial need, which takes into consideration the future annual expenses of the client?
   A. Replacement ratio estimate
   B. Expense method
   C. Tax and investment assumption
   D. Retirement age assumption

ANSWERS

1. **C.** Reasons for early retirement include financial independence goals, not financial dependence; downsizing of corporations, not corporate growth; and physical, not mental, demands of the job. (5.23a)

2. **B.** DIPP is used to provide inflation protection for income from existing sources. (5.31c)

3. **C.** Additional expenses that usually decrease in later retirement are entertainment, transportation, clothing, and housing. (5.27a(1))

4. **A.** The shorthand formula is a method of calculating the capital needed to support an individual at a constant standard of living until death. (5.32a)

5. **B.** A list of expenses must be considered, including both general expenses and expenses unique to a particular client. (5.26a)

6

Investing Before Retirement

"The best way to find yourself is to lose yourself in the service of others."

—Mahatma Gandhi

A HELICOPTER VIEW OF ASSIGNMENT 6

TERMS TO KNOW

Capital market line	Market portfolio	Standard deviation
Constant relative risk aversion	Mean reversion process	Strategic asset allocation
Dollar cost averaging	Normal distribution	Tactical asset allocation
Efficient frontier	PITI	Tax-efficient allocation
Geometric mean return	Return/return tradeoff	Time diversification
Human capital	Risk tolerance	Woerheide-Persson index
Independent stock returns		

6.1 MODERN PORTFOLIO THEORY

> **Key point**   The modern portfolio theory is based on the principle that all investments are defined by expected returns and variances of the expected returns (i.e., risk).
>
> **Key point**   Risk aversion is the willingness of an investor to accept lower returns in exchange for reduced risk.
>
> **Key point**   Diversification is a method of reducing risk.

6.11   Basic principles of modern portfolio theory.

   a. Modern portfolio theory is based on the principle that all investments are defined by two basic elements:

   (1) Expected returns of the investments.

   (2) Variances (or standard deviations) of the expected returns.

   b. Covariance of returns: variables in an investment are dependent and affect one another; measures the extent to which two variables move together over time.

   (1) Large, positive covariance between two securities:

   (a) Prices of the two securities nearly always move together.

   (b) Therefore, when one security's price dramatically increases or decreases, the price of the other security will likely have a similar jump or drop.

   (2) Large, negative covariance between two securities:

   (a) Prices of the two securities nearly always move in opposite directions.

   (3) Covariances of zero or near zero mean price changes of the two securities are most likely unrelated.

   c. **Efficient frontier:** based on the assumption that investors can earn a risk-free rate of return; represents the set of portfolios that will give you the highest return at each level of risk; can be defined in one of two ways:

   (1) For any level of risk as measured by the standard deviation of return, a set of portfolios that provides the greatest expected return.

   (2) For any level of expected return, a set of portfolios that provides the lowest level of risk as measured by the standard deviation of return.

   d. **Capital market line:** the introduction of a risk-free asset changes the original efficient frontier theory from a curve into the straight capital market line.

   (1) Represents most efficient portfolios an investor should hold, not which particular portfolio to hold.

   (2) Capital market line is made up of different combinations of only two assets: risk-free asset and portfolio M.

   (3) Under the portfolio and capital market theory, if an asset is risk free, its return does not vary; its variance and standard deviation are zero.

   (4) If an asset has no variance, its expected return does not move.

   (5) Separation theorem: theory that an investor's risk preferences when making an investment do not influence the choice of risky assets.

   (6) **Market portfolio:** Portfolio M; portfolio containing all assets where the weights on each asset are equal to the percentage of the market value of each asset to the market value of the entire market portfolio.

(a) $$\text{Stock's weight in the market portfolio} = \frac{\text{Market value of stock}}{\text{Market value of market portfolio}}$$

EXAMPLE If Cindy's market value of a stock is $100 million and the market value of the market portfolio is $5 billion, that stock's weight in the market portfolio is 2% ($100 million ÷ $5 billion).

---

e. Optimal portfolio: portfolio that gives an investor the greatest possible utility; optimal portfolio for an investor is determined by using indifference curves.

   (1) Optimal portfolio for each investor is found on the highest indifference curve that is tangent to the efficient frontier.

   (2) An investor cares about which curve touches the efficient frontier.

   (3) An investor does not care about one portfolio over another portfolio on the same indifference curve in seeking his optimal portfolio.

   (4) Indifference curve: set of portfolios with the same utility; investor's goal is to create a portfolio on the highest possible indifference curve.

   (a) Vertical axis is expected return; horizontal axis is standard deviation.

f. Risk aversion: when an investor is willing to accept a lower expected return in exchange for a portfolio of assets with less risk.

   (1) If there are two investments with equal expected returns, investors prefer the one with the lowest risk.

   (2) If there are two investments with equal risk, investors prefer the one with the greatest expected return.

g. Diversification: method of controlling investment risk by spreading funds among various investments.

   (1) The greater the number of individual investments or securities an investor holds—that is, the more diversified the investments, the less risk each poses to the overall portfolio.

   (a) Seven important principles of diversification and investment planning:

   - Financial planners should understand a client's risk tolerance so that a portfolio can be created to accurately reflect such risk tolerance.

   - Financial planners should make sure that the risky assets in a client's portfolio are diversified.

   - Total risk of a portfolio declines as more securities are added.

   - Total risk of a portfolio declines at a decreasing rate as more securities are added to the portfolio.

   - Portfolio's total risk moves toward the market portfolio's total risk.

   - Diversification of a portfolio generally cannot decrease a portfolio's total risk below the market portfolio's total risk.

   - More securities in your client's portfolio would be more favorable the lower the amount of commission your client must pay.

(2) Diversification eliminates only nonsystematic (nonmarket) risk, not systematic (market) risk.

   (a) Systematic risk: risk that events impacting the overall market will cause fluctuations in the price of a stock; also called market risk.

(3) Diversification has no effect on systematic risk because diversification affects individual securities, not the overall market.

   (a) Nonsystematic risk: risk associated with factors exclusive to a particular corporation.

   (b) Potential costs of diversifying a portfolio:

   ■ Monitoring cost: an investor who is watching the performance of his portfolio is likely to spend more time watching a higher number of stocks in a portfolio as opposed to a one- or two-stock portfolio.

   ■ Cost of adding another stock to a portfolio at a certain point exceeds the value of decreasing the portfolio's risk by diversifying the portfolio.

EXAMPLE Assume Lee has invested 100% of her capital in the stock market. Ed has invested 50% of his capital in the stock market and 50% of in cash equivalents. If the stock market drops by 30%, the loss to Lee's capital is 30%; the loss to Ed's capital is 15%. This example shows that the more diversified a portfolio, the more chance that losses on individual stocks will not adversely affect the overall performance of the portfolio.

6.2 DETERMINING CLIENT'S RISK TOLERANCE

Key point   Recommend asset allocation that reflects the client's risk tolerance.

Key point   A client's risk tolerance varies based on financial goals and time horizon.

Key point   Clients have a harder time when given too many investment choices.

6.21 **Risk tolerance**: client's feelings about risk.

   a. The financial planner must determine a client's risk tolerance.

   (1) Highly risk averse client: risk intolerant or conservative.

   (2) Mildly risk averse client: risk tolerant or aggressive.

   b. The financial planner must then recommend an asset allocation that appropriately reflects the client's level of risk.

   (1) No research relates asset allocation strategies to risk tolerance.

   (2) However, financial planners should assess a client's risk level to show due diligence and protect themselves from liability.

   (3) Financial planners often give risk tolerance questionnaires to their clients.

General Guidelines on Profiling Clients' Risk Tolerance

Certainly, risk tolerance categories cannot be applied rigidly, and every financial institution has developed its own criteria as to how investors are profiled. However, enough similarities exist among them to provide some general guidelines. The following offers an idea of how these categories are labeled and defined.

Client's Risk Tolerance Category	Description of Risk Tolerance Level
Conservative	This label usually applies to investors who desire stability and preservation of capital and current income. They are less concerned about increasing the value of their investments; they want to protect what they already have.
Moderately Conservative	Investors positioned in this category may want to see some increase in the value of their investments, but they are concerned equally about loss of principal. They seek stability and current income.
Moderate	Moderate investors likely have longer-term horizons. They seek reasonable but relatively stable rates of growth on their investments. Most moderate investors accept some fluctuations, but generally want less risk than the overall market.
Moderately Aggressive	Moderately aggressive investors have long-term horizons and seek good rates of growth. They usually don't need current income. They are willing to accept a fair amount of risk.
Aggressive	This category is reserved for those who have long-term horizons and want high rates of growth. They are comfortable with year-to-year fluctuations in the value of their investments and are willing to accept substantial risk in exchange for the potential for high returns over the long term.

    c. Clients' risk tolerance varies based on financial goals, research says.

        (1) A client with multiple investment goals can have multiple portfolios.

        (2) Each portfolio representing a different financial goal will contain a different asset allocation based on the client's particular risk tolerance level.

6.22 Client's long-term perspective on investments.

    a. Client's retirement portfolio should contain assets with more risk than assets contained in portfolios created for nonretirement reasons.

    b. Studies show that decisions about risky issues are dictated by the lag between the time of the decision and the time the decision is realized.

        (1) If an investor immediately knows the impact of his decision, the investor is more likely to be risk averse.

        (2) A client's short-term look at his financial future causes him to be more likely to make risk-averse decisions.

        (3) A client's long-term look at his financial future causes him to be more likely to choose riskier investments.

    c. Financial planners may help their clients develop a long-term perspective.

        (1) Clients should be aware of risks involved in their portfolios; more awareness causes less fear.

        (2) Clients should monitor their portfolios' performance less frequently.

6.23   Clients and the number of investment choices.

    a.   Studies show that employees offered 401(k) programs by their employers were less likely to sign up for a program when employers offered more program choices.

    b.   Financial planners should consider offering their clients a limited number of choices consistent with each client's risk tolerance level.

6.3   HUMAN CAPITAL AND RETIREMENT PLANNING

> **Key point**   Human capital is a person's ability to produce wage income.
>
> **Key point**   A young worker has little savings but much human capital.
>
> **Key point**   A good strategy: don't buy investments that are correlated with return of human capital (such as employer stock)—you could lose both a job and savings.

6.31   Human capital.

    a.   Financial planners should examine a client's total portfolio, including all of a client's liabilities and assets.

    b.   **Human capital**: an asset that is not part of a client's investment portfolio, but a significant part of a client's total portfolio.

        (1)   Client's wealth = financial assets + human capital.

        (2)   Human capital: a person's ability to produce wage income; the current value of a person's net income from wages and salaries earned in the future.

        (3)   A worker's wealth changes from consisting only of human capital at the beginning of the worker's career to consisting only of financial assets at retirement; three stages of a worker's wealth:

            (a)   Worker's human capital increases each year of employment.

            (b)   Human capital decreases as years of work decrease.

            (c)   Worker's financial assets grow as the worker contributes to investments.

        (4)   A worker's human capital value declines when the decrease in working years exceeds the increase in the present value of the other years.

6.32   Impact of diversification on human capital.

    a.   A worker who is just beginning his working life is not greatly affected by diversification because the worker's total wealth consists primarily of human capital.

> **EXAMPLE**   Sally begins working at the age of 25 after graduation from graduate school for journalism. At the end of her first year of working at a news station, she invests $2,000 into financial assets. Sally's total wealth at the end of her first working year is $502,000. Therefore, of her total wealth, her human capital is worth $500,000 and her financial assets are worth $2,000. At this point, Sally's financial asset worth is so small that any or all loss of the investment does not greatly impact Sally's total wealth. Diversification of her portfolio at this point in her working life has minimal impact on her total wealth.

    b. Diversification of human capital: a worker learns a new skill set or obtains additional education.

    c. Diversification's significance increases as the worker's years of working increase.

        (1) Because financial assets become a larger part of worker's wealth.

        (2) Diversification becomes most important to a retiree upon retirement because his total wealth is made up only of financial assets at retirement.

        (3) A beginning worker may contribute over many years of working and make up for any financial losses; as the worker's years of working come to an end, his ability to recover from losses lessens.

6.33 Human capital and financial assets.

    a. Fundamental rule of financial planning: investors should lessen the correlation between two assets if their portfolio is only a two-asset portfolio.

    b. Financial planners should recommend that clients not invest in either their own corporation or other companies within their industry.

    c. Problem occurs when employees invest in their employer's stock.

        (1) Employees could have a decline in both their human capital (i.e., get laid off) and their financial assets (i.e., stock value in the company declines) at the same time if their company's performance becomes poor.

    d. Problem occurs when employees invest in stock of companies that are a part of the employees' industry.

        (1) It is likely that an entire industry is experiencing financial woes when one company is in financial difficulty.

    e. Employers often encourage employees to invest in company stock.

        (1) Employee stock purchase plans: employers offer company stock to employees at a discounted rate of up to 15% off the present market value of the stock.

        (2) Stock options in employer's stock: increases employees' risk of decline in both human capital and financial assets at the same time.

6.4 ESTIMATING FUTURE RATES OF RETURN

> **Key point** The two types of averaging to compute return are arithmetic mean return (AMR) and geometric mean return (GMR).
>
> **Key point** Standard deviation is a measure of variances from the mean in any set of data; in the case of investment returns, the larger the standard deviation, the riskier the investment.
>
> **Key point** A long time horizon allows for riskier investments.

6.41 Portfolio projections.

    a. Begin portfolio projections by estimating future return rates.

        (1) Best way to develop an estimate:

            (a) Analyze historical return rates and historical variability.

- **(b)** Assume future return rates and related risk will equal the average historical return rates and variability.

(2) Two problems encountered with this estimation strategy:

- **(a)** Determining which asset categories will provide the historical data.
  - ■ Many financial planners use five asset types provided by Ibbotson & Associates: Treasury bills, long-term government and corporate bonds, and small and large company common stocks.

- **(b)** Determining what time frame to use in estimating future return rates:
  - ■ Mean return rates are more stable if longer time periods are used.
  - ■ Using historical data that dates back decades causes a problem in the estimation; economy was different decades ago.
  - ■ Financial planners may want to use a shorter time period when estimating future return rates based on historical information.

b. Arithmetic mean return and geometric mean return.

(1) Arithmetic mean return (AMR): adding together the rates of return and then dividing by **n**, the number of return rates; this is the averaging technique you learned in fifth grade.

(2) **Geometric mean return (GMR):** effective rate of return representing a geometric average of returns calculated as follows:

- **(a)** Step 1: Add one to each period's return rate, the sum of which is called the per period return relative (PPRR).
- **(b)** Step 2: Multiply together all of the PPRRs, the sum of which is the holding period return relative (HPRR).
- **(c)** Step 3: Take the nth root of the number in step two (HPRR), where **n** is the number of PPRRs used in the formula.
- **(d)** Step 4: Subtract 1 from the nth root.

(3) These four steps are expressed symbolically as follows (note that the steps don't appear in the same order):

$$\text{GMR} = \sqrt[n]{\text{HPRR}} - 1 \qquad \text{(Steps 3 and 4)}$$

$$\text{Where, HPRR} = \text{PPRR}^1 \times \text{PPRR}^2 \times \ldots \times \text{PPRR}_n \quad \text{(Step 2)}$$

$$\text{PPRR} = 1 + \text{each period's return rate} \qquad \text{(Step 1)}$$

And n = the number of data points (i.e., PPRRs) used in the calculation.

(4) Three ways the arithmetic mean return relates to the geometric mean return:

- **(a)** GMR equals the AMR when all the PPRRs are the same; when the individual returns are close to each other (and none are negative), GMR and AMR will be close to each other.
- **(b)** GMR will always be less than the AMR when all the PPRRs are not the same.
- **(c)** Difference between GMR and AMR increases as the difference among all the PPRRs increases.

(5) The arithmetic mean is good for predicting future performance for one year; the geometric mean is good for predicting future performance for many years.

(6) The weighted average of both the arithmetic mean and the geometric mean is best for predicted future performance; formula:

Forecast = (arithmetic mean × [1 − H/T]) + (geometric mean × [H/T])

Where H is the number of time periods forecast (i.e., horizon) and T is the number of time periods used in the historical calculation.

Note: The weighted average model should not be used if H is greater than T.

(a) Weights: the beginning value of each item in a portfolio divided by the entire value of the portfolio.

c. Standard deviation: represented by mathematical symbol sigma (σ); square root of the variance.

(1) Standard deviation formula:

$$\sigma = \sqrt{\sigma^2}$$

(2) The larger the standard deviation (σ), the larger the risk (likelihood of deviation from the mean).

(3) Variance: a measure of variability using the weighted average of squared deviations represented by the mathematical symbol sigma squared.

(4) Formula for variance: calculate and square the difference between each actual return and the return expected, then multiply by the relative probability and sum the products.

(5) The formula for variance (σ²) is shown symbolically as follows:

$$\sigma^2 = \frac{1}{n-1} \sum_{t=1}^{n} [R_t - R]^2$$

R_t = expected return

R = average of returns

t is the designator of each actual data point for return—t starts at 1 and goes up to n.

Σ is a summation symbol—it means that you repeat the operation that follows for each t, starting with 1 and going up to n and add them all together.

> **✱ EXAMPLE** A particular investment provides a 25% probability of a −3% return, a 55% probability of a 9% return, and a 20% probability of a 21% return. The expected return for the investment is 9% with deviations from the mean of −12, 0, and 12. The squares of these differences are 144, 0, and 144. The variance is equal to the relative probabilities multiplied by the squared terms:
>
> $(0.25 \times -12^2) + (0.55 \times 0) + (0.20 \times 12^2) = 64.8$, stated as 64.8%
>
> The standard deviation is the square root of 64.8 or 8.05, stated as 8.05%.

d. Probability distributions are used to assess continuous occurrences (shows possible outcomes and probabilities); differ from histograms, which assess distinct possibilities rather than infinite possibilities; used as a measure of the degree of risk or confidence in the expected return.

(1) Probabilities increase until the peak is met (R or the expected value) and decrease symmetrically thereafter.

(2) Probabilities of returns that are equal distances from R are the same.

(3) **Normal distribution**: most common assumption is that returns follow a normal distribution; there are three properties of a normal distribution:

   (a) For most distributions, the actual value will be no more than one standard deviation away from the mean 66% of the time.

   (b) Actual value will be no more than two standard deviations away from the mean 95% of the time.

   (c) Actual value will be no more than three standard deviations away from the mean 99% of the time.

6.42 **Time diversification**: belief that the risk of stocks decreases as the investment horizon increases—in other words, that the greater the age of the retiree as he is approaching retirement, the more likely the retiree will invest in more risk-free assets than risky assets.

   a. Time diversification supported: McEnally and Kockman and Goodwin: main argument that if a retiree's time horizon is long enough, a retiree most likely will accomplish a satisfactory mean rate of return.

   (1) Time horizon: also called investment horizon; time period during which an investor's money is invested; begins when the investor makes his first investment and ends when the investor needs to access his savings.

   (2) Time diversification is a good argument only if an investor is willing to assume three things:

   (a) No human capital value.

   (b) Constant relative risk aversion.

   (c) Independent stock returns.

   b. Time diversification not supported (or arguments against time diversification):

   (1) As the holding periods increase, overlapping information provides an illusion of accuracy.

   (2) The overlapping characteristic of the information causes the maximum-minimum range of annual rates of return to become smaller.

   (3) Time diversification is misleading because the total holding period is more significant to the investor than the mean annual return rate.

   (4) More risk is involved with greater holding periods; however, the risk is not proportionate to the length of the holding period.

   c. Reasons time diversification argument is incorrect.

   (1) Same allocation percentages would be recommended to a client who has chosen his risk tolerance regardless of the number of the years for the holding period (under certain situations).

   (2) Samuelson: retirees will make the same asset allocation decisions regardless of their time horizon; three assumptions for this argument.

   (a) Retiree's wealth is only worth his investment portfolio.

- Investors with long time horizons who continuously receive human capital can compensate for unsuccessful years of returns by investing new funds from human capital into their portfolio and reducing living expenses.

(b) Retirees have a constant relative risk aversion.

- **Constant relative risk aversion:** an investor's wealth is independent of the risk tolerance chosen by an investor; that is, an investor will choose a risk tolerance level independent of his current financial status.

- Evidence does not support this assumption.

- Nearly all investors have a decreasing relative risk aversion; the less wealthy the investor is, the less likely the investor is to take risks in investing.

- An investor with a longer time horizon is more likely to allocate a greater percentage of his portfolio to stock.

(c) **Independent stock return:** also known as the random walk theory that stock returns of one period are not related in any way to the previous period's stock return results; assumes stock prices follow a random walk because the prices reflect the uninfluenced expectations of future news events.

- Perfect random walk is not reflected in the market, research says.
  - Investors sometimes overact to news events.
  - Market will not immediately feel the entire impact of a news event, but will fully react to the event over time.

- **Mean reversion process:** a low (high) return rate in one period is more likely to be followed by a high (low) return rate in the following period; opposite of the momentum theory.

- **Momentum:** a low (high) return rate in one period is more likely to be followed by another low (high) return rate in the following time period; opposite of the mean reversion process.
  - Most people don't believe the market operates on a momentum.
  - Investors who believe in this theory should reduce the stock percentage in their portfolios because their stock returns become more unstable the greater their investment horizons.

6.43 Dominance: one strong argument for persons with long time horizons to set up aggressive investment portfolios.

a. Likely result when comparing the performance of a conservative all-bond portfolio to that of an aggressive diversified all-stock portfolio:

(1) The longer the life of the investment, the more likely the weak performance of the aggressive all-stock portfolio will perform better than the best performance of the conservative all-bond portfolio.

6.5 ASSET ALLOCATION DECISION MAKING

> **Key point** Asset allocation is a strategy of investing in different asset groups to reduce overall risk.
>
> **Key point** The reasons for a client's change in risk tolerance are career change, family change, change in wealth, and aging.

6.51 Asset allocation: strategy of placing an investor's funds into different asset groups to create a portfolio that will weather all kinds of markets.

  a. Method to enhance a portfolio's returns while minimizing risks.

  b. Goal of asset allocation is to build and maintain an investor's wealth in a way that is suited to the individual based on his objectives and level of risk tolerance.

6.52 **Strategic asset allocation**: more dynamic and anticipatory approach; decision that must be long-term and typically involves only a few types of assets; two-step strategy:

  a. Assignment of percentages between the risk-free and risky assets.

  b. Division of risky asset percentage into particular types of assets.

  c. Begins by assigning percentages to various asset categories and then encourages a periodic adjustment of the selected percentages—the weight—for each asset held in the investor's portfolio based on market analysis.

  d. Typical strategic asset allocation strategy: 60% stock, 30% bonds, 10% cash equivalents.

  e. This strategy includes a range of weights rather than a precise weight.

  f. Purpose: create a portfolio that accurately reflects a client's risk level.

  g. This strategy is considered successful if the allocation accurately reflects:

   (1) The market's returns.

   (2) The client's risk level.

  h. Strict strategic asset allocation approach would include the inclusion of index funds in a client's portfolio.

  i. Changes to a strategic asset allocation should represent risk level change.

   (1) Common reasons for changes to a client's level of risk:

    (a) Career changes.

    (b) Family reasons.

    (c) Change in client's wealth.

    (d) Aging.

  j. Only infrequent changes may be made to a strategic asset allocation for the allocation to remain strategic.

  k. Frequent changes to a strategic asset allocation are tactical, not strategic.

  l. Three issues to consider in strategic asset allocation decision making:

   (1) Frequency of checking the portfolio to make sure that the portfolio is strictly following the designated strategic weights.

    (2) Client's tolerance to weight ranges.

    (3) Portfolio rebalancing: purchasing assets that have not performed well and selling those that have performed well; adjusting the strategic weights of assets in a portfolio that have changed from the originally desired asset allocation due to varying returns.

6.53 **Tactical asset allocation**.

  a. Tactical asset allocation is similar to a strategic asset allocation to the extent that it is anticipatory—that is, it rebalances not so much in response to market changes, but in anticipation of them.

  b. Most aggressive asset allocation model by actively using nontraditional products like futures to meet its goals.

  c. Three principal features of a tactical asset allocation decision:

    (1) More frequent decisions.

    (2) Includes more types of assets.

    (3) Aim is to beat the market instead of determining the client's risk level.

  d. Decisions are not based on the efficient market theory.

6.54 Contribution timing: building wealth

  a. Most effective way to build wealth is the continuous contributions of new money into a client's portfolio rather than trying to choose the most successful securities.

  b. Perfect certainty: what happens if an investor waits to contribute a portion of his income into a nonqualified account at the end of each year with perfect certainty as to the average rate of return? How does this impact the investor's wealth?

    (1) The difference in contributing on the first day of each year and contributing on the last day of each year is essentially the ending value of the first contribution.

  c. Uncertainty: what happens if an investor waits to contribute a portion of his income into a nonqualified account at the end of each year with uncertainty as to the average rate of return? How does this impact the investor's wealth?

    (1) The investor would have a dramatic drop in returns if the investor missed the 10, 20, 30, and 40 best trading days of a certain time period.

    (2) The investor would have a significantly better return rate if the investor missed the 10, 20, 30, or 40 worst trading days of the period.

    (3) An investor would receive a lower return rate if he missed both the best trading day and the worst trading day.

    (4) An investor has greater success in the market when he is present for the few significantly dramatic price increase days during a certain time period.

  d. Investors who have a long-term investment strategy should make their contributions at the earliest point because they will have decreased rates of return if they miss the best trading days, weeks, or months during a certain time period.

6.55 Periodic portfolio modifications

  a. Time diversification is an erroneous principle.

    (1) Longer investment horizons mean greater differences in portfolio values.

(2) A good financial planner should meet with clients at least every one to two years to analyze the portfolio and determine any necessary changes to be made.

b. Client who becomes underfunded:

(1) Underfunded client: where the portfolio's liabilities exceed the market value of the portfolio.

(2) An underfunded client may do any of the following with his portfolio:

(a) Get a second job.

(b) Believe poor performance of portfolio was merely bad luck.

(c) Set a later retirement date.

(d) Make greater contributions to portfolio.

(e) Increase the portfolio's expected return.

(f) Set lower standard of living for retirement period.

(3) **Return/return tradeoff**: to protect underfunded client, increase the expected return by increasing the portfolio's risk.

(a) Best way to increase a portfolio's expected return is to increase risk.

c. Client who becomes overfunded:

(1) Overfunded client: where the portfolio's market value exceeds its liabilities.

(2) An overfunded client may do any of the following with his portfolio:

(a) Create a risk cushion; keep the contribution amount the same:

(b) Decrease contributions.

(c) Continue with the same plan, but more gifts or legacies to charities during retirement should be considered.

(d) Take on a more aggressive approach with the portfolio.

(e) Strategic asset allocation model could be modified into a more conservative approach so that the client will be more likely to reach desired retirement income level.

6.6 PORTFOLIO PERFORMANCE

Key point Four portfolio strategies are diversification, mutual funds, dollar cost averaging, and borrowing from plans.

Key point The benefits of placing mutual funds in a portfolio are professional management and diversification; the disadvantage to such strategy is the fees.

Key point Dollar cost averaging is a strategy of regular investment regardless of trends.

6.61 Recommending asset allocations to your client.

a. Two issues arise in making asset allocation recommendations to your client:

(1) The length of the time period that will provide the historical data.

(2) Professionalism of using unaltered historical data; planners should consider other data sources to mitigate historical data.

6.62   Quantifying diversification:

   a.   Diversification: placing additional securities into a portfolio is not enough to constitute diversification.

      (1)   Diversified portfolio contains assets that have minimal correlation.

      (2)   Completely diversified portfolio contains stocks with a correlation coefficient of –1.

   b.   Two ways to determine diversification:

      (1)   Calculate the standard deviation of portfolio's rate of return.

      (2)   Calculate the correlation coefficient between each pair of securities in the portfolio. Then, compute the average of the correlation coefficients.

   c.   Investment portfolios are not static because:

      (1)   Trades are usually made by investors over time.

      (2)   Changes are made to the portfolio's allocation over time even if no trades were made.

   d.   Problems with calculating the average correlation coefficient:

      (1)   Knowledge of standard deviations of different investments is required. This is a problem because the standard deviation will become meaningless over time as the portfolio changes.

      (2)   No standard of comparison exists for calculating correlation coefficients or covariances.

   e.   Quantifying diversification immediately:

      (1)   **Woerheide-Persson index:** index that calculates a portfolio's degree of diversification without using statistical measures based on time; index can be created by the following four steps.

         (a)   Calculate each security's market value weight.

         (b)   Square each of the security's weights.

         (c)   Add together the squared weights.

         (d)   Subtract this sum from one; difference is the value of the index.

      (2)   Interpretation of index value.

         (a)   Must compare index value to a table of index values that are determined for portfolios that are divided among all of the securities equally.

         (b)   Woerheide-Persson index = $1 - 1/n$

            If n securities in a portfolio have the same market values.

         (c)   The table below is an index for portfolios with one to 20 securities that have equal weights. Compare your calculation above with the index values below to determine the degree of portfolio diversification.

Woerheide-Persson Index Values							
#	Index Value	#	Index Value	#	Index Value	#	Index Value
1	0.0	6	.833	11	.910	16	.938
2	.5	7	.857	12	.917	17	.941
3	.667	8	.875	13	.923	18	.944
4	.75	9	.889	14	.929	19	.947
5	.80	10	.90	15	.933	20	.950

    f. Sufficient diversification.

      (1) Earlier researchers argued that at least 10 securities with equal market values was an adequate amount of diversification.

      (2) More recent researchers suggest that 15 to 20 securities are an adequate amount.

      (3) Three disadvantages of W-P Index:

        (a) Only applies to portfolios fully invested in stocks.

        (b) Index does not consider cash and cash equivalents such as Treasury bills, which diversify a portfolio without requiring the addition of new securities.

        (c) Index does not consider debit balances caused by borrowing money using a portfolio for collateral or purchasing stocks on margin.

6.63 Tax-efficient allocation strategy.

    a. **Tax-efficient allocation**: place equity investments in nonqualified accounts and have tax-deferred plans hold only fixed-income investments.

      (1) Disadvantages of placing equities in tax-deferred plans:

        (a) Would be subject to a higher ordinary income tax as opposed to a lower capital gains tax if placed in a nonqualified account; this rule applies to all tax-deferred plans except Roth IRAs.

        (b) Most tax-deferred accounts have minimum distribution rules.

      (2) Problem with standard investment strategy based on tax advantages.

        (a) Problem occurs when the investor's strategic asset allocation decision is inconsistent with his allocation based on tax advantages.

6.64 Client's objectives with retirement accounts.

    a. Your client may use his retirement account for retirement purposes or for nonretirement reasons or as a liquidity source.

    b. Two reasons cash equivalent assets should not be part of a retirement portfolio:

      (1) Low rates of return compared to other assets.

      (2) Placing them into a retirement account defeats the main purpose of cash equivalents (i.e., accessible cash reserves); severe penalty to access such assets from a tax-advantaged retirement plan (with few exceptions).

6.65 Mutual funds in portfolios.

    a. Reasons for placing mutual funds in a client's portfolio:

      (1) Professionalism and high qualifications of portfolio managers at investment companies.

      (2) Adequate diversification: the smallest holdings in an investment company are diversified, except:

        (a) Sector funds.

        (b) Specialty funds.

    b. Reasons against placing mutual funds in a client's portfolio:

      (1) Fees associated with mutual funds.

  (a) Load fund fees (front-end and back-end).

  (b) Fees paid to investment company's portfolio managers.

  (c) Fees paid for operation expenses.

  (d) According to research, mutual funds would perform in line with the market, but for the fees required to be paid by the investor.

 (2) Creating a portfolio of securities directly and individually owned by the client.

  (a) Minimizing capital gains taxes: client with many securities can sell those that have not increased significantly if client needs funds.

  (b) Tax harvesting of securities: taxpayers can deduct losses on securities, the recognition of which would reduce taxes on income (annual deduction of up to $3,000 on net capital losses).

c. Sufficiently diverse: recent research finds that a portfolio of at least 50 securities is sufficiently diverse for long-term goals, such as retirement, and that risk-averse clients should build portfolios with even more securities.

 (1) Two approaches to building a portfolio with a high number of individual stock holdings.

  (a) Begin by directly purchasing individual stocks.

   ■ Drawback: excessive risk if portfolio has only a few individual stocks (i.e., large difference in returns).

   ■ Better approach: in nonqualified plans.

  (b) Begin by buying mutual funds, selling them when value significantly increases, and purchasing individual stocks.

   ■ Drawbacks: fees, capital gains tax if initial investment does well.

   ■ Better approach: in qualified plans because a participant of such plan is not required to pay capital gains tax when switching from mutual funds to individual stock.

d. Mutual funds for retirement

 (1) Fund of funds investing: funds from one mutual fund are invested in other funds in the first fund's portfolio managed by the same portfolio manager.

  (a) Purpose is to set up a retirement portfolio for clients who wish to set a particular retirement date.

  (b) Investor owes two sets of fees:

   ■ Fee for the investor's direct investment in the first mutual fund.

   ■ Fee for the investment of funds in the other mutual funds in portfolio.

6.66 **Dollar cost averaging:** the strategy of investing a specified amount regularly into a portfolio, regardless of recent investment trends.

a. Fixed payments buy more shares and the average purchase price per share for the portfolio declines if the current stock price declines.

b. Produces a lower average price per share because fewer shares are purchased when prices are high and more shares are bought when prices are low.

    c. The long-term investor assumes the price will rise eventually, so a lower average purchase price means a greater total profit.

    d. Dividend reinvestment plans (DRIPs): stockholders' dividends are directly reinvested into the company's stock; dividends are sent by the company to the trust department of the managing bank where an account for each stockholder is created; existing stock and newly issued stock can be acquired by DRIPs.

        (1) Benefits of DRIPs to companies:

            (a) Stockholder goodwill.

            (b) Small stockholders encouraged to increase ownership.

            (c) Dividend expense savings.

            (d) Greater demand for company's stock.

            (e) Debt-to-equity ratio decreases on plans with new share purchases.

            (f) New equity is sold without related fees with plans with newly issued stock.

            (g) Equity capital is regularly produced with plans with newly issued stock.

        (2) Disadvantage of DRIPs:

            (a) Restricts investor's ability to diversify portfolio by buying other companies' stock because investors with a DRIP typically purchase more shares in the existing stock in the investors' portfolio.

    e. Direct purchase plans (DPPs): plans enable investors to set up checking or savings accounts that receive debits to buy new shares of stock.

        (1) Benefits of DPPs:

            (a) Younger investors with limited income are able to more quickly create a diversified portfolio.

            (b) Investors can transfer the DPPs to other companies and diversify their portfolio after acquiring more shares in one company.

        (2) Disadvantage of DPPs:

            (a) Limits investor's ability to diversify portfolio.

6.67 Clients' borrowing from 401(k) and 403(b) plans.

    a. Employees may borrow from qualified plans only if their employer specifically provides for it in their plans.

    b. Clients are permitted to borrow in about 82% of 401(k) plans.

    c. No tax-deductible interest on loans.

    d. Not an appropriate strategy for younger investors.

    e. Appropriate strategy for older clients who wish to change the makeup of their retirement portfolio as they are approaching retirement.

6.68 Inflation's impact on client's standard of living during retirement.

    a. Investing in securities that provide inflation protection is not a good strategy for investors during the accumulation period because this causes minimal returns.

6.7 CLIENT'S MORTGAGE AS PART OF PORTFOLIO

Key point The two ways to pay off a mortgage early are making extra payments (prepayments) and investing an amount that would have been equal to the prepayment if a greater return would result.

6.71 Clients in 20s, 30s, and 40s with mortgages.

   a. Interest-only mortgages: borrower is only required to pay interest on a loan for a certain period of time.

   b. Adjustable rate mortgages (ARMs): most interest-only mortgages offered presently are either 5/1 or 10/1 adjustable rate mortgages.

   (1) 5/1 or 10/1 ARMs: interest rate is fixed during the interest-only period, which is the first 5 or 10 years of the loan.

   (a) Interest rate is thereafter adjusted annually (i.e., the 1 of the 5/1).

   (b) ARM is amortized during the remaining years on the loan.

   c. Two reasons clients may want interest-only mortgages:

   (1) Client wants to buy a more expensive house.

   (a) Lenders typically follow the rule that a borrower should not have a monthly PITI that exceeds 28% of the borrower's gross monthly income.

   (b) **PITI:** principal and interest payment for the month (i.e., mortgage payment) plus payments on property taxes and homeowner's insurance premiums made monthly on a prorated basis.

   (c) Borrower who elects an interest-only mortgage could qualify under the 28% rule and therefore take out a larger loan amount; good financial planners would discourage such election.

   (2) Client wants to have the money that would have been used to pay the principal amounts free and available to be used to invest in new securities.

6.72 Principal payments on mortgages.

   a. Two elements of principal payments:

   (1) Same as investing that money in a savings account that pays the same interest rate as the mortgage.

   (2) The return rate obtained on a fixed-rate mortgage is risk free.

   (a) No default risk is associated with a fixed-rate mortgage.

   (b) No interest rate risk is associated with a fixed-rate mortgage.

6.73 Clients in 50s, 60s, and 70s with mortgages

   a. Advantages of having a home mortgage paid off at retirement:

   (1) Psychological benefits.

   (2) Financial benefits: interest payments on a mortgage are beneficial only to those workers who have income to protect from taxation and enjoy those interest payments as deductions on their income taxes.

    b. Disadvantages of retirees paying off a mortgage: with less income, retirees must resort to gaining additional income via the following different methods, which causes retirees to pay more taxes, and in turn, requires them to get more taxable income.

        (1) Capital gains tax is imposed on gains retiree receives from selling assets.

        (2) Income tax is imposed on withdrawals from retiree's retirement accounts.

        (3) More of the retiree's Social Security income will be taxed because the retiree's total income will increase after withdrawing from accounts and selling assets; retiree's total income determines the taxable amount of Social Security income.

    c. Two ways to pay off a mortgage early (before retirement):

        (1) Periodically make more mortgage payments on the principal (i.e., prepayments).

        (2) Invest amount equal to what would have been the prepayments to receive a return that is greater than the rate on the mortgage.

Note: Good financial planners should not advise clients to save the prepayment amounts and invest them in various investment instruments.

HIGHLIGHTS

Highlight 1: Market Portfolios

■ Market portfolio: Portfolio M; portfolio containing all assets; the weights on each asset are equal to the percentage of the market value of each asset to the market value of the entire market portfolio. (6.11d(6))

$$\text{Stock's weight in the market portfolio} = \frac{\text{Market value of stock}}{\text{Market value of market portfolio}}$$

Highlight 2: Diversification

■ Seven important principles of diversification and investment planning today:
   (1) Financial planners should understand a client's risk tolerance so that a portfolio can be created to accurately reflect such risk tolerance.
   (2) Financial planners should make sure that the risky assets in a client's portfolio are diversified.
   (3) Total risk of a portfolio generally declines as more securities are added to a client's portfolio.
   (4) Total risk of a portfolio declines at a decreasing rate as more securities are added to the portfolio.
   (5) Total risk of a portfolio generally converges downward toward the total risk of the market portfolio.
   (6) Diversification of a portfolio generally cannot decrease the total risk of a portfolio below that of the market portfolio.
   (7) More securities in your client's portfolio would be optimal the lower the amount of commission your client must pay. (6.11g)

Highlight 3: Long-Term Perspective on Investments

■ Client's retirement portfolio should contain assets with more risk than assets contained in portfolios created for nonretirement reasons.

■ Studies show that decisions about risky issues are dictated by the lag between the time of the decision and the time the decision is realized.
   (1) If the investor immediately knows the impact of his decision, the investor is more likely to be risk averse than if the decision's impact will not be realized for awhile.
   (2) A client's short-term look at his financial future causes him to be more likely to make risk-averse decisions.
   (3) A client's long-term look at his financial future will cause him to be more likely to choose riskier investments that have greater potential for a greater return. (6.22)

Highlight 4: Geometric Mean Return

- The geometric mean return (GMR) is the effective rate of return. There are four steps in calculating the GMR.
  (1) Add the number one to each period's return rate, the sum of which is called the per period return relative (PPRR).
  (2) Multiply together all of the PPRRs, the sum of which is the holding period return relative (HPRR).
  (3) Take the nth root of the number in step two (i.e., HPRR), where **n** is the number of periods used in the formula.
  (4) Subtract one from the nth root. (6.41b)

Highlight 5: Strategic Asset Allocation Changes

- Common reasons for changes to a client's level of risk:
  (1) Career changes.
  (2) Family reasons.
  (3) Change in client's wealth.
  (4) Aging.

- Only infrequent changes may be made to a strategic asset allocation for the allocation to remain strategic.

- Frequent changes to a strategic asset allocation are tactical, not strategic. (6.52)

TERMS TO KNOW DEFINITIONS

Capital market line (CML) A portfolio's return is a function of the expected standard deviations, return of the portfolio (M), and the risk-free rate. (6.11d)

Constant relative risk aversion An investor's wealth is independent of the risk tolerance chosen by an investor—that is, an investor will choose a risk tolerance level independent of his current financial status. (6.42c)

Dollar cost averaging Investment of a fixed amount of money each period; three forms of dollar cost averaging are dividend reinvestment plan, employee stock purchase plan, and direct purchase plan. (6.67)

Efficient frontier Greatest expected return that can be generated at a fixed risk level; based on the assumption that investors can earn a risk-free rate of return. Represents set of portfolios that gives investors the greatest return at each level of risk or lowest risk for each level of return. (6.11c)

Geometric mean return (GMR) Obtained by computing a series of holding period return relatives (HPRRs), taking the nth root of the product of the HPRRs, and then subtracting one from the resulting root. (6.41b)

Human capital Person's ability to produce wage income; the current value of a person's net income from wages and salaries earned in the future. (6.31b(2))

Independent stock returns Also known as the random walk theory that stock returns of one period are not related in any way to the previous period's stock return results; assumes stock prices follow a random walk because the prices reflect the uninfluenced expectations of future news events. (6.42c(2)(c))

Market portfolio Portfolio M; portfolio containing all assets; the weights on each asset are equal to the percentage of the market value of the asset to the market value of the entire market portfolio. (6.11d)

Mean reversion process A low (high) return rate in one period is more likely to be followed by a high (low) return rate in the following period; opposite of the momentum theory. (6.42c)

Normal distribution Bell-shaped curve reflecting the relationship between mean returns and standard deviations; for most distributions, the actual value will be no more than one standard deviation away from the mean 66% of the time, no more than two standard deviations 95% of the time, and no more than three standard deviations 99% of the time. (6.41d(3))

PITI Principal and interest payment for the month (i.e., mortgage payment) plus payments on property taxes and homeowners insurance premiums made monthly on a prorated basis. (6.71c)

Return/return tradeoff To protect underfunded client, increase the expected return by increasing the portfolio's risk. (6.55b(3))

Risk tolerance Client's feelings about risk. (6.21)

Standard deviation Shows how close or far an actual return is from an expected return; square root of the variance; the measure of an asset's riskiness. (6.41c)

Strategic asset allocation Purpose is to identify the portfolio's overall risk; the purpose is not to try to outperform the market; measure the success of this allocation by identifying the optimal portfolio beta and identifying an appropriate efficient frontier. (6.52)

Tactical asset allocation Purpose is to decide what specific investments should comprise the portfolio; less broad than strategic asset allocation; purpose is to outperform the market, not to identify the acceptable risk level as with strategic asset allocation; decisions must be made more often and more specific categories of assets are involved. (6.53)

Tax-efficient allocation Placing equity investments in nonqualified accounts and have tax-deferred plans hold only fixed-income investments. (6.63a)

Time diversification Belief that the risk of stocks decreases as the investment horizon increases—in other words, that the greater the age of the retiree as he is approaching retirement, the more likely the retiree will invest in more risk-free assets than risky assets. (6.42)

Woerheide-Persson index Index that calculates a portfolio's degree of diversification without using statistical measures based on time; Woerheide-Persson index = $1 - 1/n$ if n securities in a portfolio have the same market values. (6.62e)

QUESTIONS

1. A measure of how well the returns of two risky assets move together is the
   A. correlation
   B. covariance
   C. momentum
   D. standard deviation

2. All of the following are common reasons for a client to change his level of risk, and therefore change his strategic asset allocation EXCEPT
   A. career changes
   B. family reasons
   C. change in client's wealth
   D. change in client's health

3. Which of the following are benefits of dividend reinvestment plans (DRIPs)?
   I. Stockholder goodwill
   II. Greater demand for company's stock
   A. I only
   B. II only
   C. Both I and II
   D. Neither I nor II

4. What term describes the process in which a high return rate in one period is more likely to be followed by a low rate?
   A. Momentum
   B. Random walk theory
   C. Mean reversion
   D. Risk aversion

5. Which of the following statements regarding the diversification of a portfolio is(are) TRUE?
   I. A portfolio's total risk decreases as more securities are included in the portfolio.
   II. Diversification eliminates market risk.
   A. I only
   B. II only
   C. Both I and II
   D. Neither I nor II

systematic
should be
non-sys. risk

ANSWERS

1. **B.** Covariance is defined as the comovement of the returns of two assets, or how well the returns of two risky assets move together. Note that range, semi-variance, and standard deviations are measures of dispersion and measure risk, not how assets move together. (6.11b)

2. **D.** The four most common reasons a client will change his risk level, and therefore his strategic asset allocation are aging, change in career, family reasons, and change in client's wealth. (6.52i(1))

3. **C.** The following are benefits of dividend reinvestment plans: stockholder goodwill; small stockholders encouraged to increase ownership; dividend expense savings; greater demand for company's stock; debt-to-equity ratio for company is decreased on plans with new share purchases; new equity is sold without related fees with plans with newly issued stock; and equity capital is regularly produced with plans with newly issued stock. (6.66d(1))

4. **C.** Mean reversion is the long-run pattern of overreactions of stock prices followed regularly by market corrections it is the opposite of the momentum theory. (6.42c(2)(c))

5. **A.** Diversification only eliminates nonmarket risk (nonsystematic risk), not market risk (systematic risk). (6.11g(2))

7

Investing After Retirement

"Only those who will risk going too far can possibly find out how far one can go."

—T.S. Eliot

TERMS TO KNOW

Capital preservation model	Portfolio failure	Risk-free withdrawal rate
Flat annuity	Portfolio success rate	Withdrawal rate
Inflation-adjusted annuity	Purchasing power preservation model	Withdrawal strategy
Performance-based annuity	Retirement portfolio	

130

7.1 RISK-RETURN MODEL FOR PORTFOLIOS DURING DISTRIBUTION

Key point The risk-return trade-off for portfolio distributions is the increase in withdrawal rate and an increased probability that the portfolio will fail.

Key point The risk-free withdrawal rate is equal to or less than the interest the portfolio earns, resulting in no decrease in the portfolio as funds are withdrawn.

7.11 Risk-return model during the period that a retiree withdraws funds from his retirement portfolio (i.e., distribution period) is based on cash withdrawals.

    a. A retiree's goal during the distribution period is to die before all assets of his or her retirement portfolio are distributed.

        (1) Risk during the distribution period is the probability that the portfolio assets will be depleted before the retiree dies.

        (2) Return is the annual cash withdrawal amount from the retiree's portfolio.

        (3) **Retirement portfolio:** portfolio created for retirement income with the possibility that the portfolio's value will steadily decline.

    b. Withdrawals from the portfolio.

        (1) **Withdrawal rate:** the cash value that can be taken from the portfolio; the formula for the withdrawal rate is:

$$\frac{\text{Cash withdrawal amount during the first year of distribution}}{\text{Portfolio's initial value}}$$

        (2) **Withdrawal strategy:** modification of withdrawals after the retiree has made his first withdrawal from the portfolio.

        (3) Withdrawal occurrence: although impractical, most research on withdrawal rates uses yearly withdrawals that occur at the end of each year.

            (a) Assumes cash for the first year has been withdrawn before the portfolio strategy begins.

            (b) Assumes cash withdrawn at the end of the first year will cover second-year expenses.

    c. Three fundamental withdrawal strategies.

        (1) **Inflation-adjusted annuity:** the inflation rate for a particular year determines the withdrawal increase for the next year.

        (2) **Performance-based annuity:** portfolio's performance in a particular year determines the withdrawal amount for the following year.

        (3) **Flat annuity:** fixed dollar amounts of cash are withdrawn annually.

        (4) A withdrawal strategy can be a combination of these three strategies.

7.12 The risk-return trade-off for portfolio distributions is that the probability that a portfolio will fail increases as the withdrawal rate increases.

    a. **Portfolio failure:** a portfolio is considered to have failed when the withdrawal amount is equal to or greater than the value of the entire portfolio.

    b. A **risk-free withdrawal rate** is essentially the interest that the portfolio receives every time an amount is withdrawn from the portfolio.

    c. The fundamental principles of risk-return trade-off for portfolio distributions are:

        (1) When the withdrawal rate increases, the probability that the portfolio will fail increases.

        (2) A portfolio won't fail if the withdrawal rate equals the risk-free return rate.

    d. Trade-off between withdrawal rate and probability of portfolio failure.

        (1) There is an optimal debt-equity ratio for such a trade-off.

        (2) A withdrawal rate can increase without increasing the probability of portfolio failure when equity investments and bonds are included in a retirement portfolio.

    e. Trade-off between withdrawal rate and intended estate size at retiree's death.

        (1) There is no optimal debt-equity ratio for such a trade-off.

        (2) Expected estate size at the retiree's death will increase as the percentage of equity in the portfolio increases.

7.13 Two withdrawal strategies that won't deplete a retirement portfolio:

    a. **Capital preservation model.**

        (1) Account balance at life expectancy equals balance at retirement.

        (2) Model is achieved by withdrawing only the interest income from the portfolio and keeping the principal intact.

    b. **Purchasing power preservation model.**

        (1) Portfolio's purchasing power at life expectancy equals the portfolio's purchasing power at retirement.

        (2) Model is achieved by making the withdrawal rate equal the return rate minus the inflation rate.

7.14 Three theories on maximum allowable probability of portfolio failure:

    a. 1 or 2% theory: probability should not be greater than 1 or 2%.

    b. 5 to 25% theory: maximum probability should be in the range of 5 to 25%; recommended most often by planners.

    c. Unlimited risk theory: any risk amount is proper if client is informed.

7.2 OPTIMAL WITHDRAWAL RATES DURING RETIREMENT

> **Key point** Most research on optimal withdrawal rates for retirees overstates the probability of portfolio failure.

7.21 Overstating and understating the probability that a client's portfolio will fail during retirement.

    a. Some research that has studied the optimal withdrawal rates for retirees during retirement understates the probability of portfolio failure in three ways:

        (1) Exclusion of taxes and transaction fees.

(2) Exclusion of immunization of bonds.

   (a) Bond immunization would decrease the volatility of returns on the bond portion of the portfolio.

(3) Lack of ability to match index performance: two ways to match:

   (a) Purchase either an open-end index fund or a closed-end index fund.

   (b) Create a portfolio with the same securities as the index.

b. Most research on optimal withdrawal rates for retirees during retirement overstates the probability of portfolio failure for three reasons:

   (1) Underestimating retirees' willingness to rebalance their portfolios: assumed by most researchers, except Guyton.

   (2) Ignoring death of retiree's spouse: most research assumes one client and ignores the reduced need for withdrawals after a spouse dies.

   (3) Exclusion of regular decrease in living expenses as clients age.

7.22 Determining the withdrawal rate on investment portfolios.

a. General conclusions regarding optimal withdrawal rates:

   (1) No right answer about optimal withdrawal rate or optimal portfolio.

   (2) Market conditions at the start of the withdrawal period are crucial to estimating the sustainable withdrawal rate.

   (3) Portfolio failure: does not mean the portfolio is earning less than the expected return rate.

   (a) Does mean the portfolio is equal to or less than a planned withdrawal so that the portfolio is zeroed out at the next withdrawal.

   (4) Safe withdrawal rate: 3% is safe regardless of asset allocation in portfolio.

   (5) Stock percentage generally recommended in a portfolio: 40% to 70%.

   (a) More stock diversification will likely cause the portfolio to last longer.

   (6) Withdrawal rate is maximized when stock in portfolio is at least 50%.

   (7) Greater percentage of stock in a portfolio causes a portfolio's average ending value to significantly increase, according to all studies; beneficial for clients wishing to bequest portfolio assets.

   (a) Greater percentage of stock in a portfolio, however, increases the standard deviation of the distribution of terminal portfolio values.

   (b) To lower the standard deviation: bond immunization or partial annuitization instead of a bond component could be used.

   (c) Immunizing bonds almost certainly increases the withdrawal rate.

7.23 Methodologies used in retirement planning recommendations.

a. Financial planners use one of two methodologies in making retirement planning recommendations to clients.

   (1) Elements of study conducted by Cooley, Hubbard, and Walz (2003):

   (a) Two alternative methodologies:

   ■ Monte Carlo simulation.

   ■ Historical data analysis.

    (b) Each methodology has its disadvantages:

        ■ Historical data analysis is limited; successful past strategies will not necessarily be successful in the future.

        ■ Monte Carlo simulation results are only as good as the information that is inputted into the calculation.

    (c) Monte Carlo simulation: methodology assuming that distribution of assets from a portfolio is a fixed, independent process.

        ■ Returns from each time period are entirely independent of the returns from previous periods.

        ■ Mean return for each asset type is the same for each time period.

        ■ Standard deviations of returns are the same for each time period.

  (2) Study's conclusions:

    (a) Portfolio success rates were greater, on average, under the Monte Carlo simulations when monthly withdrawals were fixed.

        ■ **Portfolio success rate**: portfolio failure rate subtracted from 100%.

  (3) Study's recommendations for financial planners:

    (a) Monte Carlo simulation may be more appropriate when using longer withdrawal periods.

    (b) Overlapping periods methodology may be more appropriate when using shorter withdrawal periods.

b. Monte Carlo simulation: most studies on withdrawal rates using this method assume a lognormal distribution for returns.

  (1) Daily financial returns are likely to achieve a lognormal distribution as they are aggregated for a longer time, such as monthly or yearly.

  (2) Results from a Monte Carlo simulation are extremely sensitive to standard deviations and expected rates of return used in the calculations.

  (3) Conflicting findings concerning portfolio composition, sustainable withdrawal rate, and portfolio failure rate.

  (4) Portfolio with Treasury Inflation Protection Securities (TIPS) significantly lowers the probability that the portfolio will fail.

  (5) Portfolio failure rates will fall as the percentage of stock in the portfolio falls, according to Terry (2003).

    (a) In contrast, another study focusing on portfolios with specific asset categories found that portfolio failure rates fell as the percentage of stock in the portfolio increased; true when lognormal distribution was assumed.

c. Historical returns method: overlapping historical periods.

  (1) Bengen's study: two conclusions:

    (a) Portfolio with 40% to 70% stock will sustain for at least 30 years of retirement at a 4.15% withdrawal rate.

    (b) Safe withdrawal rate significantly falls for a portfolio with under 40% stock and over 70% bonds.

  (2) Cooley, Hubbard, and Walz (1998): conclusions differed from Bengen's findings.

(a) Portfolio with 25% to 100% stock could only sustain for 30 years of retirement at a 3% inflation-adjusted withdrawal rate.

(3) Altering how long an overlapping period lasts.

   (a) Portfolio of 25% bonds/75% stock was the only portfolio to sustain a 4% inflation-adjusted withdrawal rate for 30 years in one study.

   (b) Aggressive portfolio of 85% stock and 15% bonds is likely to perform significantly better than the more conservative portfolios in the beginning retirement periods in another study.

   (c) With portfolios of only stocks and intermediate-term government bonds, substituting 10% to 50% of large-cap stock with small-cap stock can increase the 30-year withdrawal rate to 4.5%, according to a study.

   (d) Portfolio with 30-day T-bills constituting up to 15% of the portfolio has no substantial effect on the safe withdrawal rate, reports one study.

7.24 Comparing the two methodologies.

   a. Portfolio failure rates are higher when using historical overlapping periods with the difference likely to increase over longer withdrawal periods, according to research comparing the two methods.

   b. Monte Carlo simulations: better method to use if two things are true (otherwise, historical overlapping periods is the better method):

   (1) Required amount of simulations are performed.

   (2) Distribution of returns is stable.

7.25 Appropriate stock percentage of a client's portfolio (Bengen 1996).

   a. Study's conclusions (key tested area):

   (1) Formulas to determine appropriate stock percentage of client's portfolio:

   (a) Conservative client:

   - Percentage of tax-deferred portfolio in stock = 115 minus age of client.

   - Percentage of nonqualified portfolio in stock = 125 minus age of client.

   (b) Moderate client:

   - Percentage of tax-deferred portfolio in stock = 128 minus age of client.

   - Percentage of nonqualified portfolio in stock = 138 minus age of client.

   (c) Aggressive client:

   - Percentage of tax-deferred portfolio in stock = 140 minus age of client.

   - Percentage of nonqualified portfolio in stock = 150 minus age of client.

    b. Study's recommendations:

        (1) Withdrawal rate on tax-deferred portfolio should be at least .5% more than the withdrawal rate for nonqualified portfolios.

        (2) 4% rate for tax-deferred; 3.5% for nonqualified.

        (3) As tax brackets increase, withdrawal rates should decrease.

        (4) Portfolio should be rebalanced after investor annually withdraws funds.

        (5) Maximum probability of portfolio failure should be 15%.

7.26 Four factors that affect sustainable withdrawal rates.

    a. Yearly portfolio rebalancing: assumed in most research on sustainable withdrawal rates:

        (1) Client may be withdrawing from portfolio when stock market is weak.

        (2) To replace funds withdrawn from the portfolio, the client may sell assets.

        (3) Dynamic rebalancing strategy: during a down period in the stock market, fixed-income assets and/or cash reserves can be used to fund withdrawals.

        (4) Conclusion from studies: using dynamic rebalancing strategy can increase the longevity of a portfolio by three to five years.

    b. Variable withdrawal rates: research assumes retiree will always use the initial withdrawal rate regardless of the portfolio performance:

        (1) To date, no research has considered decreases in withdrawals each year.

        (2) Evidence shows persons voluntarily lowering consumption costs as they age.

        (3) Easiest way to use a variable withdrawal rate is to use a nominal withdrawal rate (instead of an inflation-adjusted withdrawal rate).

            (a) Strategy for persons who have mostly fixed expenses and/or plan to lower their living expenses as they get older.

        (4) Second way to use a variable withdrawal rate is to use a phased withdrawal rate strategy (i.e., apply a different withdrawal rate for each phase).

        (5) Third way to use a variable withdrawal rate is to use portfolio performance factors as a trigger to change the rate.

    c. International stocks in a portfolio: early research suggested that international diversification benefited portfolios; later research has suggested the opposite.

        (1) Two studies on effect of international stocks on sustainable withdrawal rate:

            (a) Study using Monte Carlo simulation: concluded that international stocks in a portfolio for 30 years can modestly lower portfolio failure rates when a 4% to 6% inflation-adjusted withdrawal rate is used.

            (b) Study using overlapping historical periods: found that international stocks increased portfolio failure rates using all withdrawal rates.

    d. Longevity risk: most studies have used a fixed planning horizon (e.g., 30 years of retirement).

        (1) Considering life expectancy when determining the sustainable withdrawal rate can potentially better satisfy the client's needs during retirement.

            (a) Conclusion from study that tried to incorporate life expectancy: women have a higher equity requirement than men of the same age.

(2) Eliminating longevity risk: can be done by annuitizing the retirement assets at the start of the retirement period; full annuitization, however, is not popular in the United States.

  (a) Partial annuitization: due to the increase in life expectancies, partial annuitization is receiving more attention; can cause greater, sustainable withdrawal rates adjusted for inflation.

  (b) Total retirement portfolio: includes investment portfolio plus client's fixed income (i.e., fixed annuities such as pension income, Social Security income).

  ■ Buying an annuity is similar to buying a totally immunized bond investment; thus, client's total portfolio includes bond investments in which there is perfect certainty on returns.

  (c) Four effects of partial annuitization in a client's portfolio.

  ■ Clients with fixed income are likely to increase the stock in their portfolio if such income is considered a de facto bond investment.

  ■ Optimal benefits when client defers annuity payments until age 75 to 85.

  ■ Portfolio failure rate: significantly lowered with a 4.5% withdrawal rate if 25 to 50% of the initial retirement portfolio is annuitized.

  ■ Terminal portfolio value: standard deviation and mean amount of this value decreased due to partial annuitization.

7.3 SEQUENCE FOR TAPPING RETIREMENT ASSETS

Key point All things being equal, tap assets in the following sequence: (1) ordinary income, (2) assets subject to capital gains, (3) tax-exempt municipal bonds, (4) retirement accounts (tax deferred), and (5) Roth IRAs (tax free).

Key point Assets not subject to sequencing are Social Security, annuities in pay status, and retirement plans after age 70½.

Key point Other factors in determining the sequence for tapping assets are liquidity, risk, investment horizon, and growth or loss potential.

7.31 A retiree may have a variety of assets at his disposal when it comes time to establish a plan for drawing on the assets for retirement income.

  a. Life annuities (whether held on a nonqualified or qualified basis) are guaranteed for life, as is Social Security; once begun these provide income for life.

  (1) These amounts are subtracted from the estimated retirement income need before determining the sequence for tapping retirement assets.

  b. Qualified retirement plans and traditional IRAs are subject to minimum distribution requirements after age 70½.

  (1) Prior to that age, these assets should be considered to be tax-deferred assets (see below).

  (2) After that age, these assets should be considered two separate assets.

(a) The minimum required distribution amount must be taken to avoid a 50% penalty.

(b) The balance should be considered a tax-deferred asset (see below).

(c) Roth IRAs are not subject to minimum required distribution rules.

7.32 All things being equal (subject to points (a) and (b) above), you can maximize your withdrawals from various retirement assets by taking money from taxable investments first, then from tax-sheltered investments.

a. The usual sequence is as follows:

(1) Assets that provide ordinary income such as bonds or bond mutual funds (as these are subject to the most tax upon withdrawal).

(2) Assets that are subject to capital gains and little or no current income such as stocks and stock mutual funds (because the capital gains tax is lower than ordinary income rates).

(3) Tax-exempt mutual bonds (which produce tax-free income while held but are taxable when sold).

(4) Assets that are tax deferred such as qualified retirement plan accounts, traditional IRAs, and nonqualified deferred annuities that have not yet been annuitized.

(5) Tax-exempt assets such as Roth IRAs, particularly since minimum distribution requirement does not apply.

b. The main idea is to preserve tax-sheltered assets as long as possible while drawing from taxable assets.

7.33 You can do detailed analyses by computing the time that payments from the various assets will continue given different interest rate and tax rate assumptions, but the general rule of harvesting taxable assets holds in most cases.

a. This is accomplished by computing how long an individual's retirement savings will last and testing all the possible sequences; the simplest is to compare the withdrawal sequences of two assets, but it can be done with three or more.

ZOOM IN   Required Distributions and Specific Plans

In one form or another, the required distribution rules apply to virtually every type of qualified employer and individual retirement plan. In fact, to meet qualification requirements, employer plans must include provisions that reflect Section 401(a)(9) of the Code by providing that distributions will be made in accordance with the regulations. Failing to make minimum distributions according to the requirements will no necessarily cause a plan to lose its tax-favored status; however, if there is a consistent pattern of such failure, the plan could be disqualified.

Because of the complexity of the required distribution rules, there is much misunderstanding as to how they apply to different types of plans. Here we will set the record straight.

Traditional IRAs, SEP-IRAs, and SIMPLE IRAs

Traditional IRAs and IRAs used in employers plans are subject to required distributions under any and all circumstances. This is a very important point because many people incorrectly think that IRAs are not subject if the owner is still employed. Employment status is irrelevant; however, once a traditional IRA owner reaches 70½, distributions must be taken from the IRA. (It is worth noting how nondeductible IRA and SEP contributions are handled for purposes of required distributions.)

Roth IRAs

As mentioned earlier, Roth IRAs are not subject to required distribution regulations. Since there is no tax revenue created through distribution of Roth funds, there is no requirement that distribution must occur. However, at the account owner's death, the beneficiary does fall under a set of required distribution rules which mandate the time period over which the funds are to be withdrawn.

Pension, Profit-Sharing, and 401(k) Plans

Required distribution rules for pension, profit-sharing and 401(k) plans are slightly different; the required beginning date for plan participants is the later of age 70½ or the year of retirement. Consequently, the initial distribution can be delayed until April 1 following the year the participant turns 70½ or until April 1 following the year in which he or she retires. For those who own more than five percent of a business that operates such plans, the required beginning date is April 1 of the year following the year the participant turns 70½; for these individuals, there is not alternative "after retirement" option.

403(b) Tax-Sheltered Annuities

All 403(b) plans are also subject to the required minimum distribution rules, but they are somewhat distinctive in the way they are treated. Account balances accrued as of December 31, 1986 are exempt from required distribution rules. Thus the required minimum distribution rules require distributions only from the account balance that accrued after December 31, 1986, which means any earning or contributions made after this date are subject to the minimum distribution rules.

The fact that the required distribution rules do not apply to December 31, 1986 account balances can lead TSA owners to a false sense of security. They may think that the rules do not apply to their accounts at all. This, of course, is incorrect. Even if TSA participants are no longer making contributions to their plans, they are certainly still getting earnings credited to their accounts. The bottom line is that the minimum distribution rules apply to all TSA holders but the account balance to which the rules apply is reduced by the December 31, 1986 balance. The pre-1987 account balances must be distributed no later than April 1 of the year following the year the owner attains age 75.

EXAMPLE Joanne is 65. In addition to Social Security and an employer pension, she has a 401(k) plan worth $100,000 and a mutual fund worth $100,000. Social Security and the pension do not provide enough to live on. She needs $15,000 per year to live on above Social Security and her pension. Which account should she draw from first? Here are the figures.

Account	401(k) Drawn First		Mutual Fund Drawn First	
	401(k)	**Mutual Fund**	**Mutual Fund**	**401(k)**
Value of account at age 65	$100,000	$100,000	$100,000	$100,000
Value of account when withdrawals begun	$100,000	$121,903	$100,000	$146,311
Withdrawal amount	$20,833	$15,000	$15,000	$20,833
Tax rate on withdrawal	28%	0%	0%	28%
Tax on withdrawal	$5,833	$0	$0	$5,833
Net withdrawal	$15,000	$15,000	$15,000	$15,000
Interest rate in accounts	5.00%	5.00%	5.00%	5.00%
Tax on interest in account	0%	28%	28%	0.00%
After tax rate on interest in account	5.00%	3.60%	3.60%	5.00%
Years account pays before exhausted	5.6	7.8	7.8	8.8
Total years for both accounts		15.4		16.6

To do this comparison, we computed the number of years each account would pay before being exhausted using the term (or period) calculation in a computer spreadsheet or financial calculator. You can find how to do this on a financial calculator in Appendix 1.

■ For the 401(k) account, we used $20,833 as the payment amount and 5.00% as the interest factor. Joanne needs to withdraw $20,833 rather than $15,000 because she pays tax on a withdrawal from a 401(k). There is no tax on withdrawal from the mutual fund because the tax has been paid all along; it hasn't been deferred.

■ For the mutual fund, we used $15,000 as the payment amount and 3.60% as the interest factor. You need to figure the effective interest rate for the mutual fund because this is taxed as it is earned, while the interest in the 401(k) is not taxed as it is earned. The effective interest rate is the real interest rate multiplied by (1 − tax rate).

We calculated each column of numbers separately. Find the term (years account pays before exhausted) for the first column (401(k) plan) before you go on to calculate the term for the mutual fund because while Joanne draws on the 401(k), the mutual fund continues to grow. So in your calculation, you start with a larger account balance after 5.6 years (the future value of $100,000 at 3.60% interest for 5.6 years is $121,903).

E X A M P L E   (continued)

The process is repeated for the third and fourth columns.

If Joanne starts drawing on the 401(k) plan first, her two assets will be exhausted in 15.4 years. If she draws on the mutual fund and saves the tax-favored 401(k) for last, her two assets will last 16.6 years, more than a year longer.

Of course, actuarial tables show that Joanne's life expectancy is somewhat longer than either period. She might need to refigure her needs to lower the withdrawals, purchase annuities to get the guarantees, or probably both.

7.34   Impact of minimum distribution requirement:

    a.   This example suggests that Joanne should hold on to her 401(k) plan for 7.8 years before making the first withdrawal.

    b.   After 6½ years (age 70½), Joanne will be subject to a 50% penalty if she doesn't take a minimum amount from the 401(k) account.

    c.   In the last year of mutual fund withdrawals, Joanne should take the minimum required distribution from her 401(k) to avoid the penalty and complete the withdrawals from the mutual fund.

7.35   Both interest rates and tax rates tend to change over time.

    a.   You can redo the calculations assuming different tax rate and interest rate scenarios.

    b.   Most scenarios yield the conclusion that tax-preferred investments should be held as long as possible while withdrawals from taxable accounts are taken; the advantage of this strategy is greater or lesser depending on the assumptions but the strategy holds up.

    c.   An exception occurs if the client's tax rates are expected to increase significantly over time; this is rare but possible.

7.36   This tax-driven strategy applies if everything else is equal.

    a.   Everything else is not always equal.

    b.   You don't want to hold on to assets that are losing value or otherwise performing poorly even if they are sheltered from taxes.

    c.   Factors to consider are:

        (1)   How liquid is the asset?

            (a)   Liquidate liquid assets first.

            (b)   Don't pay surrender charges or withdrawal penalties just to save a comparably small amount of taxes.

        (2)   How risky is the asset? Riskier assets may be acceptable for a longer time horizon than for immediate need.

        (3)   Does the asset have growth or loss potential for the time period in question?

7.4 FACTORS RELATING TO ANNUITIES

> **Key point** For portfolio balancing, annuities should be considered like bonds (regular income).
>
> **Key point** You may have to increase stock holdings to balance annuities.

7.41 Annuities (qualified and nonqualified) and Social Security benefits have the basic characteristics of fully immunized bond investments.

  a. They represent a secure stream of regular income payments (similar to interest on the bonds).

  b. The present value of these payments should be taken into account in determining the asset allocation in a client's investment portfolio.

EXAMPLE Bill owns a conservative portfolio of investments, including $700,000 in bonds and $350,000 in stocks. These two investments provide $38,500 income (combined interest and dividends). Bill also gets $20,000 in Social Security and draws $45,000 from an annuitized pension from his former employer. Rather than looking at the income stream, let's capitalize the Social Security and pension benefit so we can see how Bill's assets are allocated.

	Income	Capitalized Value	Asset Allocation
Stocks	$3,500	$350,000	Stocks = $350,000
Bonds	$35,000	$700,000	Bond-like = $2 million
Social Security*	$20,000	$400,000	
Pension*	$45,000	$900,000	

*We computed the capitalized values of Social Security and the pension benefit by dividing the amounts by a deemed bond interest rate of 5%.

This results in a portfolio that is overly heavy in bonds. We can't reinvest the Social Security and pension benefit, but we could reinvest all of Bill's bonds in stock to give him a resulting portfolio balanced as follows:

	Income	Capitalized Value	Asset Allocation
Stocks	$10,500	$1,050,000	Stocks = $1.05 million
Social Security	$20,000	$400,000	Bond-like = $1.3 million
Pension	$45,000	$900,000	

This results in a more balanced portfolio, but since stock dividend rates are lower than bond interest rates, Bill's income is reduced by this move. That reduction may be acceptable to preserv assets for heirs, or the income could be augmented by periodically selling some stock.

7.42 Unless a guarantee feature is selected on an annuity (see Assignment 8), annuities do not leave any money to heirs; other investments offer this potential.

  a. A significant issue in the purchase of an annuity, then, is whether the client thinks he will outlive his life expectancy.

(1) If the answer is yes, an annuity would be a good investment.

(2) If the answer is no, the undistributed value would be lost at death.

(3) If the answer is maybe, are there family members who would be capable and willing to provide resources if the client purchases an investment other than an annuity and then outlives his assets?

7.43 Once an annuity is annuitized, the decision is irreversible.

a. There is a risk that alternative investments could do better—if interest rates were to rise, for example.

b. A client could purchase an alternative investment and switch to an annuity a year later; the reverse switch is not possible.

(1) By waiting to purchase the annuity, however, there is a risk that interest rates will decline.

7.5 DRAWING INCOME OUT OF THE PORTFOLIO

Key point Various plans can minimize risk and transaction costs related to withdrawing money from an investment portfolio.

7.51 Five-year safety stock plan.

a. The objective: to draw a regular income without exposing the client unnecessarily to the risk of liquidating her principal.

b. The plan: put five years' worth of money into cash equivalents; put the remainder in the stock market.

(1) If the market goes up, take the increase out of stock each year and complete the needed income out of the cash equivalents.

(2) If the market goes down, take the needed income out of the cash equivalents.

(3) The principal held in stocks is protected because no money would be taken from the stocks in years of loss and five years are covered by the amount in the cash equivalents.

> **EXAMPLE** Isabel has $1.5 million. She wants to have $60,000 in income per year. Under the five-year safety stock plan, she puts $300,000 in cash equivalents. The remaining $1.2 million is invested in stocks.
>
> If the market goes up and her stocks go to $1.3 million, she can draw the entire $60,000 from the stocks, leaving $1.24 million in stocks and the original $300,000 in cash equivalents.
>
> If the market goes down to $1.1 million, she doesn't touch the stocks, but draws her entire $60,000 from the cash equivalents, leaving $240,000.
>
> If the market goes up only slightly to $1.22 million, she draws out the $20,000 of increase from the stocks, leaving $1.2 million in stocks. She draws $40,000 from the cash equivalents (to give her a total of $60,000 to spend), leaving $260,000.

    c. Disadvantage: earnings on the cash equivalents are quite low; the cost of maintaining five year's worth of income as insurance is the lost earnings.

7.52 Laddered portfolio strategy.

    a. The objective: same as with the five-year safety stock plan, above.

    b. The plan: similar to the five-year safety stock plan, but instead of investing the five years' worth of planned income in cash equivalents:

        (1) Divide the amount among five categories of bonds, with maturities of one, two, three, four, and five years.

        (2) At the end of each year, the matured bonds are cashed in and new five-year bonds are purchased.

    c. Advantages and disadvantages.

        (1) The bonds typically will provide more income than the cash equivalents.

        (2) If the market goes down, the portfolio will become progressively weighted with bonds rather than stocks.

7.53 Strategy for minimizing transaction fees on withdrawal.

    a. The problems:

        (1) Fees for frequent withdrawals from mutual funds, from unannuitized deferred annuities, and sales of stocks or bonds may be higher than well-timed withdrawals.

        (2) Small withdrawals are typically more expensive than larger withdrawals.

    b. Two solutions:

        (1) In a nonqualified account, set up a margin account that will allow withdrawals that are transferred to the client's checking account; the debit balance can be paid off when the account is rebalanced at the end of the year.

        (2) Get a home equity line of credit.

            (a) Monthly transfers are made to the client's checking account.

            (b) Interest may be deductible with a home equity loan.

7.54 Adjusting withdrawals for inflations.

    a. Where payments are set up on a long-term basis, it might be desirable to build in an inflation adjustment.

        (1) Inflation factors (consumer price index) are provided by the Bureau of Labor Statistics; this agency maintains a Website at **www.bls.gov** to report the changes on a monthly basis.

    b. Where payments are under the control of the client, adjustments can be made as needed.

HIGHLIGHTS

Highlight 1: Risk-Return Model for Portfolios During Distribution

■ The risk-return trade-off for portfolio distributions is that the probability that a portfolio will fail increases as the withdrawal rate increases.

(1) Portfolio failure: a portfolio is considered to have failed when the withdrawal amount is equal to or greater than the value of the entire portfolio.

(2) A risk-free withdrawal rate is essentially the interest that the portfolio receives every time an amount is withdrawn from the portfolio.

(3) The fundamental principles of risk-return trade-off for portfolio distributions are:

(a) When the withdrawal rate increases, the probability that the portfolio will fail increases.

(b) A portfolio will not fail if the withdrawal rate equals the risk-free return rate. (7.12)

Highlight 2: Research on Optimal Withdrawal Rates During Retirement.

■ General conclusions regarding optimal withdrawal rates:

(1) No correct answer about optimal withdrawal rate or optimal portfolio.

(2) Market conditions at the start of the withdrawal period are crucial to estimating the sustainable withdrawal rate.

(3) Portfolio failure means the portfolio is equal to or less than a planned withdrawal so that the portfolio is zeroed out at the next withdrawal.

(4) Safe withdrawal rate: 3% is safe regardless of asset allocation in portfolio.

(5) Stock percentage generally recommended in a portfolio: 40% to 70%.

(6) Withdrawal rate is maximized when stock in portfolio is at least 50%.

(7) Greater percentage of stock in a portfolio causes a portfolio's average ending value to significantly increase, according to all studies. (7.22a)

Highlight 3: Sequence for Tapping Retirement Assets

■ Some assets are not part of the sequencing decision:

(1) Social Security and employer-provided pensions typically start at retirement with little option for delaying the start date.

(2) Annuities, once in pay status (annuitized), continue without option for change.

(3) Qualified retirement plan accounts and IRAs may be subject to a 50% penalty if withdrawals are delayed after age 70½; consequently these assets must be tapped (in preference to all others) once that age is reached or significant loss will occur. (7.31)

■ Portfolio investments (including qualified retirement plan accounts and IRAs) should be tapped to leave tax-preferred assets as long as possible: the following is a typical sequence:

(1) Assets that provide ordinary income such as bonds or bond mutual funds (as these are subject to the most tax upon withdrawal).

(2) Assets that are subject to capital gains and little or no current income such as stocks and stock mutual funds (because the capital gains tax is lower than ordinary income rates).

(3) Tax exempt mutual bonds (which produce tax-free income while held but are taxable when sold).

(4) Assets that are tax deferred such as qualified retirement plan accounts, traditional IRAs, and nonqualified deferred annuities that have not yet been annuitized.

(5) Tax-exempt assets such as Roth IRAs. (7.32)

■ Other factors are considered that may outweigh these tax items in determining withdrawal sequence, including:

(1) How liquid is the asset?

(2) How risky is the asset? Riskier assets may be acceptable for a longer time horizon than for immediate need.

(3) Does the asset have growth or loss potential for the particular time period in question? (7.36c)

Highlight 4: Factors Relating to Annuities

■ For the purpose of portfolio analysis, annuities should be treated like a bond; actual bond holding may need to be changed to equities to counterbalance annuities (including Social Security and pensions). (7.4)

Highlight 5: Drawing Income Out of the Portfolio

■ Various plans can be provided to minimize risk and transaction costs related to withdrawal of money from an investment portfolio. (7.5)

TERMS TO KNOW DEFINITIONS

Capital preservation model Retiree's account balance at life expectancy equals his account balance at retirement. Model is achieved by withdrawing only the interest income from the portfolio and keeping the principal intact. (7.13a))

Flat annuity Fixed dollar amounts of cash are withdrawn annually. (7.11c(3))

Inflation-adjusted annuity Inflation rate for a particular year determines the withdrawal increase for the next year. (7.11c(1))

Performance-based annuity Portfolio's performance in a particular year determines the withdrawal amount for the following year. (7.11c(2))

Portfolio failure A portfolio is considered to have failed when the withdrawal amount is equal to or greater than the value of the entire portfolio. (7.12a)

Portfolio success rate Portfolio failure rate subtracted from 100%. (7.23a)

Purchasing power preservation model Portfolio's purchasing power at life expectancy equals the portfolio's purchasing power at retirement; model is achieved by making the withdrawal rate equal the return rate minus the inflation rate. (7.13b)

Retirement portfolio Portfolio created for retirement income with the possibility that the portfolio's value will steadily decline. (7.11a(3))

Risk-free withdrawal rate Interest that the portfolio accumulates every time an amount is withdrawn from the portfolio. (7.12b)

Withdrawal rate Cash value that can be withdrawn from the portfolio; formula for the withdrawal rate is the cash withdrawal amount during the first year of distribution divided by the portfolio's initial value. (7.11b(1))

Withdrawal strategy Modification of withdrawals after the retiree has made his first withdrawal from the portfolio. (7.11b(2))

QUESTIONS

1. Which of the following stock percentages was considered an appropriate stock percentage of a conservative client's portfolio, according to Bengen?
   I. 115 minus the client's age for tax-deferred portfolio
   II. 135 minus the client's age for nonqualified portfolio
   A. I only
   B. II only
   C. Both I and II
   D. Neither I nor II

2. All of the following are true regarding annuities EXCEPT
   A. waiting to purchase an annuity risks that interest rates will rise
   B. in portfolio analysis, an annuity represents a secure stream of regular income payments similar to a bond
   C. once an annuity is annuitized, the decision is irreversible
   D. unless a guarantee feature is selected on an annuity, no money is left to heirs when the annuitant dies

3. Which of the following regarding the risk-return trade-off for portfolio distributions is(are) CORRECT?
   I. Probability that a portfolio will fail increases as the withdrawal rate increases
   II. A portfolio will not fail if the withdrawal rate equals the risk-free return rate
   A. I only
   B. II only
   C. Both I and II
   D. Neither I nor II

4. Which of the following statements regarding annuities is(are) TRUE?
   I. Annuities that are in pay status are considered part of the process of sequencing of retirement assets.
   II. Annuities that are in pay status are considered to be like bonds for purposes of portfolio balancing.
   A. I only
   B. II only
   C. Both I and II
   D. Neither I nor II

5. The capital preservation model, which is used to determine portfolio withdrawal rates, is based on which of the following?
   A. Retiree's account balance at life expectancy equals the amount required at retirement as adjusted for inflation.
   B. Retiree's account balance at life expectancy equals the account balance at retirement.
   C. Portfolio's purchasing power at life expectancy equals the portfolio's purchasing power at retirement.
   D. Withdrawal rate would equal the portfolio's return rate minus the inflation rate.

ANSWERS

1. **A.** In his 1996 study, Bengen concluded that the appropriate stock percentage for a conservative client's portfolio is 115 minus the client's age for a tax-deferred portfolio and 125 minus the client's age for a nonqualified portfolio. (7.25a)

2. **A.** By waiting before purchasing an annuity, the client risks that interest rates will decline. An increase in an annuity rate would be a good thing. (7.41 – 7.43)

3. **C.** When the withdrawal rate increases, the probability of portfolio failure increases. (7.12)

4. **B.** Annuities that are in pay status are not considered part of the process of sequencing of retirement assets. They are also considered to be like bonds in the portfolio balancing process. (7.31; 7.41)

5. **B.** The capital preservation model is a capital needs analysis based on the assumption that the retiree's account balance at life expectancy equals his account balance at retirement. (7.13a)

8

Annuity Basics

"Anyone who lives within their means suffers from a lack of imagination."

—Oscar Wilde

TERMS TO KNOW

Accumulation units

Accumulation value

Annual contract charges

Annual reset indexing method

Annuitant

Annuity

Annuity units

Asset allocation

Asset fee (also called spread or margin)

Back-end load

Beneficiary (of an annuity)

Bonus interest rates

Cap rate

Contract term

Death benefit (of an annuity)

Deferred annuity

Fixed-interest deferred annuity

Flexible-premium annuity

Free window period

Free-corridor amount

Front-end load

Fund expense

General account

Guaranteed minimum accumulation benefit

Guaranteed minimum income benefit

Guaranteed minimum interest rate

Guaranteed minimum return of premium benefit

High water mark indexing method

Immediate annuity

Index (equity and bond)

Indexed annuity

Interest rate guarantee period

Maturity date

Mortality and expense charges (M&E)

Nonqualified annuity

Owner (of an annuity)

Partial surrender

Participation rate

Percentage change

Point-to-point indexing method

Pre-59½ IRS penalty tax

Premium bonus

Prospectus

Qualified annuity

Rising floor death benefit

Sec. 1035 exchange

Separate account

Single-premium annuity

Stepped-up death benefit

Subaccounts

Surrender

Surrender charge period

Surrender charges

Surrender value

Tax deferral

Total expense ratio

Variable deferred annuity

8.1 ANNUITIES TERMINOLOGY

> **Key point** Annuities are used for two purposes: accumulating funds (money in) and paying out funds (money out).
>
> **Key point** The parties to an annuity are the owner, the annuitant, and the beneficiary.
>
> **Key point** Immediate annuities start paying immediately; deferred annuities are used to accumulate funds; single premiums are used with immediate annuities; flexible premiums (multiple premium payments) are used with deferred annuities.

8.11 **Annuity:** A contract to pay a stipulated sum at regular intervals during the lifetime of one or more individuals or payable for a specified period.

   a. People buy annuities for two basic reasons:

   (1) To accumulate funds for retirement.

   (2) To manage the distribution of funds after retirement.

   b. Tax treatment depends on whether they are qualified or nonqualified:

   (1) **Qualified annuity:** An annuity contract used in connection with a tax-qualified retirement plan maintained either by an employer or by an individual.

   (2) **Nonqualified annuity:** An annuity contract that is not used in connection with any tax-qualified retirement plan or IRA.

   c. Annuities are long-term investments.

   (1) Because of the length of the guarantees provided, financial strength of the insurance company is important.

   (2) The insurance company makes its money on the difference between what it earns and what it pays out; it hopes to get 1.5 to 2%.

> **EXAMPLE** Wilde Insurance Co. offers you an annuity that pays 4.5%. It expects to earn 6 to 7% on your money. Your 4.5% is guaranteed. Wilde Insurance Co.'s return is not. At the bottom of the range, the company will make 1.5%, which is profit. If the year is good, it could make 2.5%.

   d. Annuities are mainly purchased for living benefits, but also have death benefits; similarities and differences between annuity and life insurance contracts.

   (1) Two similarities:

   (a) Protect against income loss.

   (b) Pooling method.

   (2) Four differences:

   (a) Life insurance is nearly always income tax free to the beneficiary; annuity beneficiary must pay income tax on any gain over the principal amount paid by the annuity owner.

   (b) Life insurance has a net amount at risk; an annuity has none.

   (c) Life insurance has substantial mortality charges; an annuity does not.

(d) Life insurance involves medical underwriting; an annuity (except impaired risk annuities) does not.

8.12 An annuity involves three parties: the owner, the annuitant, and the beneficiary.

a. **Owner (of an annuity):** The person (or business) designated as the owner of the policy, with all rights contained in the policy; the owner:

(1) Applies for the contract.

(2) Pays the premium.

(3) Chooses features of the contract.

(4) Has the right to surrender the contract or make withdrawals.

(5) Names the annuitant (may be owner or another person) and any beneficiaries.

(6) Is also known as the contract owner or contract holder.

b. **Annuitant:** The person (or business) to whom an annuity is payable.

c. **Beneficiary (of an annuity):** The person (or business) to whom the death benefit of an annuity is paid upon the death of the owner; the beneficiary can be a single person or more than one, primary or contingent, and may be changed from time to time.

d. The owner and annuitant are frequently the same person, though this is not required.

> **EXAMPLE** Sam purchases an annuity naming himself and his wife Charlotte as joint annuitants and his daughter Teresa as beneficiary. Since the owner (Sam) is not the same as the annuitant (Sam and Charlotte), it is important to analyze the contract and understand what will happen on the deaths of Sam and Charlotte. Don't make any assumptions.

8.13 Categorizing of annuities.

a. **Immediate annuity:** An annuity contract that provides for the first payment of the annuity at the end of the first interval of payment after purchase.

> **EXAMPLE** Maya has an IRA that is invested in mutual funds. She is approaching her 70th birthday and knows that she will be required to start taking money out. She would like some assurance that the money will last as long as she lives, so she sells the mutual funds and buys an immediate annuity. This contract will meet the minimum distribution requirements by starting to pay immediately and it will protect her income for life.

b. **Deferred annuity:** An annuity contract in which the first payment is not made to the annuitant until after a specified number of years or until the annuitant attains a specified age.

c. **Single-premium annuity:** An annuity purchased with one lump-sum payment.

(1) Single-premium annuities may be deferred annuities, but more frequently are immediate annuities.

d. **Flexible-premium annuity:** An annuity purchased with more than one payment.

e. Any particular annuity can be characterized as a combination of these categories.

Categories of Annuities		
	Immediate	Deferred
Single premium	Single-premium immediate annuities are typically used to manage distribution from a retirement account that used other investments during the accumulation phase.	Single-premium deferred annuities are known as SPDAs. Competes with certificates of deposit. A guarantee is provided for a specific period, with a new offer at the next period.
Flexible premium	This type DOES NOT EXIST: Since payments (investments) are spread out over time, flexible-premium annuities are always deferred annuities.	Flexible-premium deferred annuities are known as FPDAs. This is the typical retirement annuity either in the qualified or nonqualified context, as it allows periodic deposits.

8.14 Annuities provide investors return on their investment in three ways:

a. **Fixed-interest deferred annuity:** An annuity contract that sets an interest rate to be paid on invested money that is guaranteed for a specific period of time; once the guarantee period is over, the interest rate is reset depending on prevailing interest rates. A guaranteed minimum rate is often provided.

b. **Indexed annuity:** A fixed annuity that ties the interest rate of the annuity to a published index; the Standard & Poor's 500 Index is a common index for equity-indexed annuities (EIAs) and 10-year Treasury notes is a common index for interest-indexed annuities.

c. **Variable deferred annuity:** An annuity in which payments fluctuate up and down depending on the earnings in one or more investment accounts.

8.2 CONTRACT PROVISIONS AND RIDERS

Key point An annuity accumulates funds based on an interest rate, which may be guaranteed, reduced by applicable fees.

Key point Three important riders reduce surrender charges in case of terminal illness, long-term care, or disability.

8.21 The parties to an annuity contract (owner, annuitant, beneficiary) are determined in the application; how the contract operates is determined by the contract, riders, and endorsements.

8.22 How funds accumulate is an important part of the contract:

a. How interest is credited is determined by the basic rate plus:

(1) **Bonus interest rates:** Extra interest paid to new purchasers of annuities, typically for one to five years, designed to attract people with existing annuity contracts to switch to a new contract; the bonus interest is designed to offset losses incurred by terminating the old contract.

> **EXAMPLE** Bob owns an annuity paying 4%. You are able to sell him an annuity paying 5%, but Bob is concerned about switching because of the 3% surrender charges on his current annuity. Above the basic 5%, your contract offers an additional 2% bonus interest for the first five years. This more than offsets Bob's surrender charges, so he agrees to surrender his old contract and buy yours.

    (a) Bonus interest may not be paid on early termination or surrender.

(2) **Premium bonus:** A bonus incentive to new annuity purchasers, similar to bonus interest rates, but added to the premium at the beginning and not paid as interest.

> **EXAMPLE** If the contract you offered Bob in the previous example offered a premium bonus equal to 2% of the amount invested, this amount would be added to the contract immediately. This would offset Bob's surrender charges on the old contract, but his decision would be more difficult because it is a one-time thing. What other rights would he be giving up to earn the extra 1%?

  b. How renewal rates are determined involves two questions: when and how.

    (1) **Interest rate guarantee period:** The period of time for which an insurance company's guarantee of the rate for crediting interest to an annuity in operative; a new rate for crediting interest will apply after the conclusion of the guarantee period.

> **EXAMPLE** Emerson Insurance offers an annuity that pays 5%. This rate is guaranteed for five years. After that time, a new rate will be determined that could be higher or lower or remain the same.

    (a) Surrender charges typically apply during a guarantee period because an insurance company may be taking a risk by providing a guarantee.

> **EXAMPLE** The Emerson Insurance contract from the previous example imposes a charge for withdrawals from the contract for five years. If a customer is unhappy with the rate adjustment at the end of the interest rate guarantee period, he can surrender the contract without worrying about a surrender charge.

    (2) How renewal rates are determined depends on the type of annuity.

      (a) In a fixed-interest deferred annuity, the renewal rate is at the discretion of the insurance company.

      (b) Renewal rates are determined by the index in an EIA and are not relevant in a VA.

  c. Minimum interest guarantees: A rate below which interest will never be credited.

(1) This has historically been 2% or 3%.

> **E X A M P L E** The Emerson Insurance contract from the previous example has a 3% minimum interest guarantee. It will never fall below 3%.

8.23 Other basic contract provisions:

a. Fees.

(1) With a fixed-interest annuity, the insurance company makes most of its money from the spread between what it earns and what it pays.

(a) The company may also charge a contract maintenance fee (example: 1% cash value but not exceeding $20 or $50) as a deduction from cash values.

(2) Different fees are associated with indexed annuities and variable deferred annuities, which will be discussed at those points in the outline.

b. Minimum initial premiums depend on the type of annuity:

(1) Single-premium deferred annuities (SPDAs) typically require $5,000 to $10,000.

(2) Flexible-premium deferred annuities (FPDAs) typically require a low $25 to $50 per month.

(3) Lower minimums are used in qualified annuities to allow them to be used in IRAs.

8.24 The following are some common annuity riders:

a. Terminal illness rider: An annuity rider that gives access to annuity values if the annuitant becomes terminally ill; often up to 75% may be withdrawn without surrender charges.

b. Long-term care benefit rider: An annuity rider that gives access to annuity values if the annuitant goes into a long-term care facility; often up to 50% may be withdrawn without surrender charges.

c. Disability rider: An annuity rider that waives surrender charges if the owner is totally disabled and unable to work due to injury or illness.

d. A qualified plan rider allows an annuity to function with a qualified plan.

8.3 GETTING MONEY OUT OF THE CONTRACT

Key point An annuity can be paid for a fixed period, until a fixed amount has been paid, for the life of one or more people, or based on a combination of lives and fixed payout.

Key point Before annuitization, a death benefit is paid to a beneficiary.

Key point Before annuitization, a contract may be surrendered for its accumulation value minus any applicable surrender charges.

Key point Taxes are based on the idea that interest is taxed but principal is not; however, timing is critical and a 10% tax penalty may apply before age 59½.

Sample Annuity Surrender		
Contract Year	5-Year Schedule	10-Year Schedule
1	8%	5%
2	6%	5%
3	4%	4%
4	2%	4%
5	0%	3%
6		3%
7		2%
8		2%
9		1%
10		0%

8.31 Annuities have a wide variety of settlement options:

  a. Annuitization:

  (1) Fixed-period payments.

  (2) Fixed-amount payments.

  (3) Life contingent payments.

  (4) Joint-life contingent payments.

> **EXAMPLE** Pat and Jessie are retired and own an annuity that they want to start drawing from. Pat wants the payments to continue to Jessie when he dies, so they arrange for joint-life annuity payments. This will work for Pat as well if Jessie dies first.

  b. Payment at the **maturity date** (i.e., insurer's selected maximum age when distributions must start):

  (1) Lump-sum payment.

  (2) Leaving the proceeds with the insurance company to earn interest.

  c. Surrenders or partial withdrawals.

  d. Death benefits.

8.32 **Death benefit (of an annuity):** Payment to a beneficiary upon the death of either the owner or annuitant.

  a. If the owner's death controls, the contract is called owner driven.

  b. If the annuitant's death controls, the contract is called annuitant driven.

  c. If death occurs prior to annuitization and the beneficiary is someone other than the spouse, either:

(1) The contract value must be paid out within 5 years; or

(2) The beneficiary must take a life annuity beginning within one year to be paid over the life of the beneficiary.

d. If death occurs prior to annuitization and the beneficiary is the spouse, either:

(1) The spouse may accept death benefit; or

(2) The spouse may continue the contract as the new owner, which allows the spouse to name a new beneficiary and to select settlement terms.

> **EXAMPLE** Rafael was the owner (and annuitant) of two annuities when he died. One named his wife Janice as beneficiary, the other named his daughter Lucy. Lucy took the death benefit as a life annuity. Janice, on the other hand, had other resources, so she took over the annuity as the owner. She named Lucy as beneficiary, but intends to hold on to it as long as she can before starting to take withdrawals. As long as the money remains in the contract, it grows tax-deferred.

8.33 Complete or partial surrenders provide liquidity.

a. **Surrender**: In a deferred annuity contract, the contract owner's right to withdraw all the funds in the contract prior to maturity resulting in a termination of the contract and possible surrender charge.

b. **Partial surrender:** In a deferred annuity contract, the contract owner's right to withdraw funds prior to maturity of the contract; withdrawals may incur a surrender charge.

c. **Accumulation value:** The value of an annuity before surrender charges are subtracted.

d. **Surrender value:** The value of an annuity after surrender charges are subtracted.

e. Loans are typically not available in an annuity.

f. Withdrawals can be repaid with a flexible-premium deferred annuity (FPDA) because FPDAs allow multiple premium payments; withdrawals cannot be repaid with a single-premium deferred annuity (SPDA).

g. Surrenders are not generally taken from immediate annuities because there is no deferred maturity; they are in pay status right from the beginning.

8.34 **Surrender charges**: A charge imposed on the contract owner for the surrender (or partial surrender) of an annuity contract, designed to encourage the contract owner to hold on to the contract and to protect the insurance company from losses it could incur due to an early surrender.

a. **Surrender charge period:** The period of time (typically 5 to 10 years) during which a fee is charged if the owner of an annuity makes a complete or partial surrender (two sample schedules of surrender charges appear in Figure 8-2).

> **EXAMPLE** Catherine owns a single-premium deferred annuity with an accumulation value of $120,000. It has a 10-year surrender charge schedule shown in Figure 8-2. Catherine wants to withdraw $15,000 to make a down payment on a vacation home. It is the sixth year of the contract. This withdrawal will cost her $450 (3% of $15,000).

b. Free-corridor amount: An amount that may be withdrawn from an annuity without being subject to surrender charges; the amount can range from 10 to 15%.

> **EXAMPLE** If the annuity discussed in the previous example had a free-corridor amount of 10%, Catherine would have been able to withdraw the first $12,000 without a surrender charge, but $3,000 of the withdrawal would have been subject to a $90 surrender charge (3% of $3,000).

c. Rolling surrender charges: In a flexible-premium deferred annuity, a surrender charge period that begins anew with each new investment in the contract, but applies only to the new investment.

    (1) To avoid this, money should be withdrawn from old money first.

d. Surrender charges may be waived (depending on terms of the contract):

    (1) If the contract is annuitized.

    (2) At the death of the contract owner or the annuitant (but not both).

    (3) In the event long-term care is required.

    (4) In the event of terminal illness.

    (5) In the event of unemployment.

    (6) To the extent of a required minimum distribution in a qualified plan.

8.35 Income taxes in nonqualified annuities.

a. Tax deferral: A delay of tax liability while money is invested (e.g., in an annuity); tax is deferred, not eliminated because tax will be due once money is withdrawn.

b. Annuity payments: A portion of each annuity payment is subject to tax and a portion is received tax free.

    (1) A fraction of each payment corresponding to the investment in the contract is received tax free.

    (2) This fraction is called the exclusion ratio.

> **EXAMPLE** Mitch began receiving payments under a life annuity of $18,000 a year. According to IRS life expectancy figures, Mitch can expect to receive these payments for 20 years. Over the years, Mitch invested $120,000. Mitch computes his exclusion ratio as the amount of his investment ($120,000) divided by his total expected payments ($18,000 × 20 years = $360,000), which gives him an exclusion ratio of 33.3%. Of the $18,000 annual payments, 33.3% (or one-third) is received tax free. The rest ($12,000) is subject to tax.
>
> This rule is reapplied year after year until Mitch dies or he outlives the 20-year life expectancy.

c. Partial surrenders are generally taxed on a last-in, first-out (LIFO) basis.

    (1) This results in early withdrawals being completely taxable (until all earnings have been withdrawn); subsequent withdrawals (representing the investment in the contract) are tax free.

> **EXAMPLE** Ron has invested $45,000 in a flexible-premium deferred annuity over the years. Its current accumulation value is $80,000. If Ron withdraws $30,000, the entire amount will be considered as coming from the $35,000 worth of interest in the account ($80,000 account value minus $45,000 investment).

> **EXAMPLE** Assume the same annuity. This time Ron wants to withdraw $50,000. Ron must treat the first $35,000 as coming from the interest. The remaining $15,000 he may treat as coming from the investment, which is tax free. Therefore, $35,000 of the withdrawal is subject to tax.

(2) The LIFO rule is also referred to as the interest-first rule.

(3) Contracts purchased before August 14, 1982, were subject to a cost-recovery or FIFO (first-in, first-out) rule.

(4) Only the interest portion of a complete surrender is subject to tax.

(5) **Pre-59½ IRS penalty tax:** A 10% penalty tax that applies to the taxable amount of a withdrawal of funds from an annuity or qualified plan prior to age 59½; various exceptions may apply depending on whether the investment is qualified or not.

    (a) The taxable portion of any surrender or withdrawal taken before age 59½ is subject to the 10% penalty; no penalty applies to the nontaxable portion.

> **EXAMPLE** In the prior example, Asheka took an $80,000 withdrawal, of which $64,000 was subject to tax. If Asheka was 55 when she took the withdrawal, the penalty (in addition to tax) would be $6,400, which is 10% of $64,000, not 10% of the whole amount.

d. Death benefits are subject to tax like any other distribution from an annuity (unlike the death benefit of a life insurance policy).

e. **Sec. 1035 exchange:** A tax-free transaction that allows a taxpayer to exchange the following three types of contracts without paying tax on the surrendered contract: (1) life insurance for life insurance, (2) annuity for annuity, or (3) life insurance for annuity; an exchange of an annuity contract for life insurance is not covered by this rule and is consequently subject to tax.

> **EXAMPLE** Robert owns an annuity with a current account value of $250,000. His investment in the contract was $150,000. If he surrenders the contract today, he would be taxed on $100,000 gain. If the surrender of the contract is in connection with the purchase of an equal or greater contract (i.e., he doesn't take any money out, but may put money in), the transaction is tax free. The $100,000 gain continues to be deferred until he surrenders the new contract or otherwise takes money out.

8.4 EQUITY-INDEXED ANNUITIES (EIAs)

> **Key point** EIAs are fixed-interest annuities with renewal rates based on a market index rather than an internal decision of the insurance company.
>
> **Key point** During the free-window period at the end of the contract term, the owner can annuitize, withdraw without surrender charge, exchange for another annuity, or renew for another contract term.
>
> **Key point** Three indexing methods may be used to set a new rate: annual reset, point to point, and high water mark.

8.41 Indexed annuities can be thought of as a type of fixed-interest annuity in which the renewal interest rate is set on the basis of a market index rather than by internal decisions of the insurance company.

8.42 **Index (equity and bond):** A measure of the performance of a defined group of stocks or bonds that is used by an insurance company to determine the rate for crediting interest to an annuity.

   a. Common indexes are:

      (1) S&P 500.

      (2) S&P Midcap 400.

      (3) Nasdaq 100.

      (4) Dow Jones Industrial Average (DJIA).

      (5) Lehman Brothers US Treasury Index.

      (6) Lehman Brothers Aggregate Bond Index.

      (7) Merrill Lynch All Convertibles Index.

      (8) International indexes may also be used.

   b. **Contract term:** The period of time during which the rate for crediting interest to an equity-indexed annuity remains fixed; changes are made at the conclusion of this period for the next period.

      (1) Surrender charges typically apply for the duration of the contract term. The contract term may be between 1 and 10 years.

   c. **Free window period:** The time at the end of the contract term of an equity-indexed annuity when the owner can choose to:

      (1) Annuitize.

      (2) Make withdrawals without a surrender charge.

      (3) Exchange for another type of annuity.

      (4) Renew for another contract term.

   d. **Percentage change:** index change from the start of the contract term to the contract term's end stated as a percentage.

8.43 Three basic methods for determining the new rate are:

   a. **Annual reset indexing method:** A method for determining the rate for crediting interest in an equity indexed annuity that increases the rate if the index rate increased from the beginning of the year to the end; no reduction is made if the index falls.

(1)   Main benefit: chance to profit when index recovers from a previous weak year.

(2)   Annual reset locks in gains in the index and is, therefore, also called ratcheting.

(3)   Annual reset performs well with rising or fluctuating markets.

E X A M P L E   American Refuge Insurance Co. offers an equity indexed annuity tied to the S&P 500 with an annual reset based on a specified percentage of each year's change in the index. Shannon bought this annuity when the S&P 500 was at 1,000 and the following shows the index level on each of the following five anniversary dates:

End of Contract Year	S&P 500	Year's Gain in the Index
1	1,100	10.0%
2	1,175	6.8%
3	1,080	−8.1%
4	1,125	4.2%
5	1,250	11.1%

Each year Shannon's annuity will be credited with some percentage of the year's gain in the index. No reduction will be made, however, for the loss in the index that occurred in the third year.

---

b.   **Point-to-point indexing method:** A method for determining the rate for crediting interest in an equity indexed annuity that adjusts the rate for any change in the index, up or down, between the beginning and the end of the contract term.

(1)   Main benefit: highest returns during continuously increasing markets.

(2)   Changes in the index in the middle of the contract term have no effect on the computation of a new rate for the next contract term.

E X A M P L E   Protection Insurance Co. offers an equity indexed annuity tied to the S&P 500 that uses a point-to-point interest crediting methodology. Chin purchased this annuity when the S&P 500 was at 1,000. At the end of the contract term, the S&P 500 was at 1,100. If the contract's participation rate is 80% (see below), Chin's annuity will be credited with 8%.

---

c.   **High water mark indexing method:** A method for determining the rate for crediting interest in an equity indexed annuity that adjusts the rate based on the highest value of the index determined on the anniversary dates within the contract term.

(1)   Main benefit: may credit higher interest than other methods if index hits a high point at the start or in the middle, then declines at the end of the term.

> **EXAMPLE** Health and Wealth Insurance, Inc. offers an equity indexed annuity tied to the S&P 500 that uses the high water mark method for crediting interest. Roger purchased this annuity when the S&P 500 was at 1,000, and the following shows the index level on each of the following five anniversary dates:
>
> | End of Contract Year | S&P 500 |
> | --- | --- |
> | 1 | 1,100 |
> | 2 | 1,090 |
> | 3 | 1,280 |
> | 4 | 1,150 |
> | 5 | 1,250 |
>
> The index at the end of the third year was the highest value during the contract term. The index level for that year, 1,280, was a 28% gain over when Roger purchased the annuity. The amount that will be credited to Roger will be some percentage of this figure.

8.44   The spread between the money earned by the insurance company and the money it pays to customers is not built into the indexing method; profit for the insurance company is provided based on the following:

a. **Asset fee (also called spread or margin):** An amount that is subtracted from any gain in an index before determining a change in the rate for crediting to an equity indexed annuity.

   (1) The rate is typically 2 or 3%.

   (2) The asset fee is generally adjustable; if so, the contract will set a maximum rate (for example, the asset fee could be capped at 5%).

b. **Participation rate:** A fraction that is multiplied by the change in an index before determining a change in the rate for crediting to an equity-indexed annuity.

   (1) Participation rates typically vary from 70 to 100%.

   (2) Participation rates may be used together with an asset fee or instead of it.

> **EXAMPLE** Ancillary Annuities Assn., Inc., offers an equity-indexed annuity with a participation rate of 75%. If the index goes up 8%, the annuity will be credited with 6% (75% of 8%). The insurance company can protect itself against loss by investing in assets that will perform as the index does. One-fourth of any gain will compensate the company for expenses and provide a profit.

c. Surrender fees are generally more complicated than with traditional fixed-interest annuities.

   (1) Surrender charges make annuities unsuitable for short-term investment.

How different are fixed-interest annuities and equity-indexed annuities in terms of risk and return? Not very different. Variable annuities are the different type in the crowd, and you can see this in the simple fact that you need an NASD license to sell variable annuities. No NASD license is required to sell fixed-interest or equity-indexed annuities.

Why is that?

Equity-indexed annuities are, in fact, only a special type of fixed-interest annuity. Earnings in the account are not the earnings of the investments making up the index. The index is only used to set the fixed interest rate.

It is important to remember that fixed-interest annuity rates are fixed only for the contract term. After that, the interest rate is adjusted according to market conditions. The difference between a fixed-interest annuity and an indexed annuity is that the methodology for adjusting the renewal interest rate is spelled out in the contract.

With a fixed-interest annuity, the purchaser doesn't know how the adjustment will be made and simply has to trust the insurance company. But, in fact, the insurance company has to go through many of the same steps in setting renewal rates as they go through in equity indexed annuities. And profits in fixed-interest annuities are assured to the insurance company when they invest assets in a portfolio of investments that are expected to pay better than the rate promised on the annuity. This portfolio is similar to an index. The index simply makes the process transparent.

That is how equity-indexed annuities and fixed-interest annuities are similar. How do they differ from variable annuities?

Fixed-interest and equity-indexed annuities may have periodic changes in the rate for crediting interest, but principal is protected.

This is not true in a variable annuity. In exchange for the possibility of enjoying a higher return on the investment, assets in a variable annuity are subject to the risk of losing principal—unless you buy a guarantee, but that will cost you extra.

8.45   Upper and lower limits on interest rate adjustments:

    a.   **Cap rate:** An upper limit on the rate of interest an annuity may earn.

        (1)   Caps may themselves be adjusted.

        (2)   Not all EIAs have caps.

    b.   **Guaranteed minimum interest rate:** The minimum rate for crediting interest to an annuity.

        (1)   May be expressed as a percentage (e.g., 3%).

        (2)   The indexed value and the guaranteed value are figured in two separate calculations.

            (a)   Only when surrendered do the two come together.

            (b)   You get the larger of the two amounts.

8.5 VARIABLE DEFERRED ANNUITIES

Key point The general account of a variable deferred annuity is similar to a fixed-interest deferred annuity.

Key point The separate account is made up of subaccounts investing in a wide variety of investments (such as mutual funds).

Key point Accumulation units measure the quantity of ownership in a variable deferred annuity; they are similar to shares in a mutual fund.

Key point Annuity units measure an annuitant's right to annuity payments after annuitization.

8.51 Rather than a set interest rate, variable deferred annuities grow investors' funds by allowing them to be invested in a variety of accounts:

  a. **General account:** In a variable deferred annuity, the account that is set up like a fixed-interest deferred annuity, guaranteeing principal and paying a minimum fixed rate of interest.

  (1) Typical interest rate has been 3 or 4%.

  (2) Current efforts to reduce this minimum for newly issued contracts.

  b. **Separate account:** An account that allows the owner of a variable deferred annuity to invest account values in a variety of ways to meet the owner's investment objectives and risk tolerance.

  c. **Subaccounts:** Components of the separate account, each of which allows the contract owner to invest account values in different assets; subaccounts are similar to mutual funds within the variable deferred annuity context.

  (1) The account owner receives the earnings of the underlying assets reduced by asset-based fees.

  (2) Types of investment portfolios available include:

  (a) Value.

  (b) Growth.

  (c) Aggressive.

  (d) Blue-chip.

  (e) Balanced.

  (f) Quality bond.

  (g) High-yield bond.

  (h) Zero-coupon bond.

  (i) Ginnie Mae.

  (j) Real estate.

  (3) Variable deferred annuity investors can move money around among the subaccounts and the general account.

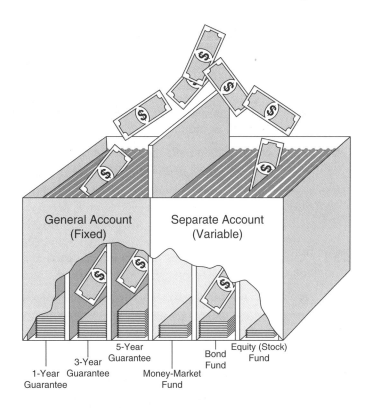

d. **Accumulation units:** The way investments are tracked in the subaccounts of a variable deferred annuity; similar to the concept of a share in a mutual fund.

(1) The number of accumulation units stays constant, but their value varies.

> ✳ **EXAMPLE** Sarah purchased a variable deferred annuity and allocates $45,000 to a growth-fund subaccount. At the time, the value of a unit is $18, so Sarah receives 2,500 accumulation units ($45,000 ÷ $18). In five years, Sarah's units are valued at $21. The value of the subaccount has, therefore, grown to $52,500 ($21 × 2,500 units). The number of units stays the same, but the value changes.

> ✳ **EXAMPLE** Assume the same annuity as the previous example, but after five years Sarah's units are valued at $15,000. Her account value has, therefore, fallen to $37,500 ($15 × 2,500 units). Again, the units stayed the same, but the value changed.

e. **Annuity units:** A measure of an annuitant's right to annuity payments under a variable deferred annuity that is in pay status (i.e., after annuitization).

(1) An annuity unit is similar to an accumulation unit except that it represents a right to current payments rather than mere accumulation.

(2) When a variable deferred annuity is annuitized, accumulation units are exchanged for annuity units.

(3) The number of annuity units you get is equal to the dollar value of the accumulation units divided by the present value of a life annuity in the amount equal to the current value of an annuity unit.

(4) Annuity units are revalued each year.

(5) The number of annuity units doesn't change as the annuity payments are made.

> **EXAMPLE** Let's say that Sarah, in the previous examples, made money in her variable deferred annuity and has $52,000 when she is ready to annuitize. Sarah is entitled to 1,300 annuity units valued at $40. This $40 represents the present value of a life annuity of $3 per year. Since Sarah will own 1,300 units, she will receive annuity payments of $3,900 per year ($3 × 1,300).
>
> The number of units Sarah has will always remain fixed at 1,300, but the value of the units may change. If the units go up, Sarah's annuity payments will go up.

f. Variable deferred annuities (through the subaccounts) offer:

(1) Professional money managers.

(2) Diversification through asset allocation.

(3) Tax-free transfers among subaccounts.

(a) Transfers may be subject to fees.

(4) Dollar cost averaging.

(5) Automatic rebalancing of portfolio.

g. **Asset allocation:** A system of allocating funds in an investment portfolio among a variety of investments to minimize risk through diversification while achieving the investor's goals most efficiently.

(1) Insurance companies offer asset allocation services.

(2) Automatic rebalancing is possible. You can't do this in taxable accounts because of taxes on the sale of assets that would occur to accomplish this, but you can do it in a variable deferred annuity.

> **EXAMPLE** Allotment Variable Deferred Annuity offers a general account plus one stock fund and one bond fund. The general account pays 3%. Let's compare how Josh and Karen did, with each investing $100,000 in different ways.
>
> | | Josh's Annuity | |
> |---|---|---|
> | | Year 1 | Year 2 |
> | General account | $10,000 | $10,300 |
> | Stock fund | $80,000 | $76,000 |
> | Bond fund | $10,000 | $10,350 |
> | Total | $100,000 | $96,650 |
>
> | | Karen's Annuity | |
> |---|---|---|
> | | Year 1 | Year 2 |
> | General account | $15,000 | $15,450 |
> | Stock fund | $40,000 | $38,000 |
> | Bond fund | $45,000 | $46,575 |
> | Total | $100,000 | $100,025 |
>
> Josh allocated most of his premium to the stock fund. When stocks went down 5%, he couldn't make up the difference from the general account, which was paying 3%, or the bond fund, which paid 3.5%.
>
> By having a more balanced allocation, Karen was able to offset stock losses with gains in the other accounts. This is a simplified example of how asset allocation works to minimize risk.

h. **Prospectus:** A document required by securities law that describes all the important information an investor might need to know about the product; in the case of a variable deferred annuity, this includes characteristics of the underlying investments, payout and other options, death benefits, taxes, fees, and other costs.

   (1) Because variable deferred annuities are registered and subject to securities law regulation, an NASD license is required to sell them.

i. Risk is borne by the investor, not the insurance company; to protect against significant losses, investors can purchase various types of guarantees discussed in the next sections, principally:

   (1) Guaranteed living benefits.

   (2) Guaranteed death benefits.

8.52 Guaranteed living benefits include the following types:

a. **Guaranteed minimum income benefit:** A guarantee in a variable deferred annuity that ensures that a minimum amount will be available to convert to annuitized income at rates specified in the contract.

   (1) This guarantee states that, after a specified period, the contract can be annuitized as if the assets had earned X%; if the account earned more, you get that; if it earned less (or lost money), you are protected against that loss.

(2)   The typical holding period is 7 to 10 years.

(3)   The typical guarantee rate is 3 to 6%.

> ✱**EXAMPLE**   Donald invested $100,000 in a variable deferred annuity. After 10 years, the account value is $120,000, not a good return for all those years. Donald purchased a guaranteed minimum income benefit with the contract, which provided that, after 10 years, he could annuitize the larger of the account value or the value he would have earned at 3%. The 3% rate would have given him an account value of $134,392. This is the value he will annuitize.

> ✱**EXAMPLE**   Let's say that Donald's account value after 10 years was $180,000, rather than $120,000. In this case, the guarantee would not come into play. Donald will annuitize the $180,000.

b.   Guaranteed minimum return of premium benefit: A guarantee in a variable deferred annuity that allows contract owners, after a specified number of years, to withdraw their premium regardless of the then current account value.

   (1)   This guarantee protects against loss of principal.

c.   Guaranteed minimum accumulation benefit: A guarantee that provides that the value of a variable deferred annuity account can be stepped up to a specified amount after a given time.

   (1)   Avoids annuitization of the guaranteed minimum income benefit.

d.   Guaranteed minimum withdrawal benefit: A guarantee that provides annual withdrawals from a variable deferred annuity of 5 to 7% of premiums annually until premiums are fully recovered regardless of the amount actually in the contract.

e.   Guaranteed payout annuity floor: A guarantee that provides that future payments from an annuitized variable deferred annuity will never be less than a specified percentage of the first payment.

   (1)   A typical payout rate is 85 to 100%.

f.   Why are guarantees a part of variable deferred annuities? Fixed-interest deferred annuities and equity indexed annuities do have a guarantee built into them. You can't lose principal with those types of annuities because of their basic characteristics as products. You can lose.

8.53   Guaranteed death benefits: The basic death benefit is the account value as of the date proof of death is received (this date is mandated by SEC rules).

   a.   Guarantees protect against declining account values.

      (1)   Issue: Is death benefit triggered by the death of the owner or the annuitant?

      (2)   A basic guarantee provides that the death benefit will be the larger of:

         (a)   Account value on date proof of death received (due to the SEC rules), or

         (b)   Total of net premiums minus partial withdrawals.

b. Rising floor death benefit: A guaranteed minimum death benefit that is equal to the sum of premiums (minus partial withdrawal) plus interest at a stated rate; the account value on the date the proof of death is received is paid if that amount is larger.

  (1) The interest rate applied in the rising floor death benefit guarantee:

  (a) In equity subaccounts is typically 4 to 6%.

  (b) In bond, money market, and guaranteed interest accounts is typically 3 to 4%.

  (2) The cost is 40 to 50 basis points.

c. Stepped-up death benefit: A guaranteed minimum death benefit that replaces the standard amount (premiums minus withdrawals) with a stepped-up amount on specified anniversary dates if the stepped-up amount is larger than the account value; also known as ratcheted death benefit.

  (1) The replacement step-up can be set to occur on the 2nd to 10th anniversaries.

  (2) The cost is 20 to 30 basis points.

d. Increases to offset income taxes on death benefit: This guarantee increases death benefit from 25 to 40% of policy gain (gain not account value).

  (1) This is intended to help the beneficiary pay the income tax on the death benefit (which is calculated on gain only).

  (2) The cost typically is 35 basis points.

e. Withdrawals will affect the death benefit guarantees in one of two ways:

  (1) The death benefit will be reduced $1 for each dollar withdrawn.

  (2) The death benefit will be reduced proportionally based on the percentage of the account withdrawn.

8.54 Fees.

a. Variable deferred annuities have a more complicated fee structure than fixed-interest deferred annuities.

  (1) The fee structure results from the fact that variable deferred annuities don't have a spread like fixed-interest deferred annuities.

b. Front-end load: A charge made for investment in a variable deferred annuity at the time of the deposit by deducting a percentage of the deposit.

  (1) Front-end loads are fairly rare.

  (2) Front-end loads can be anywhere from 2.5 to 8.5% (5.75% typically).

  (3) Disadvantage: The load reduces the amount of money going into the account that could be accumulating earnings.

c. Back-end load: A charge made for investment in a variable deferred annuity at the time of surrender or withdrawal by deducting a percentage from the amount withdrawn; also called a surrender charge or a deferred sales charge.

  (1) This is similar to surrender charges in fixed-interest deferred annuities.

  (2) Surrender charge periods, schedules, free-corridor amounts, etc. are similar.

d. Annual contract charges: An administrative fee charged by an insurance company for service provided in connection with a variable deferred annuity, typically $10 to $50 per year.

e. Mortality and expense charges (M&E): A charge made against subaccounts in a variable deferred annuity to pay for the various guarantees made in the annuity contract:

(1) Minimum guaranteed interest rate in the general account.

(2) Guarantees in connection with annuitization.

(3) Guarantees in connection with the death benefit.

(4) Average annual M&E is 1.3%, ranging from 0 to 2.1%.

f. Fund expense: A management fee charged as a percentage of assets under management in the various subaccounts of a variable deferred annuity.

(1) The average is .974%, ranging from 0 to 6.15%.

g. Total expense ratio: The ratio of asset-based expenses to the amount of assets managed in a variable deferred annuity; the asset-based expenses are the total of the fund expense and the mortality and expense charges (M&E).

(1) The total expense ratio allows comparison to fees charged in similar mutual funds.

(2) The average total expense ratio is 2.31, ranging from .33 to 8.99.

HIGHLIGHTS

Highlight 1: Basic Definitions Relating to Annuities

- Annuities are most often used for two purposes: to accumulate funds for retirement and to manage the distribution of funds after retirement. (8.11a)
  - (1) Annuities provide living benefits, such as withdrawals and regular periodic payments, but they also provide death benefits. (8.11e)

- Aside from the insurance company, there are three parties to every annuity contract you should be concerned about:
  - (1) The owner buys the contract and can make any changes in it, including withdrawals, prior to annuitization. (8.12a)
  - (2) The annuitant is the person (or persons) who will receive annuity payments after the contract is annuitized; the annuitant may be the same as the owner or different. (8.12b)
  - (3) The beneficiary is the person who receives the death benefit upon the death of the owner or annuitant, depending on how the contract is structured. (8.12c)

Highlight 2: Interest Rates, Fees, and Other Provisions

- The basic interest rate provided for in the contract may be increased by:
  - (1) Bonus interest for the first several years; (8.22a(1)) or
  - (2) A premium bonus that adds immediately to the account value. (8.22a(2))

- Renewal rates are determined:
  - (1) At the conclusion of the interest rate guarantee period to apply for the next period. (8.22b(1))
  - (2) The amount is determined by the company in the case of a fixed-interest deferred annuity and by the application of a formula to a published market index in the case of an indexed annuity. (8.22b(2))

- Fee structure differs depending on the type of annuity.
  - (1) Insurance companies earn profit on fixed-interest deferred annuities based on the spread between what it earns and what it pays, so fees are not significant. (8.23a(1))
  - (2) Fees are separately provided for in indexed and variable deferred annuities because there is no spread in the way these products are designed. (8.23a(2))

Highlight 3: Getting Money Out of the Contract

- Benefits of an annuity include single and joint life annuities, fixed-period and fixed-amount annuities, lump-sum payments, surrenders or partial withdrawals, and death benefits. (8.31)

- The surrender option or partial withdrawal gives annuity owners access to their invested funds, but surrender charges impose a penalty on withdrawals in early years. (8.33)
  - (1) Surrender charges are often set up as a schedule of charges that declines with each year the annuity is held. (8.34a)
  - (2) Often, an amount up to 10 or 15% of the account value can be withdrawn without surrender charge; this is called the free-corridor amount. (8.34b)

- Earnings distributed from an annuity are taxed, returned investment is distributed tax free; the timing of this depends on the type of payment:
  (1) Annuity payments split the taxed and untaxed portion among all the payments through application of an exclusion ratio. (8.35b)
  (2) Partial surrenders are generally taxed on a last-in, first-out (LIFO) basis. (8.35c)
  (3) A penalty tax of 10% (in addition to the regular tax) applies to the taxable portion of withdrawals taken before age 59½. (8.35c(5))
  (4) Death benefits are subject to tax like any other distribution from an annuity. (8.35d)
  (5) Annuity contracts may be exchanged tax free. (8.35e)

Highlight 4: Equity Indexed Annuities

- Equity indexed annuities are a type of fixed-interest annuity in which the renewal interest rate is determined by changes in a market index like the S&P 500. (8.41)
  (1) At the end of the contract term, the owner of an equity-indexed annuity may choose to annuitize, make withdrawals without charge, exchange for another type of annuity, or renew for another contract term; this is called the free-window period. (8.42c)

- Based on the index, there are three methods for determining the renewal rate: (8.43)
  (1) Annual reset indexing method.
  (2) Point-to-point indexing method.
  (3) High water mark indexing method.

- Factors used to provide the insurance company with a profit when an index is used include:
  (1) The asset fee (also called spread or margin), which is subtracted from any gain in an index before determining a change in the rate for crediting interest. (8.44a)
  (2) The participation rate, which scales down the percentage of change in the index before determining the new interest rate. (8.44b)

Highlight 5: Variable Deferred Annuities

- Investment in a variable deferred annuity is divided by the owner between the general account and the separate account. (8.51)
  (1) The separate account is divided into subaccounts; each subaccount invests in different types of assets in a manner similar to a mutual fund. (8.51c)
  (2) Investment amounts are tracked by accumulation units, which are similar to shares in a mutual fund and, upon annuitization, accumulation units are traded for annuity units. (8.51d, e)
  (3) Assets can be moved between the general account and subaccounts to achieve a beneficial asset allocation, but limits and fees may apply. (8.51g)

- Variable deferred annuities are subject to securities law regulation: a prospectus is required and an NASD license is required to sell them. (8.51h)

- Risk of investment in the subaccounts is borne by the investor, not the insurance company; to protect against significant losses, investors can purchase various types of guarantees.

- Although there are a number of types of fees associated with variable deferred annuities, two of the most significant include:
  (1) Back-end loads, which are similar to surrender charges and are applied to withdrawals. (8.54c)
  (2) Mortality and expense charges (M&E), which pay for various guarantees, including the minimum interest rate in the general account and guarantees in connection with annuitization and death benefits. (8.54e)

TERMS TO KNOW DEFINITIONS

Accumulation units The way investments are tracked in the subaccounts of a variable deferred annuity; similar to the concept of a share in a mutual fund. (8.51d)

Accumulation value The value of an annuity before surrender charges are subtracted. (8.33c)

Annual contract charges An administrative fee charged by an insurance company for service provided in connection with a variable deferred annuity, typically $10 to $50 per year. (8.54d)

Annual reset indexing method A method for determining the rate for crediting interest in an equity-indexed annuity that increases the rate if the index rate increased from the beginning of the year to the end; no reduction is made if the index falls. (8.43a)

Annuitant The person (or business) to whom an annuity is payable for life or for a specified period; an annuitant may be: one or more individuals (if more than one, a life annuity may be based on their joint lives); or a corporation (but not a life annuity, as a corporation has no life). (8.12b)

Annuity A contract to pay a stipulated sum at regular intervals during the lifetime of one or more individuals or payable for a specified period. (8.11)

Annuity units A measure of an annuitant's right to annuity payments under a variable deferred annuity that is in pay status (i.e., after annuitization). (8.51e)

Asset allocation A system of allocating funds in an investment portfolio among a variety of investments to minimize risk through diversification while achieving the investor's goals; most efficiently based on the expected performance of those investments. (8.51g)

Asset fee (also called spread or margin) An amount that is subtracted from any gain in an index before determining a change in the rate for crediting to an equity-indexed annuity. (8.44a)

Back-end load A charge made for investment in a variable deferred annuity at the time of surrender or withdrawal by deducting a percentage from the amount withdrawn; also called a surrender charge or a deferred sales charge. (8.54c)

Beneficiary (of an annuity) The person (or business) to whom the death benefit of an annuity is paid upon the death of the owner; the beneficiary can be a single person or more than one, primary or contingent, and may be changed from time to time. (8.12c)

Bonus interest rates Extra interest paid to new purchasers of annuities, typically for one to five years, designed to attract people with existing annuity contracts to switch to a new contract; the bonus interest is designed to offset losses incurred by terminating the old contract. (8.22a(1))

Cap rate An upper limit on the rate of interest an annuity may earn. (8.45a)

Contract term The period of time during which the rate for crediting interest to an equity-indexed annuity remains fixed; changes are made at the conclusion of this period for the next period. (8.42b)

Death benefit (of an annuity) Payment to a beneficiary upon the death of either the owner or annuitant. (8.32)

Deferred annuity An annuity contract in which the first payment is not made to the annuitant until after a specified number of years or until the annuitant attains a specified age. (8.13b)

Fixed-interest deferred annuity An annuity contract that sets an interest rate to be paid on invested money that is guaranteed for a specific period of time; once the guarantee period is over, the interest rate is reset depending on prevailing interest rates. (8.14a)

Flexible-premium annuity An annuity purchased with more than one premium payment. (8.13d)

Free window period The time at the end of the contract term of an equity-indexed annuity when the owner can choose: to annuitize, to make withdrawals without a surrender charge, to exchange for another type of annuity, or to renew for another contract term. (8.42c)

Free-corridor amount An amount that may be withdrawn from an annuity without being subject to surrender charges; the amount can range from 10 to 15% of either the initial premium or last year's accumulation value, but could be zero in some cases. (8.34b)

Front-end load A charge made for investment in a variable deferred annuity at the time of the deposit by deducting a percentage of the deposit. (8.54b)

Fund expense A management fee charged as a percentage of assets under management in the various subaccounts of a variable deferred annuity. (8.54f)

General account In a variable deferred annuity, the account that is set up like a fixed-interest deferred annuity, guaranteeing principal and paying a minimum fixed rate of interest. (8.51a)

Guaranteed minimum accumulation benefit A guarantee that provides that the value of a variable deferred annuity account can be stepped up to a specified amount after a give time. (8.52c)

Guaranteed minimum income benefit A guarantee in a variable deferred annuity that ensures that a minimum amount will be available to convert to annuitized income at rates specified in the contract. (8.52a)

Guaranteed minimum interest rate The minimum rate for crediting interest to an annuity. (8.45b)

Guaranteed minimum return of premium benefit A guarantee in a variable deferred annuity that allows contract owners, after a specified number of years, to withdraw their premium regardless of the then-current account value. (8.52b)

High water mark indexing method A method for determining the rate for crediting interest in an equity-indexed annuity that adjusts the rate based on the highest value of the index determined on the anniversary dates within the contract term. (8.43c)

Immediate annuity An annuity contract that provides for the first payment of the annuity at the end of the first interval of payment after owner deposits money with insurer. (8.13a)

Index (equity and bond) A measure of the performance of a defined group of stocks or bonds that is used by an insurance company to determine the rate for crediting interest to an annuity. (8.42)

Indexed annuity A fixed annuity that ties the interest rate of the annuity to a published index; the Standard & Poor's 500 Index is a common index for equity-indexed annuities and 10-year Treasury notes is a common index for interest-indexed annuities. (8.14b)

Interest rate guarantee period The period of time for which an insurance company's guarantee of the rate for crediting interest to an annuity in operative; a new rate for crediting interest will apply after the conclusion of the guarantee period. (8.22b(1))

Maturity date ted maximum age when distributions must start (8.31b)

Mortality and expense charge (M&E) A charge made against subaccounts in a variable deferred annuity to pay for the various guarantees made in the annuity contract: minimum deferred guaranteed interest rate in the general account, guarantees in connection with annuitization, or guarantees in connection with the death benefit. (8.54e)

Nonqualified annuity An annuity contract that is not used in connection with any tax-qualified retirement plan or IRA. (8.11b(2))

Owner (of an annuity) The person (or business) designated as the owner of the policy, with all rights contained in the policy; the owner: applies for the contract, pays the premium, chooses features of the contract, has the right to surrender the contract or make withdrawals, names the annuitant (may be owner or another person) and any beneficiaries, and is also known as the contract owner or contract holder. (8.12a)

Partial surrender In a deferred annuity contract, the contract owner's right to withdraw funds prior to maturity of the contract; withdrawals may incur a surrender charge. (8.33b)

Participation rate A fraction that is multiplied by the change in an index before determining a change in the rate for crediting to an equity-indexed annuity. (8.44b)

Percentage change Index change from the start of the contract term to the contract term's end stated as a percentage. (8.42d)

Point-to-point indexing method A method for determining the rate for crediting interest in an equity-indexed annuity that adjusts the rate for any change in the index, up or down, between the beginning and the end of the contract term. (8.43b)

Pre-59½ IRS penalty tax A 10% penalty tax that applies to the taxable amount of a withdrawal of funds from an annuity or qualified plan prior to age 59½; various exceptions may apply depending on whether the investment is qualified. (8.35c(5))

Premium bonus A bonus incentive to new annuity purchasers, similar to bonus interest rates, but added to the premium at the beginning and not paid as interest. (8.22a(2))

Prospectus A document required by securities law that describes all the important information an investor might need to know about the product; in the case of a variable deferred annuity, this includes characteristics of the underlying investments, payout and other options, death benefits, fees, and other costs. (8.51h)

Qualified annuity An annuity contract used in connection with a tax-qualified retirement plan maintained either by an employer (such as a 401(k) plan, pension plan, profit-sharing plan, 403(b) plan, SEP, or SIMPLE) or by an individual (an IRA). (8.11b(1))

Rising floor death benefit A guaranteed minimum death benefit that is equal to the sum of premiums (minus partial withdrawal) plus interest at a stated rate; the account value on the date the proof of death is received is paid if that amount is larger. (8.53b)

Section 1035 exchange A tax-free transaction that allows a taxpayer to exchange the following three types of contracts without paying tax on the surrendered contract: (1) life insurance for life insurance, (2) annuity for annuity, or (3) life insurance for annuity; an exchange of an annuity contract for life insurance is not covered by this rule and is consequently subject to tax. (8.35e)

Separate account An account that allows the owner of a variable deferred annuity to invest account values in a variety of ways to meet the owner's investment objectives and risk tolerance. (8.51b)

Single-premium annuity An annuity purchased with one lump-sum payment. (8.13c)

Stepped-up death benefit A guaranteed minimum death benefit that replaces the standard amount (premiums minus withdrawals) with a stepped-up amount on specified anniversary dates if the stepped-up amount is larger than the account value; also known as ratcheted death benefit. (8.53c)

Subaccounts Component accounts of a variable deferred annuity's separate account, each of which allows the contract owner to invest account values in different assets; subaccounts are similar to mutual funds within the variable deferred annuity context. (8.51c)

Surrender In a deferred annuity contract, the contract owner's right to withdraw all the funds in the contract prior to maturity resulting in a termination of the contract and possible surrender charge. (8.33a)

Surrender charge period The period of time (typically 5 to 10 years) during which a fee is charged if the owner of an annuity makes a complete or partial surrender of the contract; no charge is made for a withdrawal after the surrender charge period. (8.34a)

Surrender charges A charge imposed on the contract owner for the surrender (or partial surrender) of an annuity contract, designed to encourage the contract owner to hold on to the contract and to protect the insurance company from losses it could incur due to an early surrender. (8.34)

Surrender value The value of an annuity after surrender charges are subtracted. (8.33d)

Tax deferral A delay of tax liability while money is invested (e.g., in an annuity); tax is deferred, not eliminated, because tax will be due once money is withdrawn. (8.35a)

Total expense ratio The ratio of asset-based expenses to the amount of assets managed in a variable deferred annuity; the asset-based expenses are the total of the fund expense and the mortality and expense charges (M&E). (8.54g)

Variable deferred annuity An annuity in which payments fluctuate up and down depending on the earnings in one or more investment accounts. (8.14c)

QUESTIONS

1. John purchases a fixed deferred annuity with a minimum rate of return of 3% and a current rate of 5%. What percentage will John earn the first year?
   A. 3%
   B. 5%
   C. 6%
   D. 10%

2. Given the long-term nature of a variable deferred annuity contract, which of the following statements is CORRECT?
   A. The distinction between general account investment and separate account investments is irrelevant.
   B. Only annuity contracts underwritten by financially strong insurance companies should be selected.
   C. Investors should annuitize as soon as possible.
   D. Investors in fixed annuities need not worry about credit risk because their investments are in the insurer's separate account.

3. Surrender charges generally apply for how many years after an annuity is issued?
   A. 2 to 5
   B. 5 to 10
   C. 12 to 15
   D. 17 to 20

4. Deferred variable annuity premium payments purchase which of the following types of units?
   A. Value
   B. Accumulation
   C. Valuation
   D. Annuitization

5. Which of the following statements concerning equity indexed annuities is(are) CORRECT?
   A. The asset fee is an amount subtracted from any gain in an index before determining a change in the rate for crediting interest.
   B. The participation rate is the rate of regular contributions the contract holder makes to the annuity.
   C. Both A and B.
   D. Neither A nor B.

ANSWERS

1. **B.** John will earn the current rate of 5% the first year. The interest rate guarantee period is the period for which an insurance company's guarantee of the rate for crediting interest to an annuity is operative; a new rate for crediting interest will apply after the conclusion of the guarantee period. (8.22b(1))

2. **B.** Because of the length of the guarantees provided, financial strength of the insurance company is important. (8.11d)

3. **B.** Generally, surrender charges apply for the first 5 to 10 years after contract issue. (8.34a)

4. **B.** Each variable deferred annuity premium payment purchases accumulation units. (8.51d)

5. **A.** The participation rate is a fraction that is multiplied times the change in an index before determining a change in the rate for crediting to an equity indexed annuity. (8.44)

Annuities and Retirement

" *Before everything else, getting ready is the secret of success.* "

—Henry Ford

TERMS TO KNOW

Annuitization

Assumed investment return (AIR)

Exclusion ratio

Expected return

Fixed-amount annuity

Fixed-period annuity

Immediate annuity

Inflation

Joint and survivor life annuity

Joint and survivor life annuity with installment or cash refund

Joint and survivor life annuity with period certain

Life annuity with installment or cash refund

Life annuity with period certain

Life-only (straight life) annuity

Senior Protection in Annuity Transactions Model Regulation

Substandard (impaired risk) annuities

Suitability

Variable immediate annuity

9.1 IMMEDIATE ANNUITIES

Key point   Retirees purchase immediate annuities to protect against the risk of outliving their savings.

Key point   Annuities can be paid over one or more lifetimes with optional guarantees.

Key point   Exclusion ratio prevents taxation of the return of principal; interest is taxed proportionately (fractionally based on exclusion ratio) throughout the annuity period.

Key point   Annuity payments in a variable annuity depend on the returns in the investment accounts.

9.11   Purchasing an immediate annuity.

    a.   **Immediate annuity**: series of payments made to an annuitant within one month to one year after owner deposits money with insurer.

    b.   Two reasons immediate annuities are purchased:

        (1)   To protect against the risk of running out of income during life.

        (2)   To ensure the receipt of a series of payments over a fixed period of time.

    c.   Process.

        (1)   Annuity owner gives money to insurance company.

        (2)   Annuity payments must begin within a certain amount of time, within one month to one year.

    d.   Sources of funds: sale of asset, investment, inheritance, or from life insurance or deferred annuity.

9.12   Life contingencies.

    a.   Nonlife-contingent immediate annuities.

        (1)   **Fixed-period annuity:** an annuity for which annuitant (or a beneficiary) receives payments for a specified amount of time.

            (a)   Pay a premium and select time period that insurer will make periodic payments.

            (b)   Insurer determines amount that will be paid for the time period.

            (c)   If annuitant dies, payments to beneficiary continue until period ends.

> **EXAMPLE**   Gerry is the annuitant for a 5-year certain annuity with payments made monthly. At the end of the third year, Gerry dies. His beneficiary will receive the annuity payments for the remainder of the fixed period, which is two years.

        (2)   **Fixed-amount annuity:** annuity for which annuitant (or beneficiary) receives specified payments for a period determined by the insurer.

            (a)   Annuitant pays a premium and selects a periodic amount that insurer will pay.

            (b)   Insurer determines how long the periodic amount will be paid.

    (c) If annuitant dies, payments to beneficiary continue until period ends.

  b. Life-contingent immediate annuities.

    (1) Reason for purchase: fear that annuity owner's money will run out before annuitant dies.

    (2) Insurer must know date of birth and gender of annuitant to determine annuity amounts or payment periods.

  c. Types of life-contingent annuities.

    (1) **Life-only (straight life) annuity:** an annuity that pays a specified amount over the life of the annuitant.

      (a) If annuitant dies before the original deposit has been repaid, it is forfeited to the insurance company.

    (2) **Life annuity with period certain** (5, 10, 15, 20, 25, and 30 years): an annuity for which payments are made for the greater of the annuitant's lifetime or a specified period.

      (a) Payments made to a beneficiary if annuitant dies during the period certain.

> **E X A M P L E** Nicholas is the annuitant for a life with 10-year certain annuity with payments made annually. At the end of the 15th year, Nicholas dies. No further annuity payments will be made, since Nicholas died outside of the 10-year certain period. If, however, Nicholas had died after the fifth year, his beneficiary would have received annuity payments for the remainder of the fixed period, which would have been five years.

    (3) **Life annuity with installment or cash refund:** an annuity that pays the beneficiary, in installments or a lump sum, an amount equal to the unpaid balance of the original deposit should the annuitant die before the original deposit is paid out; two modes of payment:

      (a) Installment: periodic payments continue to a beneficiary until a full refund of the original deposit has been made.

      (b) Cash refund: beneficiary receives discounted present value of the remaining payments.

    (4) **Joint and survivor life annuity:** an annuity that pays income over the lives of two individuals.

      (a) Survivor may receive 100%, 75%, 66%, or 50% of payment made while both annuitants were alive.

      (b) Payments stop at the second annuitant's death.

    (5) **Joint and survivor life annuity with period certain:** an annuity for which the insurer continues payments to a beneficiary if both the annuitants die during the period certain.

    (6) **Joint and survivor life annuity with installment or cash refund:** an annuity that pays the beneficiary, in installments or a lump sum, an amount equal to the unpaid balance of the original deposit should both annuitants die before the original deposit is paid out.

> **EXAMPLE** Ben and Abby are the annuitants for a 50% joint and survivor life with installment refund annuity. They made a deposit of $100,000 to purchase the annuity. In the third year, Abby died. Ben then received 50% of the annuity payment he and Abby were receiving when Abby was alive. Four years later when a total of $80,000 had been paid out, Ben died. Max, the beneficiary, will continue to receive the annuity payment until the balance of the original $100,000 is paid out.

9.13 Annuitization and exclusion ratios.

   a. **Exclusion ratio:** a percentage of each annuity payment that is tax free to the annuitant.

   (1) The remainder is subject to ordinary income taxes.

   (2) Purpose: to allow the annuitant to receive part of the original deposit back tax free as return of premium.

   (3) Formula for life-only annuities.

$$\text{Exclusion ratio} = \frac{\text{total investment}}{\text{expected return}}$$

   (4) **Expected return**: income amount the annuitant should get back over a certain period.

   (a) Fixed-period or fixed-amount annuities: expected return equals sum of guaranteed payments.

   (b) Life expectancy annuities: expected return equals annual payments multiplied by number of years in life expectancy.

   ■ IRS Annuity Tables used for life expectancies.

   (5) Annuity payments after life expectancy.

   (a) Post-1986: exclusion ratio used until annuitant reaches life expectancy, at which point all future annuity payments are fully taxable.

> **EXAMPLE** Erin deposits $150,000 into an immediate annuity. She will receive $14,400 per year paid in monthly installments of $1,200 for the rest of her life. Erin is 68 and her Table V life expectancy is 17.6 years (see Figure 9-1).
>
> $$\text{Exclusion ratio} = \frac{\$150,000}{\$14,400 \times 17.6} = 59.19\%$$
>
> $14,400 × .5919 = 8,523 (nontaxable portion)
>
> $14,400 − $8,523 = 5,877 (taxable portion—Erin will receive a 1099 annually for this amount)

FIGURE 9-1

Extract from IRS Table V

IRS Table V—Ordinary Life Annuities One Life—Expected Return Multiples	
Age	Multiple
60	24.2
61	23.3
62	22.5
63	21.6
64	20.8
65	20.0
66	19.2
67	18.4
68	17.6
69	16.8
70	16.0

(6) Formula for life annuity with refund or period certain guarantee.

    (a) Same formula as life-only annuity, except actuarial value of the refund or period-certain guarantee must be deducted from total investment.

$$\frac{\text{Exclusion}}{\text{ratio}} = \frac{\text{total investment} - \text{value of refund or period certain}}{\text{expected return}}$$

    (b) Calculating the refund or period-certain guarantee's actuarial value is not shown because computer-generated illustrations often provide these numbers.

(7) Exclusion ratio for variable immediate annuities.

    (a) The fraction:

$$\frac{\text{Tax-free portion of}}{\text{each payment}} = \frac{\text{total investment (adjusted if necessary)}}{\text{number of years payments will be made}}$$

    (b) The tax-free portion remains the same each year regardless of fluctuations in annuity payments.

FIGURE 9-2

Extract from IRS Table VII

IRS Table VII—Percent Value of Refund Features Duration of Guaranteed Amount				
Age	Years			
Unisex	1	5	10	15
60	0	2	4	7
61	0	2	4	8
62	0	2	5	9
63	0	2	5	10
64	0	2	6	10
65	0	3	6	12

ZOOM IN   Alexander, age 62, purchases an installment refund annuity in 2007 for $130,000. He receives an annuity payment of $1,100 per month. Alexander's investment in the contract must be adjusted before calculating the exclusion ratio.

i. Unadjusted investment in the contract	$130,000
Divided by amount to be received annually	$ 13,200
Equals duration of guaranteed period	9.85 years
Rounded to nearest whole number	10 years
ii. Percentage value of guaranteed refund (Figure 9-2)	5%
iii. Value of refund feature	
5% of $130,000 rounded to the nearest dollar	$ 6,500
iv. Adjusted investment in the contract	$123,500

What is the exclusion ratio for Alexander's annuity payments?

Adjusted investment in the contract	$123,500
Guaranteed annuity payments for one year ($1,100 × 12)	$13,200
Life expectancy from Table V (see Figure 9-1)	22.5 years
Expected return ($13,200 × 22.5)	$297,000
Exclusion ratio ($123,500 ÷ $297,000)	41.6%
Annualized amount excludible from income each year (41.6% of $13,200)	$ 5,491
Amount includable in gross income ($13,200 − $5,491)	$ 7,709

EXAMPLE In 2007, Ryan, age 65, invests $110,000 in an immediate variable life annuity. In the first year, his annual variable annuity payments are $6,000. IRS Table V (see Figure 9-1) shows a life expectancy of 20 years.

$$\text{Tax-free portion of each payment} = \frac{\$110,000}{20}$$

The tax-free portion of each payment equals $5,500. During each of the first 20 years, $5,500 of the annual payments is not taxed to Ryan. Even if the variable payments fluctuate over the years, the amount excludable from income is $5,500 annually. After 20 years, Ryan's investment of $110,000 will have been returned to him and all future annuity payments are fully taxable.

9.14 Immediate annuity costs.

    a. Depends upon age and gender of annuitant, interest rates, and state premium taxes.

    b. Insurer spreads its risk over a large pool of annuitants.

        (1) Actuarial pricing model: forfeitures of those who die prematurely are used to make payments of those who live past life expectancy.

9.15 Annuity variations.

    a. Annuity/long-term care insurance (LTCI) combination.

        (1) Funded by single deposit.

        (2) Separate benefit for both needs.

        (3) LTC benefit is twice annuity account balance.

        (4) If there is a need for LTC benefit:

            (a) Annuity account is liquidated first.

            (b) LTCI pays for any remaining benefits.

        (5) If the insured dies before receiving any benefits, the beneficiary receives a death benefit equal to original deposit.

        (6) Few annuity/LTCI products exist today, but future growth is expected.

    b. Two-account annuity for LTC.

        (1) Two annuity accounts.

            (a) Fixed interest rate—similar to traditional annuity.

            (b) Significantly higher interest rate—withdrawals allowed if either is present:

              ■ Assistance with two or more activities of daily living (ADLs) is needed.

              ■ There is a cognitive impairment.

    c. **Substandard (impaired risk) immediate annuities**: special kind of immediate annuity with the following two characteristics:

        (1) Annuitant must undergo underwriting.

        (2) If health is poor, benefits may be greater due to decreased life expectancy (shorter annuity payout period).

9.16 Effects of inflation.

    a. Annuity payments are fixed and lose purchasing power during inflationary times.

> **EXAMPLE** Justin receives a $5,000 check each year, beginning in 2007. Assuming an inflation rate of 5%, in 2027, his $5,000 check will purchase an amount of goods equal to $1,884, or less than 38% of what the $5,000 purchased in 2007.

    b. Cost-of-living adjustment (COLA) rider.

        (1) Protects against inflation without the unpredictability of variable annuities.

        (2) For the same lump-sum deposit, initial annuity payments are less than payments without a COLA increase.

COLA Rider Comparison		
$50,000 Lump Sum Female Age 60	Level Payments (No COLA Rider)	Payments With 3% COLA Rider
Year 1	$325	$260
Year 5	$325	$293
Year 10	$325	$339
Year 15	$325	$393

9.17 Postannuitization liquidity.

  a. **Annuitization:** A series of payments from a deferred annuity or life insurance cash values.

  b. Risks to annuitizing.

  (1) Annuitant or beneficiary will not get back what could have been received under a different payout.

  (2) Once annuitization begins, there is no account balance from which the annuitant can withdraw if a large cash need arises.

> **E X A M P L E** Joshua makes a $100,000 lump-sum payment into an immediate annuity that will pay him $1,200 monthly for life. In year two of the annuity, he has a medical emergency and needs $10,000 cash. Since Joshua only has the right to receive $1,200 monthly (and does not own an account balance), the annuity cannot meet his $10,000 need.

  (3) Some companies have begun to allow limited access to lump-sum withdrawals under restricted circumstances.

9.18 Two considerations when comparing immediate annuities:

  a. Strength and financial stability of insurer.

  b. Dollar amount of payments for the equivalent lump sums.

  (1) Comparing interest rates only will not be helpful.

  (2) Mortality costs and other expenses must also be considered.

9.19 Variable immediate annuities.

  a. **Variable immediate annuity:** periodic annuity payments that are based on the performance of underlying investments.

  (1) Designed to compensate for loss of purchasing power due to inflation.

  (2) Annuity owner assumes more risk for higher return potential.

  (3) Insurer assumes mortality and expense risks.

  (4) Market share is small, but baby boomers needing additional retirement income may contribute to market growth.

  b. Assumed investment return (AIR).

  (1) Owner chooses from different subaccounts to create appropriate asset allocation mix.

(a) Allocation may be changed among subaccounts offered.

(2) **Assumed investment return (AIR)**: interest rate that the insurer and annuity owner presume will be earned on underlying investments of the annuity.

(a) AIR, along with expense and mortality assumptions, will determine the amount of the two initial monthly annuity checks.

(b) After first two checks, if investment accounts are:

■ Greater than AIR: monthly payments increase.

■ Less than AIR: monthly payments decrease.

c. Variable immediate annuity costs.

(1) Prospectus identifies costs.

(2) Initial annuity payments from variable immediate annuity will be less than payments from fixed immediate annuity.

(3) Expense charge percentage must be added to AIR to determine the gross interest rate.

> **EXAMPLE** Julian chooses an AIR of 4% for his immediate annuity. Assumed expenses and mortality charges equal 2%. The first two annuity checks he receives are based on the 4% AIR and assumed expenses and mortality of 2% (a gross interest rate of 6%). The annuity investment account actually earns 3% and expenses and mortality still equal 2%. Therefore, Julian's future annuity payments for the year will be down by 1%.

9.2 ANNUITIES AND RETIREMENT

Key point Concerns that seniors will outlive their assets are based on inadequate savings, increased life expectancies, and inflation.

Key point Choices in developing an annuity plan for a client include premiums (lump-sum or periodic deposits); immediate versus deferred; and whether the annuity is fixed, indexed, or variable.

9.21 Retirement problem: seniors outliving their assets. Three reasons:

a. Inadequate savings.

b. Life expectancy continues to increase.

c. **Inflation**: rise in the price of goods and services.

9.22 Annuity solution.

a. Preferential to have the guarantee of a life income from an annuity rather than depending on earnings from investments.

(1) Annuity uses principal and interest to provide income.

b. Variable or equity-indexed annuities may provide protection against inflation.

  (1) These products also have the risk of poor return during market declines.

9.23 Fact finder.

  a. Comprehensive fact finder: use in entirety to calculate retirement income needs.

  (1) Make recommendations based on cash flow, risk tolerance, and investment objectives.

  b. Dominant need approach: complete selected parts of fact finder, such as personal information, risk tolerance, and retirement income sources sections.

9.24 Designing the plan.

  a. Objective: receiving the highest value for the money deposited.

  b. Approach.

  (1) Start with straightforward plan design: immediate or deferred annuity.

  (2) Offer product choices based on risk tolerance and objectives of client.

  (3) Develop a plan that meets financial goals with the client's investment amount.

9.25 Plan criteria.

  a. Type of premium.

  (1) Single premium deferred annuity (SPDA): for a large sum of money set aside for retirement.

  (2) Flexible premium retirement annuity (FPRA): used to steadily accumulate retirement benefits by making periodic deposits.

  b. Start of annuity payments.

  (1) Deferred annuity: for clients who want money to grow tax deferred.

  (a) Most have retirement dates when deferred annuity converts to immediate annuity.

  (b) Owner can postpone this conversion by written request.

  (c) Retirees can transfer funds from a qualified retirement plan into a fixed or equity-indexed annuity that maintains qualified status.

  ■ No income taxation at time of transfer.

  ■ Continued tax deferral.

  ■ Safety of principal.

  ■ Moderate growth potential.

  (d) Reduction of Social Security benefit taxation.

  ■ Can reduce taxable income by transferring taxable investments into a tax-deferred annuity (this income not counted as income for Social Security).

  (e) Reverse mortgage (HUD) line of credit with a fixed-interest deferred annuity.

  ■ Lump-sum loan invested in deferred annuity.

  ■ Retirement is funded with line of credit until annuity payments begin.

(f) Other uses:

- Invest proceeds from sale of business or residence.

- Charitable giving strategy.

- College education funding.

(2) Immediate annuity: used for clients with large lump sums and a need for income over a long period.

(a) A conservative percentage of liquid assets invested in an immediate annuity provides guaranteed period payments within the client's investment portfolio.

(b) Can also be used to provide a guaranteed periodic income to pay for other financial products, such as long-term care insurance.

(c) Fixed immediate annuity distributions.

- Give the retiree a guarantee that income payments will remain steady over a specified period.

(d) Variable immediate annuity distributions.

- Payments keep better pace with inflation when compared to fixed income annuities.

- Can choose various accounts based on client's risk tolerance.

c. Investment of annuity funds.

(1) Fixed-interest annuity.

(a) For those who want safety of principal and a set interest rate.

(b) Can provide balance to a portfolio for moderate to aggressive investors.

(2) Equity-indexed annuity.

(a) For those who want protection of principal and potential stock market gains.

(b) Appropriate for individuals in 50s and early 60s.

(c) Good place to move matured CDs.

- Principal remains safe.

(d) These annuities are complex and can be difficult to understand.

- Formula for determining interest uses index averaging and caps.

(3) Variable annuity: recommend for clients with high risk tolerance and long investment time horizons; more likely to keep pace with inflation.

9.3 MUTUAL FUND VERSUS VARIABLE DEFERRED ANNUITY (VDA)

Key point The expense ratio for VDAs is higher than for mutual funds.

Key point The extra expense pays for the mortality feature of the annuity and for any guarantees or other features.

9.31 Average total expense ratios.

    a. Mutual fund: 1.41%.

    b. Variable deferred annuity: 2.26%.

        (1) Higher ratio due to insurance feature.

9.32 Best comparison method: pinpoint the actual mutual fund costs and compare the cost difference with the variable annuity costs.

9.33 Product feature variations.

	VDAs	Mutual Funds
Payout option guarantees	Several	None
Guaranteed death benefit	Yes	No
Death benefit amount	Greater of premium or account value	Account value
Withdrawals	Insurer surrender charges, if any; IRS penalties if under age 59½	Limits depend on class of shares; no IRS penalties
Guaranteed minimum interest account	Available	Not available
Transfers	Often allowed between sub-accounts without taxes or expenses	No charge if within fund family, but taxable
Guaranteed living benefits rider	Available	Not available
Enhanced death benefits rider	Available	Not available
Taxation of gains	100% tax deferred until death or withdrawal, then taxes as ordinary income	Tax on distribution of dividends and capital gains; tax on capital gains if sold
Excise tax on investment	Few states impose a state premium tax	None
Stepped-up cost basis at death	Not available	Yes

9.4 VARIABLE ANNUITIES REGULATION

> **Key point** Variable annuities are subject to federal securities regulation, and an NASD license is required to sell them.
>
> **Key point** Securities regulations require that a prospectus be delivered to a customer and that the product be suitable for the client.

9.41 Variable products must be deemed suitable for a client.

9.42   Client must receive a prospectus.

9.43   NASD and SEC are involved.

9.44   Also supervised by state.

9.45   Must complete investor profile form (risk tolerance, time horizon, etc.). See **www.sec.gov/investor/pubs/varannty.htm**.

9.5   SENIOR PROTECTION IN ANNUITY TRANSACTIONS MODEL REGULATION

Key point   The purpose of senior protection is to prevent abusive annuity sales.

Key point   An advisor must believe an annuity recommendation is suitable to a client's tax situation, financial condition, and investment goals.

9.51   Purposes:

    a.   **Senior Protection in Annuity Transactions Model Regulation**: Sets standards and processes for annuity product recommendations to seniors.

    b.   Safeguards seniors against abusive annuity sales.

9.52   **Suitability**: required element in selling fixed annuities and variable annuities in which registered agents must complete an investor profile form by asking potential clients about their investment goals, risk tolerance, and time horizon when filling out a policy application.

9.53   Major issues covered:

    a.   Insurance needs of seniors must be properly addressed.

    b.   Advisor must believe that an annuity is appropriate for the senior.

    c.   Protection of seniors at sale and upon surrender.

    d.   Requires insurers to set norms for compliance, training, and monitoring.

9.54   Definitions.

    a.   Annuity: any fixed or variable annuity that is individually solicited, whether for individuals or groups.

    b.   Recommendation: advice provided by an insurance producer to an individual senior consumer that results in a purchase or exchange of an annuity product based on that advice.

    c.   Senior consumer: any person aged 65 or older.

9.55   Exemptions from suitability requirement include direct response annuity solicitations, employee pension plans, 401(k) plans, government or church plans, 457 plans, structured settlement annuities, and nonqualified deferred compensation plans.

9.56   Duties of insurer and producer.

    a.   Advisor must have reason to believe that the recommendation is suitable based on the senior's:

        (1)   Tax situation.

        (2)   Financial condition.

        (3)   Investment goals.

        (4)   Other reasonable information used in making recommendations.

    b.   Advisor has no obligation to make a recommendation if the senior:

        (1)   Does not provide complete and truthful information.

        (2)   Declines to provide relevant information requested.

        (3)   Enters into a transaction not recommended by the advisor.

    c.   Insurers must have a system to oversee advisors' recommendations with:

        (1)   Written processes.

        (2)   Regular reviews of records targeted at identifying and avoiding violations of the regulation.

    d.   Insurance companies are not required to:

        (1)   Review all transactions of an advisor.

        (2)   Include recommendations for products not offered by the insurance company.

9.57   Recordkeeping.

    a.   Records of information used to make recommendations must be kept on file.

        (1)   Length of time to be kept depends on state law.

        (2)   Expectation is that information will be kept for at least five years after the annuity no longer exists.

9.6   ASSET PROTECTION

Key point   Annuities can be used to protect the owner's assets from creditors, depending on the type of annuity and applicable state law.

Key point   This protection is unique to life insurance company products, such as annuities.

9.61   Annuities can be used to protect the owner's assets from creditors, depending on the type of annuity and state law.

9.62   Check with insurance company or client's attorney before mentioning protection.

9.7 ETHICAL CONSIDERATIONS

> **Key point**   A financial services professional has three ethical obligations: (1) to match a product to the clients need, (2) to properly inform the client, and (3) to place a client's business only with companies that are financially sound.

9.71   Appropriateness.

    a.   Must try to match senior's objectives with appropriate annuity product.

    b.   State problems in a way the senior will understand.

    c.   Know the annuity products and what needs they can meet.

9.72   Prospect and client education.

    a.   Seniors will benefit most from annuities if they understand them. They should know:

        (1)   When the annuity moves from the accumulation phase to the distribution phase.

        (2)   What distribution choice best meets their needs.

        (3)   Availability of and charges for surrenders.

        (4)   How equity-indexed or variable annuities work, if they are recommended.

9.73   Due care considerations.

    a.   When recommending annuities, advisors are usually investing funds that seniors rely on.

    b.   Advisors must know about safety of insurer and use those with at least two high-quality ratings.

        (1)   Ability to pay claims.

        (2)   Investment assets.

        (3)   Ability to pay, from the general account, competitive interest and dividends on permanent life insurance and annuities.

HIGHLIGHTS

Highlight 1: Immediate Annuities

- Immediate annuities are purchased to protect against the risk of running out of income during life, or to ensure the receipt of a series of payments over a fixed period of time. (9.12)
  (1) Nonlife contingent immediate annuities can be either for a fixed period or a fixed amount.
  (2) Single life contingent immediate annuities are life-only, life with period certain, or life with installment or cash refund.
  (3) Joint life contingent immediate annuities are joint and survivor life, joint and survivor life with period certain, or joint and survivor life with installment or cash refund.

- The exclusion ratio is the percentage of each annuity payment that is tax free to the annuitant. (9.13)

- Annuity variations include annuity/long-term care insurance (LTCI), two-account annuity for long-term care, a deferred annuity with two accounts, and a substandard annuity. (9.15)

- Variable immediate annuities are designed to compensate for loss of purchasing power due to inflation. (9.19a)

Highlight 2: Annuities and Retirement

- Three reasons seniors are concerned they will outlive their assets: (9.25b(2))
  (1) Inadequate savings, since they are increasingly more dependent on this as a source of retirement income.
  (2) Increased life expectancy, which requires retirement income over a longer period of time.
  (3) Inflation, the rise in the price of goods and services, causes retirement funds to lose purchasing power.

- When designing a retirement plan funded by an annuity, the goal is for the client to receive the highest value for the money deposited.
  (1) Start with a straightforward plan design and decide whether an immediate or deferred annuity is needed.
  (2) Offer product choices based on the risk tolerance and objectives of the client.
  (3) Develop a plan that meets the financial goals with the client's investment amount.

- There are three criteria to consider when developing a plan: (9.25)
  (1) Type of premium, whether a single lump sum or periodic deposits.
  (2) The start of annuity payments, whether immediate or deferred to a later date.
  (3) The investment earnings of the funds, whether fixed, based on an equity index, or variable.

Highlight 3: Mutual Fund Versus Variable Deferred Annuity

- Average total expense ratios are lower for mutual funds (1.41%) than they are for a variable deferred annuity (2.26%).

- The best way to compare a mutual fund with a variable deferred annuity is to pinpoint the actual mutual fund costs and compare the cost difference with the variable annuity costs.

■ Product features vary when comparing a mutual fund to a variable deferred annuity. These features include payout option guarantees, guaranteed death benefits, death benefits, withdrawals, guaranteed minimum interest, and transfers. (9.3)

Highlight 4: Variable Annuities Regulation

■ Variable annuities are regulated and must be deemed suitable for a client.

■ The NASD and SEC are involved in the regulation, as are individual states.

■ All clients must complete an investor profile form, which gathers client information, such as risk tolerance and time horizons. (9.25c(3))

Highlight 5: Senior Protection in Annuity Transactions Model Regulation

■ There are three purposes of the model regulation:
(1) Safeguards seniors against abusive annuity sales.
(2) Ascertains that seniors' insurance needs and objectives are properly considered when making an annuity recommendation.
(3) Sets standards and processes for annuity product recommendations to seniors.

■ The model regulation outlines the duties of the insurer and the producer. (9.57)
(1) The advisor must have reason to believe that the recommendation is suitable based on the senior's tax situation, financial condition, and investment goals.
(2) The recommendation must be reasonable based on all of the known facts.
(3) Insurers must have a system to oversee advisors' recommendations with written processes, regular reviews of records, and other processes as needed.

■ Records of information used to make recommendations must be kept on file for a length of time to be determined by each state, which is expected to be at least five years.

Highlight 6: Asset Protection

■ Annuities can be used to protect the owner's assets from creditors, depending on the type of annuity and applicable state law.

■ This protection is unique to life insurance company products, such as annuities. (9.72)

Highlight 7: Ethical Considerations

■ There are three ethical considerations for an advisor:
(1) The appropriateness of the annuity, which is determined by how well the senior's objectives match the annuity product's features.
(2) Prospect and client education, since seniors will benefit most from annuities if they understand them.
(3) Due care considerations, which involve the advisor's responsibility to know about the safety of the insurer. (9.72)

TERMS TO KNOW DEFINITIONS

Annuitization A series of payments from a deferred annuity or life insurance cash values. (9.17a)

Assumed investment return (AIR) Interest rate that the insurer and annuity owner presume will be earned on underlying investments of the annuity. (9.19b(2))

Exclusion ratio A percentage of each annuity payment that is tax free to the annuitant; equals the total investment into an annuity divided by its expected return. (9.13a)

Expected return Income amount the annuitant should get back over a certain time period. (9.13a(4))

Fixed-amount annuity Annuity for which an annuitant (or beneficiary) receives specified payments for a period determined by the insurer. (9.12(a)(2))

Fixed-period annuity An annuity for which an annuitant (or a beneficiary) receives payments for a specified amount of time. (9.12(a)(1))

Immediate annuity An annuity contract that provides for the first payment of the annuity at the end of the first interval of payment after the owner deposits money with insurer. (9.11)

Inflation Rise in the price of goods and services. (9.21c)

Joint and survivor life annuity Provides monthly payments to the participant during the participant's lifetime; if, at the participant's death, the beneficiary is still living, a designated part of the participant's benefit continues to be paid to the beneficiary for the remainder of the beneficiary's life. (9.12c(4))

Joint and survivor life annuity with installment or cash refund An annuity that pays the beneficiary, in installments or a lump sum, an amount equal to the unpaid balance of the original deposit should both annuitants die before the original deposit is paid out. (9.12c(6))

Joint and survivor life annuity with period certain An annuity for which the insurer continues payments to a beneficiary if both the annuitants die during the period certain. (9.12c(5))

Life annuity with installment or cash refund An annuity that pays the beneficiary, in installments or a lump sum, an amount equal to the unpaid balance of the original deposit should the annuitant die before the original deposit is paid out. (9.12c(3))

Life annuity with period certain (5, 10, 15, 20, 25, and 30 years) An annuity for which payments are made for the greater of the annuitant's lifetime or a specified period. (9.12c(2))

Life-only annuity An annuity that pays a specified amount over the life of the annuitant. (9.12c(1))

Senior Protection in Annuity Transactions Model Regulation Sets standards and processes for annuity product recommendation to seniors. (9.51a)

Substandard (impaired risk) annuities Special kind of immediate annuity in which the insurer requires the annuitant to undergo underwriting and benefits may be greater due to decreased life expectancy (shorter annuity payout period) if the annuitant's health is poor. (9.15c)

Suitability Required element in selling fixed annuities and variable annuities in which registered agents must complete an investor profile form by asking potential clients about their investment goals, risk tolerance, and time horizon when filling out a policy application. (9.52)

Variable immediate annuity Periodic annuity payments that are based on the performance of underlying investments. (9.19a)

QUESTIONS

1. Andrew, age 65, purchases an installment refund annuity in 2007 for $105,000. He receives a monthly annuity payment of $900. The guaranteed refund according to IRS Table VII is 6%, and Andrew's life expectancy from IRS Table V is 20 years. On what amount of Andrew's monthly payment will he be taxed at ordinary rates?
   A. $0
   B. $411
   C. $489
   D. $900

2. Under the Senior Protection in Annuity Transactions Model Regulation, a senior consumer is defined as any person
   A. receiving Social Security
   B. retired from his job
   C. age 62 or older
   D. age 65 or older

3. Which of the following is(are) a product variation(s) of mutual funds and variable deferred annuities?
   A. Both the mutual fund and the variable deferred annuity have a guaranteed minimum interest account.
   B. Mutual funds have several payout option guarantees from which to choose.
   C. Both A and B.
   D. Neither A nor B.

4. How does a fixed-interest deferred annuity benefit a client receiving Social Security?
   A. The annuity can be exchanged for a higher Social Security benefit.
   B. It can reduce taxable income because it is not counted as income for Social Security purposes.
   C. Both A and B.
   D. Neither A nor B.

5. All of the following are required under variable annuities regulation EXCEPT
   A. the client must receive a prospectus
   B. NASD and SEC are involved
   C. the client must complete an investor profile form
   D. fixed products must be deemed suitable for a client

ANSWERS

1. **C.**

Value of refund feature (6% of $105,000)	$ 6,300
Adjusted investment in the contract ($105,000 − $6,300)	$ 98,700

Calculate the exclusion ratio:

Adjusted investment in the contract	$ 98,700
Guaranteed annuity payments for one year ($900 × 12)	$ 10,800
Life expectancy from Table V	20 years
Expected return ($10,800 × 20 years)	$216,000
Exclusion ratio ($98,700 ÷ $216,000) 45.7%	
Monthly amount excludible from income ($900 × 45.7%)	$411.00
Monthly amount includible as ordinary income	$489.00

(9.13a(6))

2. **D.** A senior consumer is defined under the Model Regulation as any person age 65 or older. (9.54c)

3. **D.** Only variable deferred annuities have a guaranteed minimum interest account and payout option guarantees. (9.33)

4. **B.** Income from funds transferred into a tax-deferred annuity can reduce taxable income because it is not counted as income for Social Security purposes. (9.25b(1)(d))

5. **D.** Fixed products are not subject to variable annuities regulations. Variable, not fixed, annuities must be deemed suitable for a client. (9.4)

6,300

6% × 105,000 = 6,300

105,000
−6,300
_____
98,700

$900 × 12 =
$10,800
× 20
_____
$216,000

98,700 / 216,000 = 45.7%

45.7% × $900 = $411.00

10

Tax Treatment of Pension Distributions

"Reflect on your present blessings—of which every man has many—not on your past misfortunes, of which all men have some."

—Charles Dickens

TERMS TO KNOW

Capital-gains provision

Cost basis

Direct rollover

Eligible rollover distribution

Lump-sum distribution

Net unrealized appreciation (NUA)

Reportable economic benefits (REBs)

Rollover

Sec. 72(t) penalty tax

Substantially equal periodic payments exception

Ten-year averaging

Trustee-to-trustee transfer

10.1 TAX TREATMENT OF DISTRIBUTIONS

Key point   Distributions are 100% taxable as ordinary income, but there is a 10% penalty in addition to tax for distributions before age 59½ (25% in first two years of a SIMPLE plan).

Key point   The three types of nontaxable distributions are recovery of nondeductible contributions, reportable economic benefits (formerly known as PS 58 costs), and rollovers.

Key point   The four exceptions to the 10% penalty in all plan types are: substantially equal periodic payments, death, disability, and medical expenses.

10.11 General income tax treatment of distributions.

  a. In the year of the distribution, the entire distribution's value will be treated as ordinary income.

  (1) Any cost basis can be recovered (e.g., after-tax contributions).

  (2) A 10% Sec. 72(t) penalty tax applies to most distributions made before the taxpayer reaches age 59½.

  b. The taxable part may be eligible for one or more special tax advantages if the distribution is a single sum.

  (1) Must be distributed from a qualified plan and meet lump-sum requirements.

  (2) Special capital gains treatment and 10-year forward averaging may be available to taxpayers born before 1936.

  c. Most distributions are eligible for rollover treatment.

  (1) Minimum distribution rules require distributions to start when the participant reaches age 70½ in most cases.

10.12 Estate taxation of pension benefits.

  a. Tax-sheltered benefits payable to a beneficiary at the participant's death will be included in the taxable estate of the participant.

  (1) Benefits payable to beneficiaries are subject to income tax.

  (2) The amount of the benefit is considered income in respect of the decedent (i.e., income taxes will be decreased by the amount of estate taxes paid as a result of the pension benefit).

10.13 **Sec. 72(t) penalty tax**: 10% tax penalty required on distributions prior to age 59½ from all types of tax-advantaged retirement plans (unless an exception applies).

  a. Penalty tax does not apply unless income tax applies; two examples of distributions not subject to income tax and, therefore, not subject to the penalty:

  (1) When the benefit rolls over from one tax-deferred plan to another.

  (2) Portion of a distribution that is nontaxable.

  b. Five exceptions allow the 10% penalty to be avoided if the distribution is:

  (1) **Substantially equal periodic payments exception**: payments made at least once per year over the life or life expectancy of the beneficiary and employee.

  (a) To qualify for substantially equal periodic payments from a qualified plan, the employee must leave employment.

(2) Made for the purpose of paying medical expenses deductible for the year under Sec. 213 (medical expenses that go beyond 7.5% of adjusted gross income).

(3) After an employee ends employment for early retirement after age 55.

(4) Result of a disability.

(5) To an employee's estate or a beneficiary on or after the employee's death.

c. Three more exceptions apply specifically to IRAs (including SEPs and SIMPLEs); IRA distributions are not subject to the penalty if the allocation is for:

(1) Payment made to purchase a first home for the participant, spouse, or any grandchild, child, or ancestor of the spouse or participant.

    (a) Lifetime limit: $10,000 per IRA participant.

    (b) Acquisition costs are considered qualified when used to build, purchase, or rebuild a first home.

    (c) The first home requirement is satisfied if the taxpayer and spouse have not owned a principal residence for the two preceding years.

(2) Payment of health insurance premiums by a person who is receiving unemployment insurance.

(3) Payment made to cover qualified higher education costs for the education of the taxpayer, the taxpayer's spouse, or any grandchild or child of the taxpayer's spouse or taxpayer at an eligible postsecondary educational facility.

    (a) Qualified educational costs include necessary supplies, fees, books, tuition, and equipment. Room and board are qualified expenses for students who are taking at least half of the full-time course load.

    (b) Qualified educational institutions include any postsecondary school that is qualified to get involved in the US Department of Education's student assistance programs.

    (c) Nearly all public, proprietary, nonprofit, and accredited postsecondary schools qualify for the exemption.

> **EXAMPLE** David, age 40, takes a distribution from his IRA to pay for his child's college education. David's distribution is not subject to the 10% penalty.

d. Three strategies for avoiding the Sec. 72(t) penalty tax:

(1) Exceptions for educational costs.

    (a) A taxpayer who qualifies for the exemption must pay qualified educational costs for a member in the taxpayer's family.

    (b) Educational expenses that are exempt from the penalty tax can be paid from IRAs, gifts, loans, wages, or an inheritance.

    (c) Qualified educational costs that are paid with certain funds are subject to the penalty tax (Pell grants, tax-free scholarships, educational aid from an employer, VA assistance, and tax-free distributions from Coverdell education accounts).

(2) Age 55 exemption.

(a) An individual must terminate employment on or after reaching age 55; the following distributions are exempt from the Sec. 72(t) penalty tax:

- Distributions from qualified plans.

- Distributions from 403(b) plans.

- Installment distributions from qualified and 403(b) plans.

- Annuity payments from qualified and 403(b) plans.

(b) Distributions in IRAs are subject to the penalty tax.

(3) Substantially equal periodic payment exception.

(a) Five reasons why this strategy is the most useful exception for planning:

- Flexible.

- Plans of all types qualify; however, participants of qualified plans must first separate from service.

- Appeals to persons needing withdrawals to meet needs.

- Works for persons needing large one-sum amounts; participants can borrow the money and repay the loan with the periodic payments.

- Substantially equal periodic payments can begin at any age if the payments are designed to continue throughout life.

(b) Three IRS-approved methods for calculating withdrawals:

- Fixed amortization method: same annual payments each year.

- Annuitization: account balance is divided by a life annuity factor based on an interest rate and mortality table.

- Required minimum distribution method: the annual account balance is divided by a number found on the life expectancy table that corresponds to that year.

(c) The interest rate used may not exceed 120% of the federal midterm rate for either of the two months directly preceding the month in which the first distribution is made.

(d) Distribution amounts are based on lifetime payments, which can stop without penalty, after the participant is 59½ years old or payments have been made for five years, whichever comes later.

(e) Amount calculated for the distribution must be distributed each year.

- Failure to make the required distribution will result in the 10% penalty tax being applied to all distributions made before the participant reached age 59½.

(f) Three types of life expectancy tables may be used: single life table, uniform lifetime table, and joint and survivor table.

10.14 Nontaxable distributions: four kinds:

a. Traditional IRAs.

(1) If an individual has made nondeductible contributions to an IRA or non-taxable amounts have been rolled into the IRA from a qualified plan, a part of each IRA distribution will be excluded from tax:

$$\text{Amount excluded} = \frac{\text{unrecovered cost basis}}{\text{total IRA account} + \text{current year's distributions}} \times \text{distribution amount}$$

   (a) Cost basis: amounts in a tax-advantaged retirement plan that have been previously taxed (e.g., employee after-tax contributions).

   (b) Calculation takes into consideration all the IRAs an individual owns.

   (c) Calculation is used each year until all nondeductible contributions have been recovered; distributions after that point are fully taxable.

b. Reportable economic benefits (REBs): formerly known as PS 58 costs; cost basis accumulated over time when a person has life insurance included in a 403(b) annuity or qualified plan; cost of term insurance part of the policy is included in income every year.

   (1) Self-employed persons: do not accumulate REBs; therefore, cannot recover them at distribution.

   (2) Recovering REBs: can be recovered only if the policy is distributed to the participant.

   (a) If participant wants to cancel the policy:

   ■ Policy's cash value can be stripped by trustee through borrowing to lower cash value to REBs; trustee can then distribute contract and cash.

   ■ Participant can then terminate the policy and recover the REBs tax free.

   ■ To avoid tax, the participant can roll over the cash to an IRA.

   (b) If participant dies and beneficiary receives proceeds from policy:

   ■ Beneficiary recovers REBs tax free.

   ■ Beneficiary must pay tax on policy's cash value minus unrecovered cost basis.

c. Rollovers from qualified plans.

   (1) When a person receives a distribution from a qualified plan that may be rolled into an IRA, the entire distribution may be rolled over.

   (a) Rolled over amounts are subject to IRA recovery rules.

   (b) The individual may choose to roll over only the taxable portion and will avoid income taxes on the rollover.

   (c) Life insurance policies cannot be rolled into an IRA.

d. Single-sum distributions.

   (1) Recovery of basis occurs at the time of the distribution when a participant receives the whole benefit and does not roll the benefit into an IRA or other tax-sheltered retirement plan.

10.15 Distribution of after-tax contributions before the starting date of the annuity.

    a. Before 1987, a participant's cash basis could be withdrawn without being taxed.

        (1) Grandfather provision allows a participant to withdraw the equivalent pre-1987 amount if the plan permitted in-service distributions.

    b. Withdrawals are now partially subject to income tax.

        (1) The fraction that is excluded from taxation is the cash basis divided by the total account balance at the time of distribution.

> **EXAMPLE**   In 2007, Elaine has $2,000 in her account. $500 of this amount can be attributed to post-1986 employee contributions and $125 can be attributed to investment earnings on $500. Elaine takes an in-service distribution of $250. Elaine can exclude $500 divided by $625 (80%) of her distribution, or $200. Therefore, Elaine receives $200 income tax free and will pay tax only on $50.

10.16 Periodic distributions from 403(b) annuities and qualified plans.

    a. Divide the cost basis by the number of expected monthly annuity payments to determine the nontaxable amount.

        (1) For life annuities, the number of months is derived from Figure 10-1.

        (2) For joint and survivor annuities, see Figure 10-2.

    b. **Cost basis**: after-tax contributions less amounts received before the annuity starting date.

    c. $\text{Tax-free amount of annuity} = \dfrac{\text{cost basis}}{\text{number of monthly payments}}$

        (1) The excluded amount remains constant, even if the payment changes.

        (2) The excluded amount may be greater than the payment, in which case the entire payment is excluded from gross income.

        (3) After the investment is recovered, remaining payments will be fully taxable.

10.17 Tax treatment of Roth IRAs and Roth account distributions.

    a. Roth IRA distributions: qualifying distributions are tax free; two requirements:

        (1) Distribution was made more than five years after the Roth IRA was created.

        (2) Distribution was made under any one of the following circumstances:

            (a) Participant is at least age 59½.

            (b) Participant dies, causing the beneficiary to receive the distribution.

            (c) Participant is disabled.

            (d) Participant uses distribution to pay qualified first-time homebuyer costs within 120 days of the distribution; $10,000 lifetime limit per IRA participant.

        (3) Nonqualified distributions: (do not meet both rules in 10.17a(1) and (2) above).

FIGURE 10-1

Single Life Annuity

Age of Participant	Number of Months
71 and over	160
66–70	210
61–65	260
56–60	310
55 and under	360

FIGURE 10-2

Joint Annuity

Combined Age of Participants	Number of Months
More than 140	210
131–140	260
121–130	310
111–120	360
110 or less	410

(a) Person's contributions (Roth IRA or converted) can be withdrawn tax free; earnings are subject to both income tax and 10% penalty tax.

(b) For converted Roth IRAs, 10% penalty tax applies for five years after conversion, even if no income tax is due.

(c) Exceptions to premature distribution penalty are the same as for traditional IRAs (see Section 4.44c in assignment 4).

b. Roth account (e.g., Roth 401(k) and Roth 403(b) plans) distributions.

(1) Similar to Roth IRAs: qualifying distributions from Roth accounts are not subject to federal income tax; qualification requirements to avoid tax are the same.

(2) Different from Roth IRAs: two differences:

(a) Tax treatment of nonqualifying distributions:

■ Roth account: recovery method applying to distributions of after-tax contributions made after 1986 also applies to nonqualifying distributions from a Roth 401(k).

■ Roth IRA: withdrawals of contributions are not subject to income tax.

(b) Applying the five-tax-year rule:

■ Roth account: no aggregation allowed (unless if a person chooses a direct rollover to one Roth 401(k) plan from another); otherwise, each Roth 401(k) must meet the rule.

10.18 Tax treatment of distributions from an IRA contributed to a charity.

    a. Distribution is taxable; charitable deduction may apply.

    b. Pension Protection Act of 2006: certain distributions from IRAs are not included in participant's income if six conditions are met (applies only to distributions made in 2006 and 2007):

        (1) $100,000 limit each taxable year for each taxpayer.

        (2) Contributions only to public charities.

        (3) Distribution may not go to participant; trustee must directly contribute to charity.

        (4) Distribution must occur when participant reaches at least 70½ years old.

        (5) Distribution must be only from IRAs or Roth IRAs.

        (6) Contribution must be deductible under the present charitable deduction rules.

    c. Four benefits of this income exclusion:

        (1) Contribution is completely excluded from income.

        (2) Other tax issues are avoided because AGI does not increase.

        (3) Distributions are considered in meeting mandatory minimum distribution rules.

        (4) Participant's taxable estate is lowered by the contribution amount.

10.2 ROLLOVERS

> **Key point** Rollovers are tax-free transfers from one retirement plan to another.
>
> **Key point** Direct rollovers are funds sent to the trustee of a new plan; indirect rollovers are funds received by a participant who can reinvest the funds within 60 days, once a year, and are subject to 20% income tax withholding.
>
> **Key point** The seven types of distributions that do not qualify for rollover are: hardship withdrawals from 401(k) plans, minimum required distributions, substantially equal periodic payments, life insurance policy expenses, loans considered distributions, dividends on employer securities, and corrective distributions.

10.21 Rollover and direct rollover rules.

    a. **Rollover**: a distribution from a plan that a participant personally receives and deposits into another plan without tax consequences (also known as an indirect rollover or regular rollover).

        (1) General rule: distributions from qualified plans, 457 plans and 403(b) plans can be rolled into an IRA free from tax and the 10% penalty if the rollover is made within 60 days after the participant receives the distribution.

        (2) Sixty-day rule: distributions not rolled over within 60 days of receipt are subject to income tax and the 10% Sec. 72(t) penalty tax, if applicable.

        (3) Waiver of 60-day requirement: applies where the absence of waiver would be inequitable or unconscionable, such as in the event of a casualty, disaster, or other event beyond a participant's reasonable control. (See Section 10.25 for more on the waiver rule.)

(4) Mandatory 20% income tax on rollovers: applies to indirect rollovers when the participant receives the distribution; participant receives only 80% of total benefit.

(5) One-year rule: only one indirect rollover is allowed per plan per year.

b. Direct rollover: a distribution from a plan sent directly by the trustee of the distributing plan to the trustee of the receiving plan without touching the hands of the participant.

(1) Qualified plans, 457 governmental plans, and 403(b) tax-sheltered annuities must give participants the option to elect a direct rollover where eligible distributions are directly transferred from one plan trustee to the trustee of another plan or an IRA (**a trustee-to-trustee transfer**).

(2) Participants can avoid the 20% mandatory withholding rule by electing a direct rollover.

(a) In an indirect rollover, the participant must pay 20% income tax withholding on the distribution and will receive only 80% of the entire benefit; the remaining 20% must be contributed from funds from other sources.

Note: Distributions from traditional IRAs, SEPs, and SIMPLEs do not fall under the direct rollover rule or the 20% withholding rule.

(3) The 60-day rollover requirement does not apply to direct rollovers because the funds are never in the participant's possession.

(4) The one-year requirement also does not apply to direct rollovers.

c. Rollovers into qualified plans versus rollovers into IRAs.

(1) Rollovers into IRAs: flexibility in withdrawing and investing the benefits.

(a) Beneficiary may withdraw benefits from an IRA during his life expectancy if participant dies when funds are in an IRA.

(b) Asset protection in bankruptcy: funds in an IRA may not be protected from creditors' claims in bankruptcy (varies by state).

(2) Rollovers into qualified plans: provide limited distribution choices to the beneficiary of the plan when the plan participant dies while the funds remain in the plan; the beneficiary may receive only restricted installment payments or a one-sum distribution.

(a) Qualified plans allow participants to borrow from the plan.

(b) Qualified plans may offer participants particular investment options.

(c) Asset protection in bankruptcy: most qualified plans are shielded from such claims.

Note: Roth IRAs may not accept rollovers from employer plans. Rollovers from employer plans may be made only to traditional IRAs or other employer plans.

10.22 Rollover rules on distributions from qualified plans, 403(b) annuities, and 457 plans.

a. Eligible rollover distribution: with a few exceptions, nearly all distributions are eligible rollover distributions; an eligible rollover distribution from a qualified plan, 403(b) annuity, or 457 plan is nontaxable if partly or completely rolled over into a qualified plan, 403(b) annuity, 457 governmental plan, or a traditional IRA.

b. Seven distributions that are not eligible rollover distributions:

(1) Hardship withdrawals from a 401(k) plan.

(2) Minimum required distributions.

(3) Distributions of substantially equal periodic payments made over one of the following three time frames:

(a) For a period of more than 10 years.

(b) For the participant's life.

(c) For the participant's and beneficiary's joint lives.

(4) Life insurance policy expenses.

(5) Loans considered distributions.

(6) Dividends on employers' securities.

(7) Specific corrective distributions.

10.23 Rollover rules on distributions from IRAs

a. The 20% mandatory income tax withholding rule does not apply to rollovers from traditional IRAs, SIMPLEs, or SEPs (as noted above in the note).

b. Distributions from SIMPLEs:

(1) Can be rolled over into another SIMPLE.

(2) May be rolled over into a traditional IRA two years after the SIMPLE's establishment.

(3) The entire distribution amount from SIMPLEs rolled over into a traditional IRA may, in turn, be rolled over into another IRA, a qualified plan, 457 governmental plan, or 403(b) tax-sheltered annuity with two exceptions:

(a) Distributions from the traditional IRA that are nontaxable may not be rolled over to a 457 plan, qualified plan, or 403(b) annuity.

(b) Minimum distributions that are mandatory may not be rolled over from the traditional IRA into another IRA, a qualified plan, 457 governmental plan, or 403(b) annuity.

c. An indirect rollover also occurs when a participant makes a withdrawal from an IRA and returns it within 60 days after the withdrawal.

10.24 Rollover rules for beneficiaries.

a. Direct rollover and 20% rules apply to eligible rollover distributions to beneficiaries.

b. A surviving spouse who is a beneficiary of a qualified plan, 457 plan, or 403(b) annuity may completely or partially roll over an eligible distribution into a qualified plan, 457 plan, or 403(b) annuity.

c. A plan participant's spouse or former spouse may roll over benefits paid out to him pursuant to a qualified domestic relations order (QDRO); the spouse is considered the participant when he rolls the benefits into a qualified plan or IRA.

d. Spouse beneficiary of the decedent participant who inherits an IRA.

(1) Spouse beneficiary may roll the benefit into an IRA in his name or have the decedent's name remain on the IRA account; tax effects:

(a) If a spouse does not change the name on the account, payments to the spouse are death benefits excluded from the 10% tax.

(b)   If a spouse under age 59½ changes the name on the account to his name, penalty taxes may apply to withdrawals before age 59½.

(c)   No deadline for a spouse to rename an inherited IRA account; a spouse under age 59½ can wait until he turns 59½ to retitle the IRA account so as to avoid the 10% tax.

(d)   Minimum distribution requirements favor a spouse who rolls over the benefit into an IRA in his name.

e.   Nonspouse death beneficiary of the decedent.

(1)   Nonspouse death beneficiary may roll 403(b), 457, or qualified plan distributions to an inherited IRA starting in 2007.

(a)   IRA is an inherited IRA if a nonspouse is the IRA's death beneficiary.

(b)   Direct trustee-to-trustee payment to the IRA from the plan is required.

(c)   Direct rollover is exempt from 20% withholding rules.

(2)   IRS Notice 2007-7: clarified rollover rules for nonspouse beneficiaries.

(a)   Qualified plans need not allow rollovers to nonspouse beneficiaries.

(b)   Minimum distribution rules applying to distributions after a participant's death apply to the rollover.

(c)   Rollover must happen by the end of the year following the participant's death if the participant dies before the start date.

(d)   Trust beneficiary may use rollover if trust meets minimum distribution rules.

(e)   Mandatory minimum distribution may not be rolled over (similar to other rollovers); rather, death beneficiary should get it.

10.25   Waiver of 60-day rollover rule. (Internal Revenue Code Sec. 402(c)(3))

a.   The IRS may waive the 60-day requirement where the IRS's failure to do so would be inequitable or unconscionable, such as in the event of a casualty, disaster, or other event beyond a participant's reasonable control.

b.   The IRS focuses on the following factors in deciding whether to grant the waiver:

(1)   Taxpayer's inability to roll over due to medical reasons.

(2)   Taxpayer's inability to roll over due to incarceration, mistakes made by the postal office or alternative delivery service, or foreign country limitations.

(3)   Financial institution's mistakes.

(4)   Time elapsing since the participant received the distribution.

(5)   Participant's use of any amount of the distribution.

c.   Five requirements for an automatic waiver of the rule (no filing required) and automatic approval of a rollover made beyond the 60 days:

(1)   A financial institution receives funds before the 60-day period ends.

(2)   The taxpayer complies with all rollover rules within the 60 days.

(3)   The rollover is not timely made solely due to the financial institution's mistake.

(4)   The rollover would have been valid if the financial institution had timely rolled over the funds as directed.

(5)   The rollover is made within one year from the first day of the 60-day period.

d.   Filing a waiver of the 60-day rule:

(1)   Participant can file a waiver if he doesn't get an automatic waiver.

ZOOM IN   Reporting Rollover Distributions and Contributions to the IRS

The Internal Revenue Service keeps track of rollovers through a system of mandatory reporting. IRA sponsors and employer plan administrators must use Form 1099-R to report any distribution to the IRS. This form, reproduced below, is coded to indicate a rollover if the sponsor or administrator is aware of it. A copy goes to the recipient for use in preparing their tax return. The IRA sponsor must also report their customer's rollover contribution to the IRS on Form 5498, which is also reproduced below, if the rollover was completed.

☐ CORRECTED (if checked)

PAYER'S name, street address, city, state, and ZIP code	**1** Gross distribution $	OMB No. 1545-0119 20**XX** Form **1099-R**	**Distributions From Pensions, Annuities, Retirement or Profit-Sharing Plans, IRAs, Insurance Contracts, etc.**
	2a Taxable amount $		
	2b Taxable amount not determined ☐	Total distribution ☐	**Copy B**
PAYER'S Federal identification number	RECIPIENT'S identification number	**3** Capital gain (included in box 2a) $	**4** Federal income tax withheld $	**Report this income on your Federal tax return. If this form shows Federal income tax withheld in box 4, attach this copy to your return.**
RECIPIENT'S name		**5** Employee contributions or insurance premiums $	**6** Net unrealized appreciation in employer's securities $	
Street address (including apt. no.)		**7** Distribution code(s)	IRA/ SEP/ SIMPLE ☐	**8** Other $ %	This information is being furnished to the Internal Revenue Service.
City, state, and ZIP code		**9a** Your percentage of total distribution %	**9b** Total employee contributions $	
Account number (optional)		**10** State tax withheld $ $	**11** State/Payer's state no.	**12** State distribution $ $
		13 Local tax withheld $ $	**14** Name of locality	**15** Local distribution $ $

Form **1099-R**   Department of the Treasury - Internal Revenue Service

☐ CORRECTED (if checked)

TRUSTEE'S or ISSUER'S name, street address, city, state, and ZIP code	**1** IRA contributions (other than amounts in boxes 2–4 and 8–10) $	OMB No. 1545-0747 20**XX** Form **5498**	**IRA Contribution Information**
	2 Rollover contributions $		
TRUSTEE'S or ISSUER'S Federal identification no.	PARTICIPANT'S social security number	**3** Roth IRA conversion amount $	**4** Recharacterized contributions $	**Copy B**
PARTICIPANT'S name		**5** Fair market value of account $	**6** Life insurance cost included in box 1 $	**For Participant**
Street address (including apt. no.)		**7** IRA ☐ SEP ☐	SIMPLE ☐ Roth IRA ☐	This information is being furnished to the Internal Revenue Service.
City, state, and ZIP code		**8** SEP contributions $	**9** SIMPLE contributions $	
Account number (optional)		**10** Roth IRA contributions $	**11** If checked required minimum distribution for 2004 ☐	

Form **5498**   (keep for your records)   Department of the Treasury - Internal Revenue Service

(2) Two requirements to file a waiver:

    (a) Use same steps for a private letter ruling.

    (b) Pay user fee (typically, $90).

e. The IRS has been willing to grant waivers of the 60-day rollover rule; the following are circumstances in which the IRS has commonly granted the waiver:

(1) Intervening causes, including weather conditions, fraud committed by the taxpayer's child, or a spouse's death.

(2) Taxpayer's medical condition.

(3) Circumstances involved a financial institution's mistake.

(4) Participant received wrong investment advice.

(5) Mistakes made by plan administrator.

(6) Taxpayer made mistakes against his intent to make a rollover.

10.3 LUMP-SUM DISTRIBUTIONS

Key point A lump-sum distribution is an alternative to periodic payments and is distributed in one tax year because of death, disability, termination of employment, or reaching age 59½.

Key point Net unrealized appreciation (NUA) occurs when employer stock is distributed and held; NUA is taxed as long-term capital gain when stock is sold.

10.31 Net unrealized appreciation (NUA): amount on which a recipient of a lump-sum distribution from a qualified plan may choose to defer paying taxes.

a. For nonlump-sum distributions, NUA is excluded to the extent that the appreciation is attributable to nondeductible contributions by the employee.

b. NUA in the employer's stock that is part of a lump-sum distribution is not included when calculating the income tax on the distribution.

(1) NUA represents the difference between the stock's cost basis and the stock's fair market value on the distribution date.

(a) The plan gives the participant the stock's cost basis.

(2) When shares are sold, NUA is taxable as a long-term capital gain to the recipient.

10.32 Lump-sum distribution: available to employees who choose not to receive periodic payments from a qualified plan at retirement.

a. To qualify, all of the participant's benefit (i.e., balance to the credit) must be distributed in one tax year for one of four reasons:

(1) Death.

(2) Disability.

(3) Termination of employment.

(4) Reaching age 59½.

b. Participant also needs to have five years of plan participation to qualify for 10-year forward averaging (but not for NUA rules).

c. A single sponsor's similar plans are one plan under balance-to-the-credit rules.

(1) All pension plans of a single sponsor (e.g., money-purchase, cash-balance, defined-benefit, target-benefit) are considered one plan.

(2) All profit-sharing plans (e.g., 401(k)) are considered one plan.

(3) All stock-bonus plans are considered one plan.

> **EXAMPLE** Clara participates in both a target-benefit plan and a money-purchase plan. Clara would have to receive both benefits in the same year to receive the balance to the credit.

d. If the tax rate using a special averaging rule is less than the capital-gains rate, a participant would want to pay tax on the NUA at distribution.

e. Stock left to an heir is taxed as income in respect of a decedent (IRD) (i.e., beneficiary receives deduction for estate taxes paid) and the unrealized appreciation does not receive a step-up in basis.

10.33 NUA rule benefits.

a. Four reasons the NUA rule has been receiving media attention:

(1) The present long-term capital-gains rate of 15% (10% in certain instances) is less than half the top marginal tax rate (35%) for ordinary income.

(2) Many plan participants are amassing large employer stock accounts with the growth of the 401(k) plan.

(3) Participants in 401(k) plans that have an employer securities account can choose NUA treatment on the employer stock and roll over any other investments tax free into an IRA.

(4) The rule is one of the few that apply to qualified plan distributions.

b. Five factors in the decision-making process when considering NUA tax treatment:

(1) How long the stock will be held before the stock is sold.

(2) How close the cost basis is to the market value when the distribution is made.

(3) Individual's present and future marginal tax bracket.

(4) Projections concerning future tax rates.

(5) Participant's attitude toward taxes.

10.34 Grandfathered special tax rules.

a. Apply to persons born before 1936 who receive lump sums from qualified plans.

b. **Ten-year averaging** may be available to individuals born before January 1, 1936, when two conditions are satisfied:

(1) The distribution meets the requirements of a lump-sum distribution.

(2) The taxpayer has not chosen 10-year averaging before.

c. The income tax rate on a lump sum qualifying for 10-year averaging depends on the lump-sum amount; the rate is determined in three steps:

(1) Calculate 10% of the distribution after considering a minimum distribution allowance on distributions under $70,000.

(2) Figure the tax on that amount using 1986 tax rates considering the lump-sum distribution as the taxpayer's sole income.

(3) Multiply the result by 10.

    d. Capital-gains election.

        (1) Capital-gains provision: allows individuals born prior to January 1, 1936, to elect to treat the portion of a lump-sum distribution attributable to pre-1974 plan participation as a capital gain.

            (a) If elected, the portion subject to capital-gains treatment is taxed at 20% (note that the current maximum capital gains rate is 15%; however, for purposes of the grandfathered capital gains rate for the 352 national exam, you must know 20%).

            (b) Election can only be made once.

        (2) When the capital-gains provision is chosen, the capital gain part of a lump-sum distribution is then excluded when the individual calculates the 10-year averaging tax.

    e. Selecting 10-year averaging and capital gains treatment.

        (1) Clients still eligible for grandfathered special tax rules have two choices:

            (a) Receive lump-sum distributions.

            (b) Receive periodic payouts from plans.

        (2) Basically, the client needs to determine whether the special tax rate looks appealing or not; three factors to consider:

            (a) Length of the potential tax deferral period.

            (b) Increases or decreases expected in the income tax rates.

            (c) Present investment climate.

        (3) Two other estate planning considerations:

            (a) If liquidity is an issue, consider taking the lump-sum distribution.

            (b) If passing wealth to the next generation is an issue, consider delaying taxes as long as possible.

HIGHLIGHTS

Highlight 1: Tax Treatment of Distributions

■ In the year of distribution, entire value of the distribution will be included as ordinary income. Taxable part may be eligible for one of several special tax benefits if the distribution is a single sum. Most distributions are eligible for rollover treatment. (10.11)

■ The Sec. 72(t) penalty tax is a 10% tax penalty required on distributions prior to age 59½. The penalty tax does not apply unless income tax applies. Two examples of distributions not subject to income tax and, therefore, not subject to penalty:
(1) When a benefit is rolled over from one tax-deferred plan to another.
(2) Nontaxable portion of a distribution. (10.13)

■ Four types of nontaxable distributions:
(1) Traditional IRAs.
(2) Reportable economic benefits (formerly known as PS 58 costs).
(3) Rollovers from qualified plans.
(4) Single-sum distributions. (10.14)

Highlight 2: Rollovers

■ Indirect rollover rule: a distribution from a plan that a participant personally receives and deposits into another plan without tax consequences; distributions from qualified plans, 457 plans, and 403(b) plans can be rolled into an IRA tax-free and free from the 10% penalty if the participant rolls over the distribution within 60 days after the date the participant receives the distribution. (10.21a)

■ Direct rollover rule: a distribution from a plan sent directly by the trustee of the distributing plan to the trustee of the receiving plan without touching the hands of the participant; qualified plans and Sec. 403(b) tax-sheltered annuities must give participants the option to have eligible benefit distributions directly transferred from one plan trustee to the trustee of another plan or an IRA. (10.21b)

■ Seven distributions do not qualify for rollover treatment:
(1) Hardship withdrawals from a 401(k) plan.
(2) Minimum required distributions.
(3) Distributions of substantially equal periodic payments.
(4) Life insurance policy expenses.
(5) Loans considered distributions.
(6) Dividends on employers' securities.
(7) Specific corrective distributions. (10.22b)

■ Rules on distributions from SIMPLEs:
(1) Distributions from SIMPLEs can be rolled over into another SIMPLE.
(2) Distributions from SIMPLEs may be rolled over into a traditional IRA two years after the SIMPLE's establishment.
(3) The entire distribution from SIMPLEs rolled over into a traditional IRA may, in turn, be rolled over into another IRA, a qualified plan, 457 governmental plan, or 403(b) tax-sheltered annuity with two exceptions. (10.23b)

■ Automatic waiver of 60-day rollover rule: five requirements for a participant to receive an automatic waiver of the 60-day rule (without needing to file a waiver with the IRS) and automatic approval of a rollover made beyond the 60 days:

(1) A financial institution receives funds before the 60-day rollover period ends.

(2) The taxpayer complies with all rules for rolling over distributions into an eligible retirement plan within the 60 days.

(3) The rollover is not made within the 60 days solely because the financial institution made a mistake.

(4) The rollover would have been valid if the financial institution had timely rolled over the funds as directed.

(5) The rollover into an eligible plan is made within one year from the first day of the 60-day rollover period. (10.25c)

Highlight 3: Lump-Sum Distributions

■ The net unrealized appreciation (NUA) is the amount on which a recipient of a lump-sum distribution from a qualified plan may choose to defer paying taxes. (10.31)

■ Lump-sum distributions are available to employees who choose not to receive periodic payments from a qualified plan at retirement. The distribution may be made for one of four reasons:

(1) Death.

(2) Disability.

(3) Termination of employment.

(4) Reaching age 59½. (10.32a)

■ Five factors in the decision-making process when considering NUA tax treatment:

(1) How long the stock will be held before the stock is sold.

(2) How close the cost basis is to the market value when the distribution is made.

(3) Individual's present and future marginal tax bracket.

(4) Projections concerning future tax rates.

(5) Participant's attitude toward taxes. (10.33b)

■ Two grandfathered special tax rules are available for some individuals born before 1936 who receive lump-sum distributions from qualified plans:

(1) Ten-year averaging.

(2) Capital-gains provision. (10.34)

TERMS TO KNOW DEFINITIONS

Capital gains provision Allows individuals born before January 1, 1936, to elect to treat the portion of a lump-sum distribution attributable to pre-1974 plan participation as capital gain. (10.34d(1))

Cost basis Amounts in a tax-advantaged retirement plan that have been previously taxed (e.g., employee after-tax contributions). (10.14a(1)(a))

Direct rollover rule A distribution from a plan sent directly by the trustee of the distributing plan to the trustee of the receiving plan without touching the hands of the participant; the one-year rule, the 60-day rollover requirement, and the 20% mandatory withholding rule do not apply to direct rollovers. (10.21b)

Eligible rollover distribution A distribution from a qualified plan, 403(b) annuity, or 457 governmental plan that is nontaxable if partially or completely rolled over into a qualified plan, 403(b) annuity, 457 plan, or a traditional IRA. (10.22a)

Lump-sum distribution Available to employees who choose not to receive periodic payments from a qualified plan at retirement; to qualify, all of participant's benefits must be distributed in one tax year due to death, disability, termination of employment, or reaching age 59½. (10.32)

Net unrealized appreciation (NUA) Amount on which a recipient of a lump-sum distribution from a qualified plan may choose to defer paying taxes; represents the difference between the stock's cost basis and the stock's fair market value on the distribution date. (10.31)

Reportable economic benefits (REBs) Formerly known as PS 58 costs; cost basis accumulated over time when person has life insurance included in a 403(b) annuity or qualified plan; cost of term insurance part of the policy is included in income every year. (10.14b)

Rollover A distribution from a tax-qualified retirement plan that a participant personally receives and deposits into another plan without tax consequences (also known as an indirect rollover or regular rollover). (10.21a)

Section 72(t) penalty tax 10% tax penalty required on distributions made prior to age 59½ from all types of tax-advantaged retirement plans unless an exception applies. (10.11; 10.13)

Substantially equal periodic payments exception Payments from all plans made at least yearly over the life or life expectancy of the employee and beneficiary are not subject to the Section 72(t) penalty tax; with qualified plans, an employee must leave employment before distributions start to qualify for the substantially equal periodic payments exception. (10.13b(1))

Ten-year averaging Special tax treatment of lump-sum distributions available to qualifying participants born before 1936 when the participants have not chosen 10-year averaging previously and the distribution satisfies the lump-sum distribution requirements. (10.34b)

Trustee-to-trustee transfer Direct rollover; eligible rollover distribution directly transferred from one plan trustee to the trustee of another plan or an IRA without ever touching the hands of the participant. (10.21b(1))

QUESTIONS

1. Which of the following statements regarding distributions qualifying for rollover treatment is CORRECT?
   A. Hardship withdrawals from a 401(k) plan are among qualifying distributions.
   B. Minimum required distributions qualify.
   C. Distributions of substantially equal periodic payments made are included as qualifying distributions.
   D. Almost all distributions are eligible rollover distributions.

2. Which of the following statements regarding the direct rollover rule is(are) CORRECT?
   I. 10% income tax is withheld if not moved to a qualified plan.
   II. Income tax is deferred only on regular rollovers.
   A. I only
   B. II only
   C. Both I and II
   D. Neither I nor II

3. Sec. 72(t) penalty tax is a 10% tax penalty required on distributions prior to which of the following ages?
   A. 59½
   B. 65
   C. 70
   D. 70½

4. Which of the following is(are) a factor(s) clients should consider in determining whether the special tax rate looks appealing?
   I. Increases or decreases expected in income tax rates
   II. Minimum required distributions
   A. I only
   B. II only
   C. Both I and II
   D. Neither I nor II

5. All of the following are IRS-approved methods for calculating withdrawals EXCEPT
   A. fixed amortization method
   B. required minimum distribution method
   C. annuitization
   D. payment method

ANSWERS

1. **D.** Almost all distributions are eligible rollover distributions. Exclusions are hardship withdrawals from a 401(k) plan, minimum required distributions, and distributions of substantially equal periodic payments. (10.22a)

2. **D.** The rule encourages direct rollovers by requiring 20% of any distribution that is not directly transferred to be withheld for income tax purposes. Participant in a qualified plan or Sec. 403(b) tax-sheltered annuity is advised to take advantage of the direct rollover option to avoid the 20% withholding. (10.21b)

3. **A.** Sec. 72(t) penalty tax is a 10% tax penalty required on distributions prior to age 59½ from all types of tax-advantaged retirement plans. (10.13)

4. **A.** Three considerations for special tax rate: length of potential period of deferral, expected increases or decreases in tax rate, and the present investment climate. (10.34e(2))

5. **D.** The three IRS-approved methods for calculating withdrawals are (1) fixed amortization method, (2) annuitization, and (3) required minimum distribution method. (10.13d(3)(b))

11

Planning Issues in Pension Distributions

"Character cannot be developed in ease and quiet. Only through experience of trial and suffering can the soul be strengthened, ambition inspired, and success achieved."

—Helen Keller

TERMS TO KNOW

Actuarial equivalent	Installment payments	Subsidized benefits
Applicable distribution period	Involuntary cash-out option	TEFRA 242(b) elections
First distribution year	Required beginning date	

11.1 MINIMUM DISTRIBUTION RULES

> **Key point** Minimum distribution rules apply to most tax-advantaged retirement plans (but not to a Roth IRA during owner's life).
>
> **Key point** Distributions must begin after age 70½ (or after retirement) and continue over lifetime or a 50% penalty is due.

11.11 Minimum distribution rules in Internal Revenue Code (IRC) Section 401(a)(9) limit the time income taxes may be deferred on funds in retirement plans.

11.12 General assessment.

    a. Four tax-deferred retirement plans to which the minimum distribution rules apply:

        (1) Qualified plans.

        (2) IRAs (including SEPs and SIMPLEs).

        (3) 403(b) annuities.

        (4) IRC Sec. 457 plans.

        (5) Roth IRAs, but only after the death of the participant.

    b. Two complicating factors related to minimum distribution rules:

        (1) Two separate minimum distribution rules apply if:

            (a) The participant lives until the required beginning date.

            (b) The participant dies prior to the required beginning date.

        (2) Code Sec. 402 permits a spouse to roll over into an IRA a benefit received at the participant's death.

    c. Failure to satisfy the minimum distribution rules can bring two severe consequences:

        (1) Under IRC Sec. 4974 the plan participant must pay a 50% excise tax on the difference between the amount actually distributed and the amount required to be distributed.

        (2) A qualified plan may have to forfeit tax-favored status.

11.13 Minimum distributions starting at the required beginning date.

    a. **Required beginning date:** the date when benefit payments must start, generally April 1 of the year after the calendar year in which the participant reaches age 70½; two important exceptions:

        (1) Any individual participating in a church or government plan may delay distributions until April 1 the year in which the participant retires.

        (2) Any participant in a qualified plan who is not a 5% owner of the plan sponsor may delay distributions until April 1 after following the year in which the participant retires.

            (a) This exception is applicable to 403(b) plans without regard to the 5% owner rule.

Note: No exceptions to the age 70½ required beginning date exist for IRAs, including SIMPLEs and SEPs.

b. First distribution year: the year in which the participant retires or the year in which the participant reaches age 70½, requiring a distribution to be made.

(1) While the distribution for the first distribution year may be delayed until the following April 1, distributions required for all ensuing distribution years are required to be made by December 31 of the applicable year.

> **EXAMPLE** IRA owner Jason Smith turned 70 on February 5, 2007. On August 5, 2007, Jason reached 70½. The initial required distribution of Jason's IRA is for the year ending December 31, 2007; however, Jason has the option to take the distribution any time in 2007 or delay the distribution up to the required beginning date of April 1, 2008. If Jason delays the distribution into 2008, a minimum distribution for the second distribution year will still have to be taken by December 31, 2008.

c. Plan distributions that occur during the participant's life.

(1) Minimum distributions must occur for each distribution year through the year of the participant's death once the participant reaches the required beginning date.

(a) Required distribution is the account balance divided by the applicable distribution period.

(b) The **applicable distribution period** is obtained from a table based on the participant's age at the end of the distribution year.

■ In most cases, the applicable distribution period is taken from the IRS Uniform Distribution Table (Figure 11-1).

■ If the participant is married and the spouse is more than 10 years younger than the participant, the applicable distribution period is taken from IRS Table VI.

d. The required beginning date occurs prior to the death of the participant.

(1) The required minimum distribution rules must continue to be satisfied for the participant who dies after the required beginning date.

(2) Heirs must receive the decedent's required distribution in the year the decedent dies based on the distribution method used by the decedent.

(a) In ensuing years, the required distributions are based on who is the designated beneficiary; four points concerning beneficiaries:

■ When the beneficiary is not the decedent's spouse, the applicable distribution period is the life expectancy of the beneficiary as of the end of the year after the decedent's death.

■ When no named beneficiary exists (or if an estate or a charity is beneficiary) as of September 30 of the year following death, the distribution period is the employee's life expectancy calculated in the year of death, decreased by one for each ensuing year.

FIGURE 11-1

Extract from IRS Uniform Distribution Table

Age	Divisor	Age	Divisor
70	27.4	77	21.2
71	26.5	78	20.3
72	25.6	79	19.5
73	24.7	80	18.7
74	23.8	81	17.9
75	22.9	82	17.1

FIGURE 11-2

Extract from IRS Table VI—Joint and Survivor Annuity Table (age/divisor)

Age	58	59	60	61	62	63	64
70	27.6	26.9					
71	27.5	26.7	26.0				
72	27.3	26.5	25.8	25.1			
73	27.1	26.4	25.6	24.9	24.2		
74	27.0	26.2	25.5	24.7	24.0	23.3	
75	26.9	26.1	25.3	24.6	23.8	23.1	22.4

> **EXAMPLE** In 2007, Peter dies at age 82, leaving an
> account balance of $310,000 (at the end of the year following
> death) to a qualified charity. The life expectancy of an 82-year-
> old person is 9.1 years. The required distribution in the year after
> death would be $310,000 ÷ (9.1–1) = $38,271.60.

■ When the participant's spouse is the named beneficiary, the spouse
usually will elect to roll the benefit into a personal IRA; in this
case, ensuing distributions are formulated with the spouse now
considered the participant.

■ If the distribution is not rolled over by the spouse, the distribution
period during the spouse's life is the spouse's life expectancy and
once the spouse dies, the distributions are based on the spouse's
life expectancy as of the year of death, decreased by one for each
following year.

e. Annuity benefits.

(1) Joint and survivor annuities and life annuities meet minimum distribution
rules in most instances; two requirements that annuities must meet:

(a) Payments must be made at least on an annual basis.

(b) Nonincreasing stream of payments: refers to annuities that increase
due to cost-of-living hikes, variable annuities, and annuities with a
cash-fund feature.

11.14 Preretirement death benefits.

    a. If a participant dies after the required beginning date, distributions continue in the same way as prior to participant's death.

    b. Different rule applies when defining the maximum length of the distribution period if the participant dies before the required beginning date.

        (1) Distributions must be made within five years after the participant's death; two exceptions:

            (a) Nonspousal beneficiary: distribution can be made over the life of the beneficiary if benefits start on or before December 31 of the calendar year after the year the participant died.

            (b) Spousal beneficiary: distribution can be made over the life of the spouse if benefits start on or before the later of two dates:

                ■ December 31 of the calendar year following the year of the participant's death.

                ■ December 31 of the calendar year following the year the participant would have attained age 70½.

11.15 Issues regarding beneficiaries.

    a. Every minimum distribution rule involves identifying the participant's beneficiary.

        (1) The required distribution is based on the beneficiary who actually receives the benefit.

        (2) Multiple beneficiaries: normally the oldest beneficiary is used to determine joint life expectancy.

        (3) Nonperson beneficiaries: naming the estate as a beneficiary is the same as naming no beneficiary.

            (a) If a trust is chosen, the trust will have the same result unless three criteria are met:

                ■ The plan's administrator receives the trust document.

                ■ The beneficiaries can be identified.

                ■ The trust may not be revoked at death (i.e., is irrevocable).

            (b) Trust beneficiaries are considered the beneficiaries for minimum distribution rules.

11.16 Other rules pertaining to minimum distributions.

    a. Multiple plans: when a person has benefits under numerous plans, minimum distribution must be measured individually subject to the rules.

        (1) Exception applies to IRAs and Section 403(b) annuity plans: minimum required distribution for each plan may be aggregated and the minimum taken from one IRA or one Section 403(b) plan.

    b. If a part of the distribution is needed to satisfy the minimum distribution requirements, that part may not be rolled over or transferred into another plan.

    c. Spousal rollovers: when the participant's spouse is the lone beneficiary, the spouse may roll the participant's benefit into an IRA in the spouse's name.

(1) The spouse may designate a beneficiary and base future minimum distributions on the joint life expectancy of the beneficiary and the spouse.

d. Grandfather provisions.

(1) **TEFRA 242(b) elections:** participants with accrued benefits as of December 31, 1983, were permitted to sign an election form specifying the method and time of distribution of the benefit of the plan.

(a) Section 242(b) elections can substantially defer the timing of distributions (later than age 70½).

(2) 403(b) plans: as long as a participant's pre-1987 account balances are accounted for, such amounts can generally be deferred until age 75.

11.17 Planning for minimum distributions.

a. Postmortem planning.

(1) Current rules allow a certain level of flexibility when determining the post-death minimum required distributions from the IRA or retirement plan.

(a) The designated beneficiary is not required to be named until September 30 of the year after the participant's death.

(b) An early distribution of a beneficiary's share or use of a qualified disclaimer could be helpful in changing the named beneficiary to contingent beneficiaries by the specified time.

(2) Separate accounts: another way to reduce problems that may occur with multiple beneficiaries.

(3) To maximize planning opportunities, many participants may want to designate multiple layers of contingent beneficiaries.

(a) The following four beneficiary elections may be applicable for a married individual with children:

- Spouse.

- Credit shelter trust having the spouse as income beneficiary and the children as remainder beneficiaries.

- Children.

- Trust having grandchildren as beneficiaries.

11.2 SELECTING A DISTRIBUTION OPTION

Key point Three forms of distribution are: annuities, installment payments, and lump-sum distributions.

Key point Three factors affecting choice of distribution option are: personal preferences, financial considerations, and tax and penalty considerations.

11.21 Three factors are involved in choosing the best distribution option at retirement:

a. Personal preferences.

b. Financial considerations.

    c. Tax incentive and tax penalty interplay.

11.22 As a financial planner, keep several factors in mind; four typical considerations:

    a. Has the client coordinated distributions from all qualified plans and IRAs?

    b. Will the distribution supplement current retirement income or will periodic distribution be used to provide necessary income for supporting the retiree?

    c. Has the client followed the rules for minimum distribution from a qualified plan?

    d. Will the retiree have an appropriate diversification of retirement resources?

11.23 Plan benefits.

    a. Qualified plans:

        (1) Possess several options with regard to the timing of payments:

            (a) Annuity payments.

            (b) Installment payments.

            (c) Lump-sum distribution.

        (2) Qualified plans specify when payments may be made and the benefit options available.

        (3) **Involuntary cash-out option:** when a participant leaves employment having a vested benefit of under $5,000, the plan can require that such small benefits be cashed out in a lump sum without providing the participant with a choice of timing or type of benefit.

        (4) Six of the more typical distribution options available:

            (a) Life annuity: provides payments on a monthly basis to the individual for the individual's lifetime; provides largest benefit compared to other life options.

            (b) Joint and survivor annuity: provides payments on a monthly basis to the participant during the participant's lifetime.

                ■ If, at the participant's death, the beneficiary is still alive, a designated part of the participant's benefit continues to be paid to the beneficiary for the rest of the beneficiary's life.

            (c) Life annuity with guaranteed payments: sometimes called a period-certain guarantee; provides benefit payments on a monthly basis to the participant during the participant's lifetime.

            (d) Annuity certain: the beneficiary receives a designated amount of guaranteed monthly payments after which time all payments cease.

            (e) Lump-sum distribution: all of the benefit is paid out at once.

            (f) **Installment payments:** distribution option that allows the participant to select a length of time for the payout and, based on earnings assumptions, the amount of the payout is also set.

        (5) The benefit's value.

            (a) Defined contribution plan: the benefit is always determined by the value of the account balance.

            (b) Defined benefit plan: the value of each benefit is nearly always the actuarial equivalent of a specified form of payment.

ZOOM IN

When advising a client on distributions, make sure you are aware of all the resources the client will have available. It is also important to be aware of the client's needs. When multiple resources are available, it is common to think about dedicating different resources for different needs. For example:

■ Select annuity payments to meet day-to-day income needs.

■ Select a lump-sum payment to meet a specific expenditure need.

■ Select installment payments to pay a regular obligation (such as a mortgage).

It is important, also, to consider the following: all things being equal, it is best to start drawing on taxable investments before you start drawing on tax-sheltered investments. Things are not always equal, so you have to consider the risk and earnings of the investment before you decide.

■ **Actuarial equivalent:** when an individual selects a lump-sum benefit, the benefit is based on the single sum value of a life annuity using the actuarial assumptions noted in the plan.

■ **Subsidized benefits:** forms of payment that carry more value than the ordinary forms of payment.

■ Actuarial assumptions must be based on the monthly PBGC long-term rate.

b. Individual retirement accounts (IRAs).

(1) Distribution options are more flexible compared to qualified plans.

(a) Participant is the beneficiary and owner.

(b) Withdrawals may be at the individual's discretion or the participant may choose to purchase one of the many annuities available.

(2) Variable annuities: benefits increase during periods of inflation.

(a) How variable annuities work: the client has a fixed number of annuity units; the value of any one unit may vary in direct relationship to the net asset value of the annuity assets the insurance company manages.

c. 403(b) annuities.

(1) Restrictions may exist on withdrawals while still employed.

(2) The plans are subject to ERISA fiduciary rules and can be subject to qualified joint and survivor annuity (QJSA) rules if employer contributions are involved.

(3) When the benefit is funded with an annuity, the participant may have more distribution alternatives than with a qualified plan.

(4) The participant can retain the account once employment has ended without choosing a certain cash-out option.

11.3 WORKING WITH CLIENTS

Key point The purpose of distribution planning is to maximize after-tax dollars available to the family.

Key point It is usually better to roll distributions from an employer plan into an IRA if the participant's other assets are sufficient to live on for the time being.

Key point Roth IRA conversion is taxable. Is the transaction worth paying the tax?

11.31 Two broad classes of clients:

    a. Those with limited funds need good planning to make funds last through retirement.

    b. Those with vast funds need good planning to finance retirement and reduce estate taxes.

11.32 Funding retirement needs is the primary concern: distribution decisions must maximize the family's after-tax dollars.

    a. Three issues essential to clients who must make funds last through retirement:

        (1) Preretirement distributions: make certain that any preretirement distributions are not spent unwisely.

        (2) Form of retirement distribution.

            (a) Lump-sum distribution rolled into an IRA provides the most flexible option, allowing the individual to withdraw money as needed.

            (b) A portion of retirement income should be a life annuity to guard against outliving pension distributions.

        (3) Qualified joint and survivor considerations: spousal consent is required when a married participant receives a pension distribution in a form other than a qualified joint and survivor annuity distribution option.

11.33 Tax issues regarding distributions.

    a. A participant receiving a distribution from a qualified plan that qualifies for special tax treatment must decide whether to elect special averaging treatment.

        (1) A client who receives a lump sum should have the sum moved directly into an IRA to escape income tax withholding.

    b. Roth IRA conversion option: complex issue that demands a full understanding of the individual's retirement and estate planning concerns.

        (1) Only available if adjusted gross income (AGI) is less than $100,000 (income limits will be eliminated starting in 2010).

        (2) Distribution is rolled into an IRA first and is then converted to a Roth IRA; the converted amount is taxable as ordinary income.

        (3) Roth IRA is more appropriate for longer distribution periods.

        (4) Individuals who cannot afford to pay taxes on the conversion may choose to contribute up to $4,000 to a Roth IRA annually (2007).

        (5) Roth IRA is more useful when income tax rates will be the same or greater at distribution than at conversion.

    c. When maximizing the estate is the primary objective, taxes should be minimized.

        (1) According to minimum distribution rules, assets can be distributed over the beneficiary's remaining life expectancy after the participant's death; two results of this approach:

            (a) Spreads out the income taxes owed.

            (b) Pension assets can continue to build income for the beneficiaries.

        (2) Purchasing life insurance can generate cash for paying estate taxes.

        (3) Three solutions for a participant who is not willing to buy insurance:

            (a) Pension distributions allow the participant to give away $11,000 per year to a beneficiary without estate or gift taxes.

            (b) Leaving the benefit to charity provides an estate tax deduction.

            (c) Converting pension benefits to a Roth IRA requires no minimum distributions during the lifetime of the participant; no distribution is required over the beneficiary-spouse's life either.

11.34 Form of distribution option.

    a. When a client's assets are significant, the IRA rollover is usually the best distribution option.

11.4 DISTRIBUTION RULES FOR VARIOUS PLAN TYPES

Key point Distributions from most tax-advantaged retirement plans are (1) taxable and (2) required to begin after age 70½.

Key point Roth IRAs are exceptions from both these rules.

11.41 Qualified plans.

    a. Distributions are considered ordinary income (i.e., are taxable) unless the distribution is in the form of a lump sum that is subject to a special tax rule or unless the participant has basis.

        (1) Special tax rules affecting lump-sum distributions include grandfathered 10-year averaging and capital gains rules as well as the deferral of gain on employer securities.

        (2) Basis includes PS 58 costs and after-tax contributions.

    b. Premature distribution penalty tax (10%) is applicable to the portion of a distribution made before age 59½ that is taxable.

        (1) Exceptions are made for payment of certain medical expenses, disability, death, distribution of substantially equal periodic payments, and distributions to a participant who is terminating employment after age 55.

    c. Minimum distribution rules apply.

        (1) Participants (excluding 5% owners) who work beyond age 70 can defer the required beginning date until April 1 of the year after the year of the participant's retirement.

    (2) If the participant made a written election in 1983, the distribution can be made under pre-TEFRA distribution rules.

d. If a beneficiary is to receive a balance payable upon the participant's death, the value of the benefit is included in the participant's taxable estate.

    (1) Beneficiaries who receive benefit payments owe income tax but may receive a deduction for estate taxes paid.

e. Qualified joint and survivor annuity (QJSA) required of most plan distributions.

f. In-service distributions are subject to three restrictions:

    (1) Limiting hardship withdrawals for 401(k) plans.

    (2) In-service withdrawals are not permitted from pension plans.

    (3) Distributions from profit sharing-type plans are permitted upon certain events.

g. Participant loan programs can be offered instead of taxable in-service withdrawals.

    (1) Loans meeting certain guidelines are not subject to income tax.

h. Choice to directly roll over distributions into another qualified plan or an IRA must be offered by qualified plans.

i. Distributions other than required minimum distributions, 401(k) hardship withdrawals, and certain annuities can be rolled over into an IRA, 457 plan, 403(b) plan, or qualified plan.

11.42 Individual retirement accounts (IRAs).

a. Distributions are considered ordinary income for tax purposes unless the participant makes after-tax contributions.

b. Premature distribution penalty (10%) applies to the portion of a distribution made before age 59½ that is taxable with seven exceptions:

    (1) Death.

    (2) Disability.

    (3) Equal periodic payments withdrawn (or substantially equal).

    (4) Education: withdrawals for post-secondary education expenses.

    (5) Withdrawals of up to $10,000 for first-time home buyer expenses.

    (6) Payment of certain medical expenses.

    (7) Insurance premiums for medical coverage for certain unemployed individuals.

c. Minimum distribution rules apply.

d. If a beneficiary is to receive a balance payable upon the participant's death, the value of the benefit is included in the participant's taxable estate.

e. IRAs are not subject to QJSA rules.

f. SIMPLE IRAs: if a withdrawal is made within the first two years of participation, the 10% premature distribution penalty balloons to 25%.

g. Unlimited withdrawals from IRAs, SEPs, and SIMPLEs are allowed at any time (the withdrawals may be subject to early-withdrawal penalties; however, the withdrawals are still permitted).

h. Distributions can be rolled over or transferred to another IRA, a 403(b) annuity, 457 plan, or qualified plan.

i. The 20% required withholding rules are not applicable to IRAs.

11.43 403(b) plans.

    a. Distributions are typically taxed as ordinary income.

        (1) No after-tax contributions; however, the participant may have a basis because of PS 58 costs recovered tax free.

    b. Premature distribution penalty is 10%.

    c. Minimum distribution rules apply.

        (1) Exception: portion of the benefit accrued before 1987 can be deferred up to age 75.

    d. If a beneficiary is to receive a balance payable upon the participant's death, the value of the benefit is included in the participant's taxable estate.

    e. In certain cases, distributions must meet QJSA requirements.

    f. In-service distributions are subject to restrictions.

        (1) If the plan is funded by annuity contracts and has a salary-deferral feature, then contributions due to the deferral election cannot be distributed until employee meets one of five criteria:

            (a) Attains age 59½.

            (b) Dies.

            (c) Becomes disabled.

            (d) Employment terminates.

            (e) Becomes a hardship case.

        (2) If the plan is funded by mutual funds, contribution amounts are subject to special distribution requirements.

            (a) Participant loan programs are allowed.

    g. Distributions can be rolled over into another 403(b) annuity, 457 plan, qualified plan or an IRA.

    h. Participants must be given the opportunity to roll over distributions directly to a new custodian or trustee.

    i. The participant can continue with 403(b) plans after termination of employment.

ZOOM IN   **Distribution Rules for Various Plan Types**

Qualified Plans	IRAs	403(b) Plans
Distribution taxed as ordinary income unless distribution is a lump sum and a special tax rule applies or unless the participant has basis.	Distributions taxed as ordinary income unless participant makes after-tax contributions; special tax rules applying to qualified plans do not apply.	Distributions are generally taxed as ordinary income.
10% premature distribution penalty applies to taxable portion of a distribution made before age 59½.	10% premature distribution penalty applies to taxable portion of a distribution made before age 59½.	10% premature distribution rule is the same as for qualified retirement plans.
Minimum distribution rules apply.	Minimum distribution rules apply to a traditional IRA; required beginning date is always April 1 following the year the participant turns age 70½.	Minimum distribution rules apply.
If participant has a balance payable at death to a beneficiary, the value of the benefit is included in the taxable estate.	If participant has an IRA account payable at death to a beneficiary, the benefit is included in the taxable estate.	If participant has a 403(b) account payable at death to a beneficiary, the value of the benefit is included in the taxable estate.
Qualified joint and survivor annuity (QJSA) requirements affect most plan distributions.	IRAs are not subject to QJSA rules.	In some cases, distributions are subject to QJSA requirements.
In-service distributions are subject to restrictions.	For SIMPLE IRAs, 10% premature distribution penalty balloons to 25% if withdrawal is made within first two years of participation.	In-service distributions subject to restrictions.
Participant loan programs can be offered instead of taxable in-service withdrawals.	Unlimited withdrawals from IRAs, SEPs, and SIMPLEs are allowed at any time.	Distributions can be rolled over into another 403(b) annuity, 457 plan, qualified plan, or an IRA.
Choice to directly roll over distributions into another qualified plan or an IRA must be offered by qualified plans.	Distributions can be rolled over or transferred into another IRA, a 403(b) annuity, 457 plan, or qualified plan.	Participants must be given the opportunity to directly roll over distributions to a new trustee or custodian.
Distributions other than required minimum distributions, 401(k) hardship withdrawals, and certain annuities can be rolled over into an IRA.	20% mandatory withholding rules do not apply to IRAs.	Participant can continue with 403(b) plans after termination of employment.

HIGHLIGHTS

Highlight 1: Minimum Distribution Rules

- Four tax-deferred retirement plans to which 401(a)(9) rules apply:
  (1) Qualified plans.
  (2) IRAs (including SEPs and SIMPLEs).
  (3) 403(b) annuities.
  (4) IRC Sec. 457 plans. (11.12a)

- Failure to satisfy the minimum distribution rules can bring two severe consequences:
  (1) Under IRC Sec. 4974, when minimum distributions are not made in a timely manner, plan participant is required to pay a 50% excise tax on the amount of shortfall between amount actually distributed and amount required to be distributed.
  (2) If the plan is a qualified plan, the plan may have to forfeit tax-favored status. (11.12c)

- Know the definition of required beginning date: the date when benefit payments must start, generally April 1 of the year after the calendar year in which the participant reaches age 70½. (11.13a)

Highlight 2: Selecting a Distribution Option

- Remember the three factors in choosing the best distribution at retirement:
  (1) Personal preferences.
  (2) Financial considerations.
  (3) Tax incentive and tax penalty interplay. (11.21)

- Three options for timing of payment:
  (1) Annuity payments.
  (2) Installment payments.
  (3) Lump-sum distribution. (11.23a(1))

Highlight 3: Working with Clients

- Three issues essential to clients who must make funds last through retirement:
  (1) Preretirement distributions.
  (2) Form of retirement distribution.
  (3) Qualified joint and survivor considerations. (11.32a)

- Understand the tax issues involved:
  (1) Participant who receives a distribution from a qualified plan and qualifies for a special tax treatment must decide whether to elect special averaging treatment.
  (2) Client who receives a lump sum but does not elect special averaging treatment should have the sum moved directly into an IRA to escape income tax withholding.
  (3) Roth IRA conversion option: complex issue that demands a full understanding of the individual's retirement and estate planning concerns.
  (4) When maximizing the estate is the primary objective, taxes should be minimized (11.33).

- Remember when a client's assets are significant, the IRA rollover is usually the best distribution option. (11.34a)

TERMS TO KNOW DEFINITIONS

Actuarial equivalent When an individual selects a lump-sum benefit, the benefit is based on the single sum value of a life annuity using the actuarial assumptions noted in the plan. (11.23a(7)(b))

Applicable distribution period Used to calculate the required minimum distribution amount and is obtained from a table; is calculated based on the participant's age at the end of the distribution year. (11.31c(1)(a); (b))

First distribution year The year in which the participant retires or the year in which the participant reaches age 70½, requiring a distribution to be made. (11.13b)

Installment payments Allows the participant to elect a payout length and, based on earnings assumptions, a payout amount also will be set. (11.23a(5)(f))

Involuntary cash-out option When the participant terminates employment with a vested benefit of less than $5,000, the plan can provide that such small benefits will be cashed out in a lump sum without giving the participant a choice in the timing or form of benefit; option simplifies plan administration. (11.23a(4))

Required beginning date The date when benefit payments must start, usually April 1 after the year the participant reached age 70½. (11.13a)

Subsidized benefits Forms of payment that carry more value than the ordinary forms of payment. (11.23a(6)(b))

TEFRA 242(b) elections Participants with accrued benefits as of December 31, 1983, were allowed to sign election form indicating the time and method of distribution of plan benefit. (11.16d(1))

QUESTIONS

1. In 403(b) plans, as long as a participant's pre-1987 account balances are accounted for, such amounts can generally be deferred until what age under grandfather provisions?
   A. 65
   B. 59½
   C. 62
   D. 75

2. Which of the following is a factor in choosing the best distribution at retirement?
   A. Financial considerations
   B. Life expectancy
   C. Grandfather provisions
   D. Designating beneficiaries

3. An essential issue to clients who must make funds last through retirement is
   A. postretirement distributions
   B. preretirement distributions
   C. investment possibilities
   D. qualified plan restrictions

4. Premature distribution penalty (10%) applies to the portion of a distribution made before age 59½ that is taxable. All of the following reasons for the distribution are exceptions to this rule EXCEPT
   A. withdrawals for post-secondary education expenses
   B. insurance premiums for medical coverage for employed individuals
   C. withdrawals of up to $10,000 for first-time home buyer expenses
   D. payment of certain medical expenses

5. All of the following statements are correct concerning the value of the benefit for qualified plans EXCEPT
   A. for a defined contribution plan, the benefit is always based on the value of the account balance
   B. actuarial assumptions must be based on the monthly PBGC long-term rate
   C. for a defined benefit plan, the value of each benefit does not depend on the form of payment
   D. subsidized benefits are forms of payment that carry more value than the ordinary forms of payment

ANSWERS

1. **D.** In 403(b) plans, as long as a participant's pre-1987 account balances are accounted for, such amounts can generally be deferred until age 75 under grandfather provisions. (11.16d(2))

2. **A.** Three factors involved in choosing the best distribution at retirement are personal preferences, financial considerations and tax incentive, and tax penalty interplay. (11.21)

3. **B.** Three issues essential to clients who want to afford retirement: (1) preretirement distributions, (2) form of retirement distribution, and (3) qualified joint and survivor considerations. (11.32a)

4. **B.** Payment of insurance premiums for medical coverage for certain unemployed individuals is another exception. (11.42b)

5. **C.** For a defined benefit plan, the value of each benefit is nearly always the actuarial equivalent of a specified form of payment (e.g., when individual selects a lump-sum benefit, the benefit is based on the single-sum value of a life annuity using the actuarial assumptions noted in the plan). (11.23a(5))

12

Housing Issues for Seniors

"In order that people may be happy in their work, these three things are needed: They must be fit for it, they must not do too much of it, and they must have a sense of success in it."

—John Ruskin

A HELICOPTER VIEW OF ASSIGNMENT 12

TERMS TO KNOW

Adjusted basis

Age-restricted housing

Amount realized

Assisted living facility

Domicile

Downsizing

Extensive contract

Fee-for-service contract

Home Equity Conversion Mortgage (HECM)

IRC Section 121

Life-care community

Modified contract

Qualified personal residence trust (QPRT)

Reverse mortgage

Sale leaseback

240

12.1 THE HOME AS A FINANCIAL ASSET

> **Key point** Housing needs change during retirement. If a client downsizes, the difference between the sale price of the old home and the cost of the new home is available for other retirement needs; this amount could be put into an annuity to spread the income over the retirement years.

12.11 Financial planners should stress four points:
- **a.** Change is inevitable.
  - **(1)** The client's friends in the neighborhood may die or move.
  - **(2)** Local development can change the community atmosphere quickly.
- **b.** Housing needs can change with retirement.
  - **(1)** Family considerations are no longer as important.
- **c.** Maintenance is expensive for a large home.
- **d.** The home can be sold to gain retirement income.
  - **(1)** If this source of retirement income is overlooked, even a mortgage-free home can take income from the retiree.
  - **(2)** **Downsizing** (moving to more economical and retirement-friendly housing) may free up assets for later years.

12.12 Planners should point out the stream of income that could be available from the sale of the home.
- **a.** Help the client understand the income available after subtracting the purchase price of the retirement home from the sale price of the preretirement home.
- **b.** Illustrate the projected installment payout, life annuity, or joint-and-survivor annuity the sale proceeds could provide.
- **c.** Recognize that psychological attachment can outweigh financial and tax wisdom.

12.2 TAX OPPORTUNITIES IN SELLING A HOME

> **Key point** Gain on the sale of a home (the difference between proceeds and cost basis) is tax free up to $250,000 for individuals, or $500,000 for a couple filing a joint return; gain above these amounts is taxed at the low capital gain rate.

> **Key point** For this exclusion to apply, the property must have been used as the principal residence for two of the last five years; both spouses must meet this two-year rule to be eligible for the $500,000 exclusion.

12.21 Exclusion provided under **Internal Revenue Code (IRC) Section 121**:
- **a.** Effective May 7, 1997, taxpayer can sell home and exclude up to $250,000 of gain.
  - **(1)** $500,000 for married taxpayers filing jointly.

(2) Gain is calculated as the **amount realized** (sale price minus selling costs) minus the taxpayer's **adjusted basis** (original purchase price plus settlement or closing expenses, such as attorney fees, recording fees, title insurance, and transfer taxes).

(a) Basis starts with the home's original sale price including closing or settlement costs (e.g., title insurance, transfer taxes, recording fees).

(b) Permanent home improvements are added to the basis (e.g., room addition, new roof).

(c) Modifications that keep the home in good repair are not added to the basis (e.g., repairing floors, repainting, repairing leaks).

12.22 Ownership and use requirement to qualify for exclusion under IRC Section 121:

a. Property must have been owned and used as the principal residence (i.e., main home or primary residence, as opposed to a vacation home) for two years out of the last five years before sale.

b. For married couples, each spouse must meet the two-year requirement, or the exclusion will be only $250,000.

(1) A couple can qualify for the full $500,000 even if just one spouse owns the home.

(2) Three cases where a taxpayer can tack on periods of ownership and use:

(a) If a taxpayer gets a home as the result of a divorce under IRC Section 1041, the taxpayer can include the transferor's ownership period.

(b) If a taxpayer's spouse dies before the date of sale, the taxpayer can add the deceased spouse's period of prior ownership and use.

(c) If a taxpayer is incapable of self-care and lives in a nursing home or similar institution, the taxpayer can apply one year of residence toward the two-year requirement.

c. If a couple plans to marry and each spouse owns a home the couple plans to sell, both homes should be sold before the marriage; if the sales take place after marriage, the two-year rule may prohibit using the exclusion for both of the homes.

d. The IRC Section 121 exclusion may be used once every two years.

(1) If a taxpayer's new spouse has used the exclusion within past two years, the taxpayer's exclusion is only $250,000 until the passage of two years from either spouse's use of the exclusion.

12.23 Reduced exclusion.

a. If a taxpayer does not meet ownership and use rules or the once every two years rule, a reduced exclusion may be allowed if the sale of the home is because of:

(1) Health change.

(2) Unforeseen situation.

(3) Employment change.

b. A reduced exclusion is based on the ratio of the amount that the period of ownership and use bears to two years.

(1) Ratio applies to the maximum allowable exclusion ($250,000/$500,000).

(2) Any depreciation claimed (e.g., rental or business purposes) on May 7, 1997, or later will reduce the amount excluded after a sale.

> **E X A M P L E** Helen is a single taxpayer and has owned her home for one year. Helen has $80,000 of gain and sells her home for a qualifying reason. Helen's total gain of $80,000 is excluded from her income because $80,000 is less than half of $250,000.

12.3 PLANNING FOR RELOCATION

Key point Three reasons to relocate in retirement: (1) reduce housing costs and transfer part of gain to cash for retirement; (2) cost of living may be lower elsewhere; and (3) take advantage of living arrangements created specifically for senior needs (e.g., safety, companionship, or special services).

12.31 Three reasons a client may want to relocate:

    a. Downsize to reduce housing costs and to transfer part of gain into cash for retirement.

    b. Take advantage of living arrangements created specifically for retirees.

    c. Cost of living may be lower elsewhere.

12.32 **Age-restricted housing**.

    a. Four reasons age-restricted housing may appeal to retirees:

        (1) Wide variety of housing options.

        (2) Companionship and safety.

        (3) Special services (e.g., recreation and leisure facilities, clubs).

        (4) Some communities are self-contained (e.g., banks, stores).

    b. The Fair Housing Act allows two exemptions from the nondiscrimination in housing rules that define age-restricted housing:

        (1) A community can restrict housing to individuals age 62 or older.

        (2) A community can limit eligibility to age 55 if 80% of all residents are 55 or older and at least one resident in each unit is age 55 or older.

12.33 Life-care communities.

    a. **Life-care community**: a combination of the two extremes of a retirement village and a nursing home, with some other features as well; also called continuing care retirement communities.

        (1) Such communities vary greatly in pricing; many are nonprofit organizations.

    b. How the life-care community works.

        (1) A one-time up-front fee is usually required, which can range from modest to substantial.

            (a) Price depends on community quality and the nature of the contract.

            (b) Fee may be nonrefundable.

        (2) Additional monthly fees can range up to $5,000.

(3) Three explanations for fee disparity:

    (a) The up-front fee and monthly fee are sometimes related to one another and to the refund policy applying to the up-front fee (i.e., a trade-off between the two types of fees).

    (b) Both fees may be high if expensive medical benefits such as long-term care are guaranteed in advance.

    (c) Both fees can vary depending on the services provided and the facility quality.

    (d) Planner must help the client look for hidden costs and understand similarities and differences between communities.

(4) Life-care contract (residential care agreement): guarantees client some level of living space, services, and lifetime health care in return for fees paid.

    (a) Living space: can be single-family residence or apartment and can change, with need, to a nursing or long-term care facility.

    (b) Services that may be included in a life-care contract:

        ■ Transportation to and from shopping and events.

        ■ Housekeeping of some type, including linen service.

        ■ Exercise and diet supervision; meal preparation.

        ■ Recreation and crafts.

        ■ Long-term care, or skilled nursing care.

    (c) Lifetime health care: a guarantee of space in a nursing home if necessary as provided for in a life-care contract; three approaches:

        ■ **Modified contract:** nursing home care is covered up to a specific amount with a per diem rate for usage over the specified amount.

        ■ **Fee-for-service contract:** covers only emergency and short-term nursing home care; provides long-term care on a per diem basis.

        ■ **Extensive contract:** client pays in advance for unlimited nursing home care at little or no increase in monthly payments.

c. Coordinating life-care community selection with long-term care insurance and Medigap coverage.

    (1) Clients in a life-care community have definite needs for long-term care insurance and Medigap coverage.

        (a) As a financial planner, you should coordinate medical and long-term care coverage provided by the community with coverage provided by insurance.

d. Two additional concerns about life-care communities:

    (1) Social interaction: many retirees enjoy the social interaction with others that is available in a community setting (e.g., having meals together).

    (2) Tax deductibility of medical costs: financial planners should find out the amount of the contract that is apportioned for medical expenses to substantiate the cost claimed for medical expenses to the IRS.

e. Financial planners should beware of hidden traps.

   (1) A client could lose the one-time up-front fee if the community goes bankrupt; three areas to investigate:

   (a) How long-term care costs are insured: self-insured or through an outside carrier.

   (b) How the community sets fees and whether medical insurance on residents encourages overuse of services.

   (c) If early residents were undercharged and more recent residents must make up the difference.

f. Some questions to ask when helping a client select a life-care community:

   (1) Who manages the community? Third-party management is less desirable.

   (2) Is there an active residence committee that can influence management?

   (3) What health care guarantees are in the contract?

   (4) Are one-time up-front fees being used to pay current costs, and what is the refund policy?

   (5) How are fee increases determined?

   (6) What are minimum and maximum age requirements?

   (7) Is the resident allowed to insist upon or refuse nursing care?

   (8) Is the community owned by a nonprofit or for-profit company?

   (9) How many units have been rented, and what is the resident population profile?

   (10) Is the facility certified by the state and/or a leading organization?

   (11) How old is the facility?

   (12) What is the facility's long-term financial outlook?

g. Four options for alternative housing:

   (1) Renting an apartment if people no longer want to maintain a home.

   (2) If a retiree owns a vacation home, selling the main residence and moving to the second home.

   (3) Buying a condominium or cooperative.

   (4) Swapping homes with someone such as a child or other relative.

h. **Assisted living facility**: multifamily housing that combines home and institutional care in a home-like setting (not a nursing home); most are privately run; aim to encourage a client's independence; not federally regulated; regulated in some states.

   (1) Common services include:

   (a) Help with activities of daily living (bathing, eating) and instrumental activities of daily living (taking medicine).

   (b) Recreational and social activities.

   (c) Health services and emergency systems.

   (d) Housekeeping (laundry).

   (e) Meals.

   (f) Transportation.

   (g) Security.

   (2) Costs: vary among facilities; include monthly rent and fees for services.

(a) Average cost is $2,500 per month.

(b) Costs: may be covered by long-term care insurance; not typically covered by Medicare or Medicaid.

12.4 RELOCATING TO ANOTHER STATE

Key point The client's domicile is his intended permanent home; factors that influence domicile location are where the client spends time, is registered to vote, has a will executed, has a driver's license, or has a financial planner.

Key point Seniors may be able to receive the following tax breaks: additional exemption or standard deduction; deferral of real estate tax; frozen property tax levels; exemption from income tax of retirement pay, unreimbursed medical expenses, or Social Security; or tax adjustments for renters.

12.41 Clients may decide to relocate based on factors such as climate, location of friends or relatives, and affection for the location.

12.42 Financial planners should advise the client regarding six concerns:

a. The decision should be made carefully because the move may be permanent.

b. If one spouse dies after the move, the other may not want to cope with moving again if the necessity arises.

c. **Domicile:** intended permanent home of the client.

(1) Domicile should be established in the state with the lowest death taxes.

(2) Five factors go into deciding which residence is the permanent home:

(a) Where the client is registered to vote.

(b) Where the client's financial planner resides.

(c) Where the client has a driver's license.

(d) Where the client's will is executed.

(e) Where the client spends time.

d. State income taxes (is pension income taxed?).

e. Property and transfer taxes.

f. Some states have tax breaks for the elderly; nine tax breaks that may be available:

(1) Adjusted real estate taxes.

(2) Frozen property tax levels for the year the retiree reaches age 65.

(3) Exemption of all or part of retirement pay from the state income tax base.

(4) Exemption of all or part of unreimbursed medical expenses from the state income tax base.

(5) Tax adjustments for renters.

(6) Income tax credit.

(7) Deferral of real estate taxes until after retiree's death; estate pays taxes from sale of home.

(8) Exemption of all or part of Social Security from the state income tax base.

(9) Additional exemption or standard deduction.

12.5 PLANNING TO REMAIN IN CURRENT HOME

> **Key point** Two ways to use a home to generate income: (1) sale leaseback is a way to access equity and stay in the home; (2) a reverse mortgage is a loan with no repayment as long as the homeowner lives in the home; it generates retirement income via either lump sum, monthly cash advance, or credit line account.
>
> **Key point** Property can be retitled through estate planning that uses a qualified personal residence trust (QPRT), which gives the home to intended heirs but retains the senior's right to live in the home.

12.51 Three advantages to remaining in the current home:

a. An extra room for visiting relatives or children.

b. Starting over would involve finding new merchants and service providers.

c. Keeping one's current social network intact.

12.52 Five areas financial planners should examine if the client wants to stay at home:

a. If the house needs to be modified for elderly living.

b. If the house should be retitled.

c. If the house could be used to create income.

d. If house sharing would be appropriate.

e. If necessary services are available.

12.53 Modifications: a client may want to modify the home for safety and to minimize maintenance (e.g., making the home safer from falls, adding siding to reduce painting costs).

a. Additional services that may be needed:

(1) Meal preparation and help with bathing and dressing.

(2) Home maintenance and cleaning services.

(3) Emergency call/response systems.

(4) Driving.

12.54 Sharing a home (two or more unrelated people share an apartment, house, or condo): helps retirees remain independent and reduces housing costs.

a. Consider carefully the client's objective (e.g., companionship, reducing expenses).

b. Check zoning and insurance implications of renting to a tenant or dividing the home into separate living areas.

c. Review the homeowner's policy to determine the ramifications if the home is shared with someone unrelated.

12.55 Two ways to use a home to generate income:

a. **Reverse mortgage:** a loan against a home that requires no repayment for as long as the homeowner continues to live in the home.

(1) Commonly available only when all the owners are age 62 or older and when the home is the principal residence.

(2) Home must either have no debt or only a small debt that can be paid off with the loan.

(3) Amount of loan payments depends on homeowner's age (or homeowners' joint ages), equity in the home, and interest rate charged.

(a) Home Equity Conversion Program (HECP): reverse annuity mortgage program sponsored by the federal Department of Housing and Urban Development (HUD); usually offers maximum loan amounts.

(4) Payment options vary; three main categories:

(a) Immediate cash advance: a lump sum payment at closing.

(b) Monthly cash advance: a monthly payment that can be stated as a definite number of years, as long as the person lives at home.

(c) Credit line account: option to take cash advances up to the maximum loan value during the life of the loan.

(5) **Home Equity Conversion Mortgage (HECM):** enables an older home-owning family to stay in the home while using some of the home's accumulated equity; six characteristics:

(a) Homeowner must be age 62 or older, have a low outstanding mortgage balance or own the home free and clear, and have received HUD-approved reverse mortgage counseling.

(b) A household can obtain an insured reverse mortgage on the principal residence through the HECM program.

(c) Property must satisfy FHA standards but the owner can pay for repairs with the reverse mortgage.

(d) Total income that an owner can receive through HECM is the maximum claim amount that is calculated using three variables:

■ Age of owner or owners.

■ Interest rate that is charged.

■ Amount of equity in the home.

(e) Several payment options are available to borrowers (homeowners making the loan).

(f) Two mortgage insurance premiums pay for a HECM:

■ An up front premium (2% of the home's value) that can be lender-financed.

■ Monthly premium that equals .5% per year of the mortgage balance.

(6) Special-purpose loans.

(a) Do not have to be repaid until after the retiree sells, moves, or dies.

(b) Typically are made by local government agencies to help low-income retirees in homes.

(c) Available for limited purposes such as home repairs or property taxes.

(d) If income exceeds minimum levels, individuals are not eligible for this type of loan.

(7) Proprietary programs (a type of reverse mortgage).

(a) Developed and owned by private companies that choose the lenders to offer the programs.

(b) Will provide greater loan advances than a HECM only on the highest value homes; expensive loans to set up.

b. Sale leaseback: an arrangement providing another means of using equity tied up in the home while allowing the client to remain in the residence.

(1) Typical arrangement: client sells home to an investor and then rents the home back from the investor under a lifetime lease; three advantages:

(a) Client can gain extra retirement resources.

(b) Client remains in the home.

(c) Home is removed from the client's estate.

(2) Most desirable type of sale leaseback: younger family members buy parents' home for investment purposes.

(a) Family relationship can make arrangement run smoothly.

(b) Caution area: IRS is likely to audit a family transaction; all areas of transaction should be handled at arm's length.

(c) New owner responsibility: lease agreement should specify responsibility for paying property taxes, special assessments, insurance, and maintenance and repairs.

12.56 Retitling property: wealthy clients need to be concerned about estate tax implications.

a. Qualified personal residence trust (QPRT): the homeowner can give away the home but retain the right to live in the home for a certain period of time without paying rent; the home is removed from the homeowner's estate.

(1) Treated as a completed gift of the remainder interest in the home.

(2) Value of the gift is based on IRS tables.

(3) Gift tax returns must be filed.

12.57 Paying off the mortgage: if a client is within a few years of paying off the mortgage, it may be economically advantageous to pay off the debt early.

a. Financial planners must help clients to carefully evaluate early payoff; five issues to consider:

(1) Client's risk tolerance and asset allocation mix.

(2) Mortgage rate; a high mortgage rate is a good reason to stop the debt sooner.

(3) Amount of principal versus interest affects the mortgage's after-tax cost.

(4) Interest rate potential for sale proceeds.

(5) Deduction itemization will also affect the mortgage's after-tax cost.

Benefits and Drawbacks of Traditional Mortgages/Home Equity Loans Compared to Reverse Mortgages

Traditional Mortgages or Home Equity Loans	Reverse Mortgages
Drawbacks:	Drawbacks:
1. Require regular, immediate repayment.	1. Not as familiar to clients.
2. Credit history is a factor.	2. More complicated than traditional mortgage or home equity loan.
	3. Generally have higher fees than traditional mortgages.
	4. Interest is not deductible until paid at the end.
	5. Interest rates can change monthly or annually depending on option selected.
	6. There may be restrictions on home upkeep.
Benefits:	Benefits:
1. Generally simpler than reverse mortgages.	1. Allow cash up front with deferred repayment.
2. Fees are generally lower than reverse mortgages.	2. Credit history is not considered.
3. Interest is tax deductible as it is paid up front.	3. Payments made are a loan and thus are not taxed.
4. Interest rates can be determined in advance and locked in.	4. Maximum liability is capped at the home's value.
5. No restrictions on home upkeep.	

HIGHLIGHTS

Highlight 1: The Home as a Financial Asset

■ The financial planner should stress four points:
(1) Change is inevitable.
(2) Housing needs can change with retirement.
(3) Maintenance is expensive for a large home.
(4) The home can be sold to gain retirement income. (12.11)

■ The financial planner should point out the stream of income that could be made available from the sale of the home.
(1) Help the client understand the income available after the purchase price of the retirement home has been subtracted from the sale price of the preretirement home.
(2) Illustrate the projected installment payout, life annuity, or joint-and-survivor annuity the sale proceeds could provide. (12.12)

Highlight 2: Tax Opportunities in Selling a Home

■ Exclusion provided under Internal Revenue Code (IRC) Section 121: taxpayers can sell homes and exclude up to $250,000 of gain.
(1) $500,000 for married taxpayers filing jointly.
(2) Effective as of May 7, 1997.
(3) Gain is calculated as the amount realized minus the adjusted basis of the taxpayer. (12.21)

■ Ownership and use requirement to qualify for exclusion under IRC Section 121:
(1) Property must have been owned and used as the principal residence for two years out of the last five years before sale.
(2) For married couples, each spouse must meet the two-year requirement or the exclusion will be only $250,000. (12.22)

Highlight 3: Planning for Relocation

■ Three reasons a client may want to relocate:
(1) Downsize to reduce housing costs and to transfer part of gain into cash for retirement.
(2) Take advantage of living arrangements created specifically for retirees.
(3) Cost of living may be lower elsewhere. (12.32)

■ Four reasons age-restricted housing may appeal to retirees:
(1) Wide variety of housing options.
(2) Companionship and safety.
(3) Special services.
(4) Some communities are self-contained. (12.33a)

Highlight 4: Relocating to Another State

■ A financial planner should advise the client regarding six concerns:
(1) The decision should be made carefully since the move may be permanent.
(2) If one spouse dies after the move, the other may not want to cope with moving again if the necessity arises.
(3) Domicile: intended permanent home of the client.
(4) State income taxes (is pension income taxed?).
(5) Property and transfer taxes.
(6) Some states have tax breaks for the elderly. (12.42)

■ Five factors go into deciding which residence is the permanent home:
(1) Where the client is registered to vote.
(2) Where the client's financial planner resides.
(3) Where the client has a driver's license.
(4) Where the client's will is executed.
(5) Where the client spends time. (12.42c(2))

Highlight 5: Planning to Remain in Current Home

■ Three advantages to remaining in the current home:
(1) An extra room for visiting relatives or children.
(2) Starting over would involve finding new merchants and service providers.
(3) Keeping one's current social network intact instead of moving away from old friends and neighbors. (12.51)

■ Qualified Personal Residence Trust (QPRT): the homeowner can give away the home but retain the right to live in the home for a certain period of time without paying rent; the home is removed from the homeowner's estate.
(1) Treated as a completed gift of the remainder interest in the home.
(2) Value of the gift is based on IRS tables.
(3) Gift tax returns must be filed. (12.56a)

TERMS TO KNOW DEFINITIONS

Adjusted basis House's original purchase price plus settlement or closing expenses, such as attorney fees, recording fees, title insurance, and transfer taxes; gain on selling a house is calculated as the amount realized minus the taxpayer's adjusted basis. (12.21a(2))

Age-restricted housing Community restricted to residents of a certain age. (12.33)

Amount realized Sale price minus selling costs; gain on selling a house is calculated as the amount realized minus the taxpayer's adjusted basis. (12.21a(2))

Assisted living facility Multifamily housing that combines home and institutional care in a homelike setting (not a nursing home); most are privately run; aims to encourage a client's independence; not federally regulated; regulated in some states. (12.33h)

Domicile Client's intended permanent home. (12.42c)

Downsizing Sell a home to free up assets for retirement use while moving to more senior-friendly housing. (12.11d)

Extensive contract Type of life-care contract in which client pays in advance for unlimited nursing home care with little or no increase in monthly payments. (12.34b)

Fee-for-service contract Type of life-care contract in which the basic agreement covers only emergency and short-term nursing home care; provides long-term care on a per diem basis. (12.34b)

Home Equity Conversion Mortgage (HECM) A type of reverse mortgage that enables an older home-owning family to stay in the home while using some of the home's accumulated equity. (12.55a)

IRC Section 121 An Internal Revenue Code provision under which taxpayers can sell their principal residence and exclude up to $500,000 of gain. (12.21)

Life-care community A combination of the two extremes of a retirement village and a nursing home, with some other features as well; also called continuing care retirement community. (12.34a)

Modified contract Type of life-care contract under which nursing home care is covered up to a specific amount, with a per diem rate paid by the client for usage over and beyond the specified amount. (12.34b)

Qualified personal residence trust (QPRT) A gift of one or two residences to an irrevocable trust for benefit of a beneficiary, often the grantor's child, with the donor (grantor) retaining the right to live in the home without rent for a specified number of years, generally for a period that is shorter than the grantor's life expectancy; as a consequence, the home is removed from the homeowner's estate. (12.56a)

Reverse mortgage A loan against a home that requires no repayment for as long as the homeowner continues to live in the home; commonly available only when all the owners are age 62 or older, when the home is the principal residence, and when there is minimal debt on the home. (12.55a)

Sale leaseback An arrangement providing a means of using equity tied up in a home while allowing the client to remain in the residence; typically involves younger family members buying the parents' home for investment purposes. (12.55b)

QUESTIONS

1. Renting an apartment if people no longer want to maintain a home is called
   A. echo housing
   B. granny flats
   C. downsizing
   D. additional flats housing

2. When a client sells the home to an investor and then rents the home back under a lifetime lease, the client is participating in a
   A. sale-leaseback
   B. reverse term mortgage
   C. reverse lease
   D. lifetime leaseback

3. Which of the following statements concerning the once every two years rule is(are) CORRECT?
   A. If a taxpayer's new spouse has used the exclusion within past 2 years, the taxpayer's exclusion is only $125,000.
   B. Property must have been owned and used as the principal residence for 2 out of last 5 years before sale.
   C. Both A and B.
   D. Neither A nor B.

4. Which of the following statements is(are) an explanation(s) for fee disparity at different life-care communities?
   A. The up-front fee and the monthly fee can interrelate with each other and the refund policy.
   B. Both fees may be high because expensive medical benefits, such as long-term care, are guaranteed in advance.
   C. Both A and B.
   D. Neither A nor B.

5. All of the following are correct regarding a client's decision to retain the current residence or relocate upon retirement EXCEPT
   A. the client may want to downsize to reduce housing costs
   B. retaining the current residence will make retirement dollars stretch further
   C. by relocating, the client can take advantage of special living arrangements that reflect changes in lifestyle that are specific to the retired population
   D. retaining the current residence allows the client to keep the current social network intact instead of moving away from old friends and neighbors

ANSWERS

1. **C.** Other options for alternative housing include buying a condominium, selling the main residence and moving to a vacation home, or swapping homes with someone. (12.11d)

2. **A.** A sale-leaseback is another means of using equity tied up in a home while allowing the client to remain in the residence. (12.55b)

3. **B.** If a taxpayer's new spouse has used the exclusion within past 2 years, the taxpayer's exclusion is only $250,000. (12.22)

4. **C.** Both fees can vary immensely because of services provided and facility quality. (12.33b)

5. **B.** Retirement dollars can be stretched further if the client relocates to an area where the cost of living is lower. (12.31)

13

Insurance Issues for Seniors

"The best thing about the future is that it only comes one day at a time."

—Abraham Lincoln

TERMS TO KNOW

Activities of daily living (ADLs)

Acute care

Benefit period (spell of illness)

Chronically ill individual

Custodial care

Guaranteed renewable

Hospice benefits

Life settlements

Lifetime reserve days

Long-term care

Long-term care insurance

Medicare medical savings account (MSA) plan

Medicare Part D

Medicare Select

Medicare supplement insurance (Medigap)

Medigap coverage

Modified endowment contract (MEC)

Policyowner's basis

Private fee-for-service plan

Respite care

Skilled nursing facility

Viatical settlement

13.1 HIGH-DEDUCTIBLE HEALTH PLANS AND HEALTH SAVINGS ACCOUNTS

> **Key point** Health care is a huge and unpredictable drain on a retiree's assets; the best protections are Medicare and health insurance.
>
> **Key point** High-deductible health plans (HDHPs) and health savings accounts (HSAs) combine insurance with savings. HDHPs protect against serious financial loss due to health care; savings in tax-deferred HSAs can pay the deductible (unused balance can be used for other needs).

13.11 2003 Medicare Modernization Act permits health savings accounts (HSAs) combined with high-deductible health plans (HDHPs).

  a. Goal: give health protection to individuals who bear more of the up-front cost by paying high deductibles ($1,100/individual; $2,200/family).

  b. Participants are encouraged to contribute to a tax-advantaged HSA (successor to Archer medical savings account, available through small employers only through 2007).

    (1) Contributions may only be made in year of participation in HDHP.

    (2) Participant cannot be a dependent on another's federal tax return.

    (3) Contribution limit to HSAs: ($2,850/individual; $5,650/family).

  c. Funds in HSA grow tax deferred and can accumulate year after year.

  d. HSA withdrawals are tax free if used to pay for qualified medical expenses.

  e. Distributions before age 65 for nonmedical expenses may have a 10% penalty.

  f. HDHP cannot provide benefits before the deductible is met.

    (1) Exception: expenses for preventive care.

    (2) Out-of-pocket limit: $5,500/individual; $11,000/family for 2007.

13.12 Consumer-directed health insurance plans.

  a. HDHPs and HSAs were allowed for the first time in 2004.

    (1) High-income, healthy individuals are more likely to participate.

    (2) HSAs may be kept after a person is covered by Medicare, but additional deductible contributions may not be made.

  b. Health reimbursement arrangement.

    (1) Combination of HDHP and employer reimbursement account.

      (a) Employer makes contributions to reimbursement account.

      (b) Employee receives reimbursement for qualified medical expenses.

    (2) Employee cannot contribute to account.

    (3) No employee reimbursements after employment ends.

    (4) No highly compensated discrimination allowed.

    (5) Self-employed cannot have a plan.

13.13 Critical illness insurance.

  a. A diagnosis of critical illness triggers payment of either a lump sum or monthly income, which may be used for any purpose.

      b. Covers specified illnesses only; provides limited protection.

      c. Can supplement comprehensive health plans.

13.14 Hospital indemnity insurance.

      a. Provides stipulated cash payout each day the insured is hospitalized.

      b. More illnesses covered than critical illness insurance but still very limited.

13.15 Ancillary health insurance.

      a. Comprehensive plans provided by employers provide basic dental and vision coverage.

13.16 The Consolidated Omnibus Budget Reconciliation Act (COBRA) of 1985.

      a. COBRA provides that a retiring employee may continue coverage through the employer's group health plan; three rules regarding the length of extended coverage:

          (1) Retirement: coverage may continue for up to 18 months after retirement.

          (2) If the coverage is through a spouse's plan and the couple divorces, the spouse dies, or the spouse becomes eligible for Medicare, the period is extended to 36 months.

          (3) Disability: period is extended to 29 months if retirement is a result of a disability.

      b. COBRA requirements apply to all health care plans of employers with 20 or more employees, except churches.

          (1) If the employer has a medical plan and COBRA does not apply, similar continuation requirements may be mandated by state law (continuation periods vary among states).

      c. The COBRA recipient pays the entire coverage premium (i.e., the full cost of group coverage); employer can charge additional 2% for administration fees.

          (1) Group coverage is frequently a bargain, especially in cases of a preexisting condition or poor health.

      d. Lapse in protection for those retiring before age 63½.

          (1) Medicare does not begin until 65, and COBRA coverage only continues for 18 months at retirement.

              (a) Expiring COBRA can be converted to an individual plan.

13.17 Employer-provided retiree health coverage.

      a. Usually available at normal retirement age but many companies are cutting back.

          (1) Employers have been sued because past benefits have been reduced or cut entirely; without a contract, employer can change benefits.

      b. Can be offered to encourage early retirement.

13.2 ORIGINAL MEDICARE

Key point Original Medicare has two parts: Part A, hospital coverage, has no premium and permits enrollment at age 65; benefits include hospital charges, hospice care, skilled nursing facilities, and home health care; Part B, supplemental coverage, charges a premium and permits enrollment at age 65; benefits include ambulance, diagnostic tests, emergency care, medical supplies, physician services (inpatient or outpatient), and surgical services.

13.21 Medicare is a federally run government program consisting of two parts:

a. Part A: Medicare's hospital coverage.

b. Part B: Medicare's supplementary medical insurance coverage.

13.22 Medicare eligibility: most individuals age 65 and older are eligible.

a. Medicare Part A benefits are free of charge to most persons age 65 and older; four groups of eligible persons:

   (1) Civilian employees of the federal government who chose not to participate in the Social Security system under the 1983 law and are at least age 65.

   (2) All individuals 65 and over who receive a monthly Social Security or survivor's benefit.

   (3) Persons age 65 and over who have deferred receiving Social Security benefits; must apply for Medicare enrollment.

   (4) Spouse, age 65 and over, of a fully insured worker of at least 62 years of age.

b. All other individuals 65 years of age and older who do not meet eligibility requirements for free Part A coverage may enroll by paying a premium.

c. Any individual enrolled in Part A of Medicare is eligible for Part B coverage; two characteristics of Part B coverage:

   (1) A monthly premium ($131 in 2007) must be paid.

   (2) The monthly premium is approximately 25% of the benefit cost; the remaining cost is financed from federal government general revenues.

d. Three key points about Medicare eligibility:

   (1) Spouses under age 65 who are married to a retiree over age 65 are not eligible for Medicare until age 65.

   (2) Persons who retire early and begin receiving Social Security at age 62 are not eligible for Medicare until age 65.

   (3) While enrollment in Part B coverage requires premium payments, the coverage is usually a good value.

13.23 Medicare enrollment.

a. Even if individuals are not planning to retire, they should sign up for Medicare by contacting the local Social Security office approximately three months before they turn 65:

b. Individuals who will receive Social Security will be automatically enrolled for Medicare when applying for Social Security benefits.

   (1) Important: early enrollment does not mean that Medicare benefits will begin before age 65.

(2)   Individual will receive a notice of automatic enrollment.

(3)   If an individual does not desire Medicare Part B coverage, the individual must reject the coverage in writing within two months of receiving the notice.

c.   If an individual is not enrolled automatically, the individual has a seven-month window for initially enrolling in Medicare Part B.

(1)   Window begins three months before the individual reaches age 65 and ends three months after the month in which the individual turns 65.

(2)   If an individual desires to receive benefits at the earliest possible date, the individual must enroll before the first day of the month in which he turns 65, delay results in delayed Medicare eligibility.

d.   Individuals who reject Part B coverage or who do not enroll when initially eligible may apply during a general enrollment period between January 1 and March 31.

(1)   Monthly premiums are increased by 10% for each 12-month period during which the individual was eligible yet did not enroll in the program.

(a)   Premium increase is due to the possibility of adverse selection.

(b)   Premium increase is waived for persons who did not enroll because of coverage under an employer plan considered primary to Medicare.

e.   Once in Medicare, a participant does not need to complete additional forms to remain in Medicare.

13.24   Medicare Part A benefits; four categories:

a.   Hospital charges.

b.   Use of hospice care (with restrictions).

c.   Skilled nursing facilities.

d.   Home health care (when needed for a condition previously treated in a skilled nursing facility or hospital).

13.25   Hospital benefits under Medicare Part A: pay for hospital services up to 90 days in each benefit period (i.e., spell of illness).

a.   **Benefit period (spell of illness):** begins the first time a Medicare patient is hospitalized and ends when he has been out of the hospital or facility for 60 consecutive days.

(1)   A new benefit period begins for any hospitalization occurring after the 60-consecutive-day period.

> **EXAMPLES** Harry is hospitalized for 80 days. He is then released from the hospital. Harry is out of the hospital for 100 days and then is hospitalized again, this time for 50 days. Because Harry has been out for more than 60 days, the second hospital stay will be covered as a new benefit period.
>
> Pete is hospitalized for 100 days. The first 90 days are covered; the last 10 days are not covered because a new benefit period has not yet begun. Pete will have to leave the hospital and be out for at least 60 days before he qualifies for a new benefit period.

b. No limit on the number of benefit periods an individual may have.

c. **Lifetime reserve days**: 60 nonrenewable days are available over an individual's lifetime in addition to 90 days of hospital coverage each benefit period.

d. Types of services covered under Medicare Part A hospital benefits:

(1) Lab tests and required x-rays.

(2) Use of regular hospital supplies, equipment, and appliances (e.g., wheelchairs, oxygen tents, surgical dressings, casts).

(3) Regular nursing and rehabilitation services.

(4) Intensive and coronary care.

(5) Diagnostic and therapeutic items and services.

(6) Hospital medical social worker services.

(7) After the first three pints of blood, blood transfusions.

(8) Biologicals and drugs normally furnished by the hospital.

(9) Operating room costs, including anesthesia.

(10) Semiprivate room and meals.

e. Deductibles and coinsurance.

(1) Hospital expenses are completely paid for first 60 days in each benefit period, subject to an initial deductible ($992 in 2007).

(2) An extra 30 days of hospitalization benefits are available; however, the patient must pay a daily coinsurance charge for days 61 to 90 ($248 per day in 2007).

(3) When using lifetime reserve days, patients must pay a daily coinsurance charge ($496 per day in 2007).

(4) Patients must also pay for items such as telephone charges, private-duty nurses, and television charges.

f. Hospitals are paid a flat fee per Medicare patient based on the patient's diagnosis versus being paid for actual charges.

(1) The flat fee payment has led to releasing patients "quicker and sicker."

(a) Patients may appeal premature discharges.

13.26 **Hospice benefits** are provided under Part A for terminally ill patients with life expectancies of six months or less.

a. Medicare benefits are primarily for hospice-type benefits provided in the patient's home (vs. at a hospice facility).

b. **Respite care:** short-term (five days or less) inpatient care to relieve the family that provides home care.

(1) Respite care in a hospice is covered.

(2) Respite care can be at the organization providing home treatment, at a hospital, in a facility, or at a facility that cooperates with the home treatment organization.

c. Hospice benefits include types of benefits provided for home health care, plus bereavement counseling, drugs, and respite care.

(1) Only drugs used to control symptoms or relieve pain are covered.

d. Some services have minimal co-payments.

e. Hospice benefits have a limit of 180 days; after 180 days, a patient must be recertified.

f. To qualify for hospice benefits, the Medicare recipient must choose hospice benefits in place of other Medicare benefits, except attending physician services and benefits not applying to the terminal condition.

13.27 Skilled nursing facility benefits under Medicare Part A are available when a patient no longer requires continuous hospital care yet is not well enough to return home.

a. Physician must certify that rehabilitative services or skilled nursing care are required for a condition treated in a hospital during the past 30 days.

   (1) Prior hospitalization must have lasted a minimum of three days.

b. Benefits are completely paid for 20 days in each benefit period.

c. An additional 80 days of coverage in each benefit period will be paid requiring a daily coinsurance charge ($124 per day in 2007).

d. Covered expenses are the same as for hospital benefits (see Section 13.25d).

e. Custodial care is not covered under any part of the Medicare program unless the patient also needs skilled nursing or rehabilitative services.

   (1) If skilled nursing or rehabilitative services are needed, custodial care may be provided for up to 100 days in a skilled nursing facility.

f. **Skilled nursing facility:** can be either a separate facility or a separate unit of a nursing home or hospital; four requirements:

   (1) One full-time registered nurse must be employed by the facility.

   (2) Physician must always be available for emergency care.

   (3) Every patient must be under a physician's supervision.

   (4) Nursing services must be provided at all times.

13.28 Medicare Parts A and B now share home health care benefits and costs; four characteristics:

a. Housekeeping, meal preparation, shopping, dressing, or bathing are not covered.

b. Three requirements to receive home health care benefits:

   (1) Physician must arrange the treatment under the home health plan.

   (2) Individual is confined at home.

   (3) Care must include speech therapy, physical therapy, or skilled-nursing services.

c. Part A pays total cost for up to 100 home visits by a home health agency.

   (1) Recipients must have already been hospitalized or have stayed in a skilled nursing facility.

   (2) Only charge to recipient is 20% co-payment for durable medical equipment.

d. Part B covers additional visits or visits prior to hospitalization; three requirements:

   (1) The individual must be confined at home.

   (2) A physician must set up the home health plan.

   (3) Care must include physical therapy, skilled nursing services, or speech therapy.

13.29 Exclusions from Medicare Part A may be in the form of not paying benefits or Medicare becoming a secondary payor.

a. Five types of services are excluded from Medicare Part A coverage:

(1) Services outside the United States and US possessions or territories (with some exceptions).

(2) Workers' compensation.

(3) Individual elects luxury services (e.g., television or private rooms).

(4) Services performed in a federal facility, including veterans' hospitals.

(5) Hospitalization for elective services (e.g., cosmetic surgery).

b. Medicare is the secondary payor of benefits in three cases:

(1) First 18 months of end-stage renal disease when coverage is provided by an employer.

(2) Employer-provided medical expense plan has been elected as primary coverage by a disabled beneficiary or an employee or spouse age 65 or older.

(3) When medical care can be paid under any liability policy, including automobile no-fault policies.

c. As secondary payor, Medicare only pays if full coverage is not available from the alternate sources and only pays to the extent that benefits are less than Medicare would normally pay.

13.2(10) Some expenses covered by Medicare Part B benefits:

a. Diagnostic tests in a hospital or doctor's office.

b. Medical supplies (e.g., splints, casts, surgical dressings) and equipment rental.

c. Occupational or physical therapy in a physician's office or other approved facility.

d. Surgical services, including anesthesia.

e. Physicians' and surgeons' fees; sometimes chiropractor, podiatrist, and optometrist services.

f. Ambulance service if required by a patient's condition; emergency room care.

g. Mammograms, Pap smears, radiation, prosthetic devices, and x-rays.

h. Home health services as listed in Medicare Part A for those without Part A coverage.

i. Various health screening tests (diabetes, blood screens for heart disease, colorectal cancer, bone mass, prostrate cancer, and a one-time physical exam within 6 months of enrolling in Part B).

13.2(11) Some significant exclusions from Medicare Part B:

a. Hearing aids, eyeglasses, and dentures.

b. Routine physical, eye, and hearing exams (except mammograms, which are covered).

c. Elective cosmetic surgery.

d. Services rendered outside the United States, except as noted under Part A.

e. Orthopedic shoes and routine foot care.

f. Dental care, except jaw and facial bone surgery or fracture setting.

   g. Individuals treated in government hospitals.

   h. Most drugs and biologicals that can be self-administered.

   i. Most prescriptions.

   j. Individuals eligible for workers' compensation.

   k. Custodial care.

13.2(12) Amount of benefits under Medicare Part B.

   a. After payment of a $131 annual deductible (2007), Medicare Part B pays 80% of approved charges.

   b. Outpatient psychiatric benefits are limited to a 50% reimbursement.

   c. Annual maximums apply to certain services (e.g., physical therapy).

   d. Five charges covered without cost sharing:

   (1) Home health services.

   (2) Pneumococcal vaccinations.

   (3) Some surgical procedures performed on an outpatient basis.

   (4) Diagnostic preadmission tests made on an outpatient basis.

   (5) Mammograms and Pap smears.

   e. Health Care Financing Administration sets the fee schedule for covered approved doctor's service charges.

   (1) Patients will be reimbursed for 80% of the approved charges above the deductible.

   (2) Doctors must submit all bills directly to Medicare, even if the doctor did not accept assignment of Medicare benefits.

   (3) Limits have been placed on the size of fees above the amount of approved charges that doctors may charge Medicare patients.

   (4) Medicare assignment procedures allow doctors to agree to accept the Medicare-approved charge amounts as payment in full.

   (a) Medicare pays 80%, which means the doctor can bill the individual for the remaining 20%.

   (b) Doctors not agreeing to accept Medicare assignments cannot charge more than 115% of the Medicare-approved charges.

13.3 MEDICARE PART C: MEDICARE ADVANTAGE

Key point   Medicare managed care provides basic Medicare benefits plus drugs, hearing aids and glasses, physicals, lower co-pays, and no deductibles.

Key point   Medicare MSAs are like a combination of a health savings account plus high-deductible insurance, both paid for by Medicare.

Key point   Medigap insurance is private insurance purchased to provide benefits not provided by Medicare.

13.31 Four alternative options for individuals eligible for Medicare who desire a greater level of coverage:

  a. Medicare managed care plans.

  b. Fee-for-service plans operated privately.

  c. Medicare medical savings account (MSA) plans.

  d. Original Medicare is used in conjunction with **Medigap coverage** (see 13.35).

13.32 Medicare participants can choose Medicare benefits provided by a managed care plan.

  a. Four types of managed care plans:

   (1) Health maintenance organization (HMO).

   (2) HMO with point-of-service (POS) option: POS option permits recipient to go outside of HMO for services but only part of charges will be reimbursed.

   (3) Provider-sponsored organization (PSO): network developed by providers (e.g., hospitals, doctors) to contract directly with employers.

   (4) Preferred provider organization (PPO): a contracting organization designed to provide services at lower price.

  b. Basic services must be equal to or better than services provided under Medicare.

  c. Five additional benefits generally include (similar to benefits under Medigap policies):

   (1) Prescription drugs.

   (2) Hearing aids.

   (3) Eyeglasses.

   (4) Routine physical exams.

   (5) Lower co-payments and no deductibles.

  d. Services must be provided by qualified providers; only in emergencies can the participant seek services from providers outside the plan.

  e. Participants pay the standard Part B premiums (plus an addition amount in a few localities); Medicare picks up the balance of the cost.

  f. Switching to regular Medicare may be problematic for individuals not healthy enough to purchase a new Medigap policy.

13.33 **Private fee-for-service plan:** private insurance plan in which the participant pays the Medicare Part B premium ($78.20 in 2005), any other monthly premium, and an amount per visit or service.

13.34 **Medicare Medical Savings Account (MSA) Plans:** an individual who is eligible under Medicare Parts A and B can choose this program, which consists of two parts:(1) MSA account: a special kind of savings account, and (2)Medicare MSA policy: high deductible insurance policy (highest deductible is $6,000) approved by Medicare.

  a. Medicare funds the plan with:

   (1) Premiums to the insurance policy.

   (2) Deposits to the MSA.

b. When a participant incurs medical expenses, he must first use the MSA until the deductible on the insurance policy is met; from that point, the insurance pays.

    (1) The annual Medicare deposit to the MSA is inadequate to meet the deductible, so if medical expenses exceed the account balance, the participant must pay the excess until the insurance policy kicks in.

    (2) Unused funds in the MSA are allowed to accumulate over the years, potentially reducing the risk that the participant would have to pay in the future.

c. Medicare MSA plans: some plans allow participants to go only to a network of providers; others allow any hospital or doctor coverage.

d. Disadvantage: no limit on the amount a provider can charge.

e. Advantage: increased flexibility; funds can be used to cover expenses that are not normally covered under Medicare.

13.35 **Medicare supplement (Medigap) insurance:** offered by private insurance planners to provide benefits not provided by the Medicare program and to relieve older individuals of all or part of the cost-sharing burdens.

a. How Medigap works.

    (1) Medigap policies provide retirees benefits not available under Medicare.

        (a) Medicare and Medigap now use consistent definitions.

        (b) Medigap coverage does not duplicate Medicare benefits.

    (2) Medigap policies must provide the following six minimum basic benefits:

        (a) Coverage for the Medicare Part A daily coinsurance amount for the 61st through the 90th day of hospitalization in each benefit period.

        (b) Coverage for Medicare Part A daily coinsurance amount for each lifetime reserve day used.

        (c) Coverage for either all of the Medicare Part A inpatient deductible or none of the deductible; partial deductible payments are not allowed.

        (d) Coverage for Medicare Part B coinsurance amount after the policyowner pays the $131 (2007) Medicare Part B annual deductible.

        (e) Reasonable and customary costs for the first three pints of blood.

        (f) Coverage for hospital charges that would otherwise have been paid by Medicare after all Medicare hospital benefits are exhausted for a lifetime maximum of 365 days.

    (3) Twelve standard policy forms lettered A through L (formerly 10 policy forms A through J) have been set up under the National Association of Insurance Commissioners' (NAIC) direction.

        (a) Insurance companies are not required to sell all 12 standardized forms.

        (b) Policy A is the standard for the base policy with lowest premium cost and minimum coverage.

        (c) Policy forms B through J must provide all components of form A plus an additional coverage as set forth in the chosen policy form.

        (d) These supplements no longer provide prescription drug coverage (now provided in Medicare Part D).

        (e) Supplements K and L provide the following.

■ Reduced benefits, but annual out-of-pocket maximum.

■ Hospital deductible and skilled nursing facility care for days 21 through 100.

b. Legal requirements.

(1) For six months after enrollment in Medicare Part B, an individual cannot be denied Medigap insurance due to health problems.

(a) A preexisting conditions clause may apply during the first six months of policy life.

(2) Both state and federal governments regulate Medigap policies, protecting consumers and providing seven benefits:

(a) Basic care benefits using the same format and terminology are offered by all insurers.

(b) Easy comparison among policies.

(c) Notice that persons eligible for Medicaid do not need a Medigap policy.

(d) Refunds: 30-day refund policy.

(e) Automatic policy changes whenever Medicare coinsurance and deductible amounts change.

(f) Notice that no individual requires more than one Medigap policy.

(g) Guaranteed renewability (although cancellation may occur in cases of nonpayment or material misrepresentation).

c. **Medicare Select:** one of the 12 standard Medigap policies that may require the recipient to use doctors or hospitals within the policy's network.

(1) Lower premiums than standard Medigap policies.

d. Medigap policies are not necessary for participants in managed care options under Medicare (see Section 13.32).

e. Congress mandated that Medigap be available to individuals dropping out of a Medicare health plan or Medicare Select, regardless of health; two limitations:

(1) Individual must leave the prior plan within one year of enrolling in that plan.

(2) Individual has 63 days to apply for Medigap after leaving the prior plan.

13.36 Eight points to consider when choosing a Medicare option.

a. Providers.

b. Cost.

(1) Part B premium is $131 per month (2007) for all beneficiaries.

(2) Medicare managed care plans have lower premiums than supplemental insurance policies and private fee-for-service plans.

(3) Managed care plans and original Medicare plan with supplemental insurance have lower out-of-pocket costs.

(4) Medicare without supplemental insurance has higher costs.

(5) Medicare MSAs have no monthly premiums.

c. Extra benefits.

(1) Dental or vision care may be offered in Medicare managed plans or private fee-for-service plans.

ZOOM IN   Comparison of the 12 Standard Medigap Policy Forms

Benefits Offered	A	B	C	D	E	F	G	H	I	J	K	L
Basic benefits	×	×	×	×	×	×	×	×	×	×	50% for Part B coinsurance and first three pints of blood *	75% for Part B coinsurance and first three pints of blood *
Part A deductible			×	×	×	×	×	×	×	×	50% *	75% *
Part B deductible			×			×				×		
Part B percentage of the excess doctor bill						100%	80%		100%	100%		
20% coinsurance	×	×	×	×	×	×	×	×	×	×		
Skilled nursing coinsurance			×	×	×	×	×	×	×	×	50% *	75% *
Extra 365 days of hospitalization	×	×	×	×	×	×	×	×	×	×		
Prescription drugs								×	×	×		
Preventive care (coinsurance for approved preventive care after deductible)	100%	100%	100%	100%	100%	100%	100%	100%	100%	100%	50%	75%
Hospice care **											50% *	75% *
Health care while abroad			×	×	×	×	×	×	×	×		
At-home recovery			×			×			×	×		
Yearly out-of-pocket maximum *											$4140	$2070

* Pays 100% of Part A and Part coinsurance for the remainder of the year after the yearly maximum has been spent. Physician charges above Medicare-approved amounts (i.e., excess charges) are not covered and do not go toward the yearly out-of-pocket limit.

** 50% (Plan K) and 75% (Plan L) of hospice cost-sharing for all Medicare Part A Medicare-covered costs and respite care are paid by the respective plans.

d. Prescription drugs.

e. Original Medicare pays providers directly based on services provided; all other Medicare health plans pay a lump sum to the health plan that oversees the services.

f. Medicare health plans can discontinue contracts with Medicare at any time.

g. Participants may unenroll from any plan at any time, except the Medicare MSA.

h. Appeal and grievance procedures are required of all Medicare health plans.

13.4 MEDICARE PART D: PRESCRIPTION DRUG COVERAGE

Key point The new Medicare drug coverage picks up part of the cost of many prescription drugs at an estimated cost of about $27 per month.

13.41 Original Medicare plan does not cover outpatient prescription drugs.

13.42 Prescription Drug, Improvement, and Modernization Act: adds a prescription drug benefit to Medicare: effective in 2006.

    a. Before 2006, a prescription drug card could be purchased by beneficiaries without drug coverage from Medicaid, TRICARE for Life, Federal Employees Health Benefits Program, or an employer plan.

    b. Part D prescription drug coverage is now in full operation, ending the drug card.

    c. Low-income individuals also eligible for subsidies of up to $600 per year.

13.43 2007 prescription drug coverage.

    a. **Medicare Part D**: prescription drug benefit program that is voluntary and available to all beneficiaries of Medicare Parts A and B; replaced Medicare drug discount cards.

    b. Estimated average premium per person (2007): $27.35 per month ($328.20 per year).

    c. Covered drugs.

        (1) Formulary (i.e., list of covered drugs) in each Medicare prescription drug plan.

        (2) Must be at least two drugs in each therapeutic category and class.

        (3) Formulary may be changed at any time.

    d. Benefits.

        (1) Standard deductible: $265 in 2007.

        (2) 75% of the next $2,135 covered prescription drug costs will be covered.

        (3) Benefits then stop until total costs (including the deductible) reach $5,451.25.

        (4) Plan will then pay 95% of drug costs in excess of $5,451.25.

    e. If an individual does not sign up when eligible, a penalty will be assessed.

        (1) Penalty amount: at least 1% higher premium for every month of later enrollment.

13.5 LONG-TERM CARE INSURANCE

Key point There are five levels of care under long-term care (LTC) insurance policies: adult day care, custodial care, home health care, intermediate care, and skilled nursing care.

Key point Eligibility for LTC benefits is usually based on activities of daily living (ADLs): bathing, continence, dressing, eating, and transferring from bed to chair.

13.51 Three reasons why long-term care (LTC) insurance is a growing market:

   a. Aging of the population: persons age 65 and over are the fastest-growing age group in the country, representing approximately 11% of the population.

   (1) This age group will be 20-25% of the population in the next 50 years.

   (2) Percentage of people age 85 and over is growing even faster: over the next two generations, the 85-and-over group will double.

   (3) The chances of needing to enter a nursing home increase significantly with age; 25% of people age 85 and over and 6% of people between 75 and 84 live in nursing homes.

   b. Family members now have difficulty providing full care; reasons:

   (1) Fewer children in the family and geographical dispersion.

   (2) Increased participation of women in the paid workforce.

   (3) Higher divorce rates.

   (4) Caretakers themselves are growing older.

   c. Rising costs of long-term care:

   (1) Each year, $103 billion is spent on nursing home care.

   (2) Annual nursing home costs of over $70,000 are typical.

13.52 History of LTC insurance; policy provisions.

   a. Three points regarding the National Association of Insurance Commissioners (NAIC) model legislation for LTC:

   (1) Discretion: model legislation establishes guidelines but insurance companies still have discretion in product design.

   (2) Early policies: many older policies written before the adoption of the model legislation or an earlier version of the model legislation are still in force.

   (3) Not all states have adopted any or all of the model legislation.

   b. Model legislation applies to any insurance policy or rider providing coverage for a minimum of 12 consecutive months in a location other than an acute care unit of a hospital for one or more of six services if medically necessary:

   (1) Therapeutic services.

   (2) Rehabilitative services.

   (3) Diagnostic services.

   (4) Preventive services.

   (5) Personal services.

   (6) Maintenance services.

   c. The 12-month period is controversial; critics argue coverage should be for at least two or three years.

   (1) 40% of people who enter nursing homes after age 65 stay longer than one year; 8% stay longer than 6 years.

   d. Policy provision criteria:

   (1) Unless state laws specify otherwise, many words or terms cannot be used in a policy (e.g., home health care services, personal care).

(2) No policy may contain renewal provisions other than noncancellable or guaranteed renewable; the company may not make any unilateral changes in any coverage provision under either provision.

(a) Under noncancellable provisions, premiums that are established in advance cannot be changed.

(b) Under guaranteed renewable provisions, the insurance company may revise the premiums based on class only.

(3) Most LTC policies contain the exclusions permitted under the NAIC model act.

(a) The exclusion for mental or nervous disorders (except Alzheimer's disease) is controversial.

(b) Other exclusions permitted are for alcoholism and drug addiction and services available under government programs.

(c) Preexisting conditions provision excludes a condition for which treatment was received or recommended within six months prior to policy purchase.

e. NAIC model legislation for LTC insurance policies does the following.

(1) Approves provisions described in 13.52d.

(2) Must offer the applicant the right to buy inflation protection (13.53g).

(3) Must offer the applicant the right to buy a nonforfeiture benefit (typically, a paid-up policy with a shortened benefit period).

(4) Requires the following standards in the marketing of LTC insurance.

(a) Outline of coverage pertaining to the specifics of the policy.

(b) Shopper's guide, in the form developed by the state Insurance Commissioner or the NAIC.

(c) 30-day free look that allows an applicant 30 days to cancel the policy after it is delivered.

13.53 LTC policies are not standardized; significant variations in terms and costs exist.

a. Age requirements:

(1) Most companies will issue policies to healthy people between ages 55 and 75 with an upper age limit of 80 or 85.

(2) If coverage is available at age 85 or older, the coverage is often accompanied by very high premiums and restrictive policy provisions.

(3) Some companies have minimum ages of 40 to 50 range, with fear of the high number of potential claims from AIDS being the reason for not issuing policies to persons under age 40.

(a) LTC insurance is often appropriate for younger people, and rates are reasonable.

b. Five ways to categorize benefits under LTC policies:

(1) Type.

(2) Amount.

(3) Duration.

(4) Ability to restore benefits.

(5) Level of inflation protection.

c. Five levels of care under **LTC insurance** (i.e., kind of health insurance commonly covering custodial care, intermediate care, and skilled care in different settings, such as adult day care, assisted-living facilities, at-home care, and nursing homes).

  (1) Custodial care: handles personal needs (e.g., bathing, dressing, eating); usually provided by someone without professional medical training or skills.

  (2) Home health care: part-time skilled nursing care, occupational and physical therapy, and speech therapy received at home.

  (3) Intermediate care: occasional rehabilitative and nursing care performed by (or under the supervision of) skilled medical personnel.

  (4) Adult day care: received at centers specifically designed for elderly persons who live at home but do not have relatives available to stay at home during the day; care levels are similar to home health care.

  (5) Skilled nursing care: daily rehabilitative and nursing care that is based on a doctor's orders and can be performed only by (or under the supervision of) skilled medical personnel.

d. Most policies cover skilled nursing, intermediate, and custodial care levels; many policies cover all five care levels.

  (1) Some policies also provide benefits for respite care.

  (2) Bed reservation benefits are becoming more common: payments to a long-term care facility are continued for a limited time (e.g., 20 days) if a patient must temporarily leave due to a hospitalization.

  (3) Some newer policies include assisted living benefits for elderly who are no longer capable of self-care but do not need a nursing home's level of care.

  (4) Some newer policies also offer benefits for hospice care.

e. Benefit amounts are usually limited to a specified amount per day that is not contingent upon long-term care's actual charges.

  (1) Insured purchases the desired benefit amounts, up to the maximum.

  (2) Benefits are sold in increments of $10 per day up to limits of $200; most companies do not offer daily benefits below $30 or $50.

  (3) All levels of institutional care usually receive the same level of benefits.

f. LTC policies contain both a maximum benefit period and an elimination (waiting) period.

  (1) Policyowner can choose a maximum period for which benefits will be paid.

    (a) Longer-term or lifetime benefits will be more expensive than short-term benefits.

    (b) In some cases, the duration chosen applies to all benefits; in other cases, the chosen duration is for nursing home benefits while home health care benefits are covered for a shorter time period.

  (2) Elimination periods keep policy costs down.

  (3) Some insurers extend the maximum period by a specified number of days for each year the insured does not use any benefits.

    (a) These extensions usually have an aggregate limit (e.g., two years).

(4) Some policies specify the maximum benefit as a stated dollar amount (e.g., $250,000 or $500,000) and are written on an indemnity basis.

(5) A few policies allow restoration of full benefits if the insured has been out of a nursing home for a specific time period (usually 180 days).

g. Inflation protection: most LTC policies offer some type of inflation protection.

(1) The inflation coverage can be chosen at the time of enrollment at a higher premium; future benefit increases are automatic.

(2) The policyowner may also buy additional benefits each year without evidence of insurability.

(3) Inflation protection is usually a specific annual increase, often 5%, but this increase does not keep pace with LTC cost increases, which run in the double digits.

(4) Two approaches to pricing additional coverage:

(a) Base premiums on the insured's original age when the policy was issued.

(b) Use the insured's age at the time each additional coverage increment is bought.

(5) Inflation coverage is usually not enough to offset actual inflation.

(a) Maximum annual benefit increase is usually 5%, yet over the last decade, LTC cost increases have been in the double digits.

h. Eligibility for benefits usually relates to **activities of daily living (ADLs)**, such as bathing, dressing, eating, transferring from bed to chair, maintaining continence, and using the toilet.

(1) **Chronically ill individual**: to qualify for long-term care benefits, a person must be a chronically ill individual, one who is certified by a licensed health care professional as satisfying one of the two rules below.

(a) Person's severe cognitive impairment requires substantial supervision to keep the person protected from threats to safety and health.

(b) Person cannot perform a minimum of two ADLs for at least 90 days without substantial assistance because of the person's loss of functional capacity.

(2) Newer policies contain criteria based on cognitive impairment; if satisfied, benefits will be paid even if activities of daily living can be performed.

(3) Most insurance companies use a form of case management because eligibility determinations can be subjective.

i. The most common preexisting conditions provision denies benefits for long-term care needed in the first six months of a policy for a condition that was either treated or recommended for treatment within six months before the policy's purchase.

j. Most LTC policies contain the exclusions permitted under the NAIC model act.

k. Underwriting of LTC policies is based on the health of the insured, focusing on situations that will cause claims in the future.

(1) Most underwriting uses questionnaires, not physical examinations, paying particular attention to the health of relatives.

(2) The company also looks for medical events, such as fainting or temporary amnesia, which might indicate future incapacities.

(3) Underwriting becomes more restrictive as the applicant's age increases.

(4) Several companies have three or four classification categories, each with a different rate structure; most insurers have a single classification for all acceptable applicants.

(5) Preexisting condition regulations and incontestability provisions have reduced the problem of insurers denying benefits because of restrictive policy provisions.

l. Current LTC policies being sold are **guaranteed renewable**: an individual's coverage cannot be cancelled except for failure to pay premiums.

(1) Premiums can be raised by class but not based on a particular applicant's claim.

m. Most LTC policies have premiums payable for life and determined by the age of insured at time of issue; if so, the premium cannot change unless the premium is raised on a class basis.

(1) These policy types have been advertised as having level premiums, which is misleading since the premium may be raised by class.

(a) NAIC model act prohibits the use of the term level premiums unless a policy is noncancellable (meaning rates cannot increase).

(2) Some policies are guaranteed renewable with scheduled premium increases that may occur every year or as rarely as every five years.

(3) Lifetime coverage can sometimes be purchased with a single premium; some companies now offer policies with premium payments of 10 to 20 years, after which the premium is paid up.

n. Even if provisions are identical, premium costs vary among companies; six factors affecting premium cost:

(1) Spouse's coverage: if both spouses purchase LTC policies from the same company, premiums are frequently discounted 10 to 15%.

(2) LTC coverage can be cheaper at a younger age.

(3) Duration: lower premiums for longer waiting periods, higher premiums for longer maximum benefit periods.

(4) Types of benefits chosen in a policy: adding home health care and other benefits coverage can increase premiums 30 to 50%.

(5) Inflation protection: purchasing inflation protection of a 5% compound annual increase will raise premiums by approximately 50%.

(6) Premium waivers: provision that waives premiums if the insured has been receiving benefits under the policy for a certain time period (often 60 or 90 days), the premium increases by about 5%.

13.54 Deductibility of premiums.

a. LTC policies are treated like health insurance under federal income tax laws.

(1) Employer LTC expenditures are deductible as a business expense.

(2) Individuals are not allowed to pay premiums through a flexible spending account (i.e., with pretax dollars).

b. Employers cannot offer LTC policies under cafeteria plans.

c. Participant may deduct LTC premiums as a medical expense if there are sufficient medical expenses to make up 7.5% of the participant's AGI.

13.55 Limited benefit taxation.

   a. Qualified long-term care policies must provide benefits that are exempt from federal income tax.

   b. An unlimited exclusion from income is specified for benefits that do not exceed actual expenses or reimburse for actual expenses; when the benefit amount exceeds actual expenses, there is a limit of $260 (2007) per day on amount exempt from income tax.

13.56 Difference between long-term care and acute care.

   a. **Long-term care**: includes custodial and social care as well as medical services to people who cannot live independently; three government programs provide LTC services (from most coverage to least).

     (1) Medicaid: largest source of LTC payments, but only available to individuals with few resources (some become eligible as their assets are depleted).

     (2) Veterans Administration: limited benefits available if disability or illness is service related or individual has low income.

     (3) Medicare: benefits are very limited.

   b. **Acute care**: includes relatively brief periods of medical care for illness or trauma.

13.6 LIFE INSURANCE FOR SENIORS

Key point Life insurance, purchased earlier in life, has many uses once the client reaches retirement, such as charitable bequests, education of children or grandchildren, funds for a spouse or minor children, funds for a business continuation plan, life benefits, paying estate taxes, or viatical or life settlements.

13.61 Goal of life insurance: to provide cash at the insured's death.

13.62 Uses of life insurance for seniors.

   a. Create funds for younger family members not inheriting assets.

   b. Meet long-term need for special children who will never be self-supporting.

   c. Give charitable bequests.

   d. Provide ongoing funds for dependent minors.

   e. Provide certainty that children from previous marriages will receive an inheritance.

   f. Provide cash to loyal household employees or other help.

   g. Pay for education of children or grandchildren.

   h. Make funds available for a business continuation plan.

   i. Provide cash to pay federal estate taxes.

13.63 Beneficiary designations.

   a. Should be reviewed periodically to make sure they achieve the desired effect.

     b. Beneficiaries who are married children undergoing a divorce: better to make payable to a trust.

     c. Problematic designations:

        (1) Wife of the insured; marital status may change and unintended person may receive benefits if insured remarries.

        (2) Children of the insured; benefit payments may be delayed as insurance company must determine the members of this class.

     d. Controlling funds after insured dies:

        (1) Specify period payments if beneficiary cannot manage money.

        (2) Pay proceeds to trust and allow trustee to determine when and how payments are to be made.

13.64 Continuing existing coverage.

     a. Group coverage may be continued when employment ends.

        (1) If amount of coverage is inadequate, an individual policy may be purchased.

     b. Existing individual policies must be assessed for their suitability and financial burden of keeping in place at current premium levels.

        (1) Policies with considerable cash value can be adjusted so no future premiums are needed.

        (2) Universal life death benefits may be reduced and maintained by cash values.

     c. Policies purchased more than two years prior provide guaranteed coverage.

        (1) New policies must start a new two-year contestable period.

13.65 Purchasing new coverage.

     a. Subject to underwriting.

        (1) Based on age and health of the senior.

        (2) If in poor health, premiums will be high.

     b. Applying to too many insurers at the same time may indicate that the prospect is too eager for coverage and may lead to rejection by insurers.

13.66 Using the living benefits from a life insurance policy.

     a. Lifetime withdrawals from a policy may be desired if:

        (1) Client no longer needs a death benefit (less likely).

        (2) Client needs retirement funds, money for LTC, or living costs (more likely).

     b. Considerations.

        (1) Because life insurance is a liquid inheritance, client may prefer to leave life policy intact and use other resources for retirement needs.

        (2) Cash surrender values may have already been assigned to another party and not be accessible.

     c. Adverse tax consequences.

        (1) Failure to meet the statutory definition of life insurance under IRC Section 7702: immediate taxation of cash surrender value (CSV) accumulation.

            (a) Solution: request statement from insurer saying policy meets statutory definition.

(2) Modified endowment contract (MEC): a policy that fails the 7-pay test, which discourages a premium schedule that would result in a paid-up policy before the end of a 7-year period.

(a) MECs are subject to last in, first out (LIFO) tax treatment regarding loans and most other distributions, plus penalty tax.

(b) Distributions are taxed until basis is left in the policy; basis is received tax free.

(c) Tax treatment of MECs discourages use of high-premium life insurance contracts as short-term investments.

(d) For each policy, a net level premium is calculated: an artificially constructed amount based on a presumed interest rate, reasonable insurance company expense, and mortality charges.

d. Determining the value of a life insurance policy.

(1) Policyowner's basis: initially, total premium paid, less:

(a) Dividends received.

(b) Nontaxable withdrawals.

(2) Amounts paid while the insured is living.

(a) Dividends: considered a tax-free return of premium.

■ Dividends that exceed premiums are taxable.

(b) Cash surrender value: taxable amount equals the total surrender value minus the policyowner's basis.

E X A M P L E Bob owns a whole life policy with a face amount of $150,000 and a cash value of $35,000. He has paid a total of $22,000 in the policy and has received $6,000 in dividends. The policy also has an outstanding loan of $10,000. Bob wants to surrender his policy for cash. Following are the tax consequences of the surrender:

Net cash value	$ 25,000
($35,000 CV less $10,000 loan)	
Less: Basis	−16,000
($22,000 premiums less $6,000 dividends)	
Taxable gain	$ 9,000

(c) Loans: full CSV less interest charges until the policy anniversary date is available.

■ Unless a MEC, loans are tax free.

■ Loan is continued as long as CSV covers the interest.

■ Policy is terminated if indebtedness equals or exceeds the CSV.

■ Indebtedness is deducted from death benefit if insured dies.

■ More preferable for seniors than partial withdrawals.

(d) Partial withdrawals: usually a proportionate reduction in death benefits.

■ Whole life policies may allow surrendering of paid-up additions without surrendering base policy.

■ If death benefit of a universal life policy is reduced within first 15 years of a policy, withdrawal may be taxed (LIFO).

(3) Exchanging for annuity: tax free even if there is gain in life insurance policy.

(a) Outstanding loan will be treated as "boot" and is taxed to the extent it exceeds investment in the contract.

(b) Policyowner can take proceeds from life insurance surrender in form of annuity and defer income taxes.

13.67 Viatical settlement of a life insurance policy.

a. **Viatical settlement:** proceeds from the sale of a life insurance policy to a third party by a terminally or chronically ill person who is expected to die within 24 months.

b. Under Health Insurance Portability and Accountability Act (HIPAA) of 1996: cash settlement received by terminally ill policyowner is not taxable income.

(1) If chronically ill:

(a) Tax free only if cash is for nonreimbursed long-term care costs.

■ Exception: per diem payments within certain limits.

(b) Contract must meet conditions of tax law that apply to chronically ill individuals.

c. Viatical settlement provider: a person who is in the business of purchasing or taking assignments of life insurance contracts on the lives of insureds.

(1) Licensed by the state where the insured resides.

13.68 Sales of policies to investors who pay premiums create **life settlements:** an investment company purchases a life insurance contract to make a profit at the death of an insured.

a. Company pays cash for the policy and pays premiums to keep it in force throughout the insured's lifetime; returns can be high—usually over 20%.

b. Usual requirements:

(1) Insured must be at least 65 years old.

(2) Policy must have considerable death benefit of $1 million or more.

c. Payment by the investor.

(1) The shorter the life expectancy, the more the investor will pay for the policy.

(2) Investor also considers:

(a) Costs of assessing the insured.

(b) Paying agent commissions.

(c) Taxes on any gain at death of the insured (unlike a beneficiary, an investor must pay taxes on the death benefit).

d. The policyowner/insured has no control over the policy once it is sold.

e. Incentive for policyowner to sell policy equals the offering price less the cash value available from the policy.

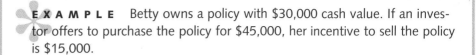

EXAMPLE   Betty owns a policy with $30,000 cash value. If an investor offers to purchase the policy for $45,000, her incentive to sell the policy is $15,000.

13.7 PROPERTY AND LIABILITY INSURANCE ISSUES

Key Point   Property and liability insurance protects against losses or liabilities that can deplete retirement savings; important areas of coverage that should be reviewed periodically include auto, homeowners, and personal liability umbrella policies.

13.71 Homeowners coverage.

a. Important to list household contents and compare with coverage limits to assess adequacy of coverage.

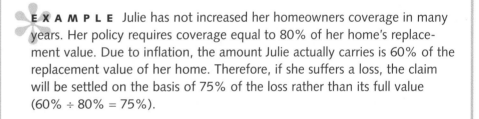

EXAMPLE   Julie has not increased her homeowners coverage in many years. Her policy requires coverage equal to 80% of her home's replacement value. Due to inflation, the amount Julie actually carries is 60% of the replacement value of her home. Therefore, if she suffers a loss, the claim will be settled on the basis of 75% of the loss rather than its full value (60% ÷ 80% = 75%).

b. A business endorsement may be needed if a person conducts a business out of the home.

13.72 Automobile insurance.

a. Seniors should take defensive driving courses.

(1) Will be less intimidated.

(2) Instructor can assess the driver's skills.

(3) Reduces insurance rates.

b. A commercial policy may be needed if the senior uses the automobile to earn income.

13.73 Personal liability umbrella policy.

a. Expands coverage provided by homeowners and automobile insurance policies.

b. Purpose: retain assets set aside for retirement in the event of a liability judgment against insured.

c. Available in increments of $1 million.

d. Premiums are reasonable.

HIGHLIGHTS

Highlight 1: High-Deductible Health Plans and Health Savings Accounts

- The 2003 Medicare and Modernization Act permits health savings accounts (HSAs) combined with high-deductible health plans (HDHPs). (13.11)

- The Consolidated Omnibus Budget Reconciliation Act (COBRA) provides that a retiring employee may continue coverage through the employer's group health plan. (13.16)

Highlight 2: Original Medicare (Parts A and B)

- Medicare is a two-part federal program for most persons age 65 and older.
  (1) Part A: hospital coverage.
  (2) Part B: supplementary medical insurance coverage. (13.21–13.23)

- Any individual enrolled in Part A of Medicare is eligible for Part B coverage.

- Part A: hospital coverage benefits are hospital charges, use of hospice care, skilled nursing facilities, and home health care.

- Part B: supplementary medical insurance coverage includes expenses for diagnostic tests, medical supplies, surgical services, physicians' and surgeon's fees from office visits or services provided in a hospital, ambulance services, emergency care, and other expenses. (13.2(10)–13.2(12))

Highlight 3: Medicare Part C: Medicare Advantage

- Four options for individuals eligible for Medicare who want greater coverage: Medicare managed care plans, fee-for-service plans operated privately, Medicare medical savings account (MSA) plans, and original Medicare in conjunction with Medigap coverage. (13.3)

- Medicare MSAs are a combination of a health savings account plus high-deductible insurance, both paid for by Medicare. (13.34)

- Medigap insurance is private insurance purchased to provide benefits not provided by Medicare. (13.35)

Highlight 4: Medicare Part D: Prescription Drug Coverage

- Effective in 2006, the Medicare Modernization Act adds a prescription benefit. (13.4)

- Medicare Part D replaces Medicare-approved drug discount cards.

- Drugs are covered under a formulary or a list of approved drugs that are covered.

Highlight 5: Long-Term Care Insurance

- There are three reasons why long-term care (LTC) is a growing market:
  (1) Aging of the population.
  (2) Inability of families to provide full care.
  (3) Rising costs of long-term care. (13.51)

■ The five levels of care under long-term care policies are:
(1) Custodial care.
(2) Home health care.
(3) Intermediate care.
(4) Adult day care.
(5) Skilled nursing care. (13.53)

■ Eligibility for benefits is now usually related to activities of daily living, which include:
(1) Bathing.
(2) Dressing.
(3) Eating.
(4) Transferring from bed to chair.
(5) Maintaining continence.
(6) Using the toilet. (13.53h)

Highlight 6: Life Insurance for Seniors

■ Some uses of life insurance for seniors include:
(1) Create funds for younger family members not inheriting assets.
(2) Meet long-term needs for special needs children who will never be self-supporting.
(3) Give charitable bequests.
(4) Provide certainty that children from previous marriages will receive an inheritance.
(5) Pay for education of children or grandchildren.
(6) Make funds available for a business continuation plan.
(7) Provide cash to pay federal estate taxes. (13.62)

■ Amounts paid from life insurance while the insured is living include:
(1) Dividends.
(2) Cash surrender value.
(3) Loans.
(4) Partial withdrawals. (13.66)

■ A viatical settlement is cash from the sale of a life insurance policy to a third party by an individual who is terminally or chronically ill and is expected to die within 24 months. (13.67)

■ A life settlement is one in which an investment company purchases a life insurance contract to make a profit upon the death of an insured. (13.68)

Highlight 7: Property and Liability Insurance Issues

■ It is important to list household contents and compare the values with the homeowners policy coverage limits to assess the adequacy of coverage. (13.71)

■ A personal liability umbrella policy can protect retirement assets in the event a liability judgment is issued against the insured. (13.73)

TERMS TO KNOW DEFINITIONS

Activities of daily living (ADLs) Bathing, dressing, eating, transferring from bed to chair, maintaining continence, and using the toilet. (13.53h)

Acute care Includes relatively brief periods of medical care for illness or trauma. (13.56b)

Benefit period (spell of illness) Begins the first time a Medicare patient is hospitalized and ends when the patient has been out of the hospital or skilled nursing facility for 60 consecutive days. (13.25a)

Chronically ill individual Person eligible to receive long-term care insurance benefits; must be certified by a licensed health care professional as satisfying one of the two rules: (1) person's severe cognitive impairment requires substantial supervision to keep the person protected from threats to safety and health, or (2) person cannot perform a minimum of two ADLs for at least 90 days without substantial assistance because of the person's loss of functional capacity. (13.53h)

Custodial care Handles personal needs (e.g., bathing, dressing, eating); usually provided by someone without professional medical training or skills. (13.53c(1))

Guaranteed renewable Coverage cannot be cancelled except for failure to pay premiums. (13.53l)

Hospice benefits Benefits provided under Medicare Part A for terminally ill patients with life expectancies of six months or less. (13.26)

Life settlement Sale by a senior insured of an existing (often unwanted) life insurance policy to a third-party company in the business of buying policies. The company purchases the life insurance contract to make a profit at the death of an insured. (13.68)

Lifetime reserve days 60 nonrenewable days are available over an individual's lifetime in addition to 90 days of hospital coverage each benefit period. (13.25c)

Long-term care Includes custodial care, social care, and medical services to people who cannot live independently. (13.56a)

Long term-care insurance Kind of health insurance commonly covering custodial care, intermediate care, and skilled care in different settings, such as adult day care, assisted-living facilities, at-home care, and nursing homes. (13.53c)

Medicare medical savings (MSA) plan For those eligible under Medicare Part A and B, a plan with (1) a savings account, and (2) a high-deductible insurance policy. (13.33b)

Medicare Part D Prescription drug benefit program that is voluntary and available to all beneficiaries of Medicare Parts A and B; replaced Medicare drug discount cards. (13.43a)

Medicare Select One of the 12 standard Medigap policies that may require the recipient to use doctors or hospitals within the policy's network. (13.35c)

Medicare supplement (Medigap) insurance Offered by private insurance planners to supplement the inadequacies of the Medicare program and to relieve older individuals of all or part of the cost-sharing burdens. (13.35)

Medigap coverage Commercial insurance that supplements Medicare. (13.31d(1))

Modified endowment contract (MEC) A policy that fails the 7-pay test; policy distributions are made on a last in, first out (LIFO) basis. (13.66c(2))

Policyowner's basis Initially, total premium paid, less (1) dividends received, and (2) nontaxable withdrawals. (13.66d(1))

Private fee-for-service plan Private insurance plan in which the participant pays the Medicare Part B premium ($131 in 2007), any other monthly premium, and an amount per visit or service. (13.33)

Respite care Temporary relief from caregiving responsibilities to relieve the caregiver who provides home care. (13.26b)

Skilled nursing facility Can be either a separate facility or a separate unit of a nursing home or hospital with (1) one full-time registered nurse employed, (2) a physician always available for emergency care, (3) physician supervision of every patient, and (4) nursing services provided at all times. (13.27f)

Viatical settlement The proceeds from the sale of a life insurance policy to a third party by an individual who is terminally or chronically ill individual and is expected to die within 24 months; intended to accelerate death benefits to the terminally ill policyholder. (13.67a)

QUESTIONS

1. A private insurance plan in which the participant pays the Medicare Part B premium, any other monthly premium, and an amount per visit or service is a
   A. supplemental premium plan
   B. private fee-for-service plan
   C. restricted service program
   D. controlled premium plan

2. In 2006, Medicare Part D: Prescription Drug Coverage will replace
   A. prescription benefits under Medicare Part A
   B. the annual prescription allowance under Medicare Part B
   C. deductibles for prescription drugs under Medicare Part C
   D. Medicare-approved drug discount cards

3. Which of the following statements concerning long-term care (LTC) policies is(are) CORRECT?
   A. Underwriting is based on the health of the insured, focusing on situation that will cause future claims.
   B. In most cases, premiums are payable for life and are determined by the age of the insured at time of issue.
   C. Both A and B.
   D. Neither A nor B.

4. The benefit period for Medicare Part A begins the first time a Medicare patient is hospitalized and ends when the patient has been out of the hospital or skilled nursing facility for how many consecutive days?
   A. 14
   B. 30
   C. 60
   D. 120

5. Regarding taxation, how are loans from modified endowment contracts (MECs) treated?
   A. They are tax free
   B. First in, first out taxation
   C. Last in, last out taxation
   D. Fully taxable

ANSWERS

1. **B.** This describes a private fee-for-service plan. (13.33)

2. **D.** Medicare-approved drug discount cards will no longer be needed since, in 2006, Medicare Part D began covering prescription drugs. (13.43)

3. **C.** Both statements are correct. (13.53)

4. **C.** A new benefit period begins for any hospitalization occurring after 60 consecutive days. (13.25a)

5. **C.** Loans from MECs are given LIFO treatment (taxable until basis is left in contract, then tax free as a return of basis). (13.66c(2))

14

Estate Planning

"Never let the estate decrease in your hands."

—Anthony Trollope

A HELICOPTER VIEW OF ASSIGNMENT 14

14.1 Basic Steps in Estate Planning for Seniors

14.2 Interpersonal Issues

14.3 Marriage Issues

14.4 Planning for Incapacity: General

14.5 Planning for Incapacity: Property and Assets

14.6 Planning for Incapacity: Health and Personal Care

14.7 Gifting

14.8 Retirement Planning for Clients with Limited Assets

14.9 Trusts and Other Estate Planning Tools

Highlights

Terms to Know Definitions

Questions

TERMS TO KNOW

Cemetery trust

Conservatorship

Coverdell Education Savings Accounts (CESAs)

Endowment care cemetery trust

Family life insurance partnerships (FLIPs)

Family limited liability company (FLLC)

Family limited partnership (FLP)

Funeral trust

Incentive trust

Intentionally defective trust

Irrevocable grandparent-grandchild insurance trust

Legacy (ethical) will

Life settlement

Look-back period

Nonspringing durable power of attorney

Qualified domestic relations order (QDRO)

Qualified personal residence trust (QPRT)

Qualified terminable interest property (QTIP) trusts

Reverse mortgage

Section 529 qualified tuition programs

Service and merchandise cemetery trusts

Special needs trust

Springing durable power of attorney

Standby trust

Upon death or incapacity letter

Viatical settlement

14.1 BASIC STEPS IN ESTATE PLANNING FOR SENIORS

Key point   Ten basic estate planning steps: make inventory; value assets; calculate net worth and potential taxes; set goals; consider most appropriate tools and forms of ownership; minimize taxes; arrange liquidity; execute documents; review periodically.

14.11 Challenges for the financial planner:

  a. Seniors feel the vulnerabilities that come with age.

  b. Planners must distinguish Depression-era seniors from younger baby-boom seniors, who are more risk tolerant.

  c. Seniors often own properties with a low basis that have greatly appreciated; from a tax standpoint, it can be unwise to use the assets for improved investment diversification.

14.12 Preventive planning approaches:

  a. Estate planning should be preventive in nature, making arrangements before long-term care is needed or clients become incapacitated.

  b. Planners should stress two things to seniors:

   (1) Estate planning goes beyond saving taxes or spending down an estate for Medicaid eligibility.

   (2) Estate planning is an issue for most seniors, not just the wealthy ones; clients should consider questions like these:

    (a) What are the consequences if I do nothing?

    (b) How will my bills get paid?

    (c) How will I be cared for if I become ill?

    (d) Can I ease the financial burdens on my spouse and children?

  c. A will is considered a fundamental estate planning document.

   (1) Having a will and a living (inter vivos) trust ensures that property not governed by the trust will be distributed through the will's residuary provisions.

   (2) If a client already has a will, the planner should review it to ensure that its objectives are current and it comports with current law.

   (3) If objectives are current but the will is over 10 years old, it should be completely re-executed to bolster the terms in the event of a will contest.

14.13 Ten key estate planning steps:

  a. Make inventory of assets and liabilities:

   (1) Many seniors are surprised both at their net worth and the fact that their estates face potential tax liabilities.

  b. Value assets using today's fair market value.

  c. Calculate net worth and potential taxes:

   (1) Value and complexity will determine whether an estate tax return or sophisticated planning is necessary.

  d. Set goals.

e. Consider alternative legal tools for lifetime care and property management, transfer, and disposition, including living trust, irrevocable trust, power of attorney, living will, health care proxy, lifetime gifts, and will.

f. Consider alternative property ownership forms, such as sole ownership, tenancy in common, joint tenancy with right of survivorship, tenancy by the entireties, or community property.

g. Investigate strategies to minimize taxes, including marital deduction, credit exclusion/equivalent bypass trust (CEBT), and annual gift tax exclusion.

h. Arrange estate liquidity to pay final costs, such as illness and funeral expenses, fees for executor, attorney, accountant, or appraiser, or personal debts.

i. Execute legal documents.

j. Review plan periodically, especially after life-changing events, such as the death of a spouse, a birth of a grandchild, grandchild's college education, sale of home, receipt of an inheritance, or serious illness.

14.2 INTERPERSONAL ISSUES

Key point   Minimize or avoid family conflicts by planning ahead; when there has been a remarriage, plan for all children.

Key point   Problems can arise with a family business if all children are not included.

14.21 Variables in family relationships can cause conflicts; planners should encourage open discussions before a crisis occurs.

a. Family-owned businesses in which children are not involved equally are an area of potential conflict.

(1) Equalize inheritances with a business-succession plan and a buy-sell agreement coupled with life insurance coverage.

14.22 Specific bequests are one way to deal with estates involving many personal items or items that are difficult to divide equally, but they can be problematic.

a. Many separate items may make specific bequests impractical; if item is later lost or destroyed or client decides on a different recipient, a new will may be necessary.

b. Some states provide that specific bequests are not subject to death taxes, which may put the tax burden on residuary beneficiaries.

14.23 Here are some ways to deal with estates involving many personal items, items difficult to divide equally, or estates involving blended families:

a. Encourage clients to keep a record of desired asset distribution.

(1) Not all states permit an external directive to be filed with a will. For those that do not recognize a letter of instruction, executor and family members usually honor a decedent's letter of wishes, if they were aware of it.

ZOOM IN   **Contents of Detailed "Upon Death or Incapacity" Letter**

1. Client's name

2. List of things to do first (with contact information):

   a. Notify family members

   b. Notify employer

   c. Make funeral arrangements

   d. Notify lawyer, bank, Social Security, Veterans' Administration

   e. Obtain and process insurance policies

3. Summary of beneficiaries' expectations:

   a. Life insurance, accident insurance, profit sharing, pension plan, other benefits from specified person/department at client's employer

   b. Total amounts from insurance companies

   c. Lump sum plus monthly benefits from Social Security and/or Veterans' Administration

   d. Amounts from other sources

4. Personal computer passwords, e-mail addresses, list of important file/document names

5. Personal papers (will, birth and marriage certificates, military records, naturalization papers)

6. Safe deposit box

7. Post office box

8. Checking and savings accounts, certificates

9. Doctors' names/addresses

10. Credit cards (Note: Give instructions to cancel all client cards)

11. Non-mortgage loans outstanding

12. Debts owed to client

13. Car

14. Income tax returns (location of prior years' returns; preparer's name contact information)

15. Investments (stocks, bonds/notes/bills, mutual funds, online accounts)

16. Funeral and burial information

17. Life insurance; other insurance

18. House, condo, co-op documents, including mortgage

19. Important warranties, receipts

20. Additional information and wishes

21. Signature

---

    b. Counsel clients who have remarried not to count on the surviving spouse to "do what is right" concerning asset distribution. Many problems can arise with this approach, including potential transfer tax liability.

    c. Make an outright lifetime gift if client can afford it.

        (1) If client has children from another marriage and plans to remarry, transferring assets during lifetime is advisable.

    d. Leave an **upon death or incapacity letter** containing relevant, up-to-date information for family and the estate representative to facilitate estate settlement.

14.3 MARRIAGE ISSUES

Key point Divorce among seniors is becoming more common, creating problems with adult children regarding anticipated inheritances.

Key point Pensions are a significant asset; a court order can direct pension distributions with a Qualified Domestic Relations Order (QDRO)

14.31 More seniors are divorcing.

  a. More divorces are occurring among couples in their 60s, 70s, and 80s, many of whom have been married for decades.

  b. Between 1990 and 2000, the divorced senior population increased by 35%.

14.32 Effects of divorce and remarriage.

  a. More strain among adult children, who realize they may have more caretaking responsibilities when one parent no longer has a spouse.

  b. If an incompetent spouse is being sued for divorce, a guardian ad litem may be appointed according to state law.

  c. Adult children may not want divorced parents to remarry for fear of losing inheritances; prenuptial agreements should be considered.

  d. A senior divorcee contemplating remarriage should consult an elder care attorney and/or a financial advisor.

14.33 Financial and property issues with divorce and remarriage.

  a. Divorce frequently lowers each former spouse's living standard.

  b. Although maintenance is often awarded along with equitable distribution of marital property, former wives generally fare less well financially than former husbands.

  c. A surviving spouse over age 60 is entitled to Social Security benefits according to the insured working spouse's earnings. Surviving divorced spouses also receive benefits if the marriage lasted at least 10 years.

  d. Pensions can be significant marital assets.

  (1) When a spouse has a qualified pension under ERISA (Employee Retirement Income Security Act), other spouse is entitled to share the pension funds.

  (2) Divorce eliminates this right unless an agreement or court order for a **qualified domestic relations order (QDRO)** exists, which allows the spouse who has not participated in the pension to be named as an alternate payee when the benefits become payable.

  (3) If other marital assets are substituted for spousal pension rights, it is crucial to have an actuary value the pension before making a property compromise.

  (4) Divorcing spouses must also confirm whether to change a pension beneficiary; if the former spouse is still the named beneficiary after divorce and the pension holder dies, the benefits could go to the former spouse instead of the new spouse or children from the first marriage.

  e. Wills, revocable trusts, and life insurance should be revisited with divorce.

14.4 PLANNING FOR INCAPACITY: GENERAL

Key point Disability is usually physical: a disabled person can be competent, whereas incapacity and incompetence involve the inability to act in a legal context, which is a mental health issue.

Key point Various arrangements can be made to appoint a representative for a person who cannot act on his own behalf.

14.41 Planners should follow the same information-gathering and assessment process in helping clients plan for potential incapacity that they follow for ordinary estate planning, with decisions based on client preferences and state law.

14.42 Terminology.

    a. Incapacity and incompetence usually mean the same thing; although both terms often involve a person's inability to act in a legal context, lack of capacity is usually determined by relatives, physicians, or mental health personnel.

    b. Disability usually pertains to daily physical impairment, such as inability to walk or talk, and is generally determined by the person or by close family members, does not mean that the disabled person is not legally competent.

    c. A guardian is responsible for personal care matters of a ward.

    d. A conservator is responsible for managing a ward's property; **conservatorship** involves court proceedings in the event an estate owner becomes disabled.

    e. A durable power of attorney (DPOA) is a legal document conveying authority to a person to carry out legal affairs on another person's behalf.

    f. A principal is the person executing the power of attorney.

    g. An attorney-in-fact, or surrogate, is the agent appointed by the principal via power of attorney.

    h. A durable power of attorney for health care (DPOAHC), sometimes called a medical proxy or medical durable power of attorney, is a form of advance medical directive that only takes effect when the patient is unable to provide consent.

    i. An advance medical directive refers to written instructions about a person's wishes concerning discontinuing medical care if the person can no longer speak for himself.

    j. A living will is a form of advance medical directive that specifies a person's wishes about medical treatment when the person is unable to give consent, generally in a terminal situation.

14.43 Having both a will and revocable trust documents helps to prevent guardianship and conservatorship proceedings if an estate owner becomes disabled or incapacitated.

    a. A will essentially pertains to the testator's death; the other documents pertain to asset and health management and incapacity while the testator is still living.

14.5 PLANNING FOR INCAPACITY: PROPERTY AND ASSETS

Key point Tools for managing the property and assets of incapacitated individuals include durable powers of attorney, living (inter vivos) trusts, guardianship or conservatorship, and special needs trusts.

14.51 Four basic, nonexclusive planning methods exist for managing an incapacitated person's assets and property: durable power of attorney (DPOA); revocable living (inter vivos) trust; guardian of property/conservator; and special needs trust.

14.52 Key points concerning durable powers of attorney for property:

a. With a **nonspringing durable power of attorney,** the power for the attorney-in-fact may become effective upon execution if the principal desires.

b. A **springing durable power of attorney** becomes operative only when the principal becomes incompetent.

c. The instrument establishing the DPOA must specify the terms upon which the document becomes effective; typically, a physician's determination is required.

d. Capacity should be documented independently at the time either type of DPOA is executed.

e. Although some third parties refuse to accept durable powers of attorney, a principal can minimize this risk by re-executing the DPOA periodically or by filing the document with an appropriate municipal office.

14.53 Key points concerning a revocable living (inter vivos) trust:

a. A revocable living trust specifies how the client (grantor) wants to consolidate assets, make financial decisions, and handle estate administration.

b. The grantor can be a trustee or co-trustee and provide as much or as little input as desired; trust document should provide for at least one successor trustee.

c. An advantage of a living trust is that trust property is not included in probate.

d. Another often-overlooked advantage is that a living trust is a good tool for planning for incapacity because the written provisions in the trust document will prevail if the grantor becomes unable to act for himself.

e. Trust can be funded either immediately after execution or later; funding takes place when the grantor re-titles the property in the name of the trustee of the trust.

(1) Ideally, the trust is funded shortly after it is created.

(2) Re-titling is necessary even when the grantor is also the trustee.

(3) **Standby trust:** term used when a trust is unfunded immediately after it is created; it is dangerous if the trust remains unfunded until the grantor is unable to act on his own behalf because at that point, the grantor will no longer be capable of carrying out the funding process.

14.54 Key points concerning guardianship or conservatorship of an estate:

a. They involve court proceedings and therefore are public.

b. A guardian or conservator must be court appointed and court supervised.

c. Proceedings can be streamlined when the ward's planning documents specify the person whom the ward, when competent, has designated as his agent.

d. Parents whose wills specify their minor children's guardian upon the parents' death should also nominate a guardian in case of the parents' incapacity.

14.55 Key points concerning **special needs trust (SNTs):** property management devices that protect the assets of persons expected to be disabled over a long term; they entail arranging beneficiaries' financial interests to maximize access to government assistance programs such as Medicaid and Supplemental Security Income (SSI).

a. Children are often the subjects of SNTs.

b. Some states consider SNTs to be void as against public policy.

c. Assets are insulated by having language in the trust document that prohibits trust principal from being used in substitution for governmental benefits.

d. There are three major types of SNTs.

(1) A common-law discretionary trust is established by nonfamily or interested parties on an incapacitated person's behalf.

(2) OBRA '93 payback trusts: distributions made at discretion of trustee with provision to reimburse the state for medical expenditures at the beneficiary's death.

(3) A pooled SNT is funded with assets that are pooled with other resources to increase investment results. Each state has a nonprofit organization to administer this fund.

14.6 PLANNING FOR INCAPACITY: HEALTH AND PERSONAL CARE

Key point Tools for handling health or personal care in the event of incapacity include a durable power of attorney for health care and a living will.

Key point While not a legal document, the values and experiences contained in a legacy or ethical will can be valuable to survivors whether or not the client becomes incapacitated.

14.61 Key points concerning a durable power of attorney for health care (DPOAHC):

a. Unlike a DPOA, a DPOAHC is always springing in its effect because the patient is assumed to speak for himself regarding medical consent; a DPOAHC only takes effect when an incapacitated person cannot give informed consent to a medical procedure, short of being terminally ill.

b. DPOAHC is broader than a living will; incapacitated person need not be terminally ill.

c. The document can either list explicit contingencies or (more commonly) give a broad declaration of power and discretion to the attorney-in-fact.

d. All states recognize some form of DPOAHC.

(1) Some states permit a DPOAHC to include the legal content of a living will.

(2) In contrast, a DPOAHC should never include the content of a traditional or financial DPOA; they involve very different situations.

(3) An efficient estate planner should offer a client a choice of separate DPOA and DPOAHC documents.

14.62 Key points concerning a living will:

a. Provisions are only triggered when a patient has been declared terminally ill in accordance with state law (unlike DPOAHC).

b. Provisions typically cover whether and how long to prolong life with artificial nourishment, separate from any life support technology decisions.

c. Provisions should be discussed with family and physicians.

d. Original document should be retained in a safe place, with a copy to the patient's closest relative, preferably the attorney-in-fact designated in the complementary DPOAHC.

14.63 Key points concerning a legacy or ethical will:

a. A **legacy or ethical will** conveys personal values, traditions, and/or experiences to succeeding generations; can be in writing or another medium.

b. It is not an estate planning document in a legal sense.

14.7 GIFTING

Key point Annual gifts to family and others can reduce the estate tax free if the gifts do not exceed the annual gift tax exclusion ($12,000 per donee per year in 2007).

Key point Trusts or special accounts (UTMAs) must be used for gifts to minors.

14.71 Gifting is a technique seniors may use to accomplish two main purposes:

a. Individuals like to benefit children and grandchildren while they are still living:

b. Properly structured gifting can reduce taxes:

(1) Estate taxes can be reduced by removing assets from the donor's estate:

(a) Asset must be transferred more than three years before donor's death or it will be included in donor's estate anyway.

(b) Gifts are potentially subject to gift tax.

(c) Gifts of $12,000 per recipient (2007 figure) are excluded each year (the annual exclusion), twice that for a married couple.

> **EXAMPLE** Rita and her husband Marco have six grandchildren. The couple may give a total of $132,000 ($22,000 per grandchild) in 2005 and reduce one or both of their estates by this amount. They can repeat similar gifts each year for additional reduction.

(d) Gifts in excess of the annual exclusion are charged first against the combined gift and estate credit, resulting in no tax; when that is used up, the gift is subject to tax.

c. Seniors should not give away assets they need to live on despite the tax benefits.

d. Source of gifts: gifts can be made from any asset:

   (1) A taxable asset.

   (2) A tax-preferred asset such as a qualified retirement plan or an IRA.

   (a) The income tax incurred is less than the estate tax that would be incurred if the asset remained in the senior's estate.

14.72 Simple gifts may create issues if the recipient is a minor.

a. If the minor is under 14, kiddie tax rules apply; above a minimal amount, the minor's income is taxed at his parent's tax rate, but the child's rate is normally lower once he reaches age 14.

b. Gifts cannot be made to minors without a special arrangement:

   (1) Totten trust: a simple trust in which the donor acts as trustee for the minor.

   (a) Assets are in bank account.

   (b) Trustee retains control.

   (c) No gift tax, as there is no complete transfer.

   (d) Assets not removed from estate.

   (2) UTMA account: a custodianship that holds an account for the benefit of a minor under the Uniform Transfers to Minors Act (UTMA); in a few states, the operative legislation is the Uniform Gifts to Minors Act (UGMA).

   (a) Gifts to an UTMA account qualify for the gift tax exclusion.

   (b) The child has access to the account at the age of majority (often 18); this often makes UTMA accounts undesirable for large amounts.

> **EXAMPLE** Over the years, Charlotte has deposited $85,000 into an UTMA account for her only grandson Tony. He is now 17. She is concerned that he will be able to access such a large amount of money next year when he reaches the age of majority. The only thing she can do at this point is threaten to discontinue the gifts if he blows the money.

   (3) For larger gifts a Section 2503(b) or 2503(c) trust may be used.

   (a) Trust instrument says how the money is to be used.

   (b) The trustee has no discretion.

   (c) The minor receives possession when the trust says:

   ■ 2503(b) requires current (annual) distribution of income but no requirement of distributing principal at age 21.

   ■ 2503(c) requires distribution of income and principal at age 21.

   (4) A Crummey trust (named after the taxpayer in an IRS case) can be used as a life insurance trust.

    (a) Donor transfers money to an irrevocable trust to purchase life insurance on the life of the donor.

    (b) Transfers to this trust may be used against the gift tax exclusion.

    (c) Assets are removed from the donor's estate.

    (d) Trust may go past the beneficiary reaching the age of majority.

14.73 Transfers for the education of a grandchild:

  a. Direct education gifts are direct tuition payments to the educational institution.

    (1) These are not considered gifts for gift tax purposes.

    (2) Amounts paid are removed from the donor's estate.

> **EXAMPLE** Mitch is proud that his grandson Josh was accepted at Trans State University. He has agreed to pay $10,000 of the tuition each year for four years. After four years, he has reduced his estate by $40,000.

  b. **Coverdell education savings accounts (CESAs):** special accounts similar to a Roth IRA but used for education expenses rather than retirement; these accounts were once called education IRAs.

    (1) Annual contributions are limited to $2,000 per beneficiary child per year; the limit is per child, not per donor.

    (2) Contributions to a grandchild's CESA count as gifts for gift tax purposes.

> **EXAMPLE** Scott wants to contribute the maximum to his grandson Joey's CESA for the year. Joey's parents already contributed $800. Scott may contribute $1,200 to make a total of $2,000. Scott can make other contributions to CESAs for his other grandchildren.

    (3) Contributions reduce the donor's estate.

    (4) Contributions are not income tax deductible.

    (5) Earnings are tax deferred.

    (6) Withdrawals are tax free if used for qualified educational expenses.

    (7) Withdrawals for other purposes are subject to tax plus a 10% penalty.

    (8) Accounts can be transferred from one beneficiary to another without tax if the new beneficiary is in the same generation as the old one.

  c. **Section 529 qualified tuition programs:** state-sponsored savings plans that allow tax-sheltered savings for higher education.

    (1) Nondeductible contributions.

    (2) Tax-deferred earnings.

    (3) Withdrawals tax free if used for qualified higher education purposes.

    (4) Tax and penalty for other types of withdrawals.

    (5) Donor maintains control of funds.

(6) Donor may aggregate up to five years of annual exclusion for a single lump-sum gift that is excludable from gift tax.

> **E X A M P L E** Richard, a single grandfather, contributed $60,000 to his granddaughter Jody's Section 529 plan in 2007. Although the annual gift tax exclusion is $12,000 in that year, he may use five years' worth of exclusions to cover this gift. As a result, he may not use the exclusion during the subsequent four years because the exclusions are considered to be already used.

14.74 Transfers to reduce a senior's estate are potentially in violation of rules designed to prevent people from fraudulently qualifying for Medicaid.

    a. Medicaid is a medical program for people with little or no income or assets.

        (1) Some people spend down their assets if they anticipate medical need in the near future, but the law makes this strategy difficult.

            (a) **Look-back period:** assets an individual transfers for less than full consideration (e.g., gifts, donations) are considered as still owned by the individual if the transfer occurred within 60 months before applying for Medicaid (reducing the motivation for spending down to qualify for Medicaid).

            (b) The Deficit Reduction Act (DRA) of 2005 set the look-back period at 60 months (formerly 36 months for most transfers) and also set $500,0000 as a maximum amount of equity an individual can have in his home and still qualify for Medicaid (individual states can raise this cap to $750,000).

        (2) Financial professionals are prohibited by federal law from advising clients to spend their assets down to qualify for Medicaid, but the US attorney general has indicated that this law will not be enforced.

        (3) Reductions intended to escape estate tax cease being beneficial when an estate drops below the estate tax exclusion amount ($2 million in 2007), so gifts for the purpose of reducing the estate to this amount will rarely make a difference for Medicaid eligibility (because an individual whose estate is equal to the estate tax exclusion amount still has a long way to go to reach Medicaid eligibility).

14.8 RETIREMENT PLANNING FOR CLIENTS WITH LIMITED ASSETS

> **Key point** Devices to consider in retirement planning for clients with limited assets include: reverse mortgages; sale-leasebacks of home to an adult child; life settlements (selling unneeded life insurance policy to a third party); or funeral trusts (to prepay funeral expenses).

14.81 **Reverse mortgage:** a loan that allows homeowners age 62 or older to take some or all of their home equity out in cash.

   a. The home must be the principal residence and have minimal debt.

   b. Amount of loan payments made to the homeowner depends on homeowner's age (or homeowners' joint ages), equity in the home, and interest rate charged.

   c. Payment options vary but usually fall into three categories:

   (1) Immediate cash advance: a lump-sum payment at closing.

   (2) Annuity: a monthly payment that can be stated as a definite number of years, as long as the person lives at home.

   (3) Credit line account: an option to take cash advances up to the maximum loan value during the life of the loan.

   d. Clients need to be alert to hidden costs, such as mortgage insurance, closing costs, and various servicing fees.

   e. For Medicaid eligibility purposes, the home only becomes a countable asset when its value is turned into cash.

14.82 A senior's sale-leaseback of home with adult child involves a financially strapped senior selling the family home to a child, perhaps as a second home, and then renting it back and remaining in the residence.

   a. Four advantages of a sale-leaseback: senior can gain extra retirement resources; senior remains in the home; home is removed from the senior's estate; and family relationships generally make the transaction and the living arrangements go smoothly.

   b. Disadvantage: IRS is likely to audit sale-leasebacks among family members.

14.83 A **life settlement** involves a senior insured selling an existing (often unwanted) life insurance policy to a third-party company in the business of buying policies.

   a. Growth market: expanded from $200 million in 1998 to $10-15 billion in 2005.

   b. Seller receives a portion of policy's net death benefit as immediate payment.

   c. The seller may be a person, corporation, or trust.

   d. Type of policy may be group, universal, variable life, survivorship, or term.

   e. Taxation:

   (1) Tax-free: payments representing basis.

   (2) Ordinary income: amounts over basis and up to cash surrender value.

   (3) Long-term capital gain: amounts in excess of cash surrender value.

   (4) No tax: if policyowner is terminally ill.

   (5) Three-year rule of IRC Section 2035 does not apply because the transaction with the funding company is a sale for value, not a gratuitous transfer.

   f. Availability:

   (1) To a policyholder age 70 or over regardless of health status.

   (2) To a policyholder age 65 in poor (not necessarily terminal) health.

   g. Distinction: life settlements are an expansion of **viatical settlements** (acceleration of death benefits to terminally ill policy holders) because a policyholder doesn't have to be terminally ill to receive a life settlement.

   h. Other considerations:

(1) Policyholder can use payments for long-term care, retirement assets, lifetime gifting, charitable contributions, and long-term health care insurance.

(2) Keep Medicaid eligibility requirements in mind.

(3) Once the policy is sold, its value is removed from the owner's gross estate except for what the recipient does not consume.

(4) Even if the life settlement amount is included in the owner's gross estate because the full amount is not consumed, the inclusion amount will be less than the full amount of the life insurance proceeds if the settlement had never occurred.

14.84 **Funeral trusts**, also called preburial or prefuneral trusts, are arrangements that seniors make with funeral directors and banks to set aside funds to prepay their funerals.

a. Many such trusts are executed for Medicaid purposes; trust funds are not considered an asset under Medicaid eligibility rules.

b. Legal compliance is essential in several areas: federal tax law, state tax and trust laws, and state preneed laws (the latter change frequently).

c. **Cemetery trusts**, which pertain to cemetery and burial plot arrangements, take various forms:

(1) **Endowment care cemetery trusts:** pool individual grantors' contributions to provide grave site maintenance; the cemetery business holds the trust in its own name and withdraws earnings regularly while the principal remains intact.

(2) **Service and merchandise cemetery trusts:** similar to funeral trusts and permit grantors to select and prefund items such as burial vaults, headstones, and the funeral service itself.

d. Federal and state tax laws govern the income taxation of funeral and cemetery trusts when trusts are paid out.

(1) Some preneed funeral trusts are revocable and are treated as grantor trusts.

(a) Income from trust assets is taxable to whoever owns or purchased the arrangement.

(b) Income attributed to the grantor from the trust might not be taxed if the grantor is below taxable thresholds.

(2) If the trust is irrevocable, it still may be treated as a grantor trust: because the funds are set aside to defray the grantor's future obligation, they are treated as a reversionary interest under Section 673 of the grantor trust rules.

(3) IRC Section 685 applies to preneed funeral trust and reporting issues.

(a) IRS form 1041, Qualified Funeral Trust (QFT), is used when electing the trust; the trustee is responsible for making the election and for complying with income tax and state filing requirements.

(b) The trust is treated as a nongrantor trust for tax purposes.

(c) A contract for a qualified funeral trust can only be established with someone engaged in the funeral business; the only permitted beneficiaries are the persons to whom the property or services apply.

14.9 TRUSTS AND OTHER ESTATE PLANNING TOOLS

> **Key point** Trusts have a variety of uses in estate planning, such as controlling the management of property, setting the timing of distributions, and reducing the amount of assets that are subject to estate tax.

> **Key point** Some trusts can also reduce current income tax for the grantor (generally irrevocable trusts); some trusts continue to expose the grantor to taxes on trust income (referred to as grantor trusts if the trust is revocable or the grantor retains certain powers over the trust).

14.91 Grantor trusts: the grantor of a grantor trust is subject to tax on the income of the trust under Sections 671–678 of the tax code.

    a. A trust is considered a grantor trust if it contains one or more of the following:

        (1) Income or principal is payable to the grantor or the grantor's spouse.

        (2) The trust is revocable or the grantor has the power to reacquire trust property or sell it for less than adequate consideration.

        (3) The trust may borrow without adequate security.

        (4) The grantor has a reversionary interest that is valued at more than 5% of the trust assets.

            (a) The younger the beneficiary, the smaller the value of the reversionary interest.

        (5) The trust uses funds to purchase life insurance on the life of the grantor or the grantor's spouse.

        (6) The amount beneficiaries are entitled to is controlled by the grantor.

        (7) These powers do not create a grantor trust if the grantor's power is subject to approval by someone who would stand to lose by the exercise of the power (an adverse party).

> **EXAMPLE** Aretha wants to set up a trust for her grandchildren and fund it with $100,000 in stock. If she adopts an irrevocable trust, the trust will pay tax on the earnings from the stock (or the grandchildren will pay tax if the income is paid out to them). If Aretha wants to change the amounts that each grandchild gets, the trust will be considered a grantor trust and she will be subject to tax.

    b. **Intentionally defective trust:** an irrevocable trust that is intentionally set up with grantor trust powers that make the grantor liable for income taxes on trust property while removing the property from the grantor's estate.

        (1) Care must be given in drafting a defective trust so as not to inadvertently bring the assets into the estate; this should be done by an experienced lawyer.

14.92 **Irrevocable grandparent-grandchild trust:** an irrevocable trust created by a grandparent for the benefit of one or more grandchildren that allows (but does not require) the trust to buy life insurance on the grandparent's adult child's life.

a. The grandchildren get the money when the adult child dies.

b. The adult child is spared paying the insurance premiums.

c. The amount of the policy is not included in the adult child's estate.

d. The grandparent's estate is reduced.

e. Transfers to the trust are applied against the lifetime gift tax credit.

f. The trust provision could provide that the adult child's estate could have access to the life insurance proceeds by selling property to the trust.

14.93 Qualified terminable interest property (QTIP) trusts: trusts that allow a senior to transfer property to a spouse that is eligible for the marital deduction while placing restrictions on how the property will pass when the spouse dies.

a. The QTIP trust provides assets to the spouse for life with remainder to the children.

b. If the spouse remarries, the new spouse (the third party) cannot have access to the QTIP property.

c. The surviving spouse must have a power to change the beneficiary (power of appointment) by will and the property will be included in the surviving spouse's estate; typically the power is not exercised.

d. A QTIP trust is often used with a second or third spouse.

e. This type of relationship often causes family friction while the client's children wait for second spouse to die.

   (1) The client could set up an irrevocable life insurance trust (ILIT) that would pay insurance proceeds to his children so they don't have to wait for second spouse to die.

14.94 Qualified personal residence trust (QPRT): a gift of one or two residences to an irrevocable trust for benefit of a beneficiary, often child, with the donor (grantor) retaining the right to live in the home without rent for a specified number of years, generally for a period that is shorter than the grantor's life expectancy.

a. The gift is equal to the fair market value of the home reduced by the value of the retained interest (the gift is reduced, so the tax is less than the estate tax would be if the home were held until the grantor's death).

   (1) The value is determined by using interest (discount) rates determined under Section 7520 of the tax code.

b. The grantor must live longer than the term specified in the trust or the estate tax savings of the arrangement is lost because the home will still be in the grantor's estate.

c. During the retained-interest period, the grantor is treated as the taxpayer and is taxed on the income of the trust.

d. At the end of the term, the grantor may rent the home for fair rental value.

14.95 Family limited partnership (FLP) or family limited liability company (FLLC): business entities in the partnership or limited liability company form held by members of a family for the purpose of holding property, often used for estate planning purposes.

a. The senior transfers property to the FLP or FLLC for ownership units.

b. The units are transferred to an irrevocable trust for the benefit of heirs.

    c. The units are valued less than the value of the property because they do not have voting rights, marketability, etc.; the discount could be 15 to 40%.

    d. These may be considered present interest gifts that qualify for the gift tax exclusion.

    e. **Family life insurance partnerships (FLIPs)**: similar to family limited partnerships but used to hold life insurance rather than other assets (used instead of an irrevocable life insurance trust [ILIT]), with the following tax savings.

        (1) Gift tax: contributions of premiums to the partnership by the insured to the FLIP qualify for the annual exclusion because they are present interest gifts.

        (2) Insured retains control; this is desirable if the repeal of the estate tax becomes permanent and the insured wants to take back the policy to use in other ways, or if other changes are desired.

        (3) Estate tax: will include proceeds of the life insurance only to the extent of the insured's share of the FLIP.

14.96 A defective trust may be used in connection with an FLP or FLLC to remove life insurance from a senior's estate.

    a. The senior sells the life insurance policy (to avoid the three-year rule that would bring life insurance proceeds into the estate if the senior dies within three years of a gratuitous transfer).

        (1) Normally, a person who buys a life insurance policy is subject to the transfer-for-value rule of Section 101 making the life insurance proceeds taxable.

        (2) An exception to this rule applies if the sale is to a partnership of which the seller is a partner or to a corporation of which he is shareholder or officer.

    b. This sale could trigger income tax if there is any gain in the policy when the senior sells it, but sale to a defective trust would eliminate that—the senior (grantor) would be considered both buyer and seller.

14.97 Private annuities: an arrangement in which one person transfers property to another (not to an insurance company) in exchange for regular annuity payments.

    a. Private annuities are used to remove low basis property from the estate.

    b. The private annuity is arranged between the senior and a younger family member.

    c. The younger family member gets a basis equal to the value of the promised annuity payments.

    d. Payments are determined based on:

        (1) Actuarial factors under Section 7520.

        (2) Fair market value of the property at the time of transfer (otherwise, the difference is treated as a taxable gift).

    e. This arrangement is beneficial if the senior dies young because the property is transferred without many of the annuity payments returned to his estate.

14.98 **Incentive trust:** a trust created with provisions that make enjoyment of the trust contingent (or partially contingent) on activities of the beneficiary (attainment of education, employment, other goals), also known as character trusts, family goals trusts, financial incentive trusts, or legacy trusts.

    a. Incentive trusts are resented if they are not flexible.

      (1) If too demanding, the child may simply forgo the trust.

      (2) If too rigid, a child who fails to reach the stated goal, but succeeds in a comparable way, would be out of luck.

b. Provisions should be made to allow distribution in case of emergencies, hardship, illness, etc.

c. If the beneficiary fails to qualify for the distribution by a certain age, the trust goes to charity or a different beneficiary.

HIGHLIGHTS

Highlight 1: Estate planning should be preventive; make arrangements before clients need long-term care or become incapacitated.

■ Key steps include making asset inventory, calculating net worth and taxes, setting goals, executing legal documents, and reviewing the plan periodically. (14.12, 14.13)

■ Many variables in family relationships must be taken into account to minimize potential conflicts. (14.21)

■ For estates involving many personal items or items that are difficult to divide equally, some options are:
(1) Leave specific bequests.
(2) Make an outright lifetime gift if client can afford it.
(3) Leave an upon death or incapacity letter containing relevant, up-to-date information for the family and estate representative. (14.22, 14.23)

■ Fact that more seniors are divorcing indicates need to be aware of financial and property issues with divorce and remarriage.
(1) Consider Social Security and pension issues.
(2) Revisit wills, revocable trusts, and life insurance in the event of divorce. (14.3)

Highlight 2: Planning for incapacity should follow the same process as ordinary estate planning.

■ Incapacity and incompetence are interchangeable terms and involve a person's inability to act in a legal context, whereas disability usually pertains to physical impairment and does not mean that a person is incompetent to transact legal matters. (14.4)

■ Four basic, nonexclusive planning methods exist for managing an incapacitated person's assets and property:
(1) Durable power of attorney (DPOA).
(2) Revocable living trust.
(3) Guardian of property/conservator.
(4) Special needs trust (SNT). (14.5)

Highlight 3: Clients can manage their health care in the event of incapacity by creating an advance medical directive.

■ Durable power of attorney for health care (DPOAHC), sometimes called a medical proxy, takes effect only when patient cannot give informed consent to a medical procedure, short of being terminally ill.
(1) All states recognize some form.
(2) Can either list explicit contingencies or (more commonly) give a broad declaration of power and discretion to the attorney-in-fact.
(3) Should never include the content of a traditional or financial DPOA. (14.61)

■ A living will's provisions are only triggered when a patient has been declared terminally ill in accord with state law.
(1) Narrower in scope than a DPOAHC; both documents complement each other. (14.62)

Highlight 4: Less affluent clients can benefit from retirement planning.

■ A reverse mortgage allows homeowners age 62 or older to take some or all of their home equity out in cash.
(1) The home must be the principal residence and have minimal debt.
(2) Payment options include a lump sum at closing, a monthly annuity, or a credit line.
(3) The home only is an asset for Medicaid purposes when its value is turned into cash. (14.81)

■ A sale-leaseback of a senior's home to an adult child or other family member removes the home from the senior's estate and creates extra retirement resources, while allowing the client to remain in his own home.
(1) Because the IRS closely scrutinizes sale-leasebacks between family members, such transactions should be handled at arm's length. (14.82)

■ Life settlements—a growth area in estate planning—are an option if a senior wants to sell an existing life insurance policy to a third-party company.
(1) Keep Medicaid eligibility requirements in mind. (14.83)

■ Funeral trusts, often executed for Medicaid eligibility purposes as well as to relieve survivors of burdens during a stressful time, offer tax benefits. (14.84)

Highlight 5: Lifetime gifting may be used to reduce a senior's taxable estate.

■ A lifetime gifting strategy takes advantage of the annual gift tax exclusion of $12,000 per donee per year (2007 figure). (14.71)

■ Gifts to minors require special treatment.
(1) Uniform Transfer to Minors Act (UTMA) accounts are simple custodial accounts that a child has access to upon reaching the age of majority.
(2) Section 2503(b) or 2503(c) trusts may be used to handle larger amounts of money and may delay access by the minor until age 21.
(3) A Crummey trust is an irrevocable trust that may be used to handle large amounts, often life insurance, and may delay access by the minor past age 21. (14.72)

■ Transfers for the education of a grandchild can reduce a senior's estate.
(1) Direct tuition payments and are not considered taxable gifts.
(2) Coverdell education savings accounts (CESAs) allow gifts of up to $2,000 per grandchild per year.
(3) Section 529 plans are state-sponsored plans that offer tax benefits similar to a CESA. (14.73)

Highlight 6: Trusts and other arrangements can reduce estate and other tax potential.

■ Grantors are not normally taxed on the income of irrevocable trusts, but grantors are taxed if certain powers are retained. (14.91)

■ Irrevocable grandparent-grandchild trusts are irrevocable trusts created by a grandparent for a grandchild.
(1) Life insurance is purchased for the adult child.
(2) Proceeds are payable to the grandchild. (14.92)

■ Qualified terminable interest property (QTIP) trusts allow a senior to transfer property to a spouse that is eligible for the marital deduction, with strings attached. (14.93)

- A qualified personal residence trust (QPRT) is an irrevocable trust holding a senior's home, allowing him to live there rent free for a limited period. (14.94)

- Family limited partnerships (FLPs) or family limited liability companies (FLLCs) can be used to remove assets from a senior's estate. (14.95)

- Private annuities are used to transfer an asset to a younger family member, removing the asset from the estate, in exchange for annuity payments. (14.97)

TERMS TO KNOW DEFINITIONS

Cemetery trust Type of funeral trust that pertains to cemetery and burial plot arrangements. (14.84c)

Conservatorship Court proceedings in the event an estate owner becomes disabled; a conservator is responsible for managing a ward's property. (14.42d)

Coverdell education savings accounts (CESAs) Special accounts similar to a Roth IRA but used for education expenses rather than retirement (formerly called education IRAs). (14.73b)

Endowment care cemetery trusts Pool individual grantors' contributions to provide grave site maintenance; the cemetery business holds the trust in its own name and withdraws earnings regularly while the principal remains intact. (14.84c(1))

Family life insurance partnerships (FLIPs) Similar to family limited partnerships but used to hold life insurance rather than other assets (used instead of an irrevocable life insurance trust [ILIT]). (14.94e)

Family limited liability company (FLLC) Business entity in the partnership or limited liability company form held by members of a family for the purpose of holding property, often used for estate planning purposes. (14.95)

Family limited partnership (FLP) Business entity in the partnership or limited liability company form held by members of a family for the purpose of holding property, often used for estate planning purposes. (14.95)

Funeral trusts Arrangements with funeral directors and banks to set aside funds to prepay funerals to avoid placing this burden on surviving family members (also called pre-burial or pre-funeral trusts). (14.84)

Incentive trust A trust created with provisions that make enjoyment of the trust contingent (or partially contingent) on activities of the beneficiary (attainment of education, employment, or other goals), also known as character trusts, family goals trusts, financial incentive trusts, or legacy trusts. (14.98)

Intentionally defective trust An irrevocable trust that is intentionally set up with grantor trust powers that make the grantor liable for income taxes on trust property while removing the property from the grantor's estate. (14.91b)

Irrevocable grandparent-grandchild insurance trust An irrevocable trust created by a grandparent for the benefit of one or more grandchildren that allows (but does not require) the trust to buy life insurance on the grandparent's adult child's life. (14.92)

Legacy (ethical) will Conveys personal values, traditions, or experiences to succeeding generations. (14.64)

Life settlement Sale by a senior insured of an existing (often unwanted) life insurance policy to a third-party company in the business of buying policies. The company purchases the life insurance contract to make a profit at the death of an insured. (14.83)

Look-back period Assets an individual transfers for less than full consideration (e.g., gifts, donations) are considered as still owned by the individual if the transfer occurred within 60 months before applying for Medicaid (reducing the motivation for spending down to qualify for Medicaid). (14.74a(1)(a))

Nonspringing durable power of attorney Power of attorney that becomes effective upon execution if the principal desires. (14.52a)

Qualified domestic relations order (QDRO) Allows a divorcing spouse who has not participated in a pension to be named as an alternate payee when the benefits become payable. (14.33d)

Qualified personal residence trust (QPRT) A gift of one or two residences to an irrevocable trust for benefit of a beneficiary, often the grantor's child, with the donor (grantor) retaining the right to live in the home without rent for a specified number of years, generally for a period that is shorter than the grantor's life expectancy; as a consequence, the home is removed from the homeowner's estate. (14.94)

Qualified terminable interest property (QTIP) trusts Trusts that allow a senior to transfer property to a spouse who is eligible for the marital deduction while placing restrictions on how the property will pass when the spouse dies. (14.93)

Reverse mortgage A loan that allows homeowners age 62 or older to take out some or all of their home equity in cash. (14.81)

Section 529 qualified tuition programs State-sponsored savings plans that allow tax-sheltered savings for higher education. (14.73c)

Service and merchandise cemetery trusts Similar to funeral trusts; permit grantors to select and prefund items such as burial vaults, headstones, and the funeral service itself. (14.84c(2))

Special needs trust (SNT) Property management device that protects the assets of persons expected to be disabled over a long term. (14.55)

Springing durable power of attorney Power of attorney that becomes operative only when the principal becomes incompetent. (14.52b)

Standby trust A living trust that is unfunded immediately after it is created. (14.53e)

Upon death or incapacity letter A written communication containing relevant, up-to-date information for family and the estate representative to facilitate estate settlement. (14.23d)

Viatical settlement The proceeds from the sale of a life insurance policy to a third party by an individual who is terminally or chronically ill and expected to die within 24 months; intended to accelerate death benefits to the terminally ill policyholder. (14.83g)

QUESTIONS

1. All of the following are basic steps of estate planning EXCEPT
   A. making an inventory of assets
   B. making a legacy will
   C. investigating tax strategies
   D. determining goals

2. Which of the following concerning guardianship or conservatorship of an estate is(are) TRUE?
   A. A guardian or conservator is not necessarily court-appointed and proceedings are not always public.
   B. Proceedings can be streamlined when the planning documents specify the person whom the ward has designated as his agent upon the ward's incapacity.
   C. Both A and B.
   D. Neither A nor B.

3. Which of the following concerning life settlements is CORRECT?
   A. The seller may only be a person, not a corporation or trust.
   B. The seller receives a portion of the policy's net death benefit immediately.
   C. The life settlement market is stagnant.
   D. Once the policy is sold, its entire value remains in the owner's gross estate.

4. A grantor trust subjects which of the following to tax?
   A. Beneficiary
   B. Grantor
   C. Trust
   D. Trustee

5. Gifts are subject to gift tax if
   A. the gift exceeds $12,000 (in 2007)
   B. the gift tax exceeds the applicable credit against gift tax
   C. both A and B
   D. neither A nor B

ANSWERS

1. **B.** A legacy will is not an estate planning document but rather conveys personal values and thoughts to survivors. (14.13, 14.63)

2. **B.** A guardian or conservator must be court appointed and court supervised; for this reason, such proceedings are public. (14.54)

3. **B.** The life settlement market is a growth area; the seller may be a person, corporation, or trust; once the policy is sold, the only portion of the value that remains in the owner's gross estate is what the recipient does not consume. (14.83)

4. **B.** Even if a trust is irrevocable, the grantor is subject to tax on the income of a grantor trust. This happens if the grantor retains one of various powers listed in Sections 671–678 of the tax code. (14.91)

5. **C.** A gift that does not exceed the annual exclusion amount is potentially subject to gift tax. However, a credit applies to the gift tax, which means that the gift is not taxed until the credit is used up. (14.71b(1))

Appendix: Using Your Calculator and the Exam

You may find a few questions on your exam that call for the use of a calculator. It is important to be comfortable with your calculator before you go to the exam. It is also important to keep calculator questions in perspective.

Most of the questions on your exam will not involve a calculator. If you read the tips at the beginning of the Study Notes, you will see that it is important to manage your test-taking time so that you can devote most of your energy to the questions that will be most productive for you.

Accordingly, we advise you to skip math questions altogether on your first pass through the exam. This will give you the time to be sure you answer all the easier questions. (Of course, if you are a math whiz, feel free to answer these questions the first time through. The point is that you should play to your strengths.)

The same strategy should also apply to your studies. Do not get hung up on the calculator questions as you study. There is a lot of material in this course to learn. If you get stuck on one part of it, you need to move on so that you cover everything during your limited study time.

One final note: The material in this appendix covers basic financial calculation for a number of different types of calculator. If you want a different perspective, consult your owner's manual or go to the Website of the manufacturer of the calculator. You can find this easily by typing the model name of your calculator into an Internet search engine.

What follows, in the remainder of this appendix, are some sample problems and a list of keystrokes you can use to solve them. In addition to the five calculators, we show values that are common to all the calculator methods.

1. FUTURE VALUE

Future Value—Annual Compounding

Today Tom purchased an investment-grade gold coin for $150,000. He expects it to increase in value at a rate of 7% compounded annually for the next 5 years. How much will the coin be worth at the end of the 5th year if his expectations are correct?

HP 17BII		HP 12C		HP 10BII	
Keystrokes	Display	Keystrokes	Display	Keystrokes	Display
[FIN]	SELECT A MENU	5 [n]	5.0000	5 [N]	5.0000
[TVM]	1 P/YR END MODE	7 [i]	7.0000	7 [I/YR]	7.0000
5 [N]	N = 5.0000	150000 [PV]	150,000.0000	150000 [PV]	150,000.0000
7 [I%YR]	I%YR = 7.0000	0 [PMT]	0.0000	0 [PMT]	0.0000
150000 [PV]	PV = 150,000.0000	[FV]	−210,382.7596	[FV]	−210,382.7596
0 [PMT]	PMT = 0.0000				
[FV]	FV = − **210,382.7596**				
[EXIT][EXIT]					

TI BA II Plus		SHARP EL 733A		COMMON VALUES	
Keystrokes	Display	Keystrokes	Display		
5 [N]	N = 5.0000	5 [n]	5.0000^FIN	PV	−150,000.0000
7 [I/Y]	I/Y = 7.0000	7 [i]	7.0000^FIN	N	5.0000
150000 [PV]	PV = 150,000.0000	150000 [PV]	150'000.0000^FIN	I	7.0000
0 [PMT]	PMT = 0.0000	0 [PMT]	0.0000^FIN	PMT	0.0000
[CPT][FV]	FV = −**210,382.7596**	[COMP][FV]	−210'382.7596^FIN	FV	**210,382.7596**

Future Value—Monthly Compounding

A client invested $20,000 in an interest-bearing promissory note earning a 9% annual rate of interest compounded monthly. How much will the note be worth at the end of 8 years assuming all interest is reinvested at the 9% rate?

HP 17BII		HP 12C		HP 10BII	
Keystrokes	Display	Keystrokes	Display	Keystrokes	Display
[FIN]	SELECT A MENU	8 [ENTER]	8.0000	8 [×]	8.0000
[TVM]	1 P/YR END MODE	12 [×][n]	96.0000	12 [=][N]	96.0000
8 [×]	8.0000×	9 [ENTER]	9.0000	9 [÷]	9.0000
12 [=][N]	N = 96.0000	12 [÷][i]	0.7500	12 [=][I/YR]	0.7500
9 [÷]	9.0000÷	20000 [PV]	20,000.0000	20000 [PV]	20,000.0000
12 [=][I%YR]	I%YR = 0.7500	0 [PMT]	0.0000	0 [PMT]	0.0000
20000 [PV]	PV = 20,000.0000	[FV]	−**40,978.4246**	[FV]	−**40,978.4246**
0 [PMT]	PMT = 0.0000				
[FV]	FV = −**40,978.4246**				
[EXIT][EXIT]					

TI BA II Plus		SHARP EL 733A		COMMON VALUES	
Keystrokes	Display	Keystrokes	Display		
8 [×]	8.0000	8 [×]	8.0000^{FIN}	PV	−20,000.0000
12 [=][N]	N = 96.0000	12 [=][n]	96.0000^{FIN}	N	96.0000 (8 × 12)
9 [÷]	9.0000	9 [÷]	9.0000^{FIN}	I	.7500 (9 ÷ 12)
12 [=][I/Y]	I/Y = 0.7500	12 [=][i]	0.7500^{FIN}	PMT	0.0000
20000 [PV]	PV = 20,000.0000	20000 [PV]	20'000.0000^{FIN}	FV	40,978.4246
0 [PMT]	PMT = 0.0000	0 [PMT]	0.0000^{FIN}		
[CPT][FV]	FV = **−40,978.4246**	[COMP][FV]	**−40,978.4246**^{FIN}		

█ 2. PRESENT VALUE

Present Value—Annual Compounding

Mary wants to give her daughter $35,000 to start her own business in 10 years. How much should she invest today at an annual interest rate of 9% compounded annually to have $35,000 in 10 years?

HP 17BII		HP 12C		HP 10BII	
Keystrokes	Display	Keystrokes	Display	Keystrokes	Display
[FIN]	SELECT A MENU	10 [n]	10.0000	10 [N]	10.0000
[TVM]	1 P/YR END MODE	9 [i]	9.0000	9 [I/YR]	9.0000
10 [N]	N = 10.0000	0 [PMT]	0.0000	0 [PMT]	0.0000
9 [I%YR]	I%YR = 9.0000	35000 [FV]	35,000.0000	35000 [FV]	35,000.0000
0 [PMT]	PMT = 0.0000	[PV]	**−14,784.3782**	[PV]	**−14,784.3782**
35000 [FV]	FV = 35,000.0000				
[PV]	PV = **−14,784.3782**				
[EXIT][EXIT]					

TI BA II Plus		SHARP EL 733A		COMMON VALUES	
Keystrokes	Display	Keystrokes	Display		
10 [N]	N = 10.0000	10 [n]	10.0000^{FIN}	FV	35,000.0000
9 [I/Y]	I/Y = 9.0000	9 [i]	9.0000^{FIN}	N	10.0000
0 [PMT]	PMT = 0.0000	0 [PMT]	0.0000^{FIN}	I	9.0000
35000 [FV]	FV = 35,000.0000	35000 [FV]	35'000.0000^{FIN}	PMT	0.0000
[CPT][PV]	FV = **−14,784.3782**	[COMP][PV]	**−14'784.3782**^{FIN}	PV	**−14,784.3782**

Present Value—Semiannual Compounding

John expects to receive $95,000 from a trust fund in 7 years. What is the current value of this fund if it is discounted at 8% compounded semiannually?

HP 17BII		HP 12C		HP 10BII	
Keystrokes	Display	Keystrokes	Display	Keystrokes	Display
[FIN]	SELECT A MENU	7 [ENTER]	7.0000	7 [×]	7.0000
[TVM]	1 P/YR END MODE	2 [×][n]	14.0000	2 [=][N]	14.0000
7 [×]	7.0000×	8 [ENTER]	8.0000	8 [÷]	8.0000
2 [=][N]	N = 14.0000	2 [÷][i]	4.0000	2 [=][I/YR]	4.0000
8 [÷]	8.0000÷	0 [PMT]	0.0000	0 [PMT]	0.0000
2 [=][I%YR]	I%YR = 4.0000	95000 [FV]	95,000.0000	95000 [FV]	95,000.0000
0 [PMT]	PMT = 0.0000	[PV]	**−54,860.1329**	[PV]	**−54,860.1329**
95000 [FV]	FV = 95,000.0000				
[PV]	PV = **−54,860.1329**				
[EXIT][EXIT]					

TI BA II Plus		SHARP EL 733A		COMMON VALUES	
Keystrokes	Display	Keystrokes	Display		
7 [×]	7.0000	7 [×]	7.0000^{FIN}	FV	95,000.0000
2 [=][N]	N = 14.0000	2 [=][n]	14.0000^{FIN}	N	14.0000 (7 × 2)
8 [÷]	8.0000	8 [÷]	8.0000^{FIN}	I	4.0000 (8 ÷ 2)
2 [=][I/Y]	I/Y = 4.0000	2 [=][i]	4.0000^{FIN}	PMT	0.0000
0 [PMT]	PMT = 0.0000	0 [PMT]	0.0000^{FIN}	PV	−54,860.1329
95000 [FV]	FV = 95,000.0000	95000 [FV]	95,000.0000^{FIN}		
[CPT][PV]	PV = **−54,860.1329**	[COMP][PV]	**−54,860.1329**^{FIN}		

Present Value—Monthly Compounding

Billy expects to receive $105,000 in 9 years. His opportunity cost is 10% compounded monthly. What is this sum worth to Billy today?

HP 17BII		HP 12C		HP 10BII	
Keystrokes	**Display**	**Keystrokes**	**Display**	**Keystrokes**	**Display**
[FIN]	SELECT A MENU	9 [ENTER]	9.0000	9 [×]	9.0000
[TVM]	1 P/YR END MODE	12 [×][n]	108.0000	12 [=][N]	108.0000
9 [×]	9.0000×	10 [ENTER]	10.0000	10 [÷]	10.0000
12 [=][N]	N = 108.0000	12 [÷][i]	0.8333	12 [=][I/YR]	0.8333
10 [÷]	10.0000÷	0 [PMT]	0.0000	0 [PMT]	0.0000
12 [=][I%YR]	I%YR = 0.8333	105000 [FV]	105,000.0000	105000 [FV]	105,000.0000
0 [PMT]	PMT = 0.0000	[PV]	**–42,849.3145**	[PV]	**–42,849.3145**
105000 [FV]	FV = 105,000.0000				
[PV]	PV = **–42,849.3145**				
[EXIT][EXIT]					

TI BA II Plus		SHARP EL 733A		COMMON VALUES	
Keystrokes	**Display**	**Keystrokes**	**Display**		
9 [×]	9.0000	9 [×]	9.0000^{FIN}	FV	–105,000.0000
12 [=][N]	N = 108.0000	12 [=][n]	108.0000^{FIN}	N	108.0000 (9 × 12)
10 [÷]	10.0000	10 [÷]	10.0000^{FIN}	I	.8333 (10 ÷ 12)
12 [=][I/Y]	I/Y = 0.8333	12 [=][i]	0.8333^{FIN}	PMT	0.0000
0 [PMT]	PMT = 0.0000	0 [PMT]	0.0000^{FIN}	PV	**42,849.3145**
105000 [FV]	FV = 105,000.0000	105000 [FV]	105'000.0000^{FIN}		
[CPT][PV]	PV = **–42,849.3145**	[COMP][PV]	**–42'849.3145**^{FIN}		

Present Value—Quarterly Compounding

Mary wants to accumulate $75,000 in 11.5 years to purchase a boat. She expects an annual rate of return of 9% compounded quarterly. How much does Mary need to invest today to meet her goal?

HP 17BII		HP 12C		HP 10BII	
Keystrokes	Display	Keystrokes	Display	Keystrokes	Display
[FIN]	SELECT A MENU	11.5 [ENTER]	11.5000	11.5 [×]	11.5000
[TVM]	1 P/YR END MODE	4 [×][n]	46.0000	4 [=][N]	46.0000
11.5 [×]	11.5000×	9 [ENTER]	9.0000	9 [÷]	9.0000
4 [=][N]	N = 46.0000	4 [÷][i]	2.2500	4 [=][I/YR]	2.2500
9 [÷]	9.0000÷	0 [PMT]	0.0000	0 [PMT]	0.0000
4 [=][I%YR]	I%YR = 2.2500	75000 [FV]	75,000.0000	75000 [FV]	75,000.0000
0 [PMT]	PMT = 0.0000	[PV]	**−26,949.3749**	[PV]	**−26,949.3749**
75000 [FV]	FV = 75,000.0000				
[PV]	PV = **−26,949.3749**				
[EXIT][EXIT]					

TI BA II Plus		SHARP EL 733A		COMMON VALUES	
Keystrokes	Display	Keystrokes	Display		
11.5 [×]	11.5000	11.5 [×]	11.5000FIN	FV	75,000.0000
4 [=][N]	N = 46.0000	4 [=][n]	46.0000FIN	N	46.0000 (11.5 × 4)
9 [÷]	9.0000	9 [÷]	9.0000FIN	I	2.2500 (9 ÷ 4)
4 [=][I/Y]	I/Y = 2.2500	4 [=][i]	2.2500FIN	PMT	0.0000
0 [PMT]	PMT = 0.0000	0 [PMT]	0.0000FIN	PV	**−26,949.3749**
75000 [FV]	FV = 75,000.0000	75000 [FV]	75'000.0000FIN		
[CPT][PV]	PV = **−26,949.3749**	[COMP][PV]	**−26'949.3749FIN**		

3. INTERNAL RATE OF RETURN (IRR)

IRR—Example 1

Jeff purchased 100 shares of an aggressive growth mutual fund for $82 per share 9 years ago. Today he sold all 100 shares for $60,000. What was his average annual compound rate of return on this investment before tax?

HP 17BII		HP 12C		HP 10BII	
Keystrokes	**Display**	**Keystrokes**	**Display**	**Keystrokes**	**Display**
[FIN]	SELECT A MENU	9 [n]	9.0000	9 [N]	9.0000
[TVM]	1 P/YR END MODE	0 [PMT]	0.0000	0 [PMT]	0.0000
9 [N]	N = 9.0000	82[CHS][ENTER]	–82.0000	82 [+\–][×]	–82.0000
0 [PMT]	PMT = 0.0000	100 [×][PV]	–8,200.0000	100 [=][PV]	–8,200.0000
82 [+\–][×]	–82.0000×	60000 [FV]	60,000.0000	60000 [FV]	60,000.0000
100 [=][PV]	PV = –8,200.0000	[i]	**24.7491**	[I/YR]	**24.7491**
60000 [FV]	FV = 60,000.0000				
[I%YR]	I%YR = **24.7491**				
[EXIT][EXIT]					

TI BA II Plus		SHARP EL 733A		COMMON VALUES	
Keystrokes	**Display**	**Keystrokes**	**Display**		
9 [N]	N = 9.0000	9 [n]	9.0000^{FIN}	N	9.0000
0 [PMT]	PMT = 0.0000	0 [PMT]	0.0000^{FIN}	PV	–8,200.0000
82 [+\–][×]	–82.0000	82 [+\–][×]	–82.0000^{FIN}	PMT	0.0000
100 [=][PV]	PV = –8,200.0000	100 [=][PV]	–8'200.0000^{FIN}	FV	60,000.0000
60000 [FV]	FV = 60,000.0000	60000 [FV]	60'000.0000^{FIN}	I	**24.7491**
[CPT][I/Y]	I/Y = **24.7491**	[COMP][i]	**24.7491**^{FIN}		

IRR—Example 2

James borrowed $1,800 from his father to purchase a mountain bike. James paid back $2,600 to his father at the end of 4 years. What was the average annual compound rate of interest on James's loan from his father?

HP 17BII		HP 12C		HP 10BII	
Keystrokes	**Display**	**Keystrokes**	**Display**	**Keystrokes**	**Display**
[FIN]	SELECT A MENU	4 [n]	4.0000	4 [N]	4.0000
[TVM]	1 P/YR END MODE	0 [PMT]	0.0000	0 [PMT]	0.0000
4 [N]	N = 4.0000	1800 [PV]	1,800.0000	1800 [PV]	1,800.0000
0 [PMT]	PMT = 0.0000	2600[CHS][FV]	–2,600.0000	2600 [+\–][FV]	–2,600.0000
1800 [PV]	PV = 1,800.0000	[i]	**9.6289**	[I/YR]	**9.6289**
2600 [+\–][FV]	FV = –2,600.0000				
[I%YR]	I%YR = **9.6289**				
[EXIT][EXIT]	SELECT A MENU				

TI BA II Plus		SHARP EL 733A		COMMON VALUES	
Keystrokes	**Display**	**Keystrokes**	**Display**		
4 [N]	N = 4.0000	4 [n]	4.0000FIN	N	4.0000
0 [PMT]	PMT = 0.0000	0 [PMT]	0.0000FIN	PV	1,800.0000
1800 [PV]	PV = 1,800.0000	1800 [PV]	1'800.0000FIN	PMT	0.0000
2600 [+\–][FV]	FV = –2,600.0000	2600 [+\–][FV]	–2'600.0000FIN	FV	–2,600.0000
[CPT][I/Y]	I/Y = **9.6289**	[COMP][i]	**9.6289FIN**	I	**9.6289**

IRR—Example 3

Susan purchased a zero-coupon bond 9½ years ago for $399.73. If the bond matures today and the face value is $1,000, what is the average annual compound rate of return that Susan realized on her investment?

HP 17BII		HP 12C		HP 10BII	
Keystrokes	**Display**	**Keystrokes**	**Display**	**Keystrokes**	**Display**
[FIN]	SELECT A MENU	9.5 [n]	9.5000	9.5 [N]	9.5000
[TVM]	1 P/YR END MODE	0 [PMT]	0.0000	0 [PMT]	0.0000
9.5 [N]	N = 9.5000	399.73 [CHS][PV]	–399.7300	399.73[+\–][PV]	–399.7300
0 [PMT]	PMT = 0.0000	1000 [FV]	1,000.0000	1000 [FV]	1,000.0000
399.73 [+\–][PV]	PV = 399.7300	[i]	**10.1200**	[I/YR]	**10.1335**
1000 [FV]	FV = 1,000.0000				
[I%YR]	I%YR = **10.1335**				
[EXIT][EXIT]					

TI BA II Plus		SHARP EL 733A		COMMON VALUES	
Keystrokes	**Display**	**Keystrokes**	**Display**		
9.5 [N]	N = 9.5000	9.5 [n]	9.5000FIN	N	9.5000
0 [PMT]	PMT = 0.0000	0 [PMT]	0.0000FIN	PV	–399.7300
399.73 [+\–][PV]	PV = –399.7300	399.73 [+\–][PV]	–399.7300FIN	PMT	0.0000
1000 [FV]	FV = 1,000.0000	1000 [FV]	1'000.0000FIN	FV	1,000.0000
[CPT][I/Y]	I/Y = **10.1335**	[COMP][i]	**10.1335FIN**	I	**10.1335**

Which answer is correct: 10.1335% or 10.12%? The correct answer is 10.1335%. The HP 12C does not calculate this correctly as illustrated below.

Proof of Internal Rate of Return with Non-Integer Compounding

By adding the internal rate of return to one and raising the sum to the power of 9.5 and multiplying the result by $399.73, you should end up with $1,000.00.

HP 17BII, HP 10BII, TI BA II Plus, SHARP EL 733A	HP 12C
$(1.101335)^{9.5} \times \$399.73 = \$1,000.00$	$(1.1012)^{9.5} \times 399.73 = \$998.84$

NOTE: The HP 12C does not handle non-integer terms very well. Thus, the HP 12C does not come up with the correct answer; however, it is reasonably close.

4. TERM CALCULATIONS

Term Calculation—Annual Compounding

Fred purchased an Oriental rug for $28,000. Today, he sold the rug for $49,345.57. Fred estimated his average annual opportunity cost on the rug was 12%. Approximately how many years did Fred own the rug (rounded to the nearest .000)?

HP 17BII		HP 12C		HP 10BII	
Keystrokes	**Display**	**Keystrokes**	**Display**	**Keystrokes**	**Display**
[FIN]	SELECT A MENU	12[i]	12.0000	12[I/YR]	12.0000
[TVM]	1 P/YR END MODE	0[PMT]	0.0000	0[PMT]	0.0000
12[I%YR]	I%YR = 12.0000	28000[CHS][PV]	−28,000.0000	28000[+\−][PV]	−28,000.0000
0[PMT]	PMT = 0.0000	49345.57[FV]	49,345.5700	49345.57 [FV]	49,345.5700
28000[+\−][PV]	PV = −28,000.0000	[n]	**5.0000**	[N]	**5.0000**
49345.57[FV]	FV = 49,345.5700				
[N]	N = **5.0000**				
[EXIT][EXIT]					

TI BA II Plus		SHARP EL 733A		COMMON VALUES	
Keystrokes	**Display**	**Keystrokes**	**Display**		
12[I/Y]	I/Y = 12.0000	12[i]	12.0000^{FIN}	I	12.0000
0[PMT]	PMT = 0.0000	0 [PMT]	0.0000^{FIN}	PV	−28,000.0000
28000[+\−][PV]	PV = −28,000.0000	28000[+\−][PV]	−28'000.0000^{FIN}	PMT	0.0000
49345.57 [FV]	FV = 49,345.5700	49345.57 [FV]	49'345.5700^{FIN}	FV	49,345.5700
[CPT][N]	N = **5.0000**	[COMP][n]	**5.0000^{FIN}**	N	**5.0000**

> NOTE: When solving for [n] on the HP 12C, only integers (whole numbers) are displayed as a solution. The HP 12C calculator cannot solve for non-integers (numbers with decimals). Therefore, your answer may be incorrect and will not match the answers of other calculators. For example, the HP 12C will give a result of N = 5 for the above problem by substituting any number between $44,084 and $49,345.57. This result will not happen with the other four calculators.

Term Calculation—Monthly Compounding

Today, Willis put all of his cash into an account earning an annual interest rate of 10% compounded monthly. Assuming he makes no withdrawals from or additions to this account, approximately how many years must Willis wait to double his money (rounded to the nearest .00)? (Suggestion: use $1 as the amount to be invested.)

HP 17BII		HP 12C		HP 10BII	
Keystrokes	Display	Keystrokes	Display	Keystrokes	Display
[FIN]	SELECT A MENU	10 [ENTER]	10.0000	10 [÷]	10.0000
[TVM]	1 P/YR END MODE	12 [÷][i]	0.8333	12 [=][I/YR]	0.8333
10 [÷]	10.0000÷	0 [PMT]	0.0000	0 [PMT]	0.0000
12 [=][I%YR]	I%YR = 0.8333	1 [CHS][PV]	−1.0000	1 [+\−][PV]	−1.0000
0 [PMT]	PMT = 0.0000	2 [FV]	2.0000	2 [FV]	2.0000
1 [+\−][PV]	PV = −1.0000	[n]	84.0000	[N]	83.5238
2 [FV]	FV = 2.0000	[ENTER]	84.0000	[÷] 12 [=]	**6.9603**
[N]	N = 83.5238	12 [÷]	**7.0000**		
[π] 12 [=]	**6.9603**				
[EXIT][EXIT]					

TI BA II Plus		SHARP EL 733A		COMMON VALUES		
Keystrokes	Display	Keystrokes	Display			
10 [÷]	10.0000	10 [÷]	10.0000^{FIN}	I		.8333 (10 ÷ 12)
12 [=][I/Y]	I/Y = 0.8333	12 [=][i]	0.8333^{FIN}	PV		−1.0000
0 [PMT]	PMT = 0.0000	0 [PMT]	0.0000^{FIN}	PMT		0.0000
1 [+\−][PV]	PV = −1.0000	1 [+\−][PV]	−1.0000^{FIN}	FV		2.0000
2 [FV]	FV = 2.0000	2 [FV]	2.0000^{FIN}	N		83.5238
[CPT][N]	N = 83.5238	[COMP][n]	83.5238^{FIN}	÷ 12		**6.9603**
[÷] 12 [=]	**6.9603**	[÷] 12 [=]	**6.9603**^{FIN}			

NOTE: As previously stated, when solving for [n] on the HP 12C, only integers (whole numbers) are displayed as a solution. The HP 12C calculator cannot solve for non-integers (numbers with decimals). In this particular problem, the solution returned by the HP 12C is not the correct answer; however, it is close.

Using the solution of 7.000 for [n] returned by the HP 12C, when calculating the FV, you do not get 2.00 as the future value as you would expect. Instead, the FV is calculated as 2.0079, because of the [n] being rounded. You can verify this by adding the following keystrokes to the end of the problem: 84[n], [FV] and the calculator will display 2.0079.

Rule of 72: The Rule of 72 states that by dividing 72 by the interest rate, you will get a reasonable approximation of the number of years it will take for your money to double. For example: 72 ÷ 10 = 7.2 years. From the above calculation, the exact answer is 6.9603 years.

5. CALCULATION OF STANDARD DEVIATION

Standard Deviation of Historical Returns

Assume Clark, Inc., has historical returns over a 12-year period as indicated below. What is the standard deviation for Clark, Inc., over the 12-year period?

Year	Average Return*	Actual Return	Difference	Difference Squared
1	12%	13.5%	−1.5%	0.0002250
2	12%	12.0%	0.0%	−
3	12%	5.0%	7.0%	0.0049000
4	12%	−2.0%	14.0%	0.0196000
5	12%	7.0%	5.0%	0.0025000
6	12%	23.0%	−11.0%	0.0121000
7	12%	6.0%	6.0%	0.0036000
8	12%	10.0%	2.0%	0.0004000
9	12%	45.0%	−33.0%	0.1089000
10	12%	10.0%	2.0%	0.0004000
11	12%	0.5%	11.5%	0.0132250
12	12%	14.0%	-2.0%	0.0004000
The sum of the squared differences:				**0.1662500**

HP 17BII		HP 12C		HP 10BII	
Keystrokes	Display	Keystrokes	Display	Keystrokes	Display
[SUM]	ITEM(_)?	[f][REG]	0.0000	[■][C ALL]	0.0000
[■][CLEAR DATA]	CLEAR THE LIST?	13.5 [Σ+]	1.0000	13.5 [Σ+]	1.0000
[YES]	ITEM(1) = ?	12 [Σ+]	2.0000	12 [Σ+]	2.0000
13.5 [INPUT]	TOTAL = 13.5000	5 [Σ+]	3.0000	5 [Σ+]	3.0000
12 [INPUT]	TOTAL = 25.5000	2 [CHS][Σ+]	4.0000	2 [+/−][Σ+]	4.0000
5 [INPUT]	TOTAL = 30.5000	7 [Σ+]	5.0000	7 [Σ+]	5.0000
2[+\−][INPUT]	TOTAL = 28.5000	23 [Σ+]	6.0000	23 [Σ+]	6.0000
7 [INPUT]	TOTAL = 35.5000	6 [Σ+]	7.0000	6 [Σ+]	7.0000
23 [INPUT]	TOTAL = 58.5000	10 [Σ+]	8.0000	10 [Σ+]	8.0000
6 [INPUT]	TOTAL = 64.5000	45 [Σ+]	9.0000	45 [Σ+]	9.0000
10 [INPUT]	TOTAL = 74.5000	10 [Σ+]	10.0000	10 [Σ+]	10.0000
45 [INPUT]	TOTAL = 119.5000	.5 [Σ+]	11.0000	.5 [Σ+]	11.0000
10 [INPUT]	TOTAL = 129.5000	14 [Σ+]	12.0000	14 [Σ+]	12.0000
.5 [INPUT]	TOTAL = 130.0000	[g][s] (located on the [.] key)	**12.2938**	[■][Sx,Sy]	**12.2938**
14 [INPUT]	TOTAL = 144.0000				
[EXIT]	ITEM(13) = ?				
[CALC]	144.0000				
[STDEV]	STDEV = **12.2938**				
[EXIT][EXIT]					
[EXIT][CLR]	0.0000				

TI BA II Plus		SHARP EL 733A		COMMON VALUES
Keystrokes	Display	Keystrokes	Display	
[2nd][Data]		[2ndF][MODE]	0.0000^{STAT}	
[2nd][CLR Work]	X01 = 0.0000	13.5 [DATA]	1.0000^{STAT}	
13.5[ENTER]	X01 = 13.50000	12 [DATA]	2.0000^{STAT}	
[↓][↓]	X02 = 0.0000	5 [DATA]	3.0000^{STAT}	
12[ENTER]	X02 = 12.0000	2 [+/−][DATA]	4.0000^{STAT}	
[↓][↓]	X03 = 0.0000	7 [DATA]	5.0000^{STAT}	
5[ENTER]	X03 = 5.0000	23 [DATA]	6.0000^{STAT}	
[↓][↓]	X04 = 0.0000	6 [DATA]	7.0000^{STAT}	
2[+/−][ENTER]	X04 = −2.0000	10 [DATA]	8.0000^{STAT}	
[↓][↓]	X05 = 0.0000	45 [DATA]	9.0000^{STAT}	
7[ENTER]	X05 = 7.0000	10 [DATA]	10.0000^{STAT}	
[↓][↓]	X06 = 0.0000	.5 [DATA]	11.0000^{STAT}	
23[ENTER]	X06 = 23.0000	14 [DATA]	12.0000^{STAT}	
[↓][↓]	X07 = 0.0000	[2nd F][Sx]	**12.2938^{STAT}**	
6[ENTER]	X07 = 6.0000	[2nd F][CA]	0.0000^{STAT}	
[↓][↓]	X08 = 0.0000	[2nd F][MODE]		
		[2nd F][MODE]	0.0000	
10[ENTER]	X08 = 10.0000		0.0000^{FIN}	
[↓][↓]	X09 = 0.0000			
45[ENTER]	X09 = 45.0000			
[↓][↓]	X10 = 0.0000			
10[ENTER]	X10 = 10.0000			
[↓][↓]	X11 = 0.0000			
.5[ENTER]	X11 = 0.5000			
[↓][↓]	X12 = 0.0000			
14[ENTER]	X12 = 14.0000			
[↓][↓]	X13 = 0.0000			
[2nd][Stat]	I–V			
[2nd][CLR Work]	LIN			
[2nd][SET]	I–V			
(Continue to press these keys until I–V is displayed.)				
[↓][↓][↓]				
	Sx = **12.2938**			

Standard Deviation of Projected Returns

A **probability distribution** can be thought of as a set of outcomes with assigned probabilities. Within investments, a probability distribution often consists of possible rates of return (outcomes) with assigned probabilities. The table below depicts an example of a probability distribution that lists the possible outcomes and assigned probabilities under different market conditions for a stock with a current market value of $100.

	Outcomes (Stock Price)	Probability	Single Period Rate of Return
Bull Market	$150	30%	50%
Slow Growth	$110	45%	10%
Bear Market	$85	25%	–15%

The expected rate of return for the probability distribution in the table above is 15.75% [(30% × .50) + (45% × .10) + (25% × (–.15))]. It is expected that an investment in this stock, priced at $100, would yield a rate of return of 15.75% or $15.75 per share based on the probability distribution.

HP 17BII		HP 12C		HP 10BII	
Keystrokes	**Display**	**Keystrokes**	**Display**	**Keystrokes**	**Display**
.3 [×]	0.3000×	.3 [ENTER]	0.3000	.3 [×]	0.3000
.5 [=]	**0.1500**	.5 [×]	**0.1500**	.5 [=]	**0.1500**
.45 [×]	0.4500×	.45 [ENTER]	0.4500	.45 [×]	0.4500
.1 [=]	**0.0450**	.1 [×]	**0.0450**	.1 [÷]	**0.0450**
.25 [×]	0.2500×	.25 [ENTER]	0.2500	.25 [×]	0.2500
.15 [+/–][=]	**–0.0375**	.15 [CHS][×]	**–0.0375**	.15 [+/–][=]	**–0.0375**
- - - - - - - - - - -	- - - - - - - - - - -	- - - - - - - - - - -	- - - - - - - - - - -	- - - - - - - - - - -	- - - - - - - - - - -
.15 [+]	0.1500+	.15 [ENTER]	0.1500	.15 [+]	0.1500
.045 [+]	0.1950+	.045 [+]	0.1950	.045 [+]	0.1950
.0375 [+/–][=]	**0.1575**	.0375 [CHS][+]	**0.1575**	.0375 [+/–][=]	**0.1575**

TI BA II Plus		SHARP EL 733A		COMMON VALUES		
Keystrokes	Display	Keystrokes	Display	Probability	E(r)	E(r)w
.3 [×]	0.3000	.3 [×]	0.3000^{FIN}	30%	50%	15.0000%
.5 [=]	**0.1500**	.5 [=]	**0.1500^{FIN}**	45%	10%	4.5000%
.45 [×]	0.4500	.45 [×]	0.4500^{FIN}	25%	−15%	−3.7500%
.1 [=]	**0.0450**	.1 [=]	**0.0450^{FIN}**	100%		15.7500%
.25 [×]	0.2500	.25 [×]	0.2500^{FIN}			
.15 [+/−][=]	**−0.0375**	.15 [+/−][=]	**−0.0375^{FIN}**			
- - - - - - - - - - -	- - - - - - - - - - -	- - - - - - - - - - -	- - - - - - - - - - -			
.15 [+]	0.1500	.15 [+]	0.1500^{FIN}			
.045 [+]	0.1950	.045 [+]	0.1950^{FIN}			
.0375 [+/−][=]	**0.1575**	.0375 [+/−][=]	**0.1575^{FIN}**			

Index of Terms to Know